The Dairy Book of HOME COOKERY

by Sonia Allison

Published by the Milk Marketing Board

The Author would like to thank the following
for their help and co-operation

Dairy Produce Advisory Service of
the Milk Marketing Board

Photographic accessories
David Mellor
Elizabeth David
Divertimenti
Craftsmen Potters

Photography by Roger Tuff

Designed and illustrated by Tony Streek

First edition published 1968
Revised edition published 1978

Printed by Purnell & Sons Limited
Paulton · Bristol

ISBN 0 900543 41 8

Contents

Important notes

Metric/Imperial Recipes
The ingredients are shown in both metric and imperial measures. However, the metric quantities are not exact conversions but calculated to give proportionately correct measurements for successful results.

All spoon measures are based on the metric spoon where a level teaspoon is 5 millilitres (5ml) and a level tablespoon is 15 millilitres (15ml).

In most recipes, level spoon measures have been recommended. This is because a level measure is more accurate and reliable than a rounded or heaped measure.

Guide to Egg Weights

Old Size	New Size	Weight
	1	70g or over
Large	2	65g – 70g
	3	60g – 65g
Standard	4	55g – 60g
	5	50g – 55g
Medium		
	6	45g – 50g
Small		
Extra Small	7	under 45g

Freezing of Recipes
This symbol indicates that the recipes are suitable to freeze.
Follow the guide lines given for the freezing of foods on page 10.

Front Cover

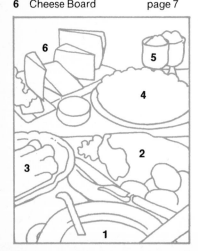

Introduction

Milk

Milk is one of today's finest bargain buys. Its versatility enables it to be taken in so many attractive forms that it can appeal to everyone. For expectant and nursing mothers, infants and children, milk is useful for nourishment and sound growth. It provides teenagers with vital energy and aids healthy physical development. Adults find it revitalising and refreshing. For invalids and the aged, milk is easily digested and a convenient way of taking nourishment.

Milk tempts, pleases and satisfies. To drink, cook and bake with it makes for better living.

Grades of milk

All milk produced in Britain today is tuberculin-tested.

Untreated
This is raw milk which has not undergone any form of heat treatment.

Untreated farm bottled
This is raw milk which must be bottled at the farm where it is produced. It may be from any breed of cow, provided the stock conditions on the farm comply with Government regulations and the producer holds a licence to use the special designation 'Untreated'.

Pasteurised
This is milk which has been subjected to heat treatment which destroys harmful bacteria and prolongs its keeping qualities. Most milk is pasteurised, which means that it is heated generally to not less than 71°C / 161°F for 15 seconds, and then rapidly cooled.

Homogenised
This is pasteurised milk, processed to break up the globules of butterfat evenly throughout the milk instead of allowing them to rise to the top.

Sterilised
This is homogenised milk which has been heat treated in the bottle at a high temperature (at least 100°C / 212°F) for 20 to 30 minutes and vacuum sealed. This extends the keeping quality of the milk. Unopened, it will keep fresh for at least 7 days, but several weeks without refrigeration is usual.

Ultra heat treated (UHT)
This long-keeping milk is homogenised milk which is raised to an ultra high temperature of 132°C / 270°F for 1 to 2 seconds. It is then aseptically packed into containers. This milk will keep for several months and is usually date stamped.

Channel Islands
Milk from Jersey and Guernsey breeds of cow —with a minimum butterfat content of 4%. It can be supplied 'pasteurised', or as 'untreated' milk bottled at the farm of production or at a dairy.

Milk Chart
See chart on page 6.

Legal standards of milk
Ordinary milk must have a minimum of 3% butterfat and 8.5% non-fat solids. Milk sold as Channel Islands, Jersey or Guernsey must contain not less than 4% butterfat.

Care of milk
Ask the milkman to leave it in a shady place away from direct sunlight and avoid leaving it on the doorstep for too long.

If you find the birds are helping themselves, invest in some discs which fit over the bottle tops. When you bring milk indoors, either put it straight into the refrigerator or stand it in a basin or bowl of water and cover with a clean cloth with its edges dipping into the water. Evaporation of the water keeps the milk cool and fresh. Always keep milk covered and well away from strong smelling foods.

Never mix new milk with old and never pour milk into anything but a spotlessly clean container.

Boiling milk
If milk must be boiled, then do it quickly, stirring all the time, and cool it immediately. Prolonged heating of milk will cause the lactose (milk sugar) to caramelise, giving the milk a cooked flavour. As milk boils over surprisingly quickly, never leave a saucepan of heating milk unwatched.

Grades of milk	Colour of bottle cap	Type and processing	Keeping qualities	Characteristics and uses
Pasteurised				
Ordinary	Silver	Subjected to mild heat treatment- 71°C/161°F for 15 seconds, then rapidly cooled to not more than 10°C/50°F	1-2 days in a cool place. 2-3 days in a domestic refrigerator	A visible creamline. Usually chosen for general use, drinking neat, in beverages, in cooking and on cereals
Homogenised	Red	Warm milk is forced through a fine aperture so that fat globules are broken down into smaller particles which do not rise to the surface, but remain evenly distributed throughout the milk. Milk is then pasteurised.	1-2 days in a cool place. 2-3 days in a domestic refrigerator	No creamline; whiter appearance than ordinary pasteurised milk. Fat globules are smaller and more easily digested, so suitable for younger children, invalids and the elderly. Also everyone has a fair share of the cream!
Channel Islands	Gold	Milk from Jersey and Guernsey breeds of cow.	1-2 days in a cool place. 2-3 days in a domestic refrigerator	Similar uses to ordinary pasteurised milk, but its high butterfat content gives it a rich, creamy flavour and colour which may be preferred by some
Sterilised				
	Crown cap or Blue foil	Homogenised, bottled and sealed, then heat treated to above boiling point – not less than 100°C/212°F for approximately 20-23 minutes – and allowed to cool.	Should keep for minimum of 7 days if unopened, but several weeks without refrigeration is usual.	Traditionally sold in a long slender necked bottle with a crown cap, but some in rigid plastic bottles with foil cap. Rich creamy appearance and slight caramel flavour. Junket will not set because of the effect of heat treatment on the milk. Makes a creamy rice pudding.
Ultra Heat Treated				
	Pink	Homogenised, heated for an extended time at lower temperatures to stabilise protein, then subjected to ultra high temperature – not less than 132°C/270°F for one second. Aseptically packed in foil lined containers or rigid plastic bottles.	Several months if unopened, then as pasteurised milk. Usually date stamped.	Similar flavour to pasteurised homogenised milk. Excellent for those on holiday and who require a milk that will keep without refrigeration.
Untreated				
Ordinary	Green	Undergoes no heat treatment. Bottled under licence at farm or at dairy.	1 day in a cool place 2-3 days in a domestic refrigerator.	Very visible creamline. May be preferred by some especially in rural areas.
Channel Islands	Green with single gold stripe			

Fresh cream

Cream is a delicious food which can be used in a wide variety of sweet and savoury dishes. There is a great range of creams available to the house-wife, each one being suited to different purposes.

Types of cream
Single This must, by law, have a minimum butter-fat content of not less than 18%. It is generally used as pouring or coffee cream and will not whip.

Whipping This must, by law, have a butterfat content of not less than 35% although most is sold with around a 40% butterfat content. It is pasteurised but not homogenised, and whips well.

Double This must, by law, have a butterfat content of not less than 48%. If desired, double cream can be whipped. When whipping, add one table-spoon milk. This lowers the butterfat content and increases the volume of whipped cream.

Clotted This usually contains about 60% butter-fat, although the legal minimum requirement is 55%.

Extended life This type of cream is heat treated and vacuum sealed and has a keeping quality of 2 to 3 weeks unopened in a refrigerator. Usually for pouring or spooning, but may be lightly whipped.

Ultra heat treated (UHT) This cream is ultra heat treated and has a long shelf life. It will not whip.

Sterilised cream This cream must, by law, have a minimum butterfat content of 23%. It is sterilised with its container to kill all the bacteria and will keep 6 to 9 months. It has a different flavour from fresh cream and will not whip.

Care of cream
Cream should always be kept cool, clean and covered and away from bright light and strong sunshine. Fresh pasteurised cream will keep 2 to 3 days in summer and 3 to 4 days in winter if refrigerated. Sterilised, extended life and UHT cream will keep for longer periods without refrig-eration, provided the containers remain unopened. All types of cream must be treated as fresh once the container is opened.

To whip cream
Everything (bowl, whisk and the cream itself) must be really cold before cream is whipped.

Cream should be whipped quickly until a matt surface appears–then slowly to avoid over whip-ping and ending up as butter.

Cheese

There are many varieties of cheese produced in the United Kingdom and although they are all made from cow's milk, they are, nevertheless, all different in flavour and texture. This is due to slight variations in the manufacturing processes, which were developed regionally over hundreds of years.

Varieties of cheese
Cheddar, the most popular UK cheese, is famed for its uniquely 'nutty' flavour which becomes deeper as the cheese matures. With its close creamy texture, it is used in a wide variety of ways.

Cheshire is a mellow, open-textured and crumbly cheese. Its keen tangy flavour is said to be due to the salty soil in Cheshire. Red and white Cheshire both have the same flavour and are delicious for 'elevenses' with fruit, cake or biscuits. Blue Cheshire has a rich flavour and is very rare.

Derby is a pale honey-coloured cheese with a close smooth texture and soft mild flavour. Derby is well suited for interesting flavour combinations such as cheese and pineapple, or for use in a salad garnished with sprigs of mint or parsley.

Sage Derby is Derby cheese flavoured with sage leaves.

Double Gloucester is a rich orange-red colour. It has a smooth velvet texture and a full but mellow flavour. Delicious with bread, butter and a glass of ale, or with fresh fruit salad and cream.

Leicester is a mild orange-coloured cheese with a soft flaky texture. It is especially recommended as a dessert cheese.

Caerphilly is creamy-white with a mild flavour and semi-smooth texture. It is a great favourite with children and excels with celery and thin slices of bread and butter.

Lancashire cheese has a mild flavour when young, but it develops a full and rather pungent flavour as it matures. Its texture makes it ideal for crumbling over soups and hotpots, and it is renowned for its toasting qualities.

Wensleydale is pale parchment in colour with a subtle and unique after-taste ideal with apple pie. Blue Wensleydale is occasionally available.

Stilton–the 'King of Cheeses'–has a close texture intermingled with blue veins which give it its special rich flavour and appearance.

White Stilton is a younger version of the Blue Stilton and is milder in flavour, chalky-white in colour and crumbly in texture.

Cottage cheese is a creamy, acid curd cheese with a distinctive, delicate flavour. It is made from pasteurised, skimmed milk inoculated with a 'starter' to develop texture and flavour. It also contains added cream and salt. Cottage cheese is a particularly valuable source of protein and riboflavin (vitamin B_2). It is easily digested and is especially useful in the feeding of babies, invalids and old people. It should always be stored in a cool place.

Cheese as a food
As all well-known UK cheeses are made from whole milk, they are rich in protein, fat, calcium, and some vitamins. They contain approximately 1,708kJ per 100g/120 Calories per ounce.

As Cottage cheese is made from skimmed milk, it contains only 480kJ per 100g/32 Calories per ounce. This makes it very useful as part of a weight-reducing diet.

Care of cheese
Hard cheeses will stay fresh and moist if wrapped in a polythene bag or aluminium foil and then stored in a cool larder or refrigerator. In the latter case it should be brought to room temperature before serving. This takes about half an hour.

UK Butter

Butter has a unique and luxurious flavour and a tremendous versatility of usage. It has always been the foundation of French haute cuisine. In ordinary, everyday cooking and baking and as a spread on bread, toast, crumpets, muffins, buns, biscuits and scones, it has no rival.

The value of butter
Butter is an energy food usually containing rather more than 80% butterfat. It also contains vitamins A and D (the amount varying with the season).

Care of butter
Butter should be kept cool, covered and away from foods with strong flavours or smells.

Yogurt

Yogurt is slightly acidic in taste, it is refreshingly stimulating and very versatile. It is available natural, in a wide variety of flavours, and with pieces of fruit added. Yogurt teams well with sweet and savoury dishes, it is particularly delicious with breakfast cereals, stewed and canned fruit and in summer drinks. When added to soups, sauces, stews and casseroles, or poured over white fish before baking, yogurt not only improves the flavour of the dish but also adds to the nutritional value.

When cooking with yogurt care should be taken not to heat it too vigorously as it might curdle.

When buying yogurt, ensure that the cartons are not blown.

Home-made soft yogurt
600ml / 1 pint UHT milk
150g / 5oz carton natural yogurt

1 Sterilise all the equipment used with a commercial sterilising solution
2 Warm milk to blood heat (about 37°C / 94°F)
3 Remove from heat
4 Gently whisk in the yogurt with a wire whisk or fork
5 Transfer to vacuum flask
6 Leave for 6 to 8 hours or until set
7 Refrigerate after it has set

For fruit yogurt
Stir small pieces of fresh, canned or frozen fruit into yogurt after it has set.

Soured (or cultured) cream
Soured cream has a piquant and refreshing taste, combined with a smooth texture. This enhances the flavour and creaminess of many made-up dishes. It is delicious with raw or cooked fruit, meat, fish and vegetable dishes, soups, stews and sauces. Salad dressings made up with soured cream are ideal for use in a cold buffet.

General Food Care

Dairy products
Always keep milk, cream, yogurt, cheese and butter in a cool pantry or larder or in the special compartments provided in the refrigerator. Make sure they are in clean, covered containers and well away from strong-smelling foods. This is important because uncovered dairy products easily pick up strong taints.

Meat and offal
Always unwrap bought meat, stand it on a clean plate, allowing cold air to get to it directly. Put it straight into the coldest part of the refrigerator. To keep raw meat as fresh as possible in a pantry or larder protect it with a loose covering of thin muslin. Most raw meat can be kept 2 or 3 days in the refrigerator or very cold pantry or larder, but minced raw meat, pork, veal, sausages and offal should be cooked within 24 hours of purchase.

Bacon, loosely wrapped in greaseproof paper in a covered container, will keep up to 7 days in a refrigerator or very cold pantry or larder.

Cooked meat should be cooled quickly, wrapped in foil or placed in non-airtight containers before being put into the refrigerator or larder. This helps to keep the meat fresh-tasting and moist and prevents dryness. Cooked meat should be eaten within 2 days.

Small frozen cuts of meat, such as chops, may be cooked successfully without thawing. However, thawing before cooking is to be recommended for larger joints, particularly boneless roasting joints, small unboned pork joints, boiling joints and meat fillings for puddings and pies. It is desirable to thaw such meat slowly overnight in a refrigerator.

Poultry
Even if kept in the refrigerator, it is advisable to cook whole fresh chickens within 36 hours of purchase and chicken joints within 24 hours of purchase. Poultry should otherwise be treated exactly as meat and offal.

Frozen poultry must be **completely** thawed before cooking.

Fish
Fresh fish bought from the fishmonger should be stiff, with shimmering scales, reddish gills, bulging eyes and a natural covering of slime. The skin of flat fish should be wrinkle-free and the spots bright. It should be prepared for storage in a similar way to meat and cooked and eaten within 24 hours of purchase.

Once frozen fish has thawed, it must be treated in exactly the same way as fresh fish. Most frozen fish can be successfully cooked from the frozen state if small and/or in fillets.

Eggs
Eggs should be stored, pointed end down, away from strong-smelling foods as they pick up odours. For freshness they should be stored in the lower part of the refrigerator, or a cold pantry or larder, where they will keep up to 3 weeks. In a cool larder they can be stored for 7 to 10 days. Eggs should be used at room temperature.

Vegetables
The fresher the better. Since vegetables do not generally store well they are best bought frequently in small quantities. However, sprouts, shredded cabbage, cauliflower, spinach, spring greens, parsley and salad greens will keep crisp and fresh for about a week if put into polythene bags or airtight plastic containers and stored in a refrigerator or cold larder. Root vegetables shrivel quickly in the warm and should therefore be kept, unwashed, in a cool, dry, airy, dark place. Plastic bags do help keep root vegetables fresh, but they must not be sealed or the vegetables will begin to rot. Tomatoes and cucumbers keep best in the least cold part of the refrigerator or larder.

Frozen vegetables, with the exception of corn on the cob, need not be thawed at all before being cooked.

Fruit
Apples, bananas, fresh pineapples, melons, pears and citrus fruits should be kept in a dry, cool and airy pantry or larder. Grapes, gooseberries, rhubarb and fresh apricots and peaches keep best in the least cold part of the refrigerator, as do soft berry fruits, which should be spread on to plates and used within 8 to 12 hours. A sprinkle of lemon juice will prevent sliced bananas, apples and pears from turning brown for a few hours.

Frozen dessert fruit should be thawed slowly before serving and stewing fruit or purée is best if partially thawed before cooking in the usual way.

Canned goods
These have a long shelf life if kept in a cool, dry, airy cupboard but do not stock cans that are dented or leaking. It is advisable to use canned goods in rotation and not to store for longer than two years after purchase. However, larger canned hams should be kept under refrigeration and used within 6 months of purchase. As soon as canned foods are opened, the food should be left in the can covered, placed in the refrigerator and treated as fresh foods, except fruit juices which should be emptied into a non-metallic container.

Dry goods
Flour should be used within 2 months of purchase and dried fruits within 3 months. Baking powder, provided the tin or jar is tightly closed, will remain active for about 6 months.

Bicarbonate of soda has a shorter life and should be used within 2 months. Cocoa should not be kept longer than 6 months and nor should cornflour, tapioca, sago, barley and rice. Cereals should be used within a month of purchase and ground coffee should be bought a little at a time and used within a week. White sugar will keep several months in a dry, dark place, but icing and brown sugar tend to harden on standing and should be used fairly soon after purchase. Packets of dried convenience foods should be stored exactly as directed by the manufacturer.

Frozen foods
Low temperature preservation is often the most satisfactory means of keeping food in good condition, provided that the basic principles of freezing are adhered to.

Freezing compartments are frequently incorporated into modern refrigerators. Star markings on packets of frozen food and correspondingly on the compartments, indicate the time that frozen food can be successfully stored –

✳ Frozen food will keep up to one week

✳ ✳ Frozen food will keep up to four weeks

✳ ✳ ✳ Frozen food will keep up to three months

If the refrigerator is an older model and has no star markings, do not keep frozen food longer than 2-3 days.

Home freezing
Only if the compartment has the following symbol –  –as the rating should you attempt to freeze your own foods. In addition the three small stars illustrate the ability to store commercially frozen foods for up to 3 months.

The following guide lines will help you to be sure of successful results when freezing your own foods:
(a) Food to be frozen must be in perfect condition
(b) Prepare the food correctly, seal in moisture / vapour-proof materials in convenient-size packages, labelled with the date, quantity and food type.
(c) Freeze the food as quickly as possible and check regularly that the temperature of the freezer remains constant.
(d) Do not re-freeze frozen food when it has thawed. If meat, poultry or vegetables which have been frozen raw are used in a cooked dish they may then be frozen.

Freezing dairy products
As there is a doorstep delivery of milk and other dairy products, there is very little need for these to be frozen. The availability of UHT milk and cream means that an extra carton can always be kept in the cupboard for emergencies. However, there are occasions when information on the keeping qualities of dairy products in the freezer may be of value.

Milk Homogenised milk can be frozen for up to 1 month in a plastic container. Do **not** freeze milk in a glass bottle.

Cheese Hard cheeses can be successfully frozen for considerable lengths of time. Most can be frozen for up to 4 months and some, particularly Cheddar, for up to 6 months. Soft cheeses such as Cottage cheese and cream cheese do not freeze successfully. Freeze cheese either in polythene or plastic containers.

Yogurt Fruit yogurts can be stored for up to 3 months with little or no deterioration. Some may separate slightly, but this disappears on stirring. Natural yogurts tend to separate. Home-made yogurt does not freeze well.

Fresh cream Single cream does not freeze well. Whipping and double cream can be frozen for up to 2 months. Best results are achieved if the cream is frozen partially whipped in plastic freezer containers. On thawing, continue whipping to the required consistency.

Butter It is not generally necessary to freeze butter as it keeps well in a refrigerator. However, salted butter can be frozen for up to 3 months in freezer polythene.

Thawing
For best results, all dairy produce should be slowly thawed for 24 hours in a domestic refrigerator.

Pressure cooking
This is a method of cooking that is becoming more popular because it is both economical and quick. Cooking times are reduced so much that less fuel is required. One pan with dividers can be used to cook different types of food, even a complete meal, since there is no transference of flavours when food is cooked in steam. Pressure cooking has further advantages in that there are reductions in the amount of steam produced in the kitchen, fewer cooking smells, and less loss of flavour and nutrients generally. When using a pressure cooker it is essential to follow the manufacturer's instructions for quantities of food and liquid to be cooked at one time, and timing should be accurate down to the last minute.

Slow cooking

Several slow cookers are now on the market and work on the old principle of the hay box. Operated electrically, food can be left **safely** all day to cook without attention, which is very useful for all busy people, but in particular working mothers and the elderly. Easy to clean and attractive to look at, the power used by a slow cooker is equivalent to between a 60-watt and 120-watt lamp bulb, making this method of cooking very economical and trouble-free.

Microwave cooking

With microwave ovens, it is now possible to thaw, cook or reheat food in minutes. This ultra-fast method of cooking is brought about by high-frequency radio waves, emitted by a magnetron and circulated through the oven by a concealed fan. The waves cause the water molecules in the food to vibrate very rapidly and so generate heat. Initial penetration of the waves (heat) is 4cm / 1½in all round, and further heating is carried out by conduction as in conventional cooking methods. As a result, cooking time can be considerably reduced but always follow the manufacturer's directions to the letter.

A guide to metrication

Oven temperature chart

°C	°F	Gas Number	Description
110	225	$\frac{1}{4}$	Very slow
120	250	$\frac{1}{2}$	Very slow
140	275	1	Slow
150	300	2	Slow
160	325	3	Moderate
180	350	4	Moderate
190	375	5	Moderately hot
200	400	6	Moderately hot
220	425	7	Hot
230	450	8	Hot
240	475	9	Very hot

The above oven temperature chart is a guide only and gives recommended equivalent settings, not exact conversions. To be absolutely sure of good results, always refer to your own cooker instruction book. Although the cooking position in the oven is given in the recipes, it is again advisable to check with your own instruction book.

Spoon measures

1 tablespoon	3 teaspoons
1 level tablespoon	15ml
1 level teaspoon	5ml

Weights and measures
Dry weight

Approximate gram (g) conversion to nearest round figure	Recommended gram (g) conversion to nearest 25g	Imperial ounce (oz)
28	25	1
57	50	2
85	75	3
113	125	4 ($\frac{1}{4}$lb)
142	150	5
170	175	6
198	200	7
227	225	8 ($\frac{1}{2}$lb)
255	250	9
284	275	10
311	300	11
340	350	12 ($\frac{3}{4}$lb)
368	375	13
396	400	14
425	425	15
453	450	16 (1lb)

Liquid measures

Approximate millilitre (ml) conversion to nearest round figure	Recommended millilitre (ml) equivalent	Imperial pint	Imperial fluid ounce (fl oz)
568	600	1	20
284	300	$\frac{1}{2}$	10
142	150	$\frac{1}{4}$	5

Handy measures
The following ingredients measured in level tablespoons give approximately 25g / 1oz weight.

3	Semolina, flour, custard powder, cornflour and other powdery starches
4	Porridge oats
2	Rice
6	Breadcrumbs (fresh)
3	Breadcrumbs (dry)
5	Grated cheese (fairly dry)
2	Granulated and caster sugar
3	Demerara sugar, icing sugar (sifted)
5	Desiccated coconut
1	Syrup, honey, treacle and jam
4	Ground almonds, hazelnuts and walnuts
2	Dried fruits (currants, sultanas and raisins)
4	Cocoa powder
1	Salt

Herbs & Spices

As interest in herbs and spices grows and their use in cooking is becoming more widespread, the following guide may be found useful.

Herbs

Basil
This mild and fragrant herb teams well with all tomato dishes, and also with mushrooms, cheese and eggs.

Bay leaves
Mild and distinctive, bay leaves are used in pickling, stews, sauces and gravies, meat and poultry casseroles and some vegetable dishes. They are often part of a 'bouquet garni' (or bag of mixed herbs).

Chives
Grass-like in appearance, chives are a much milder version of the onion and have little or no after-taste. Excellent with all foods but particularly delicious with Cottage cheese, omelettes and scrambled eggs. Snipped chives make a colourful and attractive garnish.

Marjoram
A delicate herb with a very distinctive flavour. It goes well with practically all foods but particularly with poultry, veal and lamb, fish and egg dishes, and for adding to carrots, peas, spinach and tomatoes while they are cooking.

Mint
This is used for mint sauce, which teams so admirably with lamb, and as a flavouring for potatoes and peas. A little chopped mint is excellent in poultry stuffing.

Rosemary
This has quite a pungent flavour and should be used fairly sparingly. Particularly good with poultry, lamb and mutton it can also be added to pea, chicken and spinach soup and to salad dressings.

Parsley
Probably the best known and most widely used herb of all, parsley makes a most attractive garnish and improves the flavour of any dish to which it is added.

Sage
Another popular herb, sage is strong and aromatic and is used mainly in pork dishes and in stuffings for duck and goose.

Tarragon
This is a bitter-sweet herb that is both aromatic and distinctive. Particularly good in certain sauces and with poultry, fish and shellfish dishes.

Thyme
This is a strong flavoured herb recommended for mutton and pork dishes and for adding sparingly to cream and Cottage cheese. Small amounts are good in omelettes, salads and stuffings.

Spices

Allspice
This is a dried berry of a West Indian shrub. Whole, it is used to add flavour to boiled meats, pot roasts and poached fresh-water fish. When ground, it can be added to gravies, cakes and Christmas puddings.

Cinnamon
This is the bark of a type of laurel which grows in the Far East. It can either be rolled (cinnamon sticks) or powdered. It has a sweet, fragrant and distinctive flavour, and can be added to hot drinks and punches, apple dishes, cakes, buns, biscuits, puddings and curries.

Cloves
These are the dried and unopened buds of a type of myrtle with a strong and distinctive flavour. They should be used sparingly. Traditionally used with stewed apples, they also improve the flavour of stewed pears, pickles, curries and boiled meats.

Mace
This is the golden outer husk of the nutmeg and is available in blade or ground form. It has an exotic and subtle flavour, milder than nutmeg. Blades of mace are used in some soups and sauces and also for pickling. Ground mace is especially good with veal and beef.

Nutmeg
Another popular spice from the Far East and Caribbean, nutmeg is the seed of a pulpy fruit. Apart from its use in milk puddings, nutmeg gives a flavour lift to poultry, egg dishes and egg nogs, creamed potatoes and parsnips, cakes, biscuits, buns and puddings.

Paprika
This is a mild, bright red pepper made from dried ground capsicums. It adds piquancy and colour to meat, fish and vegetable dishes and makes an ideal garnish for soups and pale-coloured savoury dishes of all descriptions.

Milk and your diet

Good health depends on a balanced diet. The body needs many nutrients such as proteins, vitamins and minerals, which must be supplied by the food we eat. Where milk and milk products are a customary part of the diet, they form a major source of valuable nutrients.

Milk is a complex mixture of proteins, fat and milk sugar or lactose. These major constituents are accompanied by various minerals and vitamins.

Milk protein The proteins of milk constitute about 3.3% of its total weight. This means that 568ml / 1 pint of milk a day will supply most people with about one-third of their daily protein requirements. Children require less protein per day and so 568ml / 1 pint of milk may provide up to half a young child's requirements. Similarly lactating women or active men need more protein each day and so 568ml / 1 pint may supply about one-quarter of their daily requirements. This protein is of high quality and is in a form which is easily digested.

Milk fat The fat content of milk varies more than any other constituent. It is lighter than the rest of the milk and so rises to the surface to give the cream. The fat in milk improves the taste, texture and palatability as well as carrying the fat-soluble vitamins. Channel Islands cows produce milk with a higher fat content. This milk (gold top) has a rich, creamy flavour and a deep cream line.

Milk sugar Lactose is a slightly sweet sugar, which is unique to milk. It is easily fermented to lactic acid and this reaction is used to produce the acidity in yogurt, cultured buttermilk, soured cream and cheese.

Vitamins Milk is an excellent source of some vitamins, especially some B group vitamins and vitamin A. The B vitamins form part of the process by which the body obtains energy from food. One B vitamin, riboflavin, can be destroyed by strong sunlight, and care should therefore be taken not to leave milk bottles outside in the sunshine after they have been delivered. Vitamin A plays an important part in vision, and aids the formation of membrane linings of the nose and throat.

Minerals Milk is a rich source of calcium and phosphorus. In growing children, minerals aid the development of bones and teeth ensuring that in later life both will remain healthy.

As milk contains most of the essential nutrients in an easily digestible form it is ideal for all members of the community. Milk is the first food given to a baby, whether it is breast milk or one of the modified cows' milk formulae. From the age of about 6 months, once mixed feeding is estab-lished, milk is an important part of the diet. The protein and calcium contained in milk are neces-sary for all growing children. This rapid growth continues through childhood and in the teens, and hence nutritional needs are high. During pregnancy and lactation a good diet is needed to provide the requirements of the developing baby. Even adults, who are no longer growing, need a well-balanced diet to maintain health. 'Middle age spread' can be prevented by knowing which foods give you the nutrients you need without adding extra Joules / Calories to the diet. Milk, cheese and yogurt are also valuable in a weight-reducing diet where the proteins, vitamins and minerals must still be included while the energy intake is reduced. In old age, milk is a very useful food in that 568ml / 1 pint provides over one-third of the daily requirement of protein and all the calcium. It is convenient, good value for money, easily digested and delivered to the door to solve shopping problems.

Milk can be seen, then, to be a very versatile product. Various ways of incorporating it into the diet can be used. Soups and sauces can be made with milk, as can porridge, egg custards, rice puddings, milk jellies, blancmanges and whips. Flavoured milk drinks, both hot and cold, are often liked by children. Cheese can be grated in sauces or on salads and sprinkled over soup. Scones and pastry can be made with cheese, or cubed cheese can be speared on cocktail sticks with chopped fruit or vegetables. A healthy wedge of cheese is very good with fruit cake or ginger-bread or crusty rolls. Other dairy products such as yogurt and buttermilk all have their place in helping to provide a well-balanced diet for all members of the community. There are many exciting recipes in this book to give you extra serving ideas.

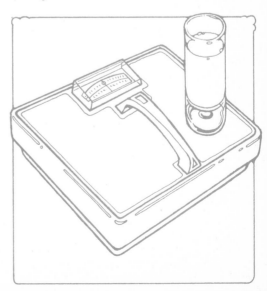

Austrian Cheese Savouries (page 14) Ham and Asparagus Rolls (page 15) Hot Sausage Crisps (page 15)

Appetisers are usually served before meals or at parties. All those in this section will serve between 4 and 10 people.

 Unless indicated as being suitable, recipes that require pastry may be partially prepared by making up the pastry and freezing baked or unbaked.

Austrian Cheese Savouries

75g / 3oz cream cheese
50g / 2oz softened butter
½ level teaspoon paprika
¼ level teaspoon caraway seeds
1 level teaspoon finely chopped capers
½ level teaspoon anchovy essence
½ level teaspoon French mustard
2 level teaspoons finely chopped chives or
   green part of leek
Savoury biscuits

Garnish
Extra capers

1 Beat cream cheese and butter together until smooth and creamy
2 Stir in paprika, caraway seeds, capers, anchovy essence, mustard and chives or leek
3 Mix well then pile on to biscuits
4 Garnish each with a whole caper

Hot Cheese Patties

1 recipe Rich Short Crust Pastry (page 212)
75g / 3oz cream cheese
25g / 1oz finely chopped lean ham
25g / 1oz stuffed olives
1 level teaspoon finely grated onion
½ level teaspoon made mustard
2 level teaspoons fresh white breadcrumbs
Salt and pepper to taste
Beaten egg for brushing

1 Roll out Pastry fairly thinly
2 Cut into twenty-eight 5cm / 2in squares
3 Mix cheese with ham, olives, onion, mustard and breadcrumbs. Season to taste with salt and pepper
4 Put equal amounts of cheese mixture (about 1 teaspoon) on to 14 squares. Moisten edges of Pastry with water
5 Cover with remaining squares
6 Press edges well together to seal. 'Ridge' with fork
7 Transfer to buttered baking tray and brush with beaten egg
8 Decorate tops of Patties with small leaves rolled and cut from trimmings. Brush leaves with more egg
9 Bake just above centre of hot oven (220°C / 425°F or Gas No 7) for 15 minutes (or until golden brown)
10 Serve hot

Cream Cheese Sticks

1 recipe Cream Cheese Pastry (page 214)
Beaten egg for brushing
Celery salt

1 Roll out Pastry fairly thinly
2 Cut into fingers and transfer to buttered baking trays
3 Brush with egg and sprinkle lightly with celery salt
4 Bake towards top of hot oven (230°C/450°F or Gas No 8) for 10 to 12 minutes (or until puffy and golden). Serve hot

Stuffed Cucumbers

1 large cucumber, unpeeled
12 heaped teaspoons cream cheese
1 level tablespoon finely chopped chives

Garnish
12 peeled prawns

1 Cut cucumber into twelve 2 to 3cm/1 to 1½in lengths
2 Scoop out some of the seedy centres, leaving fairly shallow cavities
3 Fill with cream cheese. Sprinkle with chives. Garnish each with a prawn
4 Chill lightly before serving

Cheese Aigrettes

50g/2oz finely grated Cheddar cheese (stale for preference)
1 recipe Choux Pastry (page 214)
Deep fat or oil for frying

1 Beat 25g/1oz cheese into Choux Pastry
2 Drop about 20 equal amounts, from a teaspoon, into hot fat or oil
3 Fry about 5 minutes (or until Aigrettes are golden and well puffed)
4 Remove from pan and drain on soft kitchen paper
5 Transfer to serving dish. Sprinkle with rest of cheese
6 Serve hot

Ham & Asparagus Rolls

4 slices lean ham (about 100g/4oz)
75 to 100g/3 to 4oz cream cheese
12 asparagus tips

1 Cut each slice of ham into 3 strips
2 Spread with cream cheese
3 Roll strips round asparagus tips. Skewer with cocktail sticks
4 Chill lightly before serving

Cheese-stuffed Celery

100g/4oz finely grated Cheddar cheese (stale for preference)
50g/2oz softened butter
½ level teaspoon dry mustard
1 tablespoon fresh double cream or soured cream
Well-washed celery stalks

Garnish
Paprika

1 Beat cheese, butter and mustard well together. Gradually beat in cream
2 Fill celery stalks with cheese mixture. Cut into 5cm/2in lengths
3 Chill and before serving dust lightly with paprika

Prawn-stuffed Celery

1 Follow recipe and method for Cheese-Stuffed Celery (above)
2 Fill celery stalks with Prawn Butter (page 96) instead of the cheese mixture
3 Before serving sprinkle with finely chopped parsley

Hot Sausage Crisps

250g/8oz skinless pork sausages
1 large egg
2 teaspoons milk
40g/1½oz toasted breadcrumbs
2 level teaspoons dry mustard
½ level teaspoon salt
Deep fat or oil for frying

1 Cut each sausage into 4 pieces
2 Beat egg and milk well together. Combine breadcrumbs with mustard and salt
3 Coat pieces of sausage with egg and milk. Toss in breadcrumb mixture
4 Fry in hot fat or oil until crisp and golden
5 Remove from pan, drain on soft kitchen paper
6 Serve hot

Buttered Savoury Almonds

225g/8oz blanched almonds
50g/2oz butter
2 teaspoons olive or corn oil
½ level teaspoon salt
1 level teaspoon paprika

1 Fry almonds gently in butter and oil for 3 to 4 minutes (or until pale gold), turning often
2 Remove from pan. Drain on soft kitchen paper. Sprinkle with salt mixed with paprika
3 Serve hot or cold

Cheese & Walnut Puffs

1 recipe Choux Pastry (page 214)
75g / 3oz cream cheese
50g / 2oz Blue Stilton cheese
1 tablespoon milk
25g / 1oz finely chopped shelled walnut halves

1 Using a teaspoon, place 20 equal amounts of Pastry on to buttered and lightly floured baking tray
2 Bake just above centre of moderately hot oven (200°C / 400°F or Gas No 6) for 20 minutes
3 Reduce temperature to moderate (160°C / 325°F or Gas No 3). Bake further 20 minutes
4 Cool on wire rack
5 Just before serving, beat cream cheese, Stilton and milk well together. Stir in nuts
6 Cut puffs in half. Fill bottom halves with cheese mixture. Replace tops
7 Serve immediately (if left to stand too long, the Pastry softens slightly)

Devilled Brazils

225g / 8oz shelled Brazil nuts
50g / 2oz butter
2 teaspoons olive or corn oil
1 level teaspoon *each*, dry mustard and paprika
1 level teaspoon *each*, celery and onion salt
Shake of both Cayenne pepper and garlic salt

1 Slice Brazils fairly thickly. Fry gently in butter and oil for 3 to 4 minutes (or until pale gold), turning often
2 Remove from pan. Drain on soft kitchen paper. Sprinkle with mustard mixed with paprika, celery and onion salts, Cayenne pepper and garlic salt
3 Serve hot or cold

Hot Chicken & Mushroom Puffs

Double recipe Choux Pastry (page 214)
150ml / ¼ pint Mushroom Sauce (page 130)
1 tablespoon fresh double cream
100g / 4oz cooked chopped chicken
Seasoning to taste

1 Using a teaspoon, place 40 equal amounts of Pastry on buttered and lightly floured baking trays
2 Bake just above centre of moderately hot oven (200°C / 400°F or Gas No 6) for 20 minutes
3 Reduce temperature to moderate (160°C / 325°F or Gas No 3). Bake further 20 minutes
4 Cool on wire rack
5 Combine Sauce with double cream and chicken. Season and heat through gently
6 Make slit in each Puff. Fill with chicken mixture
7 Transfer to baking trays. Heat through in moderate oven for 5 to 7 minutes. Serve immediately

Hot Cheese & Ham Puffs

1 Follow recipe and method for Hot Chicken and Mushroom Puffs (left)
2 Use Cheese Sauce (page 129) instead of Mushroom Sauce and chopped ham instead of chicken

Hot Mustard & Bacon Puffs

1 Follow recipe and method for Hot Chicken and Mushroom Puffs (left)
2 Use Mustard Sauce (page 130) instead of the Mushroom Sauce and chopped fried bacon instead of chicken

Hot Parsley & Haddock Puffs

1 Follow recipe and method for Hot Chicken and Mushroom Puffs (left)
2 Use Parsley Sauce (page 129) instead of Mushroom Sauce and cooked finely mashed smoked haddock instead of chicken

Cheese & Prawn Puffs

1 Follow recipe and method for Cheese and Walnut Puffs (left)
2 Use 75g / 3oz finely chopped peeled prawns instead of Stilton
3 Stir in ½ level teaspoon lemon rind instead of walnuts

Curried Walnuts

225g / 8oz shelled walnut halves
50g / 2oz butter
2 teaspoons olive or corn oil
½ level teaspoon salt
3 level teaspoons curry powder

1 Fry walnut halves in butter and oil for 2 to 3 minutes, turning often
2 Remove from pan. Drain on soft kitchen paper. Sprinkle with salt mixed with curry powder
3 Serve hot or cold

Dips & Dunks

Cottage Cheese and Pineapple Dip (page 18) Cheese and Olive Balls (page 20) Cheese and Tomato Flakes (page 20) Toasted Lancashire Rolls (page 20)

The Dip recipes are ideal for 'help-yourself' parties and for serving with drinks before a meal. Spoon the prepared Dips into bowls and stand on large platters or small trays. Surround with potato crisps, small savoury biscuits, thin slices of carrot, short lengths of celery and slices of peeled cucumber. Guests help themselves by dunking the crisps, biscuits or vegetables into the Dips. For more formal occasions, the Dips can be piled on to small biscuits and garnished to taste with sliced olives and gherkins, red or green peppers, paprika, curry powder, small pieces of tomato and thin slices of cucumber. Dips and dunks are also ideal to serve with fondues

Mushroom & Ham Dip

150ml / $\frac{1}{4}$ pint fresh double cream
150g / 5oz carton natural yogurt
$\frac{1}{2}$ packet mushroom soup
50g / 2oz very finely chopped or minced lean
   ham

Garnish
Cayenne pepper

1 Lightly whip cream
2 Stir in yogurt and soup
3 Chill for 2 or 3 hours
4 Before serving, stir in ham and transfer to bowl
5 Dust lightly with Cayenne pepper

Asparagus & Prawn Dip

4 tablespoons canned chopped asparagus
50 to 75g / 2 to 3oz peeled prawns, very finely
   chopped
2 × 150g / 5oz cartons natural yogurt
Seasoning to taste

Garnish
Slices of stuffed olives

1 Stir asparagus and prawns into yogurt
2 Season to taste and chill
3 Before serving, transfer to bowl. Garnish with olives

Creamed Yogurt Dip

150g / 5oz carton natural yogurt
100g / 4oz cream cheese
2 level tablespoons finely chopped peeled
   cucumber
1 level teaspoon paprika
$\frac{1}{2}$ to 1 level teaspoon salt
Good shake of pepper

1 Beat yogurt into cheese. Stir in cucumber and paprika
2 Season to taste with salt and pepper. Chill
3 Transfer to bowl before serving

Cottage Cheese, Bacon & Onion Dip

100g / 4oz back bacon
225g / 8oz Cottage cheese
1 to 2 level teaspoons finely grated onion

Garnish
Paprika

1 Chop bacon into small pieces. Fry in own fat until crisp
2 Drain on soft kitchen paper. Leave until cold
3 Combine with Cottage cheese and onion. Transfer to bowl
4 Sprinkle with paprika

Curried Cream Cheese Dip

225g / 8oz cream cheese
4 tablespoons Mayonnaise (page 126)
150g / 5oz carton natural yogurt
3 to 4 level teaspoons curry powder
2 level teaspoons finely grated onion
Salt to taste

Garnish
About 1 tablespoon sultanas

1 Beat cheese until smooth with Mayonnaise and natural yogurt
2 Stir in curry powder and onion. Season to taste with salt
3 Spoon into serving bowl. Sprinkle sultanas over the top

Leek Dip

150ml / ¼ pint fresh double cream
150g / 5oz carton natural yogurt
½ packet leek soup
50g / 2oz grated Caerphilly cheese

Garnish
Paprika

1 Lightly whip cream
2 Stir in yogurt, soup and cheese
3 Chill for 2 or 3 hours
4 Transfer to bowl before serving. Sprinkle with paprika

Avocado Dip

225g / 8oz cream cheese
4 tablespoons Mayonnaise (page 126)
150ml / ¼ pint fresh double cream
1 avocado pear, peeled and mashed
2 tablespoons chopped parsley
1 tablespoon finely grated onion

Cheddar Cheese & Celery Dip

50g / 2oz softened butter
225g / 8oz very finely grated Cheddar cheese
2 level teaspoons made mustard
100g / 4oz very finely chopped celery
150ml / ¼ pint fresh single cream
Seasoning to taste

Garnish
About 25g / 1oz chopped salted peanuts

1 Beat butter until creamy. Stir in cheese, mustard and celery
2 Very gradually beat in cream. Season to taste with salt and pepper
3 Before serving, transfer to bowl. Sprinkle top lightly with chopped nuts

Cottage Cheese & Pineapple Dip

225g / 8oz Cottage cheese
4 tablespoons soured cream
4 heaped tablespoons finely chopped canned pineapple
Seasoning to taste

Garnish
Chopped red and / or green peppers

1 Combine Cottage cheese with soured cream and pineapple
2 Season to taste with salt and a little Cayenne pepper
3 Transfer to bowl. Garnish with red or green peppers, or mixture of both

Onion Dip

150ml / ¼ pint fresh double cream
150g / 5oz carton natural yogurt
½ packet onion soup

Garnish
1 level tablespoon finely chopped parsley

1 Lightly whip cream
2 Stir in yogurt and soup
3 Chill for 2 or 3 hours
4 Transfer to bowl before serving. Sprinkle with parsley

1 crushed clove garlic
Salt and pepper to taste

1 Beat cheese until smooth with mayonnaise
2 Lightly whip cream, and stir into cheese mixture
3 Stir in remaining ingredients

Hot Cheese Fluffs

12 cream crackers
Butter
50g / 2oz finely grated Cheddar cheese (stale for preference)
4 tablespoons fresh double cream
½ level teaspoon made mustard
¼ level teaspoon salt
White of 1 standard egg

1 Spread biscuits with butter
2 Combine grated cheese and double cream. Add mustard and salt
3 Beat egg white until stiff. Gently fold into cheese mixture
4 Pile over biscuits. Grill until golden
5 Serve immediately

Cheese & Poppy Seed Flakes

1 recipe Flaky Pastry (page 214)
Beaten egg
75g / 3oz crumbled Lancashire cheese
About 4 level teaspoons poppy seeds

1 Roll out Pastry into 45cm×15cm / 18in×6in rectangle. Cut in half lengthwise (there should be 2 pieces, each measuring 45cm×7cm / 18in×3in)
2 Brush one half with egg and sprinkle with cheese
3 Cover with second half of Pastry and press down well
4 Cut into 18 strips, each about 2cm / 1in wide × 7cm / 3in long
5 Transfer to baking tray. Brush with egg. Sprinkle with poppy seeds
6 Leave in cool 20 to 30 minutes. Bake towards top of hot oven (230°C / 450°F or Gas No 8) for 8 to 10 minutes (or until well puffed and golden)
7 Serve hot

Hot Mushroom Tartlets

1 recipe Cheese Pastry (page 212)
150ml / ¼ pint Mushroom Sauce (page 130)

Garnish
10 to 12 lightly grilled button mushrooms

1 Roll out Pastry thinly. Cut into 10 to 12 rounds with biscuit cutter
2 Arrange neatly in bun tins
3 Prick well all over. Line each with aluminium foil (to prevent Pastry rising as it cooks) and bake just above centre of hot oven (220°C / 425°F or Gas No 7) for 5 minutes
4 Remove foil and return tartlet cases to oven. Bake further 5 to 7 minutes (or until golden)
5 Fill with equal amounts of hot Mushroom Sauce. Garnish each with grilled mushroom
6 Serve immediately

Cheese & Caraway Seed Flakes

1 Follow recipe and method for Cheese and Poppy Seed Flakes (left)
2 Use caraway seeds instead of poppy seeds

Cold Cucumber Tartlets

1 Follow recipe and method for Hot Mushroom Tartlets (page 19)
2 After baking, leave tartlet cases until completely cold
3 Fill with 150ml / ¼ pint carton soured cream mixed with 2 to 3 tablespoons finely grated cucumber
4 Season to taste with freshly milled pepper and salt

Prune & Bacon Savouries

12 large prunes
50 to 75g / 2 to 3oz cream cheese
12 rashers streaky bacon

1 Soak prunes in hot water for 3 to 4 hours (or until plump and soft)
2 Drain, pat dry and remove stones
3 Fill cavities with cream cheese
4 Wrap rasher of bacon round each stuffed prune. Skewer with cocktail sticks
5 Cook under hot grill until bacon is crisp and golden
6 Serve immediately

Mushroom Buttons

16 very fresh button mushrooms
50g / 2oz cream cheese
2 tablespoons fresh double cream
2 teaspoons very finely chopped chives
Salt and pepper to taste

1 Remove stalks from mushrooms
2 Gently wipe caps with clean damp cloth
3 Combine cheese with double cream and chives. Season to taste with salt and pepper
4 Fill caps with equal amounts of cream cheese mixture then spear cocktail sticks into each

Cheese & Celery Balls

1 Follow recipe and method for Cheese and Olive Balls (page 20)
2 Use 1 level tablespoon finely chopped celery instead of the olives
3 Roll in 25g / 1oz blanched, toasted and chopped almonds instead of the walnuts

Cheese & Olive Balls

100g / 4oz cream cheese
1 tablespoon fresh double cream
1 level tablespoon finely chopped stuffed olives
¼ level teaspoon paprika
50g / 2oz finely grated Cheddar cheese
Seasoning to taste
About 25g / 1oz finely chopped shelled walnut
halves

1 Beat cheese and cream together until smooth.
Stir in olives, paprika and grated cheese
2 Season to taste with salt and pepper
3 Divide into 12 to 14 equal-sized pieces. Shape
into balls
4 Roll in chopped walnuts and chill
5 Spear on to cocktail sticks just before serving

Cheese & Ham Balls

1 Follow recipe and method for Cheese and Olive
Balls (above)
2 Use 25g / 1oz finely chopped ham instead of the
olives

Cheese & Gherkin Balls

1 Follow recipe and method for Cheese and Olive
Balls (above)
2 Use 1 level tablespoon finely chopped gherkins
instead of the olives
3 Roll in 25g / 1oz salted and chopped peanuts
instead of the walnuts

Cheese & Pineapple Porcupine

1 large grapefruit
175g / 6oz Leicester cheese
175g / 6oz Derby cheese
1 medium-sized can pineapple cubes,
well-drained

1 Stand grapefruit on serving dish. (If necessary,
cut small slice off base so it stands without
toppling)
2 Cut both cheeses into 1cm / ½in cubes
3 Put on to cocktail sticks alternately with pineapple, then spear into grapefruit

Cheese & Tomato Flakes

1 recipe Flaky Pastry (page 214)
2 level tablespoons tomato purée
75g / 3oz crumbled Lancashire cheese
Beaten egg for brushing

1 Roll out Pastry into 45cm×15cm / 18in×6in
rectangle. Cut in half lengthwise (there should be
2 pieces, each 45cm×7cm / 18in×3in)
2 Brush one half with tomato purée. Sprinkle with
cheese
3 Cover with second half of Pastry and press
down well
4 Cut into 18 strips, each about 2cm / 1in in width
and 7cm / 3in long
5 Transfer to baking tray. Brush with egg. Leave
in the cool for 20 to 30 minutes
6 Bake towards top of hot oven (230°C / 450°F or
Gas No 8) for 8 to 10 minutes (or until well puffed
and golden). Serve hot

Baby Burgers

500g / 1lb lean minced beef
4 level tablespoons fresh white breadcrumbs
4 tablespoons fresh single cream
2 teaspoons Worcestershire sauce
½ to 1 level teaspoon salt
1 level teaspoon mixed herbs

1 Combine beef with breadcrumbs, cream, Worcestershire sauce, salt and herbs. Shape into 24
tiny cakes
2 Stand below hot grill and cook 4 to 5 minutes
per side
3 Spear on to cocktail sticks. Serve hot

Toasted Lancashire Rolls

8 rashers streaky bacon
16 × 1cm / ½in cubes of Lancashire cheese

1 Cut bacon rashers in half. Wrap round cubes of
cheese
2 Secure with cocktail sticks
3 Cook under hot grill until bacon is crisp and
golden
4 Serve immediately

Soups

French Onion Soup (below)

Reduce cooking of soup by 15 minutes, reduce the seasoning added and do not add garnishes or cream. After thawing, complete cooking, adjust seasoning and add cream and garnish. Cheese soups should be made up without the cheese. The cheese may be frozen separately and added after soup has been defrosted and reheated. Storage time – 3 months.

Cream of Artichoke Soup

1 Follow recipe and method for Cream of Potato Soup (page 22)
2 Use 500g / 1lb Jerusalem artichokes instead of potatoes
3 Stir in fresh double cream just before serving.
Serves 4

French Onion Soup

350g / 12oz onions
40g / 1½oz butter
900ml / 1¾ pints beef stock
Salt and freshly milled black pepper to taste
1 to 2 teaspoons dry sherry (optional)
4 slices French bread, each 2cm / 1in thick
50g / 2oz finely grated Cheddar cheese

1 Slice onions thinly. Fry gently in butter (in saucepan) until warm gold
2 Pour in stock. Season to taste with salt and pepper. Bring to boil
3 Lower heat. Cover pan and simmer 45 minutes. Add sherry if used
4 Pour into heatproof dish. Add bread (which will float on top) and sprinkle with cheese
5 Brown under hot grill and serve immediately.
Serves 4

Cream of Potato Soup

500g / 1 lb potatoes
1 large onion
2 medium-sized celery stalks
40g / 1½oz butter
450ml / ¾ pint water
1 level teaspoon salt
Shake of pepper
25g / 1oz cornflour
300ml / ½ pint milk
2-3 tablespoons fresh double cream
2 level tablespoons finely chopped parsley

1 Cut potatoes into dice
2 Thinly slice onion and celery
3 Fry vegetables very gently in butter (in saucepan) for 10 minutes. Do not allow to brown
4 Add water and salt and pepper
5 Bring to boil. Cover pan and simmer very gently for 45 minutes
6 Rub through sieve (or liquidise) and return to pan
7 Mix cornflour to smooth paste with a little of the cold milk. Stir in remainder
8 Add to Soup and bring to boil, stirring
9 Simmer 5 minutes. Ladle into 4 warm soup bowls. Whirl on fresh cream
10 Sprinkle each with parsley.
Serves 4

Cream of Cauliflower Soup

1 Follow recipe and method for Cream of Potato Soup (above)
2 Use 500g / 1 lb cauliflower (divided into small florets) instead of potatoes
3 Add large pinch of nutmeg with salt and pepper

Cabbage Soup

1 small head cabbage (about 250g / 8oz)
1 medium-sized onion
25g / 1oz butter
600ml / 1 pint beef stock
Salt and pepper to taste
4 tablespoons soured cream

Garnish
1 tablespoon very finely chopped parsley

1 Shred cabbage finely, wash well and drain
2 Coarsely grate onion. Fry gently in butter (in saucepan) until soft and pale gold
3 Add cabbage and stock. Bring to boil
4 Season to taste with salt and pepper. Reduce heat and cover pan
5 Simmer gently for 15 minutes
6 Ladle into 4 warm soup bowls. Pour tablespoon of soured cream on to each
7 Sprinkle with parsley and serve very hot.
Serves 4

Cream of Celery Soup

1 Follow recipe and method for Cream of Potato Soup (left)
2 Use a large head of celery instead of potatoes
3 Stir in 2-3 tablespoons fresh double cream just before serving. **Serves 4**

Fish Soup

1 medium-sized celery stalk
1 small lettuce
2 medium-sized tomatoes
1 shallot or small onion
1 garlic clove (optional)
600ml / 1 pint boiling water
600ml / 1 pint milk
1 blade mace
1 bay leaf
500g / 1 lb fish trimmings (bones, heads, etc.)
25g / 1oz butter
25g / 1oz flour
Seasoning to taste
Yolk of 1 standard egg
2 tablespoons fresh single cream

Garnish
2 medium-sized tomatoes, skinned and chopped
Snipped chives

1 Chop celery, lettuce, tomatoes, shallot or onion and garlic if used
2 Put into saucepan with water, milk, mace and bay leaf
3 Bring to boil. Remove scum
4 Lower heat. Cover pan
5 Simmer for 15 minutes
6 Add well-washed fish trimmings
7 Bring to boil again
8 Lower heat. Simmer slowly for further 20 minutes
9 Strain fish liquor and reserve (discarding vegetables, etc)
10 Melt butter in clean saucepan. Stir in flour. Cook for 2 minutes without browning
11 Gradually blend in fish liquor
12 Cook, stirring, until soup comes to boil and thickens
13 Season to taste. Simmer for 2 minutes
14 Remove from heat
15 Mix egg yolk and cream well together
16 Gradually beat into soup
17 Ladle into 4 or 5 warm soup bowls
18 Garnish each with chopped tomatoes and chives. **Serves 4 to 5**

Watercress Soup

2 bunches watercress
1 medium-sized onion
1 medium-sized potato
25g / 1oz butter
450ml / ¾ pint milk
300ml / ½ pint chicken stock
Salt and pepper to taste
4 tablespoons fresh double cream

1 Shred watercress, reserving some sprigs for garnish
2 Thinly dice onion and potato
3 Fry vegetables gently in butter (in saucepan) for 5 minutes. Do not allow to brown
4 Add milk and stock
5 Bring to boil stirring continuously. Cover and simmer very gently for 10 to 15 minutes
6 Rub through sieve (or liquidise) and return to pan
7 Season and reheat. Ladle into 4 warm soup bowls, whirl on a tablespoon of cream and garnish with watercress.
Serves 4

Lettuce Soup

1 Follow recipe and method for Watercress Soup (above)
2 Use 1 large lettuce (shredded) instead of watercress. **Serves 4**

Liver & Bacon Soup

1 medium-sized onion
100g / 4oz lean bacon
25g / 1oz butter
250g / 8oz ox or pigs' liver
25g / 1oz flour
900ml / 1½ pints water
½ level teaspoon salt
2 teaspoons lemon juice
½ teaspoon Worcestershire sauce

Garnish
1 level tablespoon finely chopped parsley

1 Finely chop onion and bacon. Fry gently in butter (in saucepan) for 5 to 7 minutes
2 Wash liver well and wipe dry. Cut into 1cm / ½in cubes
3 Toss in flour until each piece is well coated. Add to pan and fry with onion and bacon further 5 minutes, stirring
4 Gradually blend in water. Add salt, lemon juice and Worcestershire sauce
5 Bring slowly to boil, stirring. Lower heat and cover pan
6 Simmer gently 1½ hours. Ladle into 4 warm soup bowls. Sprinkle each with parsley. **Serves 4**

Cream of Marrow Soup

500g / 1lb marrow
1 medium-sized onion
25g / 1oz butter
Handful of parsley
450ml / ¾ pint water
Large pinch of grated nutmeg
1 level teaspoon salt
Shake of pepper
25g / 1oz cornflour
150ml / ¼ pint milk
4 tablespoons fresh double cream

Garnish
Paprika

1 Cut marrow into 2cm / 1in cubes. Chop onion finely
2 Fry both very gently in butter (in saucepan) for 10 minutes. Do not allow to brown
3 Add parsley, water, nutmeg and salt and pepper. Bring to boil
4 Lower heat, cover pan and simmer gently 1 hour
5 Rub through sieve (or liquidise) and return to pan
6 Mix cornflour to smooth paste with cold milk
7 Add to soup and bring to boil, stirring
8 Simmer for 5 minutes. Ladle into 4 warm soup bowls
9 Pour tablespoon of fresh double cream on to each. Sprinkle lightly with paprika.
Serves 4

Cheese & Onion Soup

1 large onion
25g / 1oz butter
25g / 1oz flour
1 level teaspoon dry mustard
600ml / 1 pint milk
150ml / ¼ pint chicken stock or water
Seasoning to taste
100g / 4oz finely crumbled Lancashire cheese

Garnish
Paprika

1 Chop onion finely. Fry gently in butter (in saucepan) until soft but not brown
2 Add flour and mustard. Cook slowly for 2 minutes. Gradually blend in milk and stock or water
3 Cook, stirring, until Soup comes to boil and thickens slightly
4 Season to taste with salt and pepper. Lower heat and cover pan
5 Simmer very gently for 15 minutes
6 Remove from heat. Add cheese and stir until melted
7 Ladle into 4 warm soup bowls. Dust tops of each lightly with paprika.
Serves 4

Minestrone Soup

1 medium-sized leek
1 large onion
1 medium-sized carrot
2 large celery stalks
175g/6oz white or green cabbage
1 small packet frozen green beans
400g/14oz can tomatoes
50g/2oz haricot beans, soaked overnight
2 level tablespoons finely chopped parsley
1 level teaspoon basil
1 to 2 level teaspoons salt
Freshly milled black pepper
1 level teaspoon granulated sugar
900ml/1½ pints water
50g/2oz broken macaroni
75g/3oz finely grated Cheddar cheese

1 Trim leek and cut in half lengthwise. Wash thoroughly under cold running water. Shred finely
2 Thinly slice onion, carrot and celery
3 Cut cabbage into thin strips
4 Put prepared vegetables in large pan. Add green beans, tomatoes, drained haricot beans, parsley, basil, salt, pepper, sugar and water
5 Bring to boil. Lower heat and cover pan
6 Simmer 1 hour. Add macaroni and simmer further 15 minutes (or until macaroni is plump and tender)
7 Ladle into 4 warm soup bowls. Sprinkle each thickly with cheese.
Serves 4

Paprika Beef Soup

1 medium-sized onion
1 small red or green pepper
25g/1oz butter
350g/12oz shin of beef
1 level tablespoon paprika
1 level tablespoon tomato purée
½ level teaspoon granulated sugar
1 level teaspoon salt
¼ level teaspoon caraway seeds
1 litre/1¾ pints cold water
1 large potato
150g/5oz carton natural yogurt

1 Finely chop onion and pepper. Fry gently in butter (in saucepan) for 5 minutes
2 Cut beef into small pieces and add to saucepan. Fry further 5 minutes, turning all the time
3 Stir in paprika, purée, sugar, salt, caraway seeds and water
4 Coarsely grate potato and add
5 Bring Soup to boil. Lower heat and cover
6 Simmer gently for 2 hours (or until beef is tender)
7 Remove from heat. Stir in yogurt
8 Ladle into 4 or 6 warm soup bowls.
Serves 4 to 6

Cheese & Vegetable Soup

4 medium-sized carrots
2 medium-sized onions
2 celery stalks
450ml/¾ pint water
1 level teaspoon salt
25g/1oz plain flour
300ml/½ pint milk
100g/4oz finely grated Cheddar cheese
25g/1oz butter
Seasoning to taste

1 Cut carrots into tiny dice. Chop onions and celery finely
2 Put vegetables into saucepan. Add 300ml/½ pint water and salt
3 Cook 20 to 30 minutes (or until tender). Pour in rest of water
4 Mix flour to smooth paste with milk and add to saucepan
5 Cook, stirring, until Soup comes to boil. Simmer 5 minutes
6 Remove from heat. Add 75g/3oz cheese and butter. Stir until both have melted
7 Season to taste with salt and pepper and ladle into 4 warm soup bowls. Sprinkle with rest of cheese. **Serves 4**

Cream of Lentil Soup

100g/4oz lentils
1 large carrot
1 large onion
1 celery stalk
½ small turnip
1 medium-sized potato
40g/1½oz butter
Handful of parsley
600ml/1 pint milk
300ml/½ pint chicken stock or water
Pinch of grated nutmeg
Seasoning to taste
150ml/¼ pint fresh single cream

Garnish
1 tablespoon finely chopped parsley

1 Wash lentils and drain
2 Thinly slice carrot, onion and celery. Cut turnip and potato into small dice
3 Fry very gently in butter (in saucepan) for 7 to 10 minutes
4 Add lentils and parsley. Pour in milk and stock or water
5 Bring to boil, lower heat and cover pan
6 Simmer very gently for 1 hour
7 Rub through sieve and return to pan. Add nutmeg and seasoning to taste
8 Re-heat gently. Stir in cream just before serving
9 Ladle into 4 warm soup bowls. Sprinkle each with parsley.
Serves 4

Mulligatawny Soup

1 large onion
1 small carrot
1 large celery stalk
50g / 2oz butter
25g / 1oz flour
2 level teaspoons curry powder
900ml / 1½ pints water
1 large cooking apple
2 teaspoons lemon juice
25g / 1oz boiled rice (about 15g / ½oz uncooked)
25g / 1oz finely chopped cooked chicken
    (optional)
1 level teaspoon salt
Good shake pepper
4 tablespoons fresh single cream

1 Slice onion thinly. Cut carrot into tiny dice.
Chop celery finely
2 Fry vegetables gently in butter (in saucepan) for
7 minutes. Do not allow to brown
3 Stir in flour and curry powder. Cook 2 minutes
then blend in water
4 Cook, stirring, until Soup comes to boil and
thickens slightly. Lower heat and cover pan
5 Simmer very slowly 30 minutes, stirring at least
twice
6 Peel, core and dice apple. Add to Soup with
lemon juice, rice, chicken if used, and salt and
pepper
7 Simmer further 15 minutes
8 Remove from heat. Ladle into 4 warm soup
bowls. Whirl on fresh cream. **Serves 4**

Vegetable Broth

1 medium-sized carrot
1 small parsnip
½ small turnip
1 medium-sized onion
2 large celery stalks
1 large leek
25g / 1oz butter
900ml / 1½ pints water
1 level tablespoon well-washed barley
1 to 1½ level teaspoons salt

Garnish
1 level tablespoon finely chopped parsley

1 Cut carrot, parsnip and turnip into dice. Chop
onion and celery. Cut leek into fine shreds
2 Melt butter in a saucepan. Add vegetables and
cover pan
3 Fry very gently, without browning, 7 minutes,
shaking pan frequently
4 Pour in water. Add barley and salt and bring to
boil
5 Lower heat. Cover pan and simmer very gently
for 1½ hours (or until barley is soft)
6 Ladle into 4 warm soup bowls. Sprinkle each
with parsley. **Serves 4**

Cock-a-Leekie Soup

3 medium-sized leeks
1 medium-sized joint roasting chicken
600ml / 1 pint water
1 clove   ⎫ tied
1 blade mace   ⎬ together
Sprig of parsley   in muslin
3 peppercorns   ⎭ bag
1 level teaspoon salt
50g / 2oz rice
150ml / ¼ pint fresh single cream

1 Cut off all but 5cm / 2in of green leaves from
leeks
2 Cut leeks in half lengthwise. Wash well under
cold running water then cut into fine shreds
3 Put into saucepan with chicken and water
4 Add bag of clove, mace, parsley and peppercorns. Add salt
5 Bring to boil and remove scum
6 Lower heat, cover pan and simmer gently ¾ to 1
hour (or until chicken is tender)
7 Remove chicken and cut flesh into small pieces
8 Add to Soup with rice
9 Simmer further 20 to 30 minutes (or until rice is
tender). Remove from heat and stir in cream
10 Ladle into 4 soup bowls. Serve immediately.
Serves 4

Prawn and Corn Chowder

1 large onion
15g / ½oz butter
500g / 1lb potatoes
150ml / ¼ pint stock
Salt and pepper to taste
175g / 6oz frozen prawns
200g / 7oz can sweetcorn
600ml / 1 pint milk
75g / 3oz finely grated Cheddar cheese

1 Chop onion finely and fry in butter until soft but
not coloured
2 Dice potatoes and put into saucepan with
onion. Add stock and seasoning
3 Bring to boil; cover and simmer gently for 10 to
15 minutes (or until potatoes are just cooked)
4 Add prawns, drained sweetcorn and milk and
reheat
5 Remove from heat and stir in cheese
6 Ladle into 4 warm soup bowls. Serve
immediately. **Serves 4**

Beef Broth

1 Follow recipe and method for Vegetable Broth
(left)
2 Fry 100g / 4oz lean stewing steak—cut into thin
strips—with vegetables
3 Use beef stock instead of water. **Serves 4**

Oyster Soup

25g / 1oz butter
25g / 1oz flour
600ml / 1 pint fish stock
12 oysters
1 blade mace
1 strip lemon rind
½ level teaspoon salt
Light shake of Cayenne pepper
1 teaspoon lemon juice
4 tablespoons fresh single cream

Garnish
1 level teaspoon finely grated lemon rind
2 level teaspoons finely chopped parsley

1 Melt butter in saucepan. Add flour and cook over low heat, stirring, for 2 minutes. Gradually blend in stock and liquor from oysters
2 Add mace, lemon rind, salt and Cayenne pepper
3 Cook, stirring, until Soup comes to boil and thickens slightly
4 Simmer for 5 minutes. Remove mace and strip of lemon rind. Stir in lemon juice and cream
5 Re-heat, without boiling, for 1 minute
6 Place shelled oysters in 4 warm soup bowls
7 Pour Soup into each. Sprinkle tops with lemon rind and parsley.
Serves 4

Creamed Scotch Broth

500g / 1lb scrag end neck of lamb
1 litre / 1¾ pints cold water
1 large onion
2 medium-sized celery stalks
1 medium-sized carrot
½ small turnip
1½ to 2 level teaspoons salt
25g / 1oz well-washed barley
4 tablespoons fresh single cream

Garnish
2 level tablespoons finely chopped parsley

1 Cut lamb into small neat sections. Remove as much fat as possible
2 Put into large saucepan with water
3 Bring to boil and remove scum
4 Cover and simmer gently while preparing vegetables
5 Chop onion and celery. Cut carrot and turnip into small dice
6 Add to saucepan with salt and barley
7 Bring to boil again. Lower heat and cover pan
8 Simmer very gently for 2 hours. Leave until completely cold
9 Remove fat and discard
10 Bring Soup just up to boil. Stir in cream. Ladle into 4 warm soup bowls. Sprinkle each with parsley.
Serves 4

Onion Velouté Soup

2 large onions
40g / 1½oz butter
2 level teaspoons flour
150ml / ¼ pint water
300ml / ½ pint milk
½ level teaspoon salt
Yolks of 2 standard eggs
2 tablespoons fresh double cream
Pinch of grated nutmeg
¼ level teaspoon paprika

Garnish
1 level tablespoon finely chopped parsley

1 Chop onions fairly finely. Fry very gently in butter (in saucepan) for 10 minutes. Do not allow to brown
2 Stir in flour. Cook further minute, then blend in water and milk. Add salt
3 Very slowly bring to boil, stirring, then lower heat
4 Cover pan. Simmer gently for ¾ to 1 hour (or until onions are tender)
5 Beat egg yolks with cream, nutmeg and paprika. Stir into Soup
6 Heat gently, without boiling, for 1 or 2 minutes. Ladle into 4 warm soup bowls
7 Sprinkle parsley over each.
Serves 4

Vichyssoise Soup

2 medium-sized leeks
1 small onion
25g / 1oz butter
350g / 12oz potatoes
600ml / 1 pint chicken stock
1 level teaspoon salt
Light shake of pepper
1 blade mace
300ml / ½ pint fresh double cream

Garnish
2 level tablespoons snipped chives or
   finely chopped watercress

1 Finely chop white part of leeks and onion
2 Fry gently in butter (in saucepan) for 7 to 10 minutes. Do not allow to brown
3 Thinly slice potatoes and add to saucepan with stock, salt, pepper and mace
4 Bring to boil, lower heat and cover pan
5 Simmer very gently 20 to 30 minutes (or until vegetables are tender)
6 Rub Soup through fine sieve (or liquidise). Chill thoroughly
7 Just before serving stir in cream. Transfer to 4 or 6 soup bowls
8 Sprinkle each with chives or watercress.
Serves 4 to 6

Iced Cucumber and Yogurt Soup (below)

Iced Cucumber & Yogurt Soup

1 large unpeeled cucumber
2×150g/5oz cartons natural yogurt
½ small green pepper
1 garlic clove (optional)
2 tablespoons wine vinegar
1 level tablespoon snipped chives
Seasoning to taste
300ml/½ pint chilled milk

Garnish
2 level tablespoons finely chopped parsley

1 Grate cucumber on medium grater. Transfer to bowl. Stir in yogurt
2 Finely chop green pepper (discarding pips) and garlic if used
3 Add to cucumber mixture with vinegar and chives
4 Season to taste with salt and pepper. Chill very thoroughly
5 Just before serving stir in milk
6 Ladle into 4 or 6 soup bowls. Sprinkle each with chopped parsley. **Serves 4 to 6**

Split Pea & Ham Soup

100g/4oz split peas
1 celery stalk
1 medium-sized onion
50g/2oz lean ham
40g/1½oz butter
1 medium-sized potato
900ml/1½ pints water
1 level teaspoon salt
Good shake pepper
4 tablespoons natural yogurt

1 Cover split peas with cold water. Leave to soak 2 to 3 hours. Drain
2 Finely chop celery, onion and ham. Fry gently in butter (in saucepan) for 5 minutes
3 Peel and grate potato. Add to saucepan with split peas, water and salt
4 Bring to boil. Season to taste with pepper
5 Lower heat, cover pan and simmer for 2 hours, stirring frequently
6 Ladle into 4 warm soup bowls. Pour tablespoon of natural yogurt on to each. **Serves 4**

Hot Bortsch (Russian Beet Soup)

1 large carrot
2 medium-sized onions
4 medium-sized cooked beetroots
150ml / $\frac{1}{4}$ pint water
600ml / 1 pint beef stock
100g / 4oz white cabbage
1 tablespoon lemon juice
Seasoning to taste
4 tablespoons soured cream

1 Finely grate carrot, onions and beetroots
2 Put into saucepan. Add water and bring to boil
3 Lower heat. Cover pan and simmer very slowly for 30 minutes
4 Add stock, cabbage and lemon juice. Season to taste and simmer further 20 minutes
5 Ladle into 4 warm soup bowls. Pour 1 tablespoon soured cream over each. **Serves 4**

Cold Bortsch

1 Follow recipe and method for Hot Bortsch (above)
2 Leave Soup in saucepan until completely cold
3 Strain, ladle into 4 soup bowls and chill
4 Just before serving pour tablespoon of soured cream over each. **Serves 4**

Clear Tomato Soup

1 small onion
2 medium-sized celery stalks and leaves
25g / 1oz butter
600ml / 1 pint tomato juice
1 small bay leaf
2 cloves
$\frac{1}{4}$ level teaspoon basil
1 level tablespoon coarsely chopped parsley
2 level teaspoons granulated sugar
2 teaspoons lemon juice
Salt and pepper to taste
4 tablespoons fresh single cream

1 Chop onion and celery finely. Fry very gently in butter (in saucepan) for 7 minutes. Do not allow to brown
2 Pour in tomato juice
3 Add bay leaf, cloves, basil, parsley and sugar. Bring to boil and lower heat
4 Cover pan. Simmer Soup gently 15 minutes. Strain
5 Return to clean pan. Add lemon juice and season to taste with salt and pepper
6 Re-heat 1 or 2 minutes. Ladle into 4 warm soup bowls
7 Pour 1 tablespoon cream over each.
Serves 4

Chicken Soup

1 chicken carcass
1 medium-sized onion
1 bay leaf
1 clove
600ml / 1 pint milk
1 chicken stock cube
4 tablespoons boiling water
1 level tablespoon cornflour
4 tablespoons cold water
$\frac{1}{4}$ level teaspoon nutmeg
100g / 4oz cooked chopped chicken
Season to taste

Garnish
25g / 1oz blanched, toasted and chopped almonds

1 Break up carcass and put into saucepan
2 Chop onion and add with bay leaf and clove
3 Pour in milk and stock cube dissolved in boiling water
4 Simmer slowly 20 minutes. Strain and return to pan
5 Add cornflour mixed to smooth paste with cold water. Cook, stirring, until Soup comes to boil and thickens slightly
6 Add nutmeg and chicken. Season to taste. Simmer, covered, for 15 minutes
7 Ladle into 4 warm soup bowls. Sprinkle each with almonds. **Serves 4**

Curried Chicken Soup

25g / 1oz butter
2 level teaspoons curry powder
1 level tablespoon cornflour
450ml / $\frac{3}{4}$ pint chicken stock or water
$\frac{1}{2}$ level teaspoon paprika
2 level tablespoons chutney
50g / 2oz cooked chopped chicken
Yolk of 1 standard egg
4 tablespoons fresh single cream
Seasoning to taste

Garnish
1 level tablespoon finely chopped chives

1 Melt butter in saucepan. Stir in curry powder and cornflour
2 Cook gently for 2 minutes
3 Very gradually blend in stock or water. Add paprika
4 Cook, stirring, until Soup comes to boil and thickens slightly
5 Add chutney and chicken. Cover pan and simmer 7 minutes
6 Remove from heat and stir in egg yolk beaten with cream
7 Season to taste with salt and pepper. Ladle into 4 warm soup bowls. Sprinkle each with chives.
Serves 4

Jellied Tomato Consommé

3 level teaspoons gelatine
5 tablespoons hot water
600ml / 1 pint tomato juice
1 level teaspoon finely grated onion
1 strip lemon rind
2 tablespoons lemon juice or dry sherry
1 to 2 teaspoons Worcestershire sauce

Garnish
2 level tablespoons finely chopped parsley

1 Shower gelatine into hot water. Stir until dissolved
2 Pour tomato juice into saucepan. Add onion and lemon rind. Bring just up to boil
3 Strain. Add dissolved gelatine, lemon juice or sherry and Worcestershire sauce
4 Leave until cold. Chill until softly set
5 Break up lightly with fork. Spoon into 4 or 6 soup bowls
6 Sprinkle each with parsley. **Serves 4 to 6**

Cheese & Tomato Soup

1 small onion
25g / 1oz butter
25g / 1oz flour
150ml / $\frac{1}{4}$ pint chicken stock or water
600ml / 1 pint milk
100g / 4oz skinned chopped tomatoes
Seasoning to taste
175g / 6oz finely grated Cheddar cheese

1 Chop onion finely. Fry gently in butter (in saucepan) until soft, not brown
2 Add flour and cook slowly for 2 minutes
3 Gradually blend in stock or water and milk. Cook, stirring, until Soup comes to boil and thickens slightly
4 Add tomatoes and season to taste
5 Lower heat and cover pan
6 Simmer for 10 minutes. Remove from heat and add 150g / 5oz cheese
7 Stir until cheese melts. Ladle into 4 warm soup bowls
8 Sprinkle rest of cheese on top of each. **Serves 4**

Creamy Carrot Soup

250g / 8oz carrots
1 large potato
1 medium-sized onion
25g / 1oz butter
450ml / $\frac{3}{4}$ pint water
150ml / $\frac{1}{4}$ pint milk
25g / 1oz well-washed rice
Large pinch of grated nutmeg
$\frac{1}{2}$ to 1 level teaspoon salt
2 teaspoons lemon juice
2 to 3 tablespoons fresh single cream

1 Coarsely grate carrots, potato and onion
2 Fry gently in butter (in saucepan) for 5 minutes. Do not allow to brown
3 Add water, milk, rice, nutmeg and salt
4 Bring to boil, lower heat and cover pan
5 Simmer very gently for $\frac{3}{4}$ to 1 hour
6 Stir in lemon juice and cream. Re-heat without boiling. Ladle into 4 warm soup bowls. **Serves 4**

Sweet Corn Soup

1 rasher streaky bacon
1 small finely chopped onion
25g / 1oz butter
2 large potatoes, sliced
2 stalks celery
250ml / $\frac{1}{2}$ pint chicken stock
Salt and pepper
175g / 7oz can sweet corn kernels
50g / 2oz prawns (optional)
1 level tablespoon cornflour
600ml / 1 pint milk

1 Fry bacon and onion in butter until soft. Add potato and celery
2 Add stock and seasoning and simmer until potatoes and other vegetables are soft. Drain the corn and add the kernels to the soup, with the prawns, if used
3 Blend cornflour with a little milk and add it to the rest of milk. Add to the corn mixture. Bring to the boil and simmer for 5 minutes
4 Sieve or liquidise the soup
5 Serve with croûtons. **Serves 4**

Hors-d'Œuvres

Individual Kipper Creams (page 31)

Pâtés freeze well; always defrost in the refrigerator. Storage time – 1 month. Where recipes call for pastry, eg, Vol-au-Vents, freeze pastry separately from the filling.

Grilled Grapefruits

2 grapefruits
4 teaspoons sweet sherry
8 level teaspoons caster sugar
4 teaspoons melted butter

1 Halve grapefruits and loosen flesh. Sprinkle with sherry
2 Cover with equal amounts of caster sugar. Spoon butter over each
3 Stand under hot grill. Leave until sugar just starts turning brown.
Serves 4

Buttered Buckling

1 large buckling
100g / 4oz softened butter
1 level tablespoon finely chopped parsley
2 teaspoons bottled horseradish sauce
1 tablespoon lemon juice
Freshly milled black pepper

1 Cover buckling with boiling water, leave 1 minute and drain
2 Remove skin and bones and flake up flesh very finely
3 Beat to smooth cream with softened butter. Stir in parsley, horseradish sauce and lemon juice
4 Season to taste with pepper. Arrange equal amounts on 4 serving plates
5 Shape into neat mounds with fork. Accompany with hot toast.
Serves 4

Individual Kipper Creams

250g / 8oz kipper fillets
2 teaspoons finely chopped onion
75g / 3oz softened butter
150ml / ¼ pint cold Béchamel Sauce (page 129)
2 teaspoons lemon juice
2 teaspoons dry white wine
Seasoning to taste
150ml / ¼ pint fresh double cream

Garnish
150ml / ¼ pint cold aspic jelly
4 cucumber slices

1 Skin kipper fillets. Fry gently with onion in 25g / 1oz butter for 5 to 7 minutes
2 Remove from pan and mince finely
3 Put into bowl and add pan juices. Gradually beat in rest of butter, cold sauce, lemon juice and wine. Season to taste with salt and pepper
4 Whip cream fairly stiffly. Fold into kipper mixture
5 Transfer equal amounts to 4 individual dishes. Smooth tops with a knife
6 Spoon aspic jelly over each and chill
7 Just before serving, garnish with cucumber. **Serves 4**

Hot Cheese Cups

2 standard eggs
150ml / ¼ pint fresh double cream
1 level teaspoon made mustard
Large pinch Cayenne pepper
¼ level teaspoon salt
100g / 4oz crumbled Lancashire cheese

1 Beat eggs, cream and mustard together
2 Season with Cayenne pepper and salt. Stir in 75g/3oz cheese
3 Pour into 4 individual buttered heatproof dishes, and sprinkle with rest of cheese. Bake in centre of moderately hot oven (200°C / 400°F or Gas No 6) for 20 to 25 minutes (or until top is pale gold)
4 Serve immediately with crisp toast. **Serves 4**

Potted Tongue

250g / 8oz tongue
75g / 3oz softened butter
½ level teaspoon made mustard
Seasoning to taste
25g / 1oz melted butter

1 Mince tongue finely
2 Gradually beat in 75g / 3oz butter and mustard
3 Season to taste with salt and pepper then press equal amounts into 4 small jars or pots
4 Cover tops completely with remaining butter. Leave in cool until butter is set
5 Serve with crisp toast. **Serves 4**

Potted Ham

1 Follow recipe and method for Potted Tongue (left)
2 Use 250g / 8oz ham instead of tongue. **Serves 4**

Potted Beef

1 Follow recipe and method for Potted Tongue (left)
2 Use 250g / 8oz cooked beef instead of tongue and 1 teaspoon bottled horseradish sauce instead of mustard. **Serves 4**

Egg Mayonnaise

½ box mustard and cress
4 large hard-boiled eggs, halved
8 tablespoons Chantilly Mayonnaise (page 127)
Paprika

Garnish
4 anchovy fillets, each halved lengthwise

1 Line 4 serving plates with mustard and cress
2 Arrange 2 hard-boiled egg halves on each, cut side down
3 Spoon Mayonnaise over eggs. Sprinkle lightly with paprika
4 Garnish each serving with 2 strips of anchovy. **Serves 4**

Egg & Smoked Salmon Mayonnaise

1 Follow recipe and method for Egg Mayonnaise (above)
2 Garnish each serving with small strips of smoked salmon. **Serves 4**

Liver Sausage Pâté

350g / 12oz soft liver sausage
50g / 2oz softened butter
1 level tablespoon very finely chopped parsley
2 teaspoons brandy or dry sherry
¼ level teaspoon thyme
Freshly milled black pepper and salt to taste

1 Beat sausage with butter until smooth and creamy
2 Blend in parsley, brandy or sherry and thyme
3 Season to taste with pepper and salt
4 Turn into small serving bowl. Chill 2 to 3 hours
5 Serve by spooning portions on to plates and accompanying with crisp toast.
Serves 4

Stilton-filled Eggs

4 large hard-boiled eggs
50g/2oz Blue Stilton cheese
1 level teaspoon paprika
2 tablespoons fresh single cream
Salt and pepper to taste
4 level tablespoons mustard and cress

Garnish
8 small slices of tomato

1 Halve eggs lengthwise and carefully remove yolks
2 Transfer to basin and mash finely with Stilton cheese
3 Stir in paprika and cream then season to taste with salt and pepper
4 Pile back into egg white halves
5 Cover 4 serving plates with mustard and cress and place 2 egg halves on each. Garnish each with slice of tomato
6 Chill lightly before serving
7 Accompany with brown bread and butter.
Serves 4

Curried Egg & Shrimp Cocktail

½ round lettuce, washed and dried
3 tablespoons Mayonnaise (page 126)
4 tablespoons natural yogurt
2 level teaspoons curry powder
4 level tablespoons chutney
2 tablespoons lemon juice
1 level tablespoon sultanas
100g/4oz peeled shrimps
2 standard eggs, hard-boiled and coarsely chopped

1 Shred lettuce and use to half-fill 4 large wine glasses. Leave on one side
2 Combine Mayonnaise with yogurt, curry powder, chutney and lemon juice. Stir in sultanas, shrimps and eggs
3 Mix well and chill lightly
4 Spoon equal amounts into glasses and accompany with brown bread and butter. **Serves 4**

Cream-filled Avocados

2 medium-sized ripe avocados
Lemon juice
1 recipe Cream Cheese and Celery Dressing (page 123)

1 Cut avocados in half about 5 minutes before serving
2 Remove stones. Brush avocado flesh with lemon juice to prevent browning
3 Fill cavities with Dressing
4 Serve rest of Dressing separately. **Serves 4**

Cream Cheese-filled Eggs

4 large hard-boiled eggs
50g/2oz cream cheese
1 level tablespoon finely chopped celery
1 tablespoon milk
Salt and pepper to taste
4 heaped tablespoons shredded lettuce

Garnish
8 thin strips canned pimento

1 Halve eggs lengthwise and remove yolks
2 Transfer to basin and mash finely
3 Mix well with cream cheese, celery and milk then season to taste with salt and pepper
4 Pile back into egg white halves
5 Cover 4 serving plates with shredded lettuce and place 2 egg halves on each. Garnish with pimento
6 Chill lightly before serving. **Serves 4**

Hot Sole Fritters

500g/1lb sole fillets
Salt and pepper
1 recipe Savoury Fritter Batter (page 146)
Deep fat or oil for frying
50g/2oz very finely grated Cheddar cheese
4 lemon wedges

1 Using sharp knife or kitchen scissors, cut sole into strips measuring about 5cm × 1cm / 2in × ½in
2 Sprinkle lightly with salt and pepper. Coat with Fritter Batter
3 Fry in hot fat or oil (about a quarter at a time) for 2 to 3 minutes (or until crisp and golden)
4 Remove from pan and drain on soft kitchen paper. Transfer to serving dish lined with paper napkin
5 Sprinkle with cheese. Serve immediately
6 Hand lemon separately. **Serves 4**

Avocados with Yogurt

1 Follow recipe and method for Cream-filled Avocados (left)
2 Fill cavities with Basic Yogurt Dressing (page 124)
3 Pass rest of Dressing separately. **Serves 4**

Avocados with Shellfish

1 Follow recipe and method for Cream-filled Avocados (left)
2 Fill cavities with 3 level tablespoons peeled prawns or crabmeat mixed with 3 tablespoons Thousand Island Mayonnaise (page 126).
Serves 4

Onion-stuffed Tomatoes

4 large tomatoes
3 level tablespoons fresh white breadcrumbs
1 small onion, finely grated
1 level tablespoon very finely chopped parsley
40g / 1½oz butter, melted
Salt and pepper to taste

Garnish
Parsley

1 Cut tops off tomatoes and keep for lids
2 Scoop tomato centres into basin and discard any hard pieces
3 Add breadcrumbs, onion, parsley and melted butter to tomato pulp. Mix well together
4 Season to taste with salt and pepper. Leave to stand 10 minutes
5 Pile back into tomato cases and put lid on to each
6 Transfer to lightly buttered heatproof dish and heat through towards top of moderately hot oven (200°C / 400°F or Gas No 6) for 15 minutes
7 Transfer to 4 warm serving plates and garnish with parsley. Serve hot. **Serves 4**

Ham-stuffed Tomatoes

1 Follow recipe and method for Onion-stuffed Tomatoes (above)
2 Use 50g / 2oz very finely chopped ham instead of onion
3 Add ½ level teaspoon made mustard with finely chopped parsley. **Serves 4**

Prawn-stuffed Tomatoes

1 Follow recipe and method for Onion-stuffed Tomatoes (above)
2 Use 50g / 2oz peeled and chopped prawns instead of onion. **Serves 4**

Lamb-stuffed Tomatoes

1 Follow recipe and method for Onion-stuffed Tomatoes (above)
2 Use 50g / 2oz very finely chopped cooked lamb instead of onion
3 Add ½ level teaspoon mixed herbs with finely chopped parsley. **Serves 4**

Cheese-stuffed Tomatoes

1 Follow recipe and method for Onion-stuffed Tomatoes (above)
2 Use 50g / 2oz finely crumbled Lancashire cheese instead of onion. **Serves 4**

Prawn Cocktail

½ round lettuce, washed and dried
2 tablespoons Mayonnaise (page 126)
4 tablespoons natural yogurt
3 tablespoons tomato ketchup
2 tablespoons Worcestershire sauce
2 level teaspoons bottled horseradish sauce
2 tablespoons lemon juice
250g / 8oz peeled prawns

1 Shred lettuce and use to half-fill 4 large wine glasses. Leave on one side
2 Combine Mayonnaise with natural yogurt, ketchup, Worcestershire and horseradish sauces and lemon juice
3 Add prawns and mix well. Chill lightly
4 Spoon equal amounts into glasses. Accompany with brown bread and butter. **Serves 4**

Creamed Pickled Mushrooms

500g / 1lb button mushrooms
1 tablespoon lemon juice
½ level teaspoon salt
4 tablespoons wine vinegar
1 bay leaf
2 cloves
1 small sliced onion
150ml / ¼ pint fresh double cream
Freshly milled pepper and salt

Garnish
Paprika

1 Wash mushrooms, put into pan and cover with water
2 Add lemon juice and salt. Bring to boil and drain
3 Slice thinly. Transfer to bowl
4 Pour vinegar into pan. Add bay leaf, cloves and onion and bring slowly to boil. Boil 5 minutes, then strain over mushrooms
5 Leave mushrooms to cool in liquor. Chill 2 to 3 hours
6 Before serving, lift mushrooms out of bowl with draining spoon. Transfer equal amounts to 4 serving plates
7 Combine fresh double cream with 3 tablespoons vinegar liquor. Season to taste with pepper and salt
8 Spoon over mushrooms. Dust each lightly with paprika. **Serves 4**

Avocado Creams

150ml / ¼ pint fresh double cream
1 tablespoon wine vinegar
4 finely chopped anchovy fillets
1 level teaspoon very finely chopped onion
2 level teaspoons caster sugar
2 medium-sized ripe avocados
Salt and Cayenne pepper
1 level teaspoon paprika

Garnish
4 lemon slices

1 Whip cream until thick
2 Combine vinegar with anchovies, onion and sugar
3 Halve avocados, remove flesh and mash finely
4 Combine with cream and vinegar mixture. Season to taste with salt and Cayenne pepper
5 Pile back into avocado shells and sprinkle lightly with paprika
6 Garnish each with slice of lemon. **Serves 4**

Cold Spaghetti Creams

175g / 6oz spaghetti
1 recipe Mixed Cheese Dressing (page 123)
1 level teaspoon paprika

Garnish
4 tomato slices and watercress

1 Break spaghetti into 2cm / 1in lengths and cook in boiling salted water until tender
2 Drain and leave until cold
3 Turn into large bowl, add Dressing and toss lightly together
4 Transfer to 4 individual plates. Sprinkle with paprika and garnish each with slice of tomato and watercress. **Serves 4**

Tuna Cocktail

½ round lettuce, washed and dried
150g / 5oz carton natural yogurt
2 tablespoons tomato ketchup
2 tablespoons lemon juice
2 teaspoons Worcestershire sauce
4 level tablespoons grated cucumber
200g / 7oz can middle-cut tuna

1 Shred lettuce and use to half-fill 4 large wine glasses. Leave on one side
2 Combine natural yogurt with ketchup, lemon juice, Worcestershire sauce and cucumber
3 Drain tuna, divide into small chunks and add to soured cream mixture
4 Mix well and chill lightly
5 Spoon equal amounts into glasses. Accompany with brown bread and butter. **Serves 4**

Chicken & Bacon Pâté

50g / 2oz butter
100g / 4oz pigs' liver, sliced
100g / 4oz gammon, coarsely chopped
100g / 4oz cold cooked chicken
1 garlic clove
2 teaspoons brandy or dry sherry
2 tablespoons fresh double cream
Freshly milled pepper and salt to taste

1 Melt half of the butter in pan. Add liver slices and gammon. Fry gently 7 to 10 minutes
2 Remove from heat. Mince finely with chicken and garlic
3 Stir in brandy or sherry and cream. Season to taste with pepper and salt
4 Transfer to small earthenware dish and smooth top with knife
5 Melt remaining butter and pour over top of Pâté. Chill before serving. **Serves 4**

Chicken & Mushroom Vol-au-Vents

½ recipe Puff Pastry (page 212) or 225g / 8oz bought Puff Pastry
Beaten egg for brushing

Filling
100g / 4oz cooked chicken
50g / 2oz chopped mushrooms
15g / ½oz butter
150ml / ¼ pint freshly made Béchamel Sauce (page 129)
2 teaspoons lemon juice
Seasoning to taste

1 Roll home-made Pastry out to ½cm / ¼in thickness and bought Pastry as directed on packet
2 Cut into 4 rounds with 9cm / 3½in fluted biscuit cutter dipped in hot water
3 Stand upside down on damp baking tray. Cut circle in centre of each round by pressing a quarter of the way through Pastry with 4cm / 1½in cutter
4 Brush with beaten egg and leave for 30 minutes
5 Bake just above centre of hot oven (220°C / 450°F or Gas No 8) for 10 to 15 minutes (or until well risen and crisp)
6 Lift off centre pieces from baked pastry cases and reserve for lids. Scoop out remaining soft centres underneath and discard
7 Return cases to oven (with heat switched off and door left open). Leave 5 to 10 minutes
8 Cut chicken into bite-sized pieces. Lightly fry mushrooms in butter
9 Add chicken and mushrooms to Sauce with lemon juice. Heat through gently, then adjust seasoning to taste
10 Spoon equal amounts of filling into hot Pastry cases. Top with lids and serve immediately. **Serves 4**

Chicken and Mushroom Vol-au-Vents (page 34)

Prawn Vol-au-Vents

1 Follow recipe and method for Chicken and
Mushroom Vol-au-Vents (page 34)
2 Instead of chicken and fried mushrooms, use
100g/4oz peeled prawns and 50g/2oz cooked
and flaked white fish.
Serves 4

Ham & Mushroom Vol-au-Vents

1 Follow recipe and method for Chicken and
Mushroom Vol-au-Vents (page 34)
2 Instead of chicken, use 100g/4oz coarsely
chopped ham. **Serves 4**

Large Vol-au-Vent

1 recipe Puff Pastry (page 212)
Beaten egg for brushing
Filling (double quantity) as for small Vol-au-
   Vents (pages 34, 35)

1 Roll out Pastry to 1 to 2cm/$\frac{1}{2}$ to $\frac{3}{4}$in thickness
2 Cut into 18cm/7in round (with knife dipped in
hot water), using 18cm/7in cake tin as guide
3 Stand upside down on damp baking tray. Cut
circle in centre by pressing half-way through
pastry with 10cm/4in round biscuit cutter

4 Brush with egg. Leave for $\frac{1}{2}$ an hour then bake
just above centre of hot oven (230°C/450°F or
Gas No 8) for 15 minutes
5 Reduce temperature to moderately hot
(190°C/375°F or Gas No 5). Bake further 15 to 20
minutes
6 Remove lid from baked Pastry case and reserve.
Scoop out remaining soft centre and discard
7 Return case to oven (with heat switched off and
door left open) for 5 to 10 minutes
8 Fill as for small Vol-au-Vents. **Serves 4 to 6**

Mushroom Cocktail

½ round lettuce, washed and dried
250g / 8oz button mushrooms
150ml / ¼ pint fresh double cream
2 tablespoons bottled salad cream
2 tablespoons tomato ketchup
1 tablespoon lemon juice

1 Shred lettuce and use to half-fill 4 large wine glasses
2 Wash mushrooms and stalks, cover with boiling water and leave 2 minutes
3 Drain and slice
4 Combine fresh double cream with salad cream, ketchup and lemon juice
5 Add sliced mushrooms. Mix well and chill lightly
6 Spoon equal amounts into glasses. Accompany with brown bread and butter. **Serves 4**

Crab Cocktail

½ round lettuce, washed and dried
150ml / ¼ pint Mayonnaise (page 126)
3 tablespoons tomato ketchup
½ teaspoon Tabasco sauce
1 tablespoon lemon juice
2 tablespoons fresh double cream
250g / 8oz flaked crab meat

1 Shred lettuce and use to half-fill 4 large wine glasses. Leave on one side
2 Combine Mayonnaise with ketchup, Tabasco sauce, lemon juice and cream
3 Stir in crab meat, mix well and chill lightly
4 Spoon equal amounts into glasses. Accompany with brown bread and butter. **Serves 4**

Stuffed Mushrooms

8 large mushrooms
25g / 1oz butter
1 level tablespoon finely grated onion
25g / 1 oz lean bacon, finely chopped
25g / 1oz fresh white breadcrumbs
2 level teaspoons finely chopped parsley
¼ to ½ level teaspoon salt
Freshly milled pepper

1 Wash and peel mushrooms
2 Chop stalks finely. Retain caps
3 Melt butter in pan. Add mushroom stalks, onion and bacon. Fry very gently, without browning, for 5 minutes
4 Stir in breadcrumbs and parsley. Season to taste with salt and pepper
5 Pile equal amounts on to mushroom caps. Transfer to buttered heatproof dish
6 Bake towards top of moderately hot oven (190°C / 375°F or Gas No 5) for 10 to 12 minutes
7 Serve immediately. Accompany with crisp toast and butter. **Serves 4**

Asparagus Mousse

3 level teaspoons gelatine
150ml / ¼ pint hot water
150ml / ¼ pint fresh single cream
Yolks and whites of 2 standard eggs
1 level teaspoon paprika
½ level teaspoon salt
1 tablespoon lemon juice
175g / 6oz canned asparagus tips, very finely chopped

Garnish
8 extra asparagus tips

1 Put gelatine and hot water in a basin. Stir until dissolved, over a pan of boiling water. Leave until lukewarm.
2 Warm cream then beat into egg yolks
3 Combine with dissolved gelatine and stir in paprika, salt and lemon juice
4 When cold and just beginning to thicken, stir in chopped asparagus
5 Beat egg whites to stiff snow and gently fold into asparagus mixture
6 Spoon into 4 large wine glasses and chill until firm
7 Just before serving decorate each with 2 asparagus tips. **Serves 4**

Steak Tartare

500g / 1lb rump, sirloin or fillet steak, very finely minced
1 tablespoon finely chopped capers
1 teaspoon Worcestershire sauce
½ to 1 level teaspoon salt
Freshly milled black pepper
1 small onion, peeled and coarsely grated
Yolks of 4 standard eggs

1 Combine meat with capers, Worcestershire sauce and salt. Season to taste with pepper
2 Put equal amounts on to 4 plates. Shape into neat mounds, then make hole in centre of each
3 Sprinkle with onion. Fill with egg yolks.
Serves 4

Salmon Mousse

1 Follow recipe and method for Asparagus Mousse (above)
2 Use 1 medium-sized can red salmon (about 225g / 8oz), well drained and finely mashed, instead of asparagus
3 Garnish with lemon slices and parsley. **Serves 4**

French Country-style Pâté (below)

French Country-style Pâté

175g / 6oz pigs' liver, sliced
100g / 4oz lean bacon
100g / 4oz stewing veal
1 small peeled onion
2 cloves crushed garlic
50g / 2oz fresh white breadcrumbs
1 level tablespoon finely chopped parsley
2 standard eggs, beaten
150ml / $\frac{1}{4}$ pint milk
$\frac{1}{2}$ to 1 level teaspoon salt
Freshly milled pepper
3 bay leaves

1 Cover liver with boiling water and leave 5 minutes. Drain
2 Mince with bacon, veal, onion and garlic
3 Stir in breadcrumbs and parsley. Combine with beaten eggs and milk
4 Season to taste with salt and pepper. Pack mixture into well-buttered 20cm × 10cm × 6cm / 1lb loaf tin
5 Put bay leaves on top and cover with aluminium foil. Bake in centre of moderate oven (160°C / 325°F or Gas No 3) for 1 hour
6 Leave in tin 5 minutes. Remove bay leaves then turn out
7 Serve cold, cut in slices, and accompany with crisp toast. **Serves 4 to 5**

Ingredients for Kedgeree (page 39)

Fresh white fish may be frozen whole in fillets or steaks. Fillets and steaks should be first dipped in cold salt water and drained before freezing. Whole fish should be first gutted and the tail and fins removed. Open freeze the whole fish on a baking tray, then dip the frozen fish into cold water and re-freeze for 30 minutes. Repeat this 3 more times. Then wrap well.
Storage time – 3 months.
Storage time of cooked fish dishes – 1 month.
Oily fish in steaks or fillets should be washed and drained. Interleave each steak with freezer film, wrap well. Storage time – 2 months.
Storage time of cooked fish dishes – 2 months.

Where whole fish are used, and where the method does not specify, heads can be removed or retained according to personal preferences

Fried Mackerel

1 Follow recipe and method for Fried Herrings (page 39)
2 Use mackerel instead of herrings.
Serves 4

Fried Herrings – Scots-style

1 Follow recipe and method for Fried Herrings (page 39)
2 Instead of flour, coat with 3 level tablespoons oatmeal or 4 level tablespoons porridge oats mixed with pepper and $\frac{1}{2}$ level teaspoon salt.
Serves 4

Fried Herrings

4 large herrings
About 4 level tablespoons flour
Good shake of pepper
$\frac{1}{2}$ level teaspoon salt
50g / 2oz butter
2 teaspoons olive or corn oil

Garnish
4 lemon wedges

1 Scale and wash herrings. Wipe dry
2 Coat with flour mixed with pepper and salt
3 Fry in hot butter and oil, allowing 4 to 5 minutes per side
4 Drain on soft kitchen paper
5 Transfer to serving dish and garnish with lemon.
Serves 4

Foil-wrapped Baked Herrings or Mackerel

4 herrings or mackerel
Salt and pepper
25g / 1oz butter, melted

Garnish
Lemon wedges and parsley

1 Scale and wash herrings or mackerel. Wipe dry
2 Sprinkle with salt and pepper
3 Stand each fish on piece of foil. Brush with melted butter
4 Seal foil loosely round each and stand on baking tray
5 Bake just above centre of moderately hot oven (190°C / 375°F or Gas No 5) for 20 minutes
6 Unwrap and serve each garnished with lemon and parsley. **Serves 4**

Baked Stuffed Haddock Fillet

2 fillets of fresh haddock, each about 350g / 12oz
1 recipe either Celery and Tomato Stuffing (page 98) or Lemon, Parsley and Thyme Stuffing (page 99)
2 large sliced tomatoes
2 level tablespoons chopped parsley
50g / 2oz butter, melted

1 Place 1 fillet of fish, flesh side uppermost, in buttered shallow heatproof dish
2 Cover with Stuffing
3 Put second fillet of fish, skin side uppermost, on top
4 Stand a line of tomato slices along centre. Sprinkle with parsley
5 Coat with melted butter
6 Bake, uncovered, in centre of moderate oven (180°C / 350°F or Gas No 4) for 40 minutes.
Serves 4

Kedgeree

175g / 6oz cooked smoked haddock
175g / 6oz cooked fresh haddock
75g / 3oz butter
350g / 12oz cooked long grain rice (about 175g / 6oz raw)
2 chopped large hard-boiled eggs
About 4 tablespoons fresh single cream
Salt and freshly milled pepper to taste

Garnish
2 level tablespoons finely chopped parsley

1 Flake fish with 2 forks
2 Melt butter in large saucepan
3 Add fish, rice, eggs and cream
4 Mix well. Add a little extra cream if mixture seems on dry side
5 Season well to taste with salt and pepper
6 Transfer to $\frac{3}{4}$ to 1 litre / $1\frac{1}{2}$ to 2 pint buttered heatproof dish
7 Cover with lid or aluminium foil
8 Re-heat just above centre of moderate oven (160°C / 325°F or Gas No 3) for 30 minutes
9 Uncover and sprinkle with parsley
10 Serve immediately.
Serves 4

Soused Herrings

4 large herrings
1 large onion
1 level tablespoon mixed pickling spice
2 small bay leaves, halved
5 tablespoons water
150ml / $\frac{1}{4}$ pint malt vinegar
1 level teaspoon granulated sugar
$\frac{1}{2}$ level teaspoon salt

1 Scale, bone and wash herrings
2 Roll up from head end to tail (with skin outside). Arrange in $\frac{1}{2}$ to $\frac{3}{4}$ litre / 1 to $1\frac{1}{2}$ pint heatproof dish
3 Slice onion thinly and arrange over herrings
4 Sprinkle with pickling spice and halved bay leaves
5 Combine water with vinegar, sugar and salt
6 Pour over fish
7 Cover with lid or aluminium foil
8 Bake in centre of slow oven (150°C / 300°F or Gas No 2) for $1\frac{1}{2}$ hours
9 Leave herrings to cool in dish
10 Chill thoroughly before serving.
Serves 4

Soused Herrings with Cider

1 Follow recipe and method for Soused Herrings (above)
2 Use dry cider instead of vinegar.
Serves 4

Jugged Kippers

4 medium-sized kippers
25 to 40g / 1 to 1½oz butter

1 Put kippers into tall jug and cover completely with boiling water
2 Leave for 5 minutes and drain
3 Serve immediately and top each with pieces of butter. **Serves 4**

Baked Haddock with Cream

1 whole fresh haddock (about 1kg / 2lb)
Salt and pepper
25g / 1oz softened butter
2 tablespoons lemon juice
1 level teaspoon made mustard
1 small grated onion
1 teaspoon Worcestershire sauce
150ml / ¼ pint fresh double cream

Garnish
1 level tablespoon finely chopped parsley
Paprika

1 Scale and wash haddock. Wipe dry with soft kitchen paper
2 Sprinkle inside with salt and pepper then spread with butter
3 Stand fish in buttered shallow heatproof dish
4 Combine lemon juice with mustard, onion and Worcestershire sauce. Spoon over fish
5 Coat with cream. Bake, uncovered, in centre of moderately hot oven (190°C / 375°F or Gas No 5) for 35 to 40 minutes (or until fish is tender)
6 Sprinkle with parsley and paprika.
Serves 4 to 5

If preferred, a 750g to 1kg / 1lb 8oz to 2lb portion of cod may be used instead of haddock

Smoked Haddock Florentine

1 large packet frozen spinach
350g / 12oz cooked and flaked smoked haddock
1 recipe Cheese Coating Sauce (page 129)
25g / 1oz finely grated Cheddar cheese

Garnish
Parsley

1 Cook spinach as directed on packet
2 Meanwhile, add fish to Sauce and heat through gently
3 Drain spinach well. Use to cover base of ¾ litre / 1½ pint buttered heatproof dish
4 Cover with fish and Sauce
5 Sprinkle top with cheese
6 Brown under hot grill
7 Garnish with parsley. **Serves 4**

Savoury Haddock Casserole

750g / 1lb 8oz fillet of fresh haddock
About 2 level tablespoons flour
½ level teaspoon salt
50g / 2oz butter
Juice of 1 small lemon
Freshly milled pepper
100g / 4oz mushrooms and stalks
1 medium-sized onion
250g / 8oz skinned tomatoes
1 small green pepper (optional)
3 level teaspoons soft brown sugar

Garnish
Parsley

1 Skin fish and cut flesh into 4 portions
2 Coat with flour mixed with salt
3 Fry quickly in 25g / 1oz butter until golden on both sides
4 Transfer to ¾ litre / 1½ pint buttered heatproof dish. Sprinkle with lemon juice and pepper
5 Finely chop mushrooms, onion, tomatoes and green pepper if used
6 Mix well together and spread over fish
7 Scatter brown sugar over vegetables. Dot with remaining butter
8 Cover dish with lid or aluminium foil. Bake in centre of moderately hot oven (190°C / 375°F or Gas No 5) for 30 to 40 minutes
9 Uncover and garnish with parsley. **Serves 4**

Fish Quenelles

250g / 8oz haddock, hake or whiting fillet (weighed after boning and skinning)
1 recipe freshly made Choux Pastry (page 214)
¼ level teaspoon nutmeg
½ level teaspoon salt
2 tablespoons fresh double cream

1 Mince raw fish finely
2 Beat into Choux Pastry with nutmeg and salt
3 Chill for at least 2 hours. Beat in cream
4 Half-fill large, fairly shallow pan with water and bring slowly to boil
5 Reduce heat. Gently lower spoonfuls of fish mixture into pan, allowing room between each for swelling
6 Poach very gently for 15 to 20 minutes
7 Lift out of water and drain
8 Serve hot with suitable savoury sauce (see Sauce Section, page 128). **Serves 4**

Cheese-baked Haddock

750g / 1lb 8oz fillet of fresh haddock
Salt and pepper
1 medium-sized onion
1 garlic clove (optional)
1 medium-sized can (about 425g / 15oz)
  tomatoes
25g / 1oz butter
$\frac{1}{4}$ level teaspoon thyme
2 level tablespoons finely chopped parsley
25g / 1oz fresh white breadcrumbs
50g / 2oz crumbled Lancashire cheese

1 Skin fish and cut flesh into 4 portions
2 Arrange in shallow heatproof dish. Sprinkle with salt and pepper
3 Finely chop onion and garlic if used
4 Put into saucepan with tomatoes, butter, thyme and parsley
5 Simmer slowly for 10 minutes
6 Cover fish with tomato mixture
7 Sprinkle with breadcrumbs mixed with crumbled cheese
8 Bake just above centre of moderate oven (180°C / 350°F or Gas No 4) for 30 minutes.
Serves 4

Skate with Cider Sauce

300ml / $\frac{1}{2}$ pint dry cider
1 small sliced onion
1 small bay leaf
1 parsley sprig
1 tablespoon vinegar
$\frac{1}{2}$ level teaspoon salt
1kg / 2lb skate
25g / 1oz butter
25g / 1oz flour
2 tablespoons fresh double cream

Garnish
4 slices unpeeled orange
Watercress

1 Put cider into large, fairly shallow, pan
2 Add onion, bay leaf, parsley, vinegar and salt
3 Bring to boil. Carefully put in fish (cut into 4 portions)
4 Lower heat. Cover pan and simmer very gently for 25 minutes
5 Drain and reserve 300ml / $\frac{1}{2}$ pint liquor. If preferred, take bones out of skate. Transfer fish to heatproof dish. Keep warm
6 Melt butter in pan. Stir in flour. Cook gently, without browning, 1 minute
7 Gradually blend in cider liquor
8 Cook, stirring, until sauce comes to boil and thickens
9 Simmer for 3 minutes. Stir in cream
10 Pour over skate
11 Garnish with orange slices and watercress.
Serves 4

Lemon Buttered Skate

1 small sliced onion
1 small bay leaf
1 parsley sprig
1 tablespoon vinegar
$\frac{1}{2}$ level teaspoon salt
1kg / 2lb skate
1 recipe Lemon Butter Sauce (page 135)

Garnish
4 lemon wedges
Parsley

1 Pour about 8cm / 3in water into large, fairly shallow, saucepan
2 Add onion, bay leaf, parsley sprig, vinegar and salt
3 Bring to boil. Carefully put in fish (cut into 4 portions)
4 Lower heat, cover pan and simmer gently for 25 minutes
5 Drain skate. If preferred, remove bones
6 Transfer to serving dish. Coat with Lemon Butter Sauce
7 Garnish with lemon and parsley
8 Serve immediately. Serves 4

Halibut au Gratin

1 small onion
100g / 4oz mushrooms and stalks
2 level tablespoons finely chopped parsley
4 halibut steaks (each about 175g / 6oz)
Salt and pepper
1 teaspoon lemon juice
4 tablespoons fresh single cream
3 level tablespoons toasted breadcrumbs
50g / 2oz butter

Garnish
4 lemon wedges
Watercress

1 Finely chop onion and mushrooms with stalks
2 Arrange, with parsley, over base of buttered shallow heatproof dish
3 Stand fish on top. Sprinkle with salt, pepper and lemon juice
4 Pour cream into dish. Coat fish with breadcrumbs
5 Dot with small pieces of butter
6 Bake in centre of moderately hot oven (190°C / 375°F or Gas No 5) for 30 to 35 minutes
7 Garnish with lemon and watercress. Serves 4

Turbot au Gratin

1 Follow recipe and method for Halibut au Gratin (above)
2 Use turbot steaks instead of halibut. Serves 4

Trout with Almonds

4 medium-sized trout
4 level tablespoons flour
½ level teaspoon salt
Shake of Cayenne pepper
100g / 4oz butter
2 teaspoons olive or corn oil
75g / 3oz blanched and halved almonds

Garnish
Lemon wedges
Parsley

1 Wash trout. Wipe dry with soft kitchen paper
2 Coat well with flour mixed with salt and pepper
3 Fry in the oil and 75g / 3oz butter until cooked through and golden (about 4 to 5 minutes per side)
4 Remove to serving dish and keep warm
5 Add remaining butter to pan and stand over low heat until melted
6 Add almonds and fry gently until golden
7 Pour hot butter and almonds over fish
8 Garnish with lemon and parsley
9 Serve immediately. **Serves 4**

Fish Fritters

1 recipe Savoury Fritter Batter (page 146)
250g / 8oz cooked and finely flaked fish
2 level tablespoons finely chopped drained capers
Deep fat or oil for frying
25g / 1oz finely grated Cheddar cheese

1 Make up Batter as directed but, before folding in beaten egg white, stir in flaked fish and capers
2 Drop spoonfuls of mixture into hot fat or oil
3 Fry until well puffed and golden (2 to 3 minutes)
4 Drain on soft kitchen paper
5 Transfer to serving plate and sprinkle with cheese
6 Accompany with suitable savoury sauce (see Sauce Section, page 128). **Serves 4**

Salmon Fish Cakes

500g / 1lb potatoes (after peeling)
75g / 3oz butter
1 medium-sized can (about 225g / 8oz) red salmon
1 level tablespoon finely chopped parsley
1 level teaspoon finely grated lemon rind
Onion salt to taste
Pepper
1 tablespoon olive or corn oil

Garnish
Parsley
Lemon slices

Scalloped Hake

500g / 1lb hake
1 recipe Cheese Pouring Sauce (page 129)
100g / 4oz fresh white breadcrumbs
1 level teaspoon celery salt
50g / 2oz crumbled Lancashire cheese

Garnish
Parsley

1 Poach hake gently in boiling salted water for 8 to 10 minutes
2 Lift out of pan. Remove skin and bones. Flake up flesh with fork
3 Fill ¾ litre / 1½ pint buttered heatproof dish with alternate layers fish, Sauce and breadcrumbs mixed with celery salt
4 Finish with layer of breadcrumbs. Sprinkle cheese over top
5 Re-heat just above centre of moderately hot oven (190°C / 375°F or Gas No 5) for 20 to 30 minutes or until top is golden
6 Garnish with parsley. **Serves 4**

Danish-style Cod

100g / 4oz streaky bacon
100g / 4oz button mushrooms
100g / 4oz cooked peas
4 cod cutlets (each about 100 to 175g / 4 to 6oz)
Salt and pepper
25g / 1oz butter

1 Chop bacon and arrange, with whole mushrooms and peas, over base of well-buttered shallow heatproof dish
2 Sprinkle cod with salt and pepper. Place on top of bacon and vegetables
3 Put a piece of butter on each cutlet
4 Cover dish with lid or aluminium foil
5 Bake just above centre of moderate oven (180°C / 350°F or Gas No 4) for 20 minutes
6 Remove lid or foil. Continue to bake for further 20 minutes. **Serves 4**

1 Cook potatoes in boiling salted water until tender
2 Mash finely with 25g / 1oz butter, drained salmon, parsley and lemon rind
3 Season to taste with onion salt and pepper. Leave mixture to cool
4 Turn out on to floured board. Divide into 8 equal-sized pieces
5 Shape into cakes. Fry in remaining butter and oil until crisp and golden, allowing about 3 to 4 minutes per side
6 Drain on soft kitchen paper
7 Garnish with parsley and lemon. **Serves 4**

Cod with Orange & Walnuts

50g / 2oz butter
75g / 3oz fresh brown breadcrumbs
1 finely chopped garlic clove (optional)
25g / 1oz very finely chopped shelled walnut
    halves
Finely grated rind and juice of 1 medium orange
4 cod cutlets (each about 100 to 175g / 4 to 6oz)
Salt and pepper

Garnish
Watercress

1 Melt butter in pan. Stir in breadcrumbs, garlic if
used, walnuts and orange rind
2 Leave over low heat, stirring frequently, until
butter has been absorbed by crumbs
3 Sprinkle fish with salt and pepper. Stand in
buttered shallow heatproof dish
4 Moisten with orange juice. Cover with breadcrumb mixture
5 Bake, uncovered, just above centre of moderate
oven (180°C / 350°F or Gas No 4) for 20 to 30
minutes (or until fish is tender)
6 Garnish with watercress. **Serves 4**

Baked Stuffed Cod Cutlets

4 cod cutlets (each about 100 to 175g / 4 to 6oz)
Salt and pepper
1 small onion
15g / ½oz butter
25g / 1oz fresh white breadcrumbs
1 level teaspoon finely chopped parsley
2 teaspoons lemon juice
300ml / ½ pint Cheese Coating Sauce (page 129)

1 Sprinkle fish with salt and pepper. Stand each
on large square of aluminium foil
2 Chop onion finely. Fry gently in butter until pale
gold
3 Stir in breadcrumbs, parsley and lemon juice.
Season if necessary with salt and pepper
4 Divide into 4 equal portions and use to fill fish
cavities
5 Seal foil loosely round each cutlet. Transfer to
baking tray
6 Bake just above centre of moderate oven
(180°C / 350°F or Gas No 4) for 30 minutes
7 Unwrap and accompany with Cheese Sauce.
Serves 4

Creamed Halibut

750g / 1lb 8oz boned halibut
Salt and pepper
Juice of ½ medium-sized lemon
150ml / ¼ pint fresh double cream
50g / 2oz grated Cheddar cheese
40g / 1½oz butter

Garnish
1 level tablespoon finely chopped parsley

1 Skin fish. Cut flesh into 4 serving portions
2 Arrange in buttered shallow heatproof dish
3 Sprinkle with salt, pepper and lemon juice
4 Coat fish with cream. Sprinkle with grated
cheese
5 Cover top with flakes of butter. Bake uncovered,
in centre of moderate oven (180°C / 350°F or Gas
No 4) for 25 to 30 minutes
6 Scatter parsley over top
7 Serve immediately. **Serves 4**

Baked Halibut Royal

2 tablespoons lemon juice
½ level teaspoon salt
½ level teaspoon paprika
4 halibut steaks (each about 175g / 6oz)
1 small chopped onion
50g / 2oz butter
½ small green pepper, cut into strips

Accompaniment
1 recipe Hot Tartare Sauce (page 131)
4 lemon wedges

1 Combine lemon juice, salt and paprika. Pour
into shallow heatproof dish
2 Add halibut. Leave to marinate for 1 hour,
turning steaks over after 30 minutes
3 Fry onion slowly in butter until soft but not
brown
4 Top halibut with pepper strips
5 Sprinkle with onion and remaining butter from
pan. Bake, uncovered, towards top of hot oven
(220°C / 425°F or Gas No 7) for 15 minutes (or until
fish flakes easily with fork)
6 Serve Tartare Sauce and lemon wedges
separately. **Serves 4**

Buttered Plaice with Bananas (below)

Buttered Plaice with Bananas

4 large plaice fillets (each about 175g / 6oz)
Salt and pepper
75g / 3oz butter
25g / 1oz salted cashew nuts
2 medium-sized bananas
Juice of 1 lemon

1 Arrange plaice fillets in buttered shallow heat-proof dish. Season with salt and pepper
2 Melt 25g / 1oz butter. Pour over fish

3 Cover dish with lid or aluminium foil. Bake in centre of moderate oven (180°C / 350°F or Gas No 4) for 20 minutes
4 After 15 minutes, melt remaining butter in pan. Add nuts and slice in bananas
5 Fry very gently for 3 minutes
6 Remove dish from oven and uncover. Arrange nuts and banana slices on top of fish
7 Sprinkle with lemon juice. Serve immediately.
Serves 4

Grilled Whole Plaice

4 whole plaice (each about 175g / 6oz)
50g / 2oz butter, melted
Salt and pepper

Garnish
4 lemon wedges
Parsley

1 Line grill pan or grill rack with aluminium foil
2 Arrange 2 plaice on top
3 Brush with melted butter. Sprinkle with salt and pepper
4 Grill for 5 to 6 minutes
5 Turn over. Brush with more butter. Sprinkle with salt and pepper
6 Grill for further 5 to 6 minutes. Transfer to warm platter and keep hot
7 Cook remaining 2 plaice and transfer to platter
8 Garnish with lemon and parsley. **Serves 4**

Plaice with Stilton Sauce

4 large plaice fillets (each about 175g / 6oz)
2 level tablespoons flour
½ level teaspoon salt
40g / 1½oz butter
2 teaspoons olive or corn oil
300ml / ½ pint freshly made Basic White Coating Sauce (page 129)
75g / 3oz Blue Stilton cheese, finely chopped
2 level tablespoons toasted breadcrumbs

Garnish
Watercress

1 Cut each fillet into 4 pieces. Coat with flour mixed with salt
2 Fry fairly briskly in butter and oil, allowing 3 minutes per side
3 Transfer to ¾ litre / 1½ pint buttered heatproof dish
4 Stand Sauce over low heat. Add cheese
5 Whisk gently until smooth. Pour over fish
6 Sprinkle breadcrumbs over top
7 Re-heat in centre of moderately hot oven (190°C / 375°F or Gas No 5) for 20 minutes
8 Garnish with watercress. **Serves 4**

Portuguese Plaice

8 sardines (canned)
8 level tablespoons fresh white breadcrumbs
2 level tablespoons finely chopped parsley
Finely grated rind and juice of 1 medium-sized lemon
1 level teaspoon finely grated onion
¼ level teaspoon salt
Beaten egg to bind
8 small plaice fillets (each about 75g / 3oz)
25g / 1oz butter, melted

1 Mash sardines finely. Combine with crumbs, parsley, lemon rind, onion and salt
2 Bind loosely with egg
3 Spread sardine mixture over plaice fillets. Roll up
4 Arrange in buttered shallow heatproof dish. Coat with lemon juice combined with melted butter
5 Cover dish with lid or aluminium foil
6 Bake just above centre of moderate oven (180°C / 350°F or Gas No 4) for 30 minutes.
Serves 4

Grecian Sole

225g / 8oz freshly boiled rice (about 100g / 4oz raw)
8 sole fillets (each about 75g / 3oz)
2 level tablespoons flour
½ level teaspoon salt
50g / 2oz butter
2 teaspoons olive or corn oil
1 recipe Tomato Sauce (page 134)

Garnish
1 canned red pepper

1 Arrange rice on serving platter. Keep warm and dry in very cool oven
2 Coat sole fillets with flour mixed with salt
3 Fry until crisp and golden in butter and oil, allowing 3 to 4 minutes per side
4 Place on top of rice
5 Coat with hot Tomato Sauce
6 Garnish with red pepper, cut into strips.
Serves 4

Sole with Cucumber Sauce

4 large sole fillets (each about 175g / 6oz)
2 tablespoons dry white wine
1 small sliced onion
½ small bay leaf
½ level teaspoon salt
1 recipe freshly made Cucumber Sauce (page 131)

Garnish
Paprika

1 With skin outside, roll up sole fillets. Secure with wooden sticks
2 Stand in shallow pan. Cover with water
3 Add wine, onion, bay leaf and salt. Slowly bring to boil
4 Reduce heat. Cover pan. Simmer fish for 6 to 7 minutes
5 Transfer to warm serving dish. Remove sticks
6 Coat with hot Cucumber Sauce
7 Sprinkle lightly with paprika. **Serves 4**

Grilled Sole

1 Follow recipe and method for Grilled Plaice (page 45)
2 Use 4 medium-sized soles, skinned on both sides, instead of plaice
3 Whether the heads are left on is a matter of personal choice. **Serves 4**

Crumbed Whiting Meunière

4 medium-sized boned whiting
2 level tablespoons flour
½ level teaspoon salt
Shake of pepper
1 small egg, beaten
8 level tablespoons fresh white breadcrumbs
100g / 4oz butter
2 teaspoons olive or corn oil
Juice of ½ medium-sized lemon

Garnish
Parsley

1 Cut head and tail off each fish
2 Wash fish well. Pat dry with soft kitchen paper
3 Toss in flour mixed with salt and pepper
4 Coat with beaten egg and crumbs
5 Fry in the oil and 75g / 3oz butter until crisp and golden, allowing 3 to 4 minutes per side
6 Remove from pan. Transfer to warm serving dish
7 Add rest of butter to pan. Heat gently until it just begins to turn brown
8 Add lemon juice and pour over whiting
9 Garnish with parsley. **Serves 4**

Normandy Whiting

4 medium-sized boned whiting
Salt and pepper
1 small onion
1 level tablespoon French mustard
4 tablespoons dry white wine or cider
Juice of ½ medium-sized lemon
40g / 1½oz butter
1 level tablespoon finely chopped parsley

Garnish
Parsley

1 Wash whiting. Arrange in buttered shallow heatproof dish. Season with salt and pepper
2 Chop onion very finely. Sprinkle over fish
3 Put mustard, wine or cider, lemon juice, butter and parsley into small saucepan
4 Leave over low heat until butter has melted
5 Pour over fish
6 Cover dish with lid or aluminium foil
7 Bake in centre of moderate oven (180°C / 350°F or Gas No 4) for 15 minutes
8 Uncover and continue to bake for further 10 minutes
9 Garnish with parsley. **Serves 4**

Fried Fish

4 cutlets of fish or 8 medium-sized fillets (about 750g / 1lb 8oz)
Deep fat or oil for frying
Coating Batter (page 146)

Garnish
Lemon wedges

1 Wash fish well. Wipe dry with soft kitchen paper
2 Half-fill deep frying pan with melted fat or oil
3 Heat until faint haze rises from it (or until bread cube sinks to bottom of pan, rises to top immediately and turns golden in 50 seconds)
4 Coat fish with Batter. Lift into pan with fork or kitchen tongs
5 Fry until crisp and golden, allowing about 6 to 8 minutes for cutlets and 4 to 5 minutes for fillets
6 Remove from pan
7 Drain on soft kitchen paper
8 Garnish with lemon. **Serves 4**

Shellfish

Scallops

Creamed Scallops (below)

It is not recommended to freeze shellfish.

Scallops are in season during the winter months, from about November to March. If they have not already been opened and cleaned by the fishmonger, put them into a hot oven and leave for a few minutes until the shells open. Remove dark frill (beard) which is round the scallop, then carefully wash the white portion and bright orange roe

Creamed Scallops

8 scallops
½ level teaspoon salt
150ml / ¼ pint fresh double cream
Yolk of 1 standard egg
1 level tablespoon finely chopped parsley
Salt and pepper
1 level tablespoon toasted breadcrumbs
25g / 1oz butter

1 Put washed scallops into pan. Cover with cold water. Add salt
2 Slowly bring to boil. Cover pan and lower heat
3 Poach for 5 minutes in water that is barely simmering
4 Lift out and drain on soft kitchen paper
5 Cut each scallop, depending on size, into 4 or 6 pieces. Transfer to buttered heatproof dish
6 Combine cream with egg yolk, parsley and seasoning to taste. Heat through gently without boiling
7 Pour over scallops
8 Sprinkle with breadcrumbs. Add flakes of butter and brown under hot grill.
Serves 4

Crumbed & Fried Scallops

8 scallops
Salt and pepper
1 tablespoon lemon juice
3 level tablespoons flour
2 standard eggs, beaten
Fresh white breadcrumbs
75g / 3oz butter
2 teaspoons olive or corn oil

Garnish
Lemon wedges

1 Cut washed scallops in half. Pat dry with soft kitchen paper
2 Season well with salt and pepper. Sprinkle with lemon juice
3 Toss in flour. Coat twice with egg and bread-crumbs
4 Leave 15 minutes in the cool
5 Fry in hot butter and oil until golden, allowing about 4 minutes per side
6 Drain on soft kitchen paper and transfer to warm serving dish
7 Garnish with lemon wedges. **Serves 4**

Fried Scallops

8 scallops
Salt and pepper
1 tablespoon lemon juice
3 level tablespoons flour
50g / 2oz butter
2 teaspoons olive or corn oil

Garnish
Lemon wedges

1 Cut washed scallops in half. Pat dry with soft kitchen paper
2 Season well with salt and pepper. Sprinkle with lemon juice
3 Toss in flour
4 Fry in hot butter and oil until golden, allowing about 4 minutes per side
5 Transfer to warm dish
6 Garnish with lemon. **Serves 4**

Oysters

Oysters are in season from September to April. Like mussels, their shells should be tightly closed and intact

Oysters in Cream Sauce

24 oysters
25g / 1oz butter
25g / 1oz flour
150ml / $\frac{1}{4}$ pint milk
1 tablespoon dry sherry
2 tablespoons fresh double cream
$\frac{1}{2}$ level teaspoon salt
Pinch of Cayenne pepper
4 slices hot buttered toast

Garnish
Paprika

1 Open oysters and reserve liquor
2 Melt butter in pan. Add flour. Cook gently, without browning, for 1 minute
3 Gradually blend in oyster liquor and milk
4 Cook, stirring, until sauce comes to boil and thickens
5 Add oysters, sherry and cream. Season to taste with salt and Cayenne pepper
6 Simmer for 4 minutes. Spoon on to hot toast
7 Sprinkle with paprika
8 Serve immediately. **Serves 4**

Butter-fried Oysters

24 oysters
1 large egg
2 tablespoons fresh single cream
$\frac{1}{4}$ level teaspoon salt
Freshly milled black pepper
Fresh white breadcrumbs
100g / 4oz butter
2 tablespoons olive or corn oil

Garnish
Lemon wedges

1 Shell oysters. Dry well with soft kitchen paper
2 Beat egg with cream and salt. Season to taste with pepper
3 Coat oysters with egg mixture. Toss in crumbs. Repeat coating and toss once more
4 Leave oysters for $\frac{1}{2}$ hour in the cool
5 Fry in hot butter and oil until crisp and golden (about 4 to 5 minutes)
6 Serve immediately and garnish with lemon. **Serves 4**

Angels on Horseback

rashers streaky bacon
6 shelled oysters
slices hot buttered toast

Cut each bacon rasher in half
Wrap round oysters. Secure with cocktail sticks
Grill until bacon is crisp, turning once
Stand 4 on each slice of toast
Remove sticks
Serve immediately.
Serves 4

Mussels

These are in season from about October to March. The shells of fresh mussels must be tightly closed and intact. Any that are cracked, or remain open after tapping with a knife, should be thrown away: this indicates that the mussels inside are dead. Mussels have beards. These may be left on or cut away with scissors. To clean mussels, put into colander and wash under cold running water. Shake the colander all the time to prevent mussel shells from opening. Scrub with a stiff brush and wash again

Moules Marinière

50g / 2oz butter
chopped shallots or chopped small onions
garlic clove
150ml / ¼ pint dry white wine
small bay leaf
3 litres / 2½ to 3 quarts washed and bearded mussels
3 level tablespoons fresh white breadcrumbs
level tablespoons finely chopped parsley

1 Melt butter in large saucepan
2 Add shallots or onions and garlic. Fry gently until pale gold
3 Pour in wine. Add bay leaf. Simmer gently for 7 minutes
4 Add mussels. Cook over brisk heat, shaking pan all the time, until shells open (about 6 to 8 minutes)
5 Stir in breadcrumbs. Pour into 4 warm serving dishes
6 Sprinkle with parsley. Serve immediately.
Serves 4

Paella

4 small joints roasting chicken
50g / 2oz butter
1 tablespoon olive oil
1 small onion
1 garlic clove
225g / 8oz long grain rice
½ level teaspoon saffron strands
600ml / 1 pint warm chicken stock or water
1 bay leaf
175g / 6oz cooked peas
100g / 4oz peeled prawns
100g / 4oz cooked lobster meat (optional)
8 cooked and shelled mussels
1 canned or bottled pimento, cut into strips

1 Skin chicken joints. Fry in butter and oil until light brown and crisp
2 Transfer to plate
3 Chop onion and garlic. Add to remaining butter in pan. Fry slowly until pale gold
4 Add rice and fry further minute
5 Mix saffron with chicken stock or water. Pour into pan
6 Add bay leaf, bring to boil and cover pan
7 Simmer slowly for 10 minutes. Transfer to large heatproof dish, about 8cm / 3in deep
8 Stand chicken joints on top. Cover with lid or aluminium foil and cook just above centre of moderate oven (180°C / 350°F or Gas No 4) for 30 minutes
9 Uncover and arrange peas, prawns, lobster meat, mussels and strips of pimento attractively over rice and chicken
10 Return to oven and cook, uncovered, for 10 to 15 minutes (or until chicken is tender and rice grains have absorbed all the liquid)
11 Serve immediately. **Serves 4**

Scampi & Prawns

Creamed Scampi with Wine

**24 large frozen or fresh scampi
3 level tablespoons flour
$\frac{1}{2}$ level teaspoon salt
Freshly milled pepper
75g / 3oz butter
2 tablespoons dry white wine
150ml / $\frac{1}{4}$ pint fresh single cream
2 level tablespoons finely chopped parsley
225g / 8oz freshly boiled rice (about 100g / 4oz
raw)**

1 Defrost scampi if frozen. Dry well with kitchen paper
2 Coat thickly with flour mixed with salt and pepper
3 Melt butter in shallow frying pan
4 Add scampi. Fry gently for 7 minutes, turning at least twice
5 Pour in wine and cream. Add parsley
6 Cook, stirring, until liquor thickens. Adjust seasoning to taste
7 Cover 4 warm serving plates with rice
8 Put equal amounts of scampi and sauce on to centres of each
9 Serve immediately. **Serves 4**

Creamed Scampi with Lemon

1 Follow recipe and method for Creamed Scampi with Wine (above)
2 Use 1 tablespoon lemon juice instead of wine.
Serves 4

Prawns in Soured Cream Sauce

**250g / 8oz peeled prawns
50g / 2oz butter
2 teaspoons lemon juice
4 tablespoons soured cream
Yolks of 2 standard eggs
Salt and pepper
4 slices hot dry toast**

Garnish
Paprika

1 Put prawns and butter into frying pan. Warm through gently for 5 minutes
2 Stir in lemon juice, soured cream and egg yolks
3 Cook over very low heat, stirring, until sauce thickens. Do not allow to boil
4 Season to taste with salt and pepper
5 Spoon equal amounts on to hot toast
6 Sprinkle lightly with paprika. **Serves 4**

Fried Scampi

**24 large frozen or fresh scampi
1 recipe Savoury Fritter Batter (page 146)
Deep fat or oil for frying**

Garnish
Lemon wedges

Accompaniment
Tartare Mayonnaise (page 127)

1 Defrost scampi if frozen. Dry well with kitchen paper
2 Coat with Batter
3 Fry in hot fat or oil until pale gold (about 3 to 4 minutes)
4 Drain thoroughly. Transfer to warm serving dish
5 Garnish with lemon wedges
6 Serve Tartare Mayonnaise separately. **Serves 4**

Curried Prawns

**400 to 500g / 12oz to 1lb peeled prawns
1 recipe Curry Sauce (page 134)
350g / 12oz freshly boiled rice (about 175g / 6oz
raw)**

Accompaniments
**1 large banana
1 tablespoon lemon juice
2 tomatoes
1 small onion
2 tablespoons desiccated coconut
Chutney**

1 Add prawns to Curry Sauce. Heat through gently
2 Cover base of large serving platter with rice. Top with prawns and Curry Sauce
3 Accompany with separate dishes of sliced banana sprinkled with lemon juice, sliced tomatoes covered with onion rings, coconut and chutney. **Serves 4**

Crabs

Fresh crabs are at their best between May and September. They should have rough shells and large claws and feel heavy for their size. When

buying a cooked crab from the fishmonger make sure that it has been freshly boiled.

Devilled Crab (below)

Devilled Crab

1 small onion or 2 shallots
50g / 2oz butter
150ml / ¼ pint freshly made Béchamel Sauce
  (page 129)
1 tablespoon brandy, dry sherry or lemon juice
1 teaspoon Worcestershire sauce
1 level teaspoon Dijon mustard
1 level tablespoon finely chopped parsley
400 to 500g / 12oz to 1lb cooked crabmeat
Salt to taste
25g / 1oz finely grated Cheddar cheese
1 level tablespoon fresh white
  breadcrumbs

1 Chop onion or shallots finely. Fry very gently in butter until soft
2 Stir in Sauce, brandy, sherry or lemon juice, Worcestershire sauce, mustard, parsley and crabmeat
3 Mix well and season. Transfer to buttered shallow heatproof dish
4 Sprinkle with cheese mixed with crumbs
5 Bake towards top of hot oven (220°C / 425°F or Gas No 7) for 10 to 15 minutes. **Serves 4**

Crab Tartare

400 to 500g / 12oz to 1lb cooked crabmeat
1 recipe freshly made Hot Tartare Sauce
  (page 131)
1 tablespoon toasted breadcrumbs
25g / 1oz melted butter

Garnish
Parsley

1 Combine crabmeat with Sauce. Heat through gently without boiling
2 Transfer to shallow heatproof dish
3 Sprinkle with crumbs and melted butter
4 Brown under hot grill
5 Garnish with parsley. **Serves 4**

Crab Newburg

1 Follow recipe and method for Lobster Newburg (page 52)
2 Use 400 to 500g / 12oz to 1lb crabmeat instead of lobster. **Serves 4**

Lobsters

These are in season from March to October. Cooked lobsters should be bright red, feel heavy for their size and have their tails curled tightly under their bodies. Although the female or hen lobster is held in greater esteem than the male, the flesh of the male lobster is firmer in texture and therefore more suitable for cooked lobster dishes. A 500 to 750g / 1lb to 1lb 8oz lobster serves 2.

Lobster Thermidor

2 cooked lobsters (each about 500g / 1lb)
300ml / ½ pint freshly made Béchamel Sauce (page 129)
3 tablespoons fresh double cream
1 level teaspoon dry mustard
Salt and pepper
6 level tablespoons finely grated Cheddar cheese

1 Halve lobsters lengthwise. Discard stomachs
2 Remove meat and cut into neat cubes
3 Combine Sauce with cream and mustard. Heat through gently without boiling. Season to taste
4 Cover base of lobster shells with a little sauce. Arrange lobster meat on top
5 Coat with remaining Sauce
6 Sprinkle with cheese
7 Brown under hot grill. **Serves 4**

Lobster Newburg

2 cooked lobsters (each about 450g / 1lb)
Salt and freshly milled pepper
75g / 3oz butter
5 tablespoons dry sherry
150ml / ¼ pint fresh double cream
Yolks of 3 standard eggs
225g / 8oz freshly boiled rice (about 100g / 4oz raw)

Garnish
Paprika

1 Cut lobsters in half and discard stomachs
2 Remove meat from shells. Cut into neat cubes
3 Season with salt and pepper. Fry gently in butter for about 4 to 5 minutes
4 Pour in sherry. Simmer slowly until liquid is reduced by about half
5 Put cream and egg yolks (broken) into double saucepan (or into basin standing over saucepan of gently simmering water)
6 Cook, stirring, until sufficiently thick to coat back of a wooden spoon. Do not allow to boil. Adjust seasoning to taste
7 Arrange hot rice on 4 warm serving plates. Place equal amounts of lobster meat and liquor from pan on to centre of each
8 Pour cream and egg yolk sauce over each
9 Sprinkle lightly with paprika. **Serves 4**

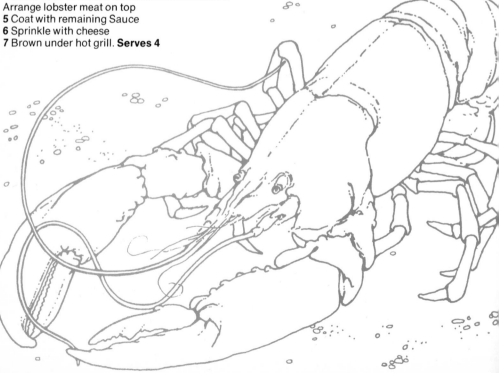

Lamb & Mutton

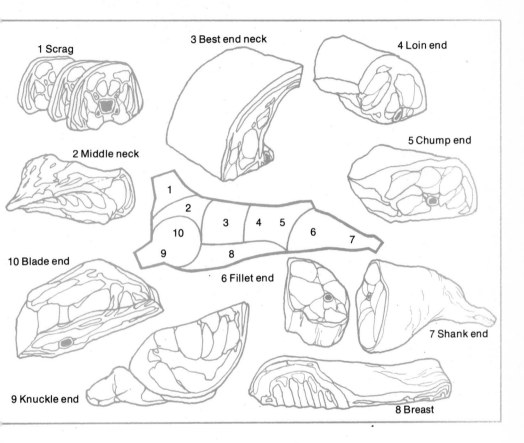

1 Scrag
3 Best end neck
4 Loin end
2 Middle neck
5 Chump end
10 Blade end
1
2
3 4 5
10
6
9
8
7
6 Fillet end
7 Shank end
9 Knuckle end
8 Breast

F Boned meat is more economical in terms of freezer space. Storage time – 9 to 12 months. Freeze chops with freezer film between each. Storage time – 4 to 6 months. When cooking stews and casseroles for freezing, reduce cooking time by 30 minutes. Allow to become cold, then place in a foil lined casserole dish and open freeze. Remove from dish, re-pack and freeze as a block. Storage time – 3 months

Roast Lamb

Choose leg, shoulder, loin, best end neck or stuffed boned breast

25g / 1oz butter, melted

Quantity
Allow approximately 250 to 400g / 8 to 12oz per person with bone

Accompaniments
Gravy (page 133)
Mint Sauce (page 133) or Onion Sauce (page 129)
Roast and/or Boiled Potatoes
Green vegetables

1 Tie or skewer joint into neat shape
2 Stand in roasting tin
3 Brush with butter
4 Put into centre of hot oven (230°C / 450°F or Gas No 8)
5 Immediately reduce temperature to moderate (180°C / 350°F or Gas No 4)
6 Continue roasting for required amount of time, allowing 25 minutes per 500g / 1lb and 25 minutes over
7 Do not baste
8 Transfer joint to carving board or dish. Remove string or skewers
9 Serve with accompaniments

Roast Mutton

1 Follow recipe and method for Roast Lamb (page 53)
2 Allow 30 minutes per 500g/1lb roasting time and 30 minutes over

Lancashire Hot Pot

750g/1lb 8oz best end neck of lamb
2 lambs' kidneys
500g/1lb potatoes
250g/8oz onions
Salt and pepper
150ml/¼ pint stock or water
25g/1oz butter, melted

1 Cut lamb into cutlets. Remove surplus fat
2 Peel and core kidneys. Cut into slices
3 Thinly slice potatoes and onions
4 Cover base of 1 to1½ litre/2 to 3 pint casserole dish with some of potato slices
5 Stand lamb on top
6 Cover with kidneys and onions
7 Sprinkle with salt and pepper
8 Arrange overlapping rings of rest of potatoes attractively on top. Pour in stock or water
9 Brush heavily with butter
10 Cover dish with lid or aluminium foil
11 Cook in centre of moderate oven (180°C/350°F or Gas No 4) for 1¼ hours
12 Uncover. Continue to cook for further 30 minutes (or until potatoes are golden brown).
Serves 4

8 shelled oysters may be added if desired

Lamb Stew

1¼kg/2lb 8oz scrag neck of lamb
2 level tablespoons flour
Salt and pepper
25g/1oz butter
1 large chopped onion
2 level tablespoons pearl barley
450ml/¾ pint stock or water
Seasoning to taste

1 Divide lamb into neat pieces. Cut away surplus fat
2 Toss in flour seasoned with salt and pepper
3 Fry briskly (in saucepan) in hot butter until crisp and brown, turning all the time
4 Transfer to plate
5 Add onion to remaining butter in pan. Fry slowly until pale gold
6 Replace lamb. Add barley, stock or water and salt and pepper to taste
7 Bring slowly to boil. Lower heat
8 Cover pan. Simmer gently for 1½ to 2 hours (or until meat is tender). **Serves 4**

Crown Roast of Lamb

1 crown of lamb
Suitable Stuffing (see Stuffings Section, page 97)
25g/1oz butter, melted
6 or 7 glacé cherries
6 or 7 cutlet frills

Garnish
Parsley sprigs

Accompaniments
Same as Roast Lamb (page 53)

1 Ask butcher (in advance if possible) to prepare crown from 2 best end necks of lamb, each with 6 or 7 cutlets
2 Alternatively, to make crown yourself, buy 2 best end necks, already chined
3 Cut half way down between each bone to separate cutlets
4 Scrape fat from upper parts of bones, leaving 5 to 8cm/2 to 3in bare
5 With skin side inside, curve both necks round to form crown
6 Hold together by stitching ends with fine string or thick thread
7 Transfer to roasting tin. Pack Stuffing into centre of crown
8 Cover tops of bones with squares of fat, or pieces of aluminium foil, to prevent over-browning
9 Brush joints with butter. Roast exactly as for Roast Lamb (page 53)
10 Remove from oven. Transfer to carving board or plate
11 Take fat or foil off bones
12 Put glacé cherries on to alternate bones and cutlet frills on to remainder
13 Serve with accompaniments. **Serves 6**

Grilled Lamb Cutlets

8 best end neck cutlets
25g/1oz butter

Garnish
Curry, Maître d'Hôtel, Mustard or Tomato Butter (see Savoury Butters Section, page 94)
4 grilled mushrooms and/or tomato halves
Watercress

1 Trim away surplus fat from cutlets
2 Stand in grill pan. Brush with melted butter
3 Cook under pre-heated hot grill for 1 minute
4 Turn over. Brush with more butter
5 Grill for further minute
6 Continue to grill for total of 7 to 9 minutes, turning cutlets frequently
7 Transfer to 4 individual plates or warm serving dish
8 Top each with piece of savoury butter. Garnish with mushrooms and/or tomatoes and watercress. **Serves 4**

Crown Roast of Lamb (page 54)

Grilled Lamb Chops

1 Follow recipe and method for Grilled Lamb
Cutlets (page 54)
2 Use 4 loin chops instead of cutlets
3 Grill for total of 10 to 18 minutes, depending on
thickness. **Serves 4**

Lamb & Mushroom Hot Pot

1 Follow recipe and method for Lancashire Hot
Pot (page 54)
2 Add 75 to 100g / 3 to 4oz sliced mushrooms and
stalks with kidneys and onions.
Serves 4

Cheshire Lamb Crumble

50g / 2oz butter
115g / 4½oz sifted flour
50g / 2oz crumbled Cheshire cheese
½ level teaspoon mixed herbs
Salt and pepper
350g / 12oz cold roast lamb
75g / 3oz onions
2 level tablespoons tomato purée
300ml / ½ pint stock
1 level tablespoon cornflour

1 Rub butter finely into 100g / 4oz flour. Add
cheese, herbs and seasoning
2 Mince meat and onions together. Stir in remaining ingredients. Slowly bring to boil, stirring
3 Place in pie dish and cover with crumble
4 Bake in a moderately hot oven (190°C / 375°F or
Gas No 5) for 45 minutes to 1 hour. **Serves 4**

Shepherd's (or Cottage) Pie

350g/12oz cold cooked lamb (or other cold
  minced meat)
1 recipe Brown Sauce (page 133)
Creamed Potatoes (page 100)
50g/2oz crumbled Lancashire cheese

1 Finely mince meat. Combine with Sauce
2 Turn into $\frac{3}{4}$ litre/$1\frac{1}{2}$ pint pie dish
3 Cover with Creamed Potatoes
4 Sprinkle with cheese
5 Re-heat and brown towards top of hot oven
(220°C/425°F or Gas No 7) for 15 to 20 minutes.
Serves 4

Mixed Grill

4 best end neck cutlets
4 lambs' kidneys, peeled and cored
40g/1$\frac{1}{2}$oz butter, melted
4 small pork or beef sausages
8 mushrooms
4 medium-sized halved tomatoes
4 rashers back bacon
Maître d'Hôtel Butter (page 95)

Garnish
Watercress
Potato crisps

1 Trim away surplus fat from cutlets
2 Stand in grill pan with kidneys
3 Brush with some of the butter
4 Cook under pre-heated hot grill for 3 minutes.
Turn
5 Add sausages and mushrooms
6 Brush all ingredients with butter. Grill for 4
minutes
7 Turn and add tomatoes and bacon
8 Brush all ingredients with remaining butter.
Grill for further 4 minutes
9 Transfer to warm serving dish
10 Top cutlets and kidneys with small pieces of
Maître d'Hôtel Butter
11 Garnish with watercress and crisps.
Serves 4

Golden Lancashire Lamb

250g/8oz cold cooked lamb
450ml/$\frac{3}{4}$ pint Basic White Coating Sauce (page
  129)
250g/8oz cooked diced carrots and peas
50g/2oz crumbled Lancashire cheese

1 Chop lamb. Add to sauce with carrots and peas
2 Turn into $\frac{3}{4}$ litre/$1\frac{1}{2}$ pint buttered heatproof dish
3 Sprinkle cheese over top
4 Brown towards top of moderately hot oven
(200°C/400°F or Gas No 6) for 15 to 20 minutes.
Serves 4

Braised Shoulder of Mutton or Lamb

50g/2oz butter
250g/8oz chopped onions
1 chopped garlic clove
100g/4oz chopped lean bacon
250g/8oz sliced carrots
100g/4oz diced turnip
2 large chopped celery stalks
150ml/$\frac{1}{4}$ pint red wine
150ml/$\frac{1}{4}$ pint water
1 level teaspoon crushed rosemary
1 level teaspoon salt
1$\frac{1}{2}$kg/3lb shoulder of mutton or lamb, boned and
  rolled

Accompaniments
Boiled potatoes
Green vegetables

1 Heat butter in large saucepan
2 Add onions, garlic, bacon, carrots, turnip and
celery
3 Cover pan. Fry gently for 10 minutes, shaking
pan frequently
4 Pour in wine and water. Add rosemary and salt
5 Bring to boil. Stand lamb on top
6 Cover saucepan
7 Simmer very gently for 2 to 2$\frac{1}{2}$ hours (or until
meat is tender)
8 Transfer lamb to warm serving dish and surround with vegetables from saucepan
9 Strain liquor and pour into clean saucepan
10 Boil briskly until reduced by half
11 Pour over meat
12 Serve with accompaniments. **Serves 4 to 5**

Boiled Mutton with Caper Sauce

1$\frac{1}{2}$kg/3lb piece of mutton, cut from leg
1 level teaspoon salt
2 medium-sized sliced onions
2 large sliced carrots
100g/4oz diced swede
100g/4oz diced turnip

Accompaniments
Caper Sauce (page 132)
Boiled potatoes

1 Put mutton into large saucepan
2 Cover with cold water
3 Bring slowly to boil. Remove scum
4 Add salt and vegetables
5 Lower heat and cover pan
6 Simmer for required amount of time, allowing
25 minutes per 500g/1lb and 25 minutes over
7 Transfer mutton to warm dish
8 Surround with vegetables
9 Serve with accompaniments.
Serves 4

Moussaka

medium-sized aubergines
alt
5g / 3oz butter
tablespoon olive or corn oil
large onions
50g / 12oz cooked minced lamb or beef
level tablespoons fresh white breadcrumbs
50ml / ¼ pint water
level tablespoon tomato purée
easoning to taste
standard egg, beaten
recipe freshly made Cheese Coating Sauce
(page 129)
0g / 2oz grated Cheddar cheese

Cut aubergines into ½cm / ¼in thick slices.
prinkle with salt and leave ½ an hour. Drain
noroughly. Fry quickly in butter and oil until
olden on both sides
Remove from pan and leave on one side
Slice onions thinly. Fry in remaining butter and
il until pale gold. Remove from heat
Combine meat with breadcrumbs, water and
omato purée. Season to taste
Line base of oblong or square heatproof dish
vith half the fried aubergine slices
Cover with meat mixture and onions. Arrange
emaining aubergine slices attractively on the top
Gradually beat egg into Cheese Sauce. Pour
to dish over aubergine slices
Sprinkle with cheese. Bake, uncovered, in
entre of moderate oven (180°C / 350°F or
as No 4) for 45 minutes to 1 hour.
erves 4

Lamb Kebabs

00g / 1lb fillet of lamb (cut from leg)
recipe Yogurt Marinade (page 93)
shallots or small onions
rashers long back bacon
small skinned tomatoes
button mushrooms
0g / 1½oz butter
50g / 12oz freshly boiled rice (about 175g / 6oz
raw)

Cut lamb into 2cm / 1in cubes
Soak in Yogurt Marinade for 3 hours
Cook shallots or onions in boiling salted water
or 10 minutes. Drain and halve
Cut bacon rashers in half. Roll up each one like
Swiss roll
Put lamb on to 4 skewers alternately with halved
nions, bacon rolls, whole tomatoes and mush-
ooms
Stand in grill pan. Brush well with melted butter
Cook under pre-heated hot grill for 8 minutes
Turn and brush with more butter
Grill for further 8 minutes
0 Serve on bed of rice. **Serves 4**

Lamb Curry

1kg / 2lb middle neck of lamb
2 medium-sized onions
1 garlic clove (optional)
25g / 1oz butter
1 level tablespoon curry powder
1 level tablespoon flour
2 large tomatoes, skinned and chopped
1 bay leaf
4 cloves
1 level teaspoon cinnamon
25g / 1oz sultanas or seedless raisins
1 large cooking apple, peeled and grated
1 level tablespoon sweet pickle
1 level teaspoon salt
300ml / ½ pint stock or water

Accompaniments
350g / 12oz freshly boiled rice (about 175g / 6oz
raw)
150g / 5oz carton natural yogurt
Chopped salted peanuts
Thinly sliced cucumber
Chutney

1 Cut lamb into neat pieces. Remove as much
surplus fat as possible
2 Thinly slice onions and garlic if used
3 Fry gently in hot butter (in saucepan) until pale
gold
4 Stir in curry powder, flour, tomatoes, bay leaf,
cloves, cinnamon, sultanas or raisins, apple,
sweet pickle and salt
5 Gradually blend in stock or water
6 Add lamb and bring slowly to boil
7 Lower heat. Cover pan
8 Simmer gently for 1¼ to 1¾ hours (or until meat is
tender)
9 Serve with accompaniments. **Serves 4**

Beef

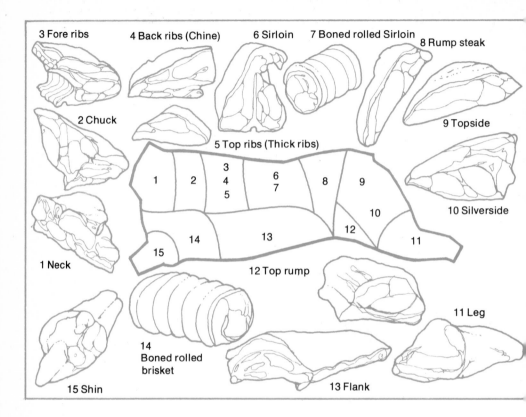

3 Fore ribs 4 Back ribs (Chine) 6 Sirloin 7 Boned rolled Sirloin 8 Rump steak

2 Chuck

9 Topside

5 Top ribs (Thick ribs)

10 Silverside

1 Neck

12 Top rump

14 Boned rolled brisket

11 Leg

15 Shin 13 Flank

See Lamb and Mutton. Freeze steaks as chops. Storage time – 4 to 6 months. Minced beef may be frozen raw or cooked, eg, hamburgers.
Storage time – raw 2 months, cooked 3 months.

Storage time for sausages – 1 month.
Pies with cooked fillings may be frozen baked or unbaked.
Storage time – baked 6 months, unbaked 3 months.

Roast Beef

Choose sirloin, all the rib cuts, topside, rump or fillet in one piece

50g / 2oz butter, melted

Quantities
Allow 250 to 400g / 8 to 12oz per person for beef with bone
Allow 100 to 175g / 4 to 6oz per person for beef without bone

Accompaniments
Gravy (page 133)
Yorkshire Pudding (page 144)
Whipped Cream Horseradish Dressing (page 124)
Roast and/or boiled potatoes
Green vegetables

1 Tie or skewer joint into neat shape
2 Stand in roasting tin
3 Brush with butter
4 Pour remaining butter into tin
5 Put into centre of hot oven (230°C / 450°F or Gas No 8)
6 Immediately reduce heat to moderate (180°C / 350°F or Gas No 4)
7 Continue roasting for required amount of time, allowing 20 minutes per 500g / 1lb and 20 minutes over
8 Baste frequently
9 Stand joint on carving board
10 Remove string or skewers
11 Serve with accompaniments

Stewed Beef

750g / 1lb 8oz stewing beef (shin, flank, skirt or chuck)
2 level tablespoons flour
Salt and pepper
40g / 1½oz butter
2 medium-sized chopped onions
3 medium-sized sliced carrots
½ small diced turnip (optional)
450ml / ¾ pint water

1 Cut beef into 2cm / 1in cubes
2 Toss in flour seasoned with salt and pepper
3 Fry briskly in hot butter until well browned, turning all the time
4 Remove to plate
5 Add onions, carrots and turnip (if used) to remaining butter in pan. Fry for 7 minutes (or until pale gold)
6 Replace meat. Pour in water
7 Bring slowly to boil
8 Lower heat. Cover pan
9 Simmer very gently for 1¾ to 2¼ hours (or until meat is tender)
10 Stir occasionally.
Serves 4

Stewed Beef with Beer

1 Follow recipe and method for Stewed Beef (above)
2 Use ½ beer and ½ water instead of all water
3 If liked, a small chopped garlic clove may also be added.
Serves 4

Stewed Beef with Tomato

1 Follow recipe and method for Stewed Beef (above)
2 Use 300ml / ½ pint tomato juice instead of water, or 250g / 8oz skinned and chopped tomatoes and 150ml / ¼ pint water
3 Add also 1 level teaspoon sugar.
Serves 4

Beef Casserole

1 Follow recipe and method for Stewed Beef (above)
2 After frying meat and vegetables, transfer to heatproof casserole dish
3 Pour in water and cover dish
4 Cook in centre of moderate oven (160°C / 325°F or Gas No 3) for 3 to 3½ hours (or until meat is tender). **Serves 4**

Stewed Beef with Dumplings

1 Follow recipe and method for Stewed Beef (left)
2 Twenty minutes before serving, add 8 small dumplings, made from ½ recipe Suet Crust Pastry (page 212)
3 Simmer with meat. **Serves 4**

Sea Pie

1 Follow recipe and method for Stewed Beef (left). Stewed Beef with Beer (left) or Stewed Beef with Tomato (left)
2 Half an hour before serving, remove lid of saucepan
3 Cover top of meat with ½ recipe Suet Crust Pastry (page 212), rolled into a round a little smaller than top of saucepan
4 Cover with lid
5 Continue to simmer for further ½ hour
6 Cut pastry into 4 portions before serving.
Serves 4

Beef Crumble

1 Follow recipe and method for Stewed Beef (left), Stewed Beef with Beer (left) or Stewed Beef with Tomato (left)
2 Transfer cooked meat to 1 litre / 2 pint pie dish
3 Cover with crumble made by rubbing 75g / 3oz butter into 150g / 6oz plain flour
4 Add 75g / 3oz crumbled Lancashire cheese
5 Put into centre of moderately hot oven (190°C / 375°F or Gas No 5). Bake for 30 to 35 minutes (or until top is pale gold). **Serves 4**

Hamburgers

500g / 1lb raw lean minced beef
50g / 2oz fresh white breadcrumbs
4 tablespoons milk
1 small finely grated onion
½ level teaspoon made mustard
1 teaspoon Worcestershire sauce
Seasoning to taste
40g / 1½oz butter

1 Combine all ingredients (except butter) well together
2 Divide into 8 equal-sized pieces. Shape each into 1cm / ½in thick cake
3 Heat butter in frying pan
4 Add Hamburgers, 3 or 4 at a time
5 Fry briskly for 1 minute each side
6 Reduce heat. Cook more slowly for further 6 to 8 minutes, turning twice.
Serves 4

Deep Dish Steak Pie (page 61)

Meat & Vegetable Pasties

175g/6oz rump steak
100g/4oz ox liver or kidney
1 medium-sized chopped onion
1 large diced potato
1 tablespoon water
½ level teaspoon salt
Shake of pepper
1 recipe Short Crust Pastry (page 211)
Milk for brushing

1 Cut steak and liver or kidney into very small pieces
2 Combine with onion, potato dice, water, salt and pepper
3 Divide pastry into 4 equal-sized pieces
4 Roll each out into 15 to 18cm/6 to 7in round
5 Moisten edges with water
6 Put equal amounts of filling into centres of each
7 Fold rounds in half over filling to form semi-circles
8 Press edges well together to seal. Ridge with fork
9 Transfer to lightly buttered baking tray
10 Brush with milk ·
11 Bake just above centre of hot oven (220°C/425°F or Gas No 7) for 20 minutes
12 Reduce heat to moderate (160°C/325°F or Gas No 3). Bake for further 45 minutes. Serve hot or cold. **Serves 4**

Boiled Silverside & Carrots

1kg/2lb salted silverside
3 cloves
1 large onion
1 large chopped celery stalk
Sprig of parsley
250g/8oz sliced carrots
½ recipe Suet Crust Pastry (page 212)

Accompaniment
1 recipe Parsley Coating Sauce (page 129)

1 Cover beef with cold water. Soak for 8 to 12 hours, changing water as often as possible (to remove excess salt)
2 Drain. Put into saucepan
3 Cover with fresh water. Slowly bring to boil
4 Remove scum
5 Press cloves into onion. Add to pan with celery and parsley
6 Lower heat. Cover pan
7 Simmer gently for 1½ hours. Add carrots. Continue to simmer for further 1 to 1½ hours (or until meat is tender)
8 Twenty minutes before serving shape pastry into 8 small dumplings. Lower into pan
9 Simmer with meat
10 Transfer beef to warm platter
11 Surround with carrot slices and dumplings
12 Serve Parsley Coating Sauce separately. **Serves 4**

Deep Dish Steak Pie

750g / 1lb 8oz stewing beef (shin, flank, skirt or chuck)
2 level tablespoons plain flour
Salt and pepper
1 large sliced onion
150ml / ¼ pint stock or water
1 level teaspoon salt
1 recipe Milk 'Puff' Pastry (page 214), Rough Puff Pastry (page 213) or Flaky Pastry (page 214)
Milk for brushing

1 Cut meat into small cubes
2 Toss in flour seasoned with salt and pepper
3 Put into ½ litre / 1 pint lipped pie dish with sliced onion. Dome meat in centre of dish
4 Combine stock or water with salt. Pour into dish over meat
5 Roll out pastry to just under 1cm / ½in thickness
6 From it cut lid, 4cm / 1½in larger all the way round than top of dish
7 Moisten edge of dish with water. Line with strip of pastry
8 Moisten strip with water. Cover with lid
9 Press edges well together to seal. Flake by cutting with back of knife
10 Press into flutes
11 Stand pie on baking tray
12 Brush with milk. Decorate with pastry leaves, rolled and cut from trimmings
13 Brush leaves with more milk
14 Make small hole in centre to allow steam to escape
15 Bake just above centre of hot oven (230°C / 450°F or Gas No 8) for 15 minutes
16 Reduce temperature to moderate (180°C / 350°F or Gas No 4). Continue to cook for further 2 hours
17 Cover pastry with piece of greaseproof paper during the latter part of cooking if it seems to be browning too much. **Serves 4**

Fried Steak & Onions

400g / 12oz onions
50g / 2oz butter
4 pieces rump steak, each about 175g / 6oz

1 Slice onions thinly. Fry gently in butter until golden, turning frequently
2 Transfer to warm plate and keep hot
3 Add steak to pan. Fry briskly for 1 minute each side
4 Lower heat. Continue to fry further for 3 to 4 minutes for underdone steak; 4 to 5 minutes for medium-cooked steak; about 7 to 8 minutes for well-done steak
5 Turn steaks about every minute to ensure even cooking
6 Transfer to 4 individual warm plates
7 Top with fried onions.
Serves 4

Deep Dish Steak & Mushroom Pie

1 Follow recipe and method for Deep Dish Steak Pie (left)
2 Use small onion instead of large
3 Include 50 to 75g / 2 to 3oz mushrooms and stalks. **Serves 4**

Steak & Kidney Pudding

1 recipe Suet Crust Pastry (page 212)
500g / 1lb stewing steak (flank, shin or chuck)
175g / 6oz ox kidney
1 level tablespoon flour
Salt and pepper
1 large chopped onion
3 tablespoons cold water

1 Roll out two-thirds pastry
2 Use to line well-buttered ¾ litre / 1½ pint pudding basin
3 Cut steak and kidney into cubes
4 Toss in flour seasoned with salt and pepper
5 Put into pastry-lined basin alternately with layers of onion
6 Pour in water
7 Moisten edges of lining pastry with water
8 Cover with lid, rolled from rest of pastry
9 Press pastry edges well together to seal
10 Cover with double thickness of buttered greaseproof paper or single thickness of buttered aluminium foil
11 Steam steadily for 3½ hours. Replenish boiling water if necessary
12 Serve from the basin with clean table napkin folded round it. **Serves 4**

Steak, Kidney & Oyster Pudding

1 Follow recipe and method for Steak and Kidney Pudding (above)
2 Reduce kidneys to 100g / 4oz
3 Include 12 shelled oysters with meat filling.
Serves 4

Quick-baking Steak & Kidney Pie

1 Prepare meat and kidney filling as in recipe for Steak and Kidney Plate Pie (page 62)
2 Transfer to ½ litre / 1 pint pie dish
3 Cover with Milk 'Puff' Pastry (page 214), Rough Puff Pastry (page 213) or Flaky Pastry (page 214)
4 Bake towards top of hot oven (230°C / 450°F or Gas No 8) for 15 to 20 minutes (or until pastry is well puffed and golden).
Serves 4

Steak & Kidney Plate Pie

**500g / 1lb stewing beef (shin, flank, skirt or
    chuck)**
175g / 6oz ox kidney
2 level tablespoons flour
Salt and pepper
40g / 1½oz butter
1 tablespoon oil
1 large chopped onion
300ml / ½ pint stock or water
1 recipe Milk 'Puff' Pastry (page 214)
Milk for brushing

1 Cut stewing steak and kidney into small cubes
2 Toss in flour seasoned with salt and pepper
3 Fry briskly in hot butter and oil until well
browned, turning all the time
4 Remove to plate
5 Add onion to remaining butter in pan. Fry gently
until pale gold
6 Replace meat. Pour in stock or water
7 Bring to boil. Lower heat
8 Cover pan. Simmer gently for 1¾ to 2 hours (or
until meat is tender), stirring occasionally
9 Leave until completely cold
10 Roll out half the pastry. Use to cover
lightly buttered 20 to 23cm / 8 to 9in heatproof
plate
11 Pile cold meat filling in centre
12 Moisten edges of pastry with water
13 Cover with lid, rolled from rest of pastry
14 Press edges well together to seal. Flake by
cutting with back of knife
15 Press into flutes
16 Stand pie on baking tray
17 Brush with milk
18 Bake just above centre of hot oven
(220°C / 425°F or Gas No 7) for 25 to 30 minutes (or
until golden brown). **Serves 4**

Meat Balls in Tomato Sauce

1 Follow recipe and method for Hamburgers
(page 59)
2 Shape mixture into 16 small balls
3 Drop into saucepan containing freshly made
Tomato Sauce (page 134)
4 Cover and simmer for 30 minutes
5 Serve with freshly boiled rice, noodles or
potatoes. **Serves 4**

Grilled Steak au Poivre

1 Follow recipe and method for Grilled Steak
(right)
2 An hour before grilling, press 2 tablespoons
crushed black peppercorns (use rolling pin for
crushing) well into steaks with palm of hand
3 Leave in a cool place until ready to cook.
Serves 4

Grilled Steak

**4 pieces of either fillet, rump or sirloin steak,
    each at least 2cm / 1in thick and weighing
    100 to 175g / 4 to 6 oz**
25g / 1oz butter, melted

Garnish
**Anchovy, Chive, Garlic, Horseradish or Mustard
    Butter (see Savoury Butters Section, page 94)**
4 whole grilled tomatoes
Watercress
Potato crisps
8 whole mushrooms lightly fried in butter

1 Stand steak on grill rack
2 Brush with butter
3 Stand under pre-heated hot grill
4 Grill for 1 minute
5 Turn over. Brush with more butter
6 Grill for 1 minute
7 Turn over. Grill for further 2 to 3 minutes each
side for rare or underdone steak; 4 to 5 minutes
each side for medium-cooked steak; up to
6 or 7 minutes each side for well-done steak
8 Transfer to 4 individual plates
9 Top each with piece of savoury butter
10 Garnish with tomatoes, watercress, crisps and
mushrooms. **Serves 4**

Beef Curry

**400g / 12oz cold cooked beef (such as
    remains of joint)**
1 recipe Curry Sauce (page 134)

Accompaniments
**350g / 12oz freshly boiled rice (about 175g / 6oz
    raw)**
25g / 1oz desiccated coconut
Chutney
4 skinned and sliced tomatoes
150g / 5oz carton natural yogurt
2 sliced bananas in lemon juice

1 Chop beef coarsely
2 Add to Sauce. Boil gently for 15 minutes,
stirring occasionally
3 Arrange border of rice on warm serving dish
4 Fill centre with Hot Beef Curry
5 Serve with accompaniments.
Serves 4

Grilled Tournedo Steak

1 Follow recipe and method for Grilled Steak
(above)
2 Allow 2 steaks per person, each about 5cm / 2in
thick and approximately 75g / 3oz in weight
3 Allow approximately 1 to 3 extra minutes grilling
time each side.
Serves 4

Beef Stroganoff

550 to 750g / 1lb 4oz to 1lb 8oz rump or fillet steak
1 small grated onion
75g / 3oz butter
400g / 12oz sliced button mushrooms
Salt and pepper
3 tablespoons white wine
150ml / ¼ pint fresh double cream

Accompaniment
Freshly boiled rice or noodles

1 Cut steak into 1cm / ½in thick slices
2 Beat until very thin with rolling pin
3 Cut into 1cm / ½in wide strips
4 Fry onion gently in 40g / 1½oz butter for 5 minutes
5 Add steak strips. Fry for further 5 minutes, turning all the time
6 Remove steak to plate
7 Add rest of butter to pan and heat
8 Add mushrooms. Fry for 3 minutes, turning
9 Replace steak. Sprinkle with salt and pepper
10 Gently stir in wine and cream
11 Re-heat gently without boiling
12 Serve with rice or noodles. **Serves 4**

Pot Roasted Beef

1kg / 2lb topside or thick flank of beef
50g / 2oz butter
2 teaspoons olive or corn oil
1 medium-sized chopped onion
2 large sliced carrots
2 large chopped celery stalks
1 large skinned and chopped tomato
300ml / ½ pint stock or water
1 wine glass red wine (optional)
1 level teaspoon salt
Shake of pepper
12 small peeled onions or shallots

1 Brown joint briskly in hot butter and oil (in large saucepan or flameproof casserole)
2 Transfer to plate
3 Add onion, carrots and celery to remaining butter in pan. Fry gently until golden
4 Replace beef. Add tomatoes, stock or water, wine if used, and salt and pepper
5 Bring to boil. Lower heat
6 Cover pan tightly
7 Simmer very gently for 1 hour, turning at least twice
8 Add whole onions. Continue to simmer further for 45 minutes to 1 hour (or until meat is tender)
9 Serve with vegetables from pan. **Serves 4**

Chilli Con Carne

225g / 8oz haricot or red kidney beans, soaked
   overnight
2 medium-sized onions
2 garlic cloves
50g / 2oz butter
2 teaspoons olive or corn oil
500g / 1lb lean minced beef
250g / 8oz skinned tomatoes
1 medium-sized green pepper
1 level teaspoon chilli powder
¼ level teaspoon salt
1 level teaspoon caraway seeds
150ml / ¼ pint water
1 level tablespoon flour
4 tablespoons fresh single cream

1 Drain beans. Cook in boiling salted water until almost tender. Strain and keep on one side
2 Chop onion and garlic finely. Fry gently in butter and oil until gold
3 Add meat and fry 5 minutes (or until brown), breaking it up with fork and turning it over all the time
4 Chop tomatoes and green pepper (remove and discard seeds of pepper first). Add to pan with beans, chilli powder, salt, caraway seeds and half the quantity of water
5 Cover and cook over very low heat for 45 minutes to 1 hour (or until beans are soft), stirring occasionally
6 Combine flour with rest of water. Pour into pan
7 Cook and stir until mixture thickens. Remove from heat and stir in cream
8 Serve immediately. **Serves 4**

This is a very fiery dish! It may be made stronger or milder by adjusting the quantity of chilli powder

Pork

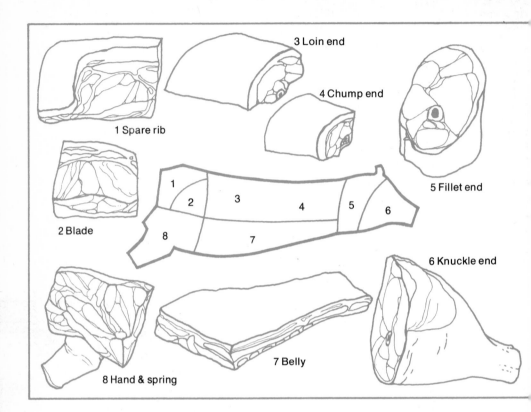

3 Loin end

4 Chump end

1 Spare rib

5 Fillet end

2 Blade

6 Knuckle end

8 Hand & spring

7 Belly

 As Lamb and Beef. Storage time–6 to 9 months. Bacon joints may be frozen.
Storage time–smoked joints 2 months, unsmoked 1 month, rashers 1 month.

Roast Pork

Choose hand and spring, blade, loin, leg or spare rib

25g / 1oz butter, melted
Salt

Quantities
Allow 250 to 400g / 8 to 12oz per person for pork with bone
Allow 100 to 175g / 4 to 6oz per person for pork without bone

Accompaniments
Gravy (page 133)
Apple Sauce (page 132) or Cranberry Sauce (page 134)
Sage and Onion Stuffing (page 98)
Creamed or roast potatoes
Green vegetables

1 Tie or skewer joint into neat shape
2 For crisp crackling, score skin at $\frac{1}{2}$cm / $\frac{1}{4}$in intervals across the joint (or ask butcher to do this for you)
3 Brush with butter. Sprinkle thickly with salt
4 Stand joint on rack in roasting tin (this helps to keep crackling dry and crisp)
5 Put into centre of hot oven (230°C / 450°F or Gas No 8)
6 Immediately reduce temperature to moderate (180°C / 350°F or Gas No 4)
7 Continue roasting for required amount of time, allowing total of 30 minutes per 500g / 1lb and 30 minutes over
8 Stand roast on carving board and remove string or skewers
9 Serve with accompaniments

Pork & Pineapple Curry

2 large chopped onions
1 chopped garlic clove
40g / 1½oz butter
600g / 1lb 4oz lean diced pork (weighed without bone)
1 level tablespoon flour
1 to 2 level tablespoons curry powder (depending on strength preferred)
4 canned pineapple rings, drained and chopped
1 level tablespoon tomato purée
50g / 2oz seedless raisins or sultanas
1 tablespoon lemon juice
1 bay leaf
1 level teaspoon ground ginger
1 level teaspoon salt
300ml / ½ pint water
150ml / ¼ pint milk

Accompaniments
350g / 12oz freshly boiled rice (175g / 6oz raw)
Chutney
Wedges of lemon

1 Fry onion and garlic gently in butter until pale gold
2 Add pork. Fry briskly for 5 minutes, turning all the time
3 Stir in flour and curry powder
4 Add remaining ingredients and bring to boil, stirring
5 Lower heat. Cover pan
6 Simmer slowly for 2 to 2¼ hours (or until pork is cooked through and tender)
7 Stir frequently
8 Serve with accompaniments.
Serves 4

Pork with Fried Peaches

4 loin of pork chops, each about 175g / 6oz
50g / 2oz butter, melted
4 canned peach halves, well drained
4 canned or glacé cherries

Garnish
Watercress

1 Stand chops in grill pan. Brush with melted butter
2 Grill for 7 to 10 minutes, depending on thickness
3 Turn over. Brush with more butter
4 Grill for further 7 to 10 minutes
5 Meanwhile, pour rest of butter into frying pan
6 Add peach halves. Fry gently until golden on both sides
7 Arrange chops on warm serving dish
8 Top each with peach half, cut side up
9 Fill centres of peaches with cherries
10 Garnish with watercress.
Serves 4

Pork with Fried Pineapple

1 Follow recipe and method for Pork with Fried Peaches (left)
2 Use 4 fried pineapple rings instead of peaches
3 Fill centres of rings with 4 grilled button mushrooms instead of cherries
4 Garnish with grilled or fried tomatoes. **Serves 4**

Chinese-style Fried Pork

500g / 1lb pork fillet
1 tablespoon soy sauce
1 level teaspoon salt
1 level teaspoon brown sugar
1 tablespoon dry white wine
1 level tablespoon flour
75g / 3oz butter
1 medium-sized chopped onion
100g / 4oz sliced mushrooms and stalks
2 large tomatoes, skinned and chopped
4 tablespoons cooked peas

Accompaniments
Freshly boiled cabbage
350g / 12oz freshly boiled flat noodles

1 Cut pork into wafer-thin slices
2 Cut slices into 2cm / 1in squares
3 Combine soy sauce, salt, sugar, wine and flour
4 Add pork squares. Toss well in soy sauce mixture
5 Melt 50g / 2oz butter in frying pan
6 Add onion. Fry gently until soft (but not brown)
7 Transfer to plate
8 Melt rest of butter in pan
9 Add pork. Fry fairly briskly for 5 minutes, turning all the time
10 Add fried onion, mushrooms and stalks, tomatoes and peas. Cook gently for further 10 minutes, stirring and turning frequently
11 Serve with accompaniments. **Serves 4**

Grilled Gammon with Tomato Butter

4 gammon rashers, each 100 to 175g / 4 to 6oz
25g / 1oz butter, melted
1 recipe Tomato Butter (page 96)

1 Remove rinds from gammon
2 Snip fat with scissors at 2cm / 1in intervals to prevent gammon from curling as it cooks
3 Stand in grill pan. Brush with melted butter
4 Grill for 5 to 7 minutes (or until fat becomes transparent)
5 Turn over. Brush with more melted butter
6 Grill for further 5 to 7 minutes
7 Transfer to warm dish
8 Top each with pat of Tomato Butter.
Serves 4

Grilled Gammon with Mustard or Devilled Butter

1 Follow recipe and method for Grilled Gammon with Tomato Butter (page 65)
2 Use Mustard Butter (page 96) or Devilled Butter (page 94) instead of Tomato Butter.
Serves 4

Grilled Gammon Maryland

1 Grill gammon as in recipe for Grilled Gammon with Tomato Butter (page 65)
2 Transfer to warm platter and surround with hot Corn Fritters (page 104) and halved bananas fried in butter. **Serves 4**

Pork Pie

1 recipe Hot Water Crust Pastry (page 213)
500g/1lb lean diced pork (weighed without bone)
1 small grated onion
1 level teaspoon sage
Large pinch of nutmeg
Good shake of pepper
150ml/¼ pint water
Beaten egg for brushing
1¼ level teaspoons gelatine

1 Roll out two-thirds pastry
2 Mould over outside of well floured 15cm/6in round cake tin, covering base and sides completely
3 Turn over on to buttered baking tray. Carefully remove cake tin
4 Combine diced pork with onion, sage, nutmeg, pepper and 4 tablespoons water
5 Pack into pastry case. Moisten edges of pastry with water
6 Roll out rest of pastry into lid. Cover pie, pressing pastry edges well together to seal
7 Tie strip of double-thickness aluminium foil round outside of pie to keep it in shape
8 Make hole in the top to allow steam to escape
9 Brush with beaten egg
10 Decorate with pastry leaves, cut from trimmings. Brush with more egg
11 Bake pie in centre of moderately hot oven (200°C/400°F or Gas No 6) for 15 minutes
12 Reduce temperature to moderate (180°C/350°F or Gas No 4) and bake for further 1¾ hours
13 Remove from oven
14 Heat rest of water. Add gelatine. Stir briskly until dissolved
15 Pour into hot pie through hole in top, using small plastic or paper funnel
16 Leave until completely cold before cutting.
Serves 4 to 6

Party Gammon

1 piece corner or middle cut of gammon, 1½ to 1¾kg/3lb 8oz to 4lb after boning
Cloves

Glaze
75g/3oz soft brown sugar
2 level teaspoons dry mustard
50g/2oz butter, melted
2 tablespoons cider or apple juice
1 teaspoon Worcestershire sauce

1 Put gammon into large pan. Cover with cold water
2 Soak for 8 to 10 hours, changing water at least 3 times to get rid of excess salt
3 Drain. Cover with fresh cold water
4 Bring slowly to boil. Remove scum
5 Lower heat. Cover pan
6 Simmer very slowly, allowing 30 minutes per 500g/lb
7 Drain and cool slightly
8 Strip off skin. Score fat into diamond pattern with sharp knife
9 Press a clove into each alternate diamond
10 Put joint into roasting tin
11 Combine sugar with mustard, melted butter, cider or apple juice and Worcestershire sauce
12 Coat fat with mixture
13 Cook in centre of moderately hot oven (190°C/375°F or Gas No 5) for 30 minutes (or until fat is golden brown). Baste 3 or 4 times
14 Serve hot or cold. **Serves 12 to 14**

Pipérade

400g/12oz onions
75g/3oz butter
2 teaspoons olive oil
3 medium-sized green peppers
500g/1lb skinned tomatoes
¼ level teaspoon marjoram or basil
Salt and freshly milled pepper to taste
6 standard eggs
4 tablespoons fresh double cream
4 gammon rashers, freshly grilled

1 Chop onion. Fry gently in butter and oil until soft but not brown
2 Meanwhile, remove seeds and inside fibres from green peppers and discard. Cut peppers into strips and add to pan. Cook slowly with onion until soft
3 Chop tomatoes. Add to pan with marjoram or basil and salt and pepper to taste. Cover and simmer for 20 minutes
4 Beat eggs lightly with cream. Pour over vegetable mixture
5 Cook slowly, stirring, until eggs are lightly scrambled
6 Transfer to warm serving dish and top with gammon. **Serves 4**

Party Gammon (page 66)

Baked Pork Creole

500g / 1lb fillet of pork
4 level tablespoons flour
Salt and pepper
40g / 1½oz butter
1 large chopped onion
250g / 8oz skinned tomatoes
1 large chopped celery stalk
1 small chopped green pepper
½ level teaspoon salt
4 tablespoons tomato juice

1 Cut pork into thin slices
2 Toss in flour seasoned with salt and pepper
3 Fry briskly in butter until golden. Transfer to plate
4 Add onion to remaining butter in pan. Fry gently until pale gold
5 Arrange pork in casserole dish
6 Cover with fried onion, tomatoes, celery and green pepper
7 Sprinkle with salt
8 Pour tomato juice into dish. Cover with lid or aluminium foil
9 Bake in centre of moderate oven (180°C / 350°F or Gas No 4) for 1 hour
10 Uncover. Continue to cook for further 15 minutes. **Serves 4**

Braised Pork Chops

4 loin of pork chops, each about 175g / 6oz
2 tablespoons flour
1 level teaspoon salt
Shake of pepper
40g / 1½oz butter
1 large chopped onion
4 medium-sized potatoes, sliced
2 large chopped celery stalks
250g / 8oz skinned and chopped tomatoes
2 level teaspoons granulated sugar
1 teaspoon Worcestershire sauce

1 Toss chops in flour seasoned with salt and pepper
2 Fry briskly in butter until crisp and golden on both sides. Transfer to plate
3 Add onion to remaining butter in pan. Fry gently until golden
4 Cover base of fairly shallow heatproof dish with potatoes
5 Add celery, tomatoes, sugar and Worcestershire sauce to onion in pan
6 Mix well. Pour over potatoes
7 Arrange chops on top
8 Cover with lid or aluminium foil
9 Bake in centre of moderate oven (180°C / 350°F or Gas No 4) for 1 to 1¼ hours. **Serves 4**

Pork Loaf

150ml / ¼ pint milk
1 teaspoon Worcestershire sauce
2 standard eggs
100g / 4oz fresh white breadcrumbs
1 medium-sized chopped onion
1 finely chopped garlic clove (optional)
25g / 1oz butter
350g / 12oz cold cooked pork, finely minced
½ level teaspoon mixed herbs
Seasoning to taste

Accompaniment
Mushroom Sauce (page 130) or Onion Sauce (page 129)

1 Beat milk with Worcestershire sauce and eggs
2 Combine with breadcrumbs
3 Fry onion and garlic (if used) gently in butter until pale gold
4 Add to breadcrumb mixture with minced pork and herbs
5 Season to taste. Mix well
6 Transfer to 20cm × 13cm × 9cm / 2lb buttered loaf tin
7 Bake in centre of moderate oven (180°C / 350°F or Gas No 4) for ¾ to 1 hour (or until firm)
8 Serve hot with Sauce. **Serves 4**

Somerset Pork Chops

4 lean pork chops
25g / 1oz butter
1 medium-sized, thinly sliced onion
25g / 1oz flour
150ml / ¼ pint cider
75ml / ⅛ pint water
1 clove garlic (optional)
Salt and pepper
Pinch of sage
2 tablespoons fresh cream

1 Fry the pork chops in butter together with the onion. When the chops are brown, remove from the pan. Continue cooking the onions until they are soft
2 Add the flour to the pan and cook gently until brown. Stir in the cider, water, garlic, salt, pepper and sage
3 Place the pork chops and onions in a shallow dish. Pour the sauce over. Bake, covered, in a moderately hot oven (190°C / 375°F or Gas No 5) for 30-40 minutes
4 Pour the cream over the chops and serve immediately. **Serves 4**

Steamed Bacon Pudding

500g / 1lb streaky bacon
300g / 12oz self-raising flour
Good shake of pepper
100g / 4oz butter
100g / 4oz grated onions
½ level teaspoon mixed herbs
1 level tablespoon finely chopped parsley
2 large eggs, beaten
4 to 5 tablespoons cold milk

Accompaniments
Gravy (page 133)
Grilled tomato halves
Apple Sauce (page 132)

1 Line 1 litre / 2 pint lightly buttered pudding basin with 8 to 10 bacon rashers. Chop rest of bacon finely
2 Sift flour and pepper into bowl
3 Rub in butter finely
4 Add chopped bacon, onions, herbs and parsley
5 Mix to soft batter with eggs and milk, stirring briskly without beating
6 Transfer to prepared basin
7 Cover securely with buttered greaseproof paper or aluminium foil
8 Steam steadily for 2 hours
9 Turn out on to warm dish
10 Serve with accompaniments. **Serves 4**

Baked Gammon Steak with Apples

2 level tablespoons soft brown sugar
1 level teaspoon dry mustard
Pepper
4cm / 1½in thick gammon steak (about 600g / 1lb 4oz)
12 very small onions or shallots
150ml / ¼ pint apple juice or cider
2 medium-sized cooking apples
3 cloves
25g / 1oz butter

1 Combine 1 tablespoon brown sugar with mustard and shake of pepper
2 Rub on to both sides of gammon steak
3 Transfer to buttered heatproof dish. Surround with whole onions or shallots
4 Pour in apple juice
5 Cover tightly with lid or aluminium foil
6 Bake in centre of hot oven (220°C / 425°F or Gas No 7) for 30 minutes
7 Turn gammon steak over
8 Cover with peeled, cored and sliced apples, rest of sugar and 3 cloves
9 Dot with butter and re-cover
10 Continue to cook in moderate oven (180°C / 350°F or Gas No 4) for further hour. Uncover during the last 15 minutes.
Serves 4

Pork with Cheese & Beer

4 loin of pork chops, each about 175g / 6oz
25g / 1oz butter, melted
175g / 6oz crumbled Lancashire cheese
2 level teaspoons made mustard
4 tablespoons brown ale

Garnish
4 grilled tomato halves

1 Stand chops in grill pan. Brush with melted butter
2 Grill for 7 to 10 minutes, depending on thickness
3 Turn over. Brush with more butter
4 Grill for further 7 to 10 minutes
5 Combine cheese with mustard and beer
6 Spread equal amounts over chops
7 Grill until brown
8 Transfer to warm serving dish and garnish each with a grilled ½ tomato. **Serves 4**

Boiled Spare Ribs

1kg / 2lb spare ribs of pork
1 large onion
1 large carrot
2 celery stalks
1 bay leaf
6 peppercorns
1 level teaspoon salt

Accompaniments
Sweet Sour White Cabbage (page 104)
Pease Pudding (page 103)
Creamed Potatoes (page 100)

1 Divide spare ribs into cutlets
2 Put into large saucepan. Cover with boiling water
3 Add whole onion, carrot, halved celery stalks, bay leaf, peppercorns and salt
4 Bring to boil and remove scum
5 Lower heat. Cover pan
6 Simmer gently for 1½ to 2 hours (or until tender)
7 Drain
8 Arrange cabbage on warm plate
9 Place spare ribs on top
10 Serve with accompaniments. **Serves 4**

Devilled Pork Sausages

500g / 1lb skinless pork sausages
25g / 1oz butter
1 medium-sized chopped onion
2 level tablespoons flour
150ml / ¼ pint water
2 level tablespoons sweet pickle
2 teaspoons Worcestershire sauce
2 tablespoons tomato ketchup
1 level teaspoon made mustard
1 tablespoon vinegar
½ level teaspoon salt

1 Fry sausages briskly in butter until golden
2 Remove to plate
3 Add onion to remaining butter in pan. Fry gently until pale gold
4 Stir in flour. Cook for 1 minute
5 Gradually blend in water
6 Add all remaining ingredients
7 Slowly bring to boil, stirring
8 Replace sausages. Lower heat. Cover pan
9 Simmer gently for 30 minutes. **Serves 4**

Pork Patties

225g / 8oz cooked minced pork
100g / 4oz finely chopped or minced lean bacon
100g / 4oz fresh white breadcrumbs
½ level teaspoon sage or mixed herbs
1 standard egg
150ml / ¼ pint milk
Seasoning to taste
300ml / ½ pint Mustard Coating Sauce (page 130)

1 Combine pork with bacon, breadcrumbs and sage or mixed herbs
2 Beat egg and milk well together
3 Add to breadcrumb mixture. Mix well
4 Season to taste with salt and pepper
5 Turn mixture out on to lightly floured board
6 Divide into 8 equal-sized pieces. Shape each into a 2cm / 1in thick cake
7 Transfer to heatproof dish
8 Coat with Mustard Sauce
9 Bake, uncovered, in centre of moderately hot oven (190°C / 375°F or Gas No 5) for 20 minutes. **Serves 4**

Veal

Veal Casserole with Cream (below)

 As Lamb and Beef.
Storage time–6 to 9 months.

Veal Casserole with Cream

750g / 1lb 8oz boned breast or knuckle of veal
50g / 2oz butter
1 medium-sized chopped onion
1 large chopped celery stalk
100g / 4oz sliced mushrooms and stalks
125ml / ¼ pint chicken stock
1 level teaspoon paprika
½ level teaspoon mixed herbs
2 tablespoons lemon juice or dry sherry
½ to 1 level teaspoon salt
Shake of pepper
150ml / ¼ pint fresh double cream

1 Cut veal into 2cm / 1in cubes
2 Fry gently in butter with onion, celery and mushrooms until pale gold
3 Transfer to casserole dish. Add stock
4 Stir in paprika, herbs, lemon juice or sherry and salt and pepper
5 Cover dish with lid or aluminium foil
6 Cook in centre of moderate oven (180°C / 350°F or Gas No 4) for 1 to 1¼ hours (or until veal is tender). Stir in cream
7 Serve immediately. **Serves 4**

Escalopes with Yogurt Sauce

4 pieces of veal fillet, each 100 to 175g / 4 to 6oz
50g / 2oz butter
2 teaspoons olive or corn oil
150g / 5oz carton natural yogurt
1 level teaspoon paprika

1 Beat each piece of veal until very thin
2 Nick edges with scissors to prevent meat from curling up as it cooks
3 Fry gently in hot butter and oil, allowing about 5 minutes per side
4 Transfer to warm plate. Keep warm
5 Add yogurt and paprika to remaining butter in pan. Heat through gently
6 Pour over veal
7 Serve immediately.
Serves 4

Escalopes in Lemon Sauce

1 Follow recipe and method for Escalopes with Yogurt Sauce (above)
2 Coat fried veal with 300ml / ½ pint Lemon Coating Sauce (page 129) instead of Yogurt Sauce
3 Garnish by sprinkling with finely chopped parsley.
Serves 4

Wiener Schnitzel

4 pieces of veal fillet, each 100 to 175g / 4 to 6oz
4 level tablespoons flour
½ level teaspoon salt
1 large egg, beaten
8 slightly rounded tablespoons fine white bread-
crumbs
75g / 3oz butter
1 tablespoon olive or corn oil

Garnish
4 slices lemon
2 teaspoons capers

1 Beat each piece of veal until very very thin
2 Nick edges with scissors to prevent meat from curling up as it cooks
3 Toss in flour seasoned with salt
4 Dip in beaten egg and coat with crumbs
5 Shake off surplus crumbs
6 Heat butter and oil in frying pan
7 Add no more than 1 or 2 pieces of veal at a time so that there is sufficient room for them to float about
8 Fry gently for 8 to 10 minutes, turning once
9 Drain on soft kitchen paper
10 Transfer to warm dish
11 Garnish centres of each with slices of lemon topped with capers. **Serves 4**

Veal Marengo

750g / 1lb 8oz boned breast or knuckle of veal
3 level tablespoons flour
1 level teaspoon salt
50g / 2oz butter
1 tablespoon olive or corn oil
1 large chopped onion
1 chopped garlic clove
150ml / ¼ pint water
1 wine glass dry white wine
400g / 12oz skinned and chopped tomatoes
250g / 8oz sliced mushrooms and stalks
1 level teaspoon granulated sugar
2 level tablespoons finely chopped parsley
350g / 12oz freshly boiled rice (about 175g / 6oz raw)

1 Cut veal into 2cm / 1in cubes
2 Toss in flour seasoned with salt
3 Fry in hot butter and oil until crisp and golden, turning all the time
4 Remove to plate
5 Add onion and garlic to remaining butter in pan. Fry gently until pale gold
6 Return veal to pan
7 Pour in water and wine
8 Add tomatoes, mushrooms and sugar
9 Bring slowly to boil. Lower heat. Cover pan
10 Simmer gently for 1 to 1¼ hours (or until veal is tender)
11 Transfer to a warm dish. Sprinkle with parsley
12 Serve rice separately. **Serves 4**

Wiener Schnitzel Holstein

1 Follow recipe and method for Wiener Schnitzel (left) but omit garnish
2 Top each Schnitzel with fried egg and accompany with lemon wedges. **Serves 4**

Italian Veal

1 Follow recipe and method for Wiener Schnitzel (left)
2 After dipping veal in egg, coat with 5 level tablespoons breadcrumbs mixed with 4 level tablespoons finely grated Cheddar cheese
3 Omit capers. Garnish each with lemon slices and 2 black or stuffed olives. Accompany with Tomato Sauce (page 134). **Serves 4**

Swiss Veal

1 Follow recipe and method for Wiener Schnitzel (left) but omit garnish
2 Coat Schnitzel with sauce made by heating gently 150ml / 5fl oz carton soured cream with yolks of 2 standard eggs
3 Dust lightly with chopped parsley. **Serves 4**

Roast Veal

Choose loin, leg, boned shoulder, stuffed breast

50g / 2oz butter

Quantities
Allow 250g to 400g / 8 to 12oz per person for veal with bone
Allow 100 to 175g / 4 to 6oz per person for veal without bone

Accompaniments
Gravy (page 133)
Grilled bacon rolls
Lemon wedges
Roast or boiled potatoes
Peas, beans, cauliflower, carrots or mixture of vegetables

1 Skewer or tie joint into neat shape
2 Stand in roasting tin
3 Brush with butter
4 Pour remaining butter into tin
5 Put into centre of hot oven (230°C / 450°F or Gas No 8)
6 Immediately reduce to moderate (180°C / 350°F or Gas No 4)
7 Continue roasting for required amount of time, allowing 30 minutes per 500g / 1lb and 30 minutes over. Baste frequently
8 Stand joint on carving board
9 Remove string or skewers
10 Serve with accompaniments

Veal & Egg Pie

Double recipe Cheese Pastry (page 212)
**300ml / ½ pint cold Basic White Coating Sauce
  (page 129)**
250g / 8oz cooked chopped veal
2 large chopped hard-boiled eggs
2 tablespoons cooked peas
Seasoning to taste
Milk for brushing

1 Divide pastry into 2 equal portions
2 Roll out 1 portion. Use to line lightly buttered
20cm / 8in heatproof plate
3 Combine Sauce with veal, eggs and peas
4 Season to taste with salt and pepper
5 Spread over pastry to within 2cm / 1in of edges
6 Moisten edges with water
7 Cover with lid, rolled from rest of pastry
8 Press edges well together to seal. Ridge with
fork
9 Brush with milk. Stand Pie on baking tray
10 Bake just above centre of hot oven
(220°C / 425°F or Gas No 7) for 25 to 30 minutes
(or until golden). Serve hot or cold.
Serves 4 to 6

Veal Goulash

250g / 8oz chopped onions
1 chopped garlic clove
50g / 2oz lean chopped bacon
75g / 3oz butter
750g / 1lb 8oz boned breast or knuckle of veal
1 level tablespoon paprika
1 large chopped green pepper
175g / 6oz skinned tomatoes, chopped
¼ level teaspoon caraway seeds
1 level teaspoon salt
150g / 5oz carton natural yogurt

Accompaniment
Boiled potatoes or noodles

1 Gently fry onion, garlic and bacon in butter (in
saucepan) until pale gold
2 Cut veal into 5cm / 2in cubes and add
3 Fry fairly briskly for 5 minutes, turning all the
time
4 Stir in paprika
5 Add all remaining ingredients except yogurt
6 Very slowly bring to boil
7 Lower heat. Cover pan
8 Simmer gently for 1 to 1¼ hours (or until veal is
tender)
9 Remove from heat. Stir in yogurt
10 Serve with potatoes or noodles.
Serves 4

An authentic Goulash has no liquid added to it;
the meat and vegetables provide their own. However, by adding 300ml / ½ pint chicken stock and
4 chopped Frankfurter sausages, a delicious
Goulash soup can be made. This is a meal in itself

Pot-roasted Veal Breast

1¼kg / 2lb 8oz boned veal breast
1 recipe Celery and Tomato Stuffing (page 98)
75g / 3oz butter
1 tablespoon olive or corn oil

Accompaniment
Gravy (page 133)

1 Spread veal with Stuffing
2 Roll up. Tie at 4cm / 1½in intervals with fine
string or thick thread
3 Heat butter and oil in flameproof casserole or
heavy saucepan
4 Add joint. Brown well all over
5 Cover pan tightly. Cook over very low heat,
allowing 45 minutes per 500g / 1lb
6 Turn occasionally
7 Transfer to carving board
8 Remove string or thread
9 Accompany with gravy. **Serves 4 to 6**

Fricassée of Veal

750g / 1lb 8oz boned breast or knuckle of veal
300ml / ½ pint stock or water
300ml / ½ pint milk
3 cloves
1 large onion
½ small bay leaf
1 blade mace
1 sprig parsley
1 level teaspoon salt
25g / 1oz butter
25g / 1oz flour
100g / 4oz button mushrooms
Seasoning to taste

Garnish
8 grilled bacon rolls
4 lemon wedges
Parsley sprigs

1 Cut veal into 5cm / 2in cubes. Put into saucepan
2 Pour in stock or water and milk
3 Press cloves into onion. Add to saucepan with
bay leaf, mace, parsley and salt
4 Bring to boil. Remove scum
5 Lower heat. Cover pan
6 Simmer gently for 1 to 1¼ hours (or until veal is
tender)
7 Strain liquor and reserve
8 Transfer veal to warm platter. Keep hot
9 Melt butter in clean saucepan
10 Stir in flour. Cook for 2 minutes without
browning
11 Gradually blend in veal liquor
12 Cook, stirring, until sauce comes to boil and
thickens
13 Add mushrooms. Simmer for 5 minutes.
Season to taste. Pour over veal
14 Garnish with bacon, lemon and parsley.
Serves 4

Offal

Devilled Kidneys   Baked Stuffed Hearts (below)

 Best frozen as made-up dish but reduce cooking time. Finish cooking when thawed. Storage time – 2 to 3 months.

Baked Stuffed Hearts

4 calves' hearts
½ recipe Pork Sausage Stuffing (page 98)
50g / 2oz butter
3 tablespoons stock or water

Accompaniments
Creamed Potatoes (page 100)
Brown Sauce (page 133)
Redcurrant jelly

1 Wash hearts well
2 Remove veins and fat. Dry thoroughly
3 Cut through centre divisions to make 1 cavity in each heart
4 Fill loosely with equal amounts of Stuffing
5 Transfer to casserole dish
6 Dot with butter. Pour in stock or water
7 Cook, tightly covered, in centre of moderate oven (160°C / 325°F or Gas No 3) for 1½ hours
8 Baste well
9 Continue to cook, uncovered, for further 30 minutes (or until tender)
10 Serve with accompaniments. **Serves 4**

Devilled Kidneys

4 pigs' kidneys
2 level tablespoons flour
Salt and pepper
50g / 2oz butter
1 medium-sized chopped onion
300ml / ½ pint water
2 teaspoons Worcestershire sauce
2 level teaspoons made mustard
2 teaspoons tomato purée
1 level tablespoon finely chopped parsley
4 slices hot buttered toast

1 Skin and core kidneys
2 Cut into ½cm / ¼in thick slices
3 Toss in flour seasoned with salt and pepper
4 Melt butter in saucepan
5 Add onion. Fry until pale gold
6 Add kidney and any remaining flour. Cook slowly for further 5 minutes, turning frequently
7 Combine water with Worcestershire sauce, mustard, purée and parsley
8 Pour into pan
9 Cook slowly, stirring, until mixture comes to boil and thickens
10 Lower heat. Cover pan
11 Simmer for 15 minutes
12 Serve on toast.
Serves 4

Tripe & Onions

1kg/2lb dressed tripe
250g/8oz onions
450ml/¾ pint milk
1 level teaspoon salt
1 level tablespoon cornflour
3 extra tablespoons cold milk
15g/½oz butter
Pepper to taste

Accompaniment
Creamed Potatoes (page 100)

1 Wash tripe well. Cut into 5cm/2in squares
2 Slice onions thinly
3 Put both into saucepan
4 Add milk and salt
5 Bring to boil. Lower heat
6 Cover pan. Simmer very gently for 35 to 45 minutes (or until tripe is tender)
7 Mix cornflour to smooth paste with extra cold milk
8 Add to tripe and onions in saucepan. Cook, stirring, until mixture comes to boil and thickens
9 Add butter. Season to taste with pepper
10 Serve with Creamed Potatoes.
Serves 4

Buttered Tripe with Cheese

1kg/2lb dressed tripe
600ml/1 pint water (or 600ml/1 pint milk, if preferred)
1 level teaspoon salt
50g/2oz butter
1 garlic clove
225g/8oz crumbled Lancashire cheese
150ml/¼ pint extra milk (unless tripe is cooked in milk)

Accompaniment
Salad (see Salad Section, page 114)

1 Wash tripe well. Cut into strips
2 Put into saucepan with water or milk and salt
3 Bring to boil. Lower heat
4 Cover pan. Simmer very gently for 35 to 45 minutes (or until tripe is tender). Drain. (If milk used in cooking, reserve 150ml/¼ pint tripe liquor)
5 Put butter and halved garlic clove into saucepan
6 Melt over low heat. Remove garlic
7 Add tripe. Cook briskly in butter for 1 minute, shaking pan frequently
8 Arrange layers of tripe and crumbled cheese in heatproof dish, beginning with tripe and ending with cheese
9 Pour in tripe liquor (or extra milk)
10 Re-heat towards top of moderately hot oven (190°C/375°F or Gas No 5) for 20 to 25 minutes
11 Serve hot and accompany with salad.
Serves 4

Fried Savoury Tripe

1kg/2lb dressed tripe
600ml/1 pint water (or 600ml/1 pint milk if preferred)
1 level teaspoon salt
1 large onion
1 garlic clove
50g/2oz butter
1 level tablespoon finely chopped parsley
2 teaspoons malt vinegar

Accompaniments
4 slices hot fried bread

1 Wash tripe well. Cut into 2cm/1in squares
2 Put into saucepan. Add water or milk and salt
3 Bring to boil. Lower heat
4 Cover pan. Simmer very gently for 35 to 45 minutes (or until tripe is tender). Drain
5 Chop onion and garlic. Fry gently in butter until pale gold
6 Add tripe, parsley and vinegar. Heat briskly for 2 to 3 minutes, shaking pan frequently
7 Pile equal amounts on to fried bread
8 Serve immediately. **Serves 4**

Kidneys Espagnole

4 calves' kidneys
50g/2oz butter
1 recipe Espagnole Sauce (page 133)
350g/12oz freshly boiled rice (about 175g/6oz raw)
1 level tablespoon finely chopped parsley

1 Skin and core kidneys
2 Cut into slices. Fry in hot butter for 5 minutes, turning frequently
3 Remove from pan. Add to Espagnole Sauce
4 Heat through gently
5 Arrange border of rice on warm serving dish
6 Fill centre with kidney mixture
7 Sprinkle with chopped parsley. **Serves 4**

Creamed Liver

250g/8oz calves' or lambs' liver
2 level tablespoons flour
Salt and pepper
25g/1oz butter
300ml/½ pint milk
2-3 tablespoons fresh double cream

1 Cut liver into small pieces
2 Roll in flour seasoned with salt and pepper
3 Fry gently in hot butter until cooked through and golden brown. Stir in remaining flour
4 Gradually blend in milk. Cook slowly, stirring, until mixture thickens. Simmer gently for 5 minutes
5 Stir in cream. **Serves 4**

Kidneys en Brochette

8 lambs' kidneys
Cold milk
8 rashers streaky bacon
225g/8oz freshly boiled rice (about 100g/4oz raw)

1 Skin and core kidneys
2 Cut each in half
3 Put into saucepan. Cover with milk. Bring slowly to boil
4 Reduce heat. Simmer for 3 minutes
5 Lift out of pan. Drain on soft kitchen paper
6 Cut bacon rashers in half. Wrap round pieces of kidney
7 Thread on to 4 skewers
8 Brown under hot grill for 2 to 3 minutes
9 Turn over and grill for further 2 to 3 minutes
10 Serve with rice. **Serves 4**

Tongue with Mustard Sauce

1 fresh ox tongue (1¼ to 1½kg/2lb 8oz to 3lb)
250g/8oz onions
2 medium-sized carrots
3 celery stalks
Handful of parsley
1 bay leaf
8 peppercorns
1 level teaspoon salt
Double recipe Mustard Coating Sauce (page 130)

1 Remove excess fat from root end of tongue
2 Put tongue into large bowl. Cover with cold water
3 Soak for 2 hours. Drain
4 Transfer to large saucepan. Cover with cold water
5 Bring slowly to boil. Drain
6 Cover with fresh water. Add whole onions, thickly sliced carrots, halved celery stalks, parsley, bay leaf, peppercorns and salt
7 Bring slowly to boil. Lower heat
8 Cover pan. Simmer for 3 to 3½ hours (or until tongue is tender)
9 Drain. Leave until cool enough to handle
10 Remove wind and food pipe, small bones and gristle at root end
11 Strip off skin
12 Carve hot tongue into thin slices
13 Serve with Mustard Sauce.
Serves 6 to 8

Tongue with Madeira Sauce

1 Follow recipe and method for Tongue with Mustard Sauce (above)
2 Serve tongue with Madeira Sauce (page 133) instead of Mustard Sauce. **Serves 6 to 8**

Grilled Liver

500g/1lb calves' liver
Cold milk
25g/1oz butter, melted

1 Slice liver thinly
2 Put into soup plate or shallow dish. Cover with milk
3 Soak for 30 minutes
4 Drain. Pat dry with soft kitchen paper
5 Stand on grill rack. Brush with melted butter
6 Cook under hot grill for 1½ minutes
7 Turn over. Brush with more butter
8 Grill for further 1½ minutes
9 Serve immediately.
Serves 4

Stewed Oxtail

1 medium-sized oxtail (900g to 1¼kg/2lb to 2lb 8oz)
25g/1oz butter
1 large sliced onion
1 medium-sized sliced carrot
½ small turnip, diced
1 bay leaf
6 peppercorns } **tied together in**
3 cloves } **muslin bag**
3 parsley sprigs }
450ml/¾ pint boiling water
1 level teaspoon salt
2 level tablespoons flour
3 tablespoons cold water
2 teaspoons vinegar
Seasoning to taste

Garnish
2 level tablespoons finely chopped parsley

1 Wash and dry oxtail
2 Cut into neat joints. Remove excess fat
3 Heat butter in large saucepan
4 Add onion. Fry gently until pale gold
5 Add oxtail and rest of vegetables
6 Fry briskly for 5 minutes, turning all the time
7 Add bag of herbs, boiling water and salt
8 Bring to boil. Lower heat
9 Cover pan. Simmer for 3 hours (or until oxtail is tender)
10 Remove bag of herbs
11 Leave overnight in cold place
12 Before serving, remove hard layer of fat from surface and discard
13 Bring oxtail up to the boil
14 Pour in flour mixed to smooth paste with cold water and vinegar
15 Cook, stirring, until liquor comes to boil and thickens
16 Simmer for 5 minutes. Season
17 Transfer to warm dish
18 Sprinkle with parsley.
Serves 4

Fried Liver

500g / 1lb lambs' or pigs' liver
Cold milk
4 level tablespoons flour
Salt and pepper
1 large egg, beaten
6 to 8 level tablespoons toasted breadcrumbs
75g / 3oz butter

Garnish
Lemon slices
Watercress

1 Cut liver into thin slices
2 Put into soup plate or shallow dish. Cover with milk
3 Soak for 30 minutes
4 Drain. Pat dry with soft kitchen paper
5 Toss in flour seasoned with salt and pepper
6 Coat twice in egg and breadcrumbs. Leave for 15 minutes
7 Heat butter in frying pan
8 Add liver, 1 or 2 pieces at a time
9 Fry until crisp and golden, allowing 2 to 3 minutes per side
10 Drain on soft kitchen paper
11 Transfer to warm platter
12 Garnish with lemon and parsley. **Serves 4**

Braised Liver

500g / 1lb ox liver
4 level tablespoons flour
Salt and pepper
50g / 2oz butter
1 medium-sized chopped onion
2 medium-sized grated carrots
1 large grated potato
2 chopped celery stalks
2 level tablespoons chopped parsley
½ level teaspoon salt
300ml / ½ pint water
1 medium-sized sliced lemon

1 Cut liver into 2cm / 1in cubes
2 Toss in flour seasoned with salt and pepper
3 Fry briskly (in saucepan) in hot butter until crisp and well sealed, turning all the time
4 Remove to plate
5 Add onion to remaining butter. Fry slowly until pale gold
6 Stir in any left-over flour, together with carrots, potato, celery, parsley, salt and water
7 Mix well. Bring slowly to boil
8 Replace liver. Top with lemon slices
9 Lower heat. Cover pan
10 Simmer for 30 to 40 minutes (or until liver is tender). **Serves 4**

Poached Sweetbreads in Cream Sauce

500g / 1lb calves' sweetbreads
2 teaspoons lemon juice
300ml / ½ pint milk
1 small chopped onion
2 peppercorns
1 small celery stalk
25g / 1oz butter
25g / 1oz flour
¼ level teaspoon finely grated lemon rind
Salt and pepper
2-3 tablespoons fresh double cream
4 slices hot buttered toast

1 Soak sweetbreads in lukewarm salted water for 1 hour. Drain
2 Put into saucepan. Cover with cold water
3 Add lemon juice. Bring slowly to boil
4 Boil for 5 minutes. Drain
5 Plunge at once into cold water
6 When sweetbreads are cool enough to handle, lift out of water. Cut away gristle and tissues
7 Bring milk to boil
8 Lower heat. Add sweetbreads, onions, peppercorns and halved celery stalk
9 Simmer gently for 15 to 20 minutes
10 Strain sweetbread liquor. Make up to 300ml / ½ pint with extra cold milk if necessary
11 Melt butter in clean saucepan and stir in flour
12 Cook slowly for 2 minutes, without browning
13 Gradually blend in sweetbread liquor. Add lemon rind
14 Cook, stirring, until sauce comes to boil and thickens. Add sweetbreads. Season to taste
15 Heat through gently for 5 minutes. Stir in fresh cream
16 Arrange on buttered toast and serve immediately. **Serves 4**

Crumbed & Fried Sweetbreads

1 Prepare sweetbreads as in recipe for Poached Sweetbreads in Cream Sauce (above)
2 After simmering sweetbreads in milk for 15 to 20 minutes, remove from saucepan and drain
3 Toss in 4 to 5 level teaspoons flour seasoned with salt and pepper
4 Coat twice in 1 large beaten egg and 5 to 6 level tablespoons toasted breadcrumbs
5 Fry until crisp and golden in 50g / 2oz butter. Drain on soft kitchen paper
6 Serve with Mock Hollandaise Sauce (page 131). **Serves 4**

Chicken

Coq au Vin (below)

Chicken may be frozen whole or jointed, raw or cooked. Poultry should not be stuffed and frozen. Always ensure that poultry is **completely** thawed before cooking. Storage time – uncooked – 12 months, cooked – 4 months.

Coq au Vin

4 medium-sized joints roasting chicken, washed and dried
4 level tablespoons flour
1 level teaspoon salt
50g / 2oz butter
1 tablespoon olive or corn oil
1 large chopped onion
1 chopped garlic clove
100g / 4oz chopped lean bacon
8 small onions or 10 shallots
2 level tablespoons finely chopped parsley
1 small bay leaf
300ml / $\frac{1}{2}$ pint dry red wine
4 tablespoons water
100g / 4oz sliced mushrooms and stalks

1 Toss chicken joints in flour seasoned with salt
2 Heat butter and oil in large saucepan
3 Add chicken. Fry until crisp and golden on both sides
4 Remove to plate
5 Add chopped onion, garlic and bacon to remaining butter and oil in pan
6 Fry gently until pale gold
7 Replace chicken
8 Add small onions or shallots, parsley, bay leaf, wine and water
9 Bring to boil and lower heat
10 Cover pan. Simmer for 1 hour
11 Add mushrooms and simmer for further 15 minutes. **Serves 4**

Chicken & Parsley Casserole

4 medium-sized joints roasting chicken, washed and dried
75g / 3oz butter
100g / 4oz streaky bacon
2 large onions
50g / 2oz flour
600ml / 1 pint milk
1 bay leaf
1 level teaspoon mixed herbs
1 chicken stock cube
Seasoning to taste
100g / 4oz sliced mushrooms and stalks

Garnish
2 level tablespoons finely chopped parsley

1 Fry chicken joints in 50g / 2oz butter until golden on both sides
2 Transfer to large casserole
3 Chop bacon and onions. Add to butter in pan. Fry gently until pale gold
4 Sprinkle over chicken
5 Melt remaining butter in frying pan. Stir in flour
6 Cook, without browning, for 2 minutes
7 Gradually blend in milk
8 Add bay leaf, herbs and crumbled stock cube
9 Cook, stirring, until sauce comes to boil and thickens. Season to taste
10 Pour over chicken. Cover casserole with lid or aluminium foil
11 Cook in centre of moderate oven (160°C / 325°F or Gas No 3) for 1 hour
12 Add mushrooms and stalks. Cook, covered, for further 30 minutes
13 Sprinkle with chopped parsley. **Serves 4**

Fried Chicken

4 medium-sized joints roasting chicken, washed and dried
Milk
2 level tablespoons flour
Salt and pepper
75g / 3oz butter
1 tablespoon olive or corn oil
1 tablespoon lemon juice
1 level tablespoon finely chopped parsley

1 Dip chicken joints in milk
2 Coat with flour seasoned with salt and pepper
3 Heat butter and oil in large frying pan
4 Add chicken joints, skin side up
5 Fry until golden
6 Turn over and cover pan
7 Continue to fry gently until tender (20 to 30 minutes). Turn joints at least twice
8 Transfer to warm serving dish. Keep hot
9 Add lemon juice and parsley to remaining butter and oil in pan. Heat through quickly. Pour over chicken. **Serves 4**

Grilled Chicken

4 medium-sized joints roasting chicken, washed and dried
50g / 2oz butter, melted
1 tablespoon lemon juice
$\frac{1}{4}$ level teaspoon paprika
$\frac{1}{4}$ level teaspoon mixed herbs (optional)
Shake of pepper

Garnish
Watercress

1 Brush chicken joints with some of the melted butter
2 Stand in grill pan, skin side down
3 Stand below pre-heated hot grill
4 Grill for about 30 minutes, turning frequently and brushing with rest of butter mixed with lemon juice, paprika, herbs and pepper
5 Transfer to warm serving dish
6 Garnish with watercress. **Serves 4**

Devilled Chicken

1 Follow recipe and method for Grilled Chicken (above)
2 Mix melted butter with $\frac{1}{2}$ level teaspoon dry mustard, 2 teaspoons Worcestershire sauce, 1 level teaspoon paprika and large pinch Cayenne pepper. **Serves 4**

Chicken with Almonds

25g / 1oz blanched and toasted almonds
1 small chopped onion
50g / 2oz sliced mushrooms and stalks
25g / 1oz butter
2 level teaspoons cornflour
150ml / $\frac{1}{4}$ pint milk
350g / 12oz cooked chicken
$\frac{1}{4}$ level teaspoon ground ginger
$\frac{1}{4}$ level teaspoon grated nutmeg
150g / 5oz carton natural yogurt
Yolks of 2 standard eggs
Salt and pepper

1 Cut almonds into strips
2 Fry onion and mushrooms in butter (in saucepan) until pale gold
3 Add cornflour. Cook for 1 minute
4 Gradually blend in milk
5 Cook, stirring, until sauce comes to boil
6 Add chicken (cut into bite-size pieces), ginger and grated nutmeg. Boil gently for 5 to 7 minutes
7 Beat yogurt and egg yolks well together
8 Add to chicken mixture. Cook very slowly, without boiling, until thickened
9 Season to taste and pour into warm serving dish
10 Scatter almonds over the top.
Serves 4

Fricassée of Chicken

1 **roasting chicken (about 1½ to 1¾kg / 3 to 4lb)**
300ml / ½ pint stock or water
300ml / ½ pint milk
100g / 4oz streaky bacon, chopped
4 cloves
1 large onion
¼ level teaspoon grated nutmeg
50g / 2oz mushrooms and stalks
¼ level teaspoon mixed herbs
½ level teaspoon salt
25g / 1oz butter
25g / 1oz flour

Garnish
4 rashers streaky bacon, halved, rolled and grilled
4 lemon wedges
1 level tablespoon finely chopped parsley

1 Cut chicken into 8 joints
2 Put into saucepan with stock or water and milk
3 Add chopped bacon
4 Press cloves into onion. Add to pan with grated nutmeg, mushrooms and stalks, herbs and salt
5 Bring to boil. Remove scum
6 Lower heat. Cover pan. Simmer gently for 1¼ to 1¾ hours (or until chicken is tender)
7 Strain liquor and reserve. Transfer chicken to warm plate and keep hot
8 Melt butter in clean saucepan. Add flour. Cook for 2 minutes without browning
9 Gradually blend in chicken liquor
10 Cook, stirring, until sauce comes to boil and thickens
11 Simmer for 2 minutes. Pour over chicken
12 Garnish with bacon rolls, lemon and parsley. **Serves 4**

Blanquette of Chicken

1 Follow recipe and method for Fricassée of Chicken (above)
2 After sauce has cooked for 2 minutes remove from heat and cool slightly
3 Stir in yolks of 2 standard eggs and 2 teaspoons lemon juice
4 Pour over chicken. **Serves 4**

Chicken Pie

4 joints boiling fowl (about 1½kg / 3lb)
2 medium-sized carrots
2 medium-sized onions
2 medium-sized celery stalks
1 litre / 2 pints water
2 level teaspoons salt
40g / 1½oz butter
40g / 1½oz flour
300ml / ½ pint milk
4 tablespoons fresh double cream
Seasoning to taste
1 recipe Milk 'Puff' Pastry (page 214)
Beaten egg for brushing

1 Put chicken joints into saucepan
2 Add whole carrots, onions and celery broken into small lengths
3 Pour in water and salt
4 Bring to boil. Remove scum
5 Lower heat. Cover pan. Simmer for 2¼ to 2¾ hours (or until chicken is tender). If preferred, pressure-cook for 30 minutes at high (or according to manufacturer's instructions)
6 Lift chicken out of saucepan. Discard skin and bones. Cut chicken meat into bite-size pieces
7 Strain chicken liquor and reserve 150ml / ¼ pint (if liked, retain vegetables for soup)
8 Melt butter in clean saucepan. Add flour. Cook for 2 minutes without browning
9 Gradually blend in chicken stock and milk
10 Cook, stirring, until sauce comes to boil and thickens
11 Remove from heat. Stir in chicken and cream
12 Adjust seasoning to taste. Transfer to ¾ litre / 1½ pint pie dish
13 Roll out Pastry to ½cm / ¼in thickness. From it, cut lid about 3cm / 1½in wider, all the way round, than top of dish
14 Moisten edge of dish with water. Line with strip of pastry
15 Moisten strip. Cover with lid
16 Press edges well together to seal
17 Flake by cutting lightly with back of knife
18 Flute edges or ridge with fork
19 Brush with beaten egg
20 Stand Pie on baking tray
21 Bake just above centre of hot oven (220°C / 425°F or Gas No 7) for 25 to 30 minutes (or until golden). **Serves 4 to 6**

Buttered Roast Chicken

1¾kg/4lb roasting chicken
75g/3oz butter
Salt and pepper

Accompaniments
Gravy (page 133)
Bread Sauce (page 132)
Small cooked sausages
Grilled bacon rolls
Roast and boiled potatoes
Assorted vegetables

1 If chicken is frozen, thaw completely and remove giblet pack
2 Wash fresh or thawed bird well. Dry thoroughly with soft kitchen paper
3 Stand in roasting tin
4 Put 40g/1½oz butter into body cavity
5 Melt rest of butter. Pour over chicken
6 Cover bird loosely with aluminium foil
7 Put into centre of hot oven (230°C/450°F or Gas No 8)
8 Immediately reduce heat to moderate (180°C/350°F or Gas No 4)
9 Continue to roast, allowing 25 minutes per 500g/1lb
10 Uncover half way through cooking time and baste well
11 Sprinkle with salt and pepper and replace foil
12 Uncover for last 30 minutes to brown bird
13 Transfer to board or carving dish. Leave for 5 minutes before carving
14 Serve with accompaniments. **Serves 4 to 6**

Roast Stuffed Chicken

1 Follow recipe and method for Buttered Roast Chicken (above)
2 Instead of butter, fill crop cavity with suitable stuffing (see Stuffings Section, page 97)
3 Allow extra 5 minutes per 500g/1lb roasting time. **Serves 4 to 6**

French-style Roast Chicken

1 Follow recipe and method for Buttered Roast Chicken (above)
2 Fill body cavity with 40g/1½oz butter creamed with 1 level teaspoon finely crushed rosemary and ½ to 1 level teaspoon French mustard.
Serves 4 to 6

Chicken Cacciatore

4 medium-sized joints roasting chicken, washed and dried
4 level tablespoons flour
1 level teaspoon salt
50g/2oz butter
1 tablespoon olive or corn oil
1 large chopped onion
1 chopped garlic clove
500g/1lb skinned and chopped tomatoes
1 level teaspoon sugar
150ml/¼ pint chicken stock
100g/4oz sliced mushrooms and stalks

1 Toss chicken in flour seasoned with salt
2 Heat butter and oil in large pan
3 Add chicken. Fry until crisp and golden on both sides
4 Remove to plate
5 Fry onion and garlic in remaining butter and oil in pan until pale gold
6 Add tomatoes, sugar and stock
7 Replace chicken
8 Slowly bring to boil. Cover pan
9 Lower heat. Simmer for 45 minutes
10 Add mushrooms. Simmer for further 15 to 25 minutes (or until chicken is tender)
11 Serve with noodles, macaroni or spaghetti.
Serves 4

Chicken Maryland

4 medium-sized joints roasting chicken, washed and dried
Milk
4 to 5 level tablespoons flour
Salt and pepper
6 level tablespoons toasted breadcrumbs
75g/3oz butter
1 tablespoon olive or corn oil

Garnish
Watercress

Accompaniments
Gravy (page 133)
Corn Fritters (page 104)
Halved bananas fried in butter

1 Dip chicken joints in milk
2 Toss in flour seasoned with salt and pepper. Leave to dry for 30 minutes
3 Dip in milk again. Coat with breadcrumbs
4 Shake surplus crumbs from each portion
5 Put butter and oil into roasting tin. Heat for 10 minutes just above centre of moderately hot oven (190°C/375°F or Gas No 5)
6 Add chicken and baste with hot butter and oil
7 Return to oven. Cook, uncovered, for 30 minutes (or until chicken is tender)
8 Drain well on soft kitchen paper
9 Garnish with watercress
10 Serve with accompaniments. **Serves 4**

Chicken Cacciatore (page 80)

Curried Chicken

4 medium-sized joints roasting chicken, washed and dried
4 level tablespoons flour
1 level teaspoon salt
40g / 1½oz butter
1 tablespoon olive or corn oil
2 large chopped onions
1 large peeled and chopped cooking apple
1 chopped garlic clove (optional)
½ level teaspoon salt
1 level tablespoon curry powder
½ level teaspoon ground ginger
½ level teaspoon cinnamon
1 level tablespoon chutney
150ml / ¼ pint milk
150ml / ¼ pint water
150g / 5oz carton natural yogurt

Accompaniments
350g / 12oz freshly boiled rice (about 175g / 6oz raw)

2 large sliced tomatoes
50g / 2oz chopped salted peanuts
Chutney

1 Toss chicken joints in flour seasoned with salt
2 Heat butter and oil in large saucepan
3 Add chicken. Fry until crisp and golden on both sides
4 Remove to plate
5 Add onions, apples and garlic (if used) to remaining butter and oil in pan
6 Fry gently until pale gold
7 Stir in salt, curry powder, ginger, cinnamon, chutney, milk and water
8 Bring to boil. Replace chicken
9 Cover pan
10 Simmer slowly for 45 minutes to 1 hour (or until chicken is tender)
11 Stir in yogurt. Heat through for further 5 minutes
12 Serve immediately with accompaniments.
Serves 4

Duckling & Goose

Duckling with Orange Sauce (below)

Duckling and Goose may be frozen whole or jointed, raw or cooked. Poultry should not be stuffed and frozen. Always ensure that poultry is **completely** thawed before cooking.
Storage time – uncooked – 6 months, cooked – 3 months

Roasting time Allow 25 minutes per 500g/1lb

Quantity Allow 500 to 600g/1lb to 1lb 4oz raw weight per person

Duckling with Orange Sauce

1 duckling (1¾ to 2¼kg/4 to 5lb)
1 level tablespoon flour
Coarsely grated rind and juice of 2 medium-
   sized oranges
2 tablespoons dry red wine
2 level tablespoons redcurrant jelly
½ wine glass dry sherry
Seasoning to taste

Garnish
2 thinly sliced oranges
Watercress

1 Roast duckling for required amount of time (see Roasting time above)
2 Transfer to warm platter and keep hot
3 Pour off all but 1 tablespoon fat from roasting tin
4 Stand tin over medium heat
5 Stir in flour
6 Cook for 2 minutes without browning
7 Add orange rind, juice, wine, jelly and sherry
8 Cook gently, stirring, until jelly dissolves and sauce comes to boil and thickens. Season to taste
9 Simmer for 2 minutes. Pour over duck
10 Garnish with border of orange slices. Place watercress at either end of dish. **Serves 4**

Roast Duckling or Goose

1 duckling or goose
Stuffing (see Stuffings Section, page 97)
Salt

Accompaniments
Gravy (page 133)
Apple Sauce (page 132)
Roast and/or boiled potatoes
Cooked green peas

1 Wash duckling or goose inside and out under cold running water
2 Dry with soft kitchen paper
3 Fill crop cavity with stuffing (or leave unstuffed if preferred)
4 Stand in roasting tin
5 Prick skin all over with fork. Sprinkle well with salt
6 Stand bird (on grid) in roasting tin
7 Put into centre of moderate oven (180°C / 350°F or Gas No 4). Roast for required amount of time. Do not baste or cover
8 Transfer to board or carving dish and carve
9 Serve with accompaniments

Duckling Provençale-style

1 × 2kg / 4lb duckling or 4 duckling portions
4 level tablespoons flour
50g / 2oz butter
250g / 8oz onions
2 small garlic cloves
1 medium-sized green pepper
50g / 2oz stuffed olives
1 level tablespoon tomato purée
2 level teaspoons caster sugar
450ml / ¾ pint water
1 medium-sized lemon
½ level teaspoon salt

Accompaniments
Boiled rice or potatoes
Salad (see Salad Section, page 114)

1 Cut whole duckling into 4 joints
2 Wash and dry joints (or portions if used)
3 Coat thickly with flour
4 Fry briskly in butter until crisp and golden. Remove to plate
5 Chop onions, garlic and green pepper
6 Add to butter in pan. Fry gently until soft and golden
7 Slice olives thinly. Add with purée and sugar
8 Blend in water. Bring to boil
9 Replace duckling
10 Slice lemon thinly. Add to saucepan with salt
11 Cover. Simmer very slowly for 1½ to 1¾ hours (or until duckling is tender)
12 Serve with accompaniments.
Serves 4

Duckling or Goose Bigarrade

1 Follow recipe and method for Roast Duckling or Goose (left)
2 After carving meat transfer to warm platter
3 Coat with hot Bigarrade Sauce (page 133)
4 Garnish edge of dish with Duchesse Potatoes (page 101)

Duckling or Goose with Apples & Prunes

1 Follow recipe and method for Roast Duckling or Goose (left)
2 Before roasting, stuff bird with 500g to 1kg / 1 to 2lb peeled, cored and thickly sliced cooking apples and 8 to 12 soaked, stoned and halved prunes
3 Accompany with Cranberry Sauce (page 134) or pickled red cabbage instead of Apple Sauce

Duckling & Apple Casserole

1 × 2kg / 4lb duckling or 4 duckling portions
1 medium-sized onion
250g / 8oz cooking apples
25g / 1oz butter
1 level tablespoon flour
300ml / ½ pint apple juice
2 level tablespoons raisins
¼ level teaspoon sage
Salt and pepper to taste

Garnish
2 level tablespoons chopped parsley

1 Cut whole duckling into 4 joints
2 Wash and dry joints (or portions if used)
3 Cut away excess fat from either. Stand duckling in casserole dish
4 Chop onion and peeled and cored apples
5 Fry gently in butter until pale gold and soft
6 Stir in flour. Cook for 2 minutes
7 Gradually blend in apple juice
8 Cook, stirring, until sauce comes to boil and thickens
9 Add raisins and sage
10 Season to taste with salt and pepper
11 Pour into dish over duckling
12 Cover casserole with lid or aluminium foil
13 Cook in centre of moderate oven (180°C / 350°F or Gas No 4) until duckling is tender (about 1½ to 2 hours)
14 Uncover. Sprinkle with parsley. **Serves 4**

Duck & Ham Loaf

175g / 6oz cooked minced duck meat
175g / 6oz lean minced ham
100g / 4oz fresh white breadcrumbs
½ level teaspoon finely grated orange rind
1 small minced onion
75g / 3oz finely chopped mushrooms and stalks
½ level teaspoon sage
2 level tablespoons finely chopped parsley
2 large beaten eggs
150ml / ¼ pint milk
Seasoning to taste

1 Combine duck, ham, breadcrumbs, orange rind,
onion, mushrooms and stalks, sage and parsley
2 Add beaten eggs and milk
3 Season to taste with salt and pepper. Mix well
4 Transfer to well-buttered
20cm×13cm×9cm / 2lb loaf tin
5 Smooth top with knife
6 Bake in centre of moderate oven (180°C / 350°F
or Gas No 4) for 1 hour (or until firm)
7 Leave in tin for 5 minutes
8 Turn out on to serving dish
9 Serve hot or cold. **Serves 4 to 6**

Sauté of Duck

4 duckling portions
15g / ½oz butter
1 medium-sized, finely sliced onion
225g / 8oz button mushrooms
250ml / ½ pint red Burgundy
125ml / ¼ pint jellied stock
Salt and pepper

Garnish
Fried croûtes of bread

1 Brown the duck in the butter quickly (this helps
to extract some of the fat, making the sauce less
greasy). Remove from the pan and allow to cool
2 Fry the onion in 2 tablespoons duck fat, and
allow it to brown slightly, add the mushrooms and
sauté for 2-3 minutes
3 Add the wine and stock to the pan. Stir until it
boils. Season, and replace pieces of duck in the
sauce
4 Simmer, covered, for 30-35 minutes or until bird
is tender

Duckling & Celery Casserole

1 × 2kg / 4lb duckling or 4 duckling portions
1 medium-sized onion
3 rashers lean bacon
25g / 1oz butter
1 level tablespoon flour
300ml / ½ pint water
Salt and pepper
¼ level teaspoon mixed herbs
1 small head celery

1 Cut whole duckling into 4 joints
2 Wash and dry joints (or portions if used)
3 Cut away excess fat from either. Stand duckling
in large casserole dish
4 Chop onion and bacon. Fry gently in butter until
pale gold
5 Stir in flour and cook for 2 minutes
6 Gradually blend in water
7 Cook, stirring, until sauce comes to boil and
thickens
8 Season to taste with salt and pepper
9 Add herbs. Pour sauce over duckling
10 Cut celery into 2cm / 1in lengths and add to
casserole
11 Cover with lid or aluminium foil
12 Cook in centre of moderate oven (180°C / 350°F
or Gas No 4) until duckling is tender (about 1½ to
2 hours). **Serves 4**

Duckling with Pineapple & Cherries

1 duckling (1¾ to 2¼kg / 4 to 5lb)
1 level tablespoon flour
4 canned pineapple rings, chopped
150ml / ¼ pint pineapple syrup (taken from can)
1 wine glass dry white wine
Seasoning to taste

Garnish
2 halved pineapple rings
Canned red cherries

1 Roast duckling for required amount of time (see
Roasting time page 82)
2 Transfer to warm platter and keep hot
3 Pour off all but 1 tablespoon fat from roasting
tin
4 Stand tin over medium heat and stir in flour
5 Cook for 2 minutes without browning
6 Add chopped pineapple, pineapple syrup and
wine
7 Cook gently, stirring, until sauce comes to boil
and thickens
8 Simmer for 2 minutes. Season to taste
9 Pour over duckling
10 Garnish dish with pineapple and small mounds
of cherries.
Serves 4

Turkey

Turkey à la King (below)

Turkey may be frozen whole or jointed, raw or cooked. Poultry should not be stuffed and frozen. Always ensure that poultry is **completely** thawed before cooking.
Storage time – uncooked – 12 months, cooked – 4 months

Quantity Allow 400g/12oz raw weight per person for small and medium-sized turkeys. Allow 250g/8oz raw weight per person for turkeys weighing 7¼kg/16lb and over

Roasting times For small turkeys weighing between 2¾ and 5½kg/6 and 12lb allow 25 minutes per 500g/1lb
For medium-sized turkeys weighing between 5½ and 7¼kg/12 to 16lb allow 20 minutes per 500g/1lb
For large turkeys weighing between 7¼ and 11¼kg/16 and 25lb allow 15 to 18 minutes per 500g/1lb

Turkey à la King

1 medium-sized chopped green pepper
50g/2oz butter
2 teaspoons olive or corn oil
100g/4oz sliced mushrooms and stalks
25g/1oz flour
150ml/¼ pint turkey stock or water
150ml/¼ pint milk
400g/12oz cooked turkey, cut into bite-size pieces
150ml/¼ pint fresh single cream
Yolks of 2 standard eggs
1 tablespoon dry sherry or lemon juice
Seasoning to taste

1 Fry green pepper gently in butter and oil for 5 minutes

2 Add mushrooms and stalks. Fry gently with pepper for further 5 minutes
3 Remove from pan and transfer to plate
4 Stir flour into remaining butter and oil in pan. Cook for 2 minutes without browning
5 Gradually blend in stock or water and milk
6 Cook, stirring, until sauce comes to boil and thickens
7 Lower heat. Add green pepper, mushrooms and turkey
8 Cover pan. Heat through gently for 10 minutes
9 Beat cream with egg yolks and sherry or lemon juice
10 Add to turkey mixture
11 Cook for further 2 to 3 minutes without boiling
12 Season to taste with salt and pepper. **Serves 4**

Roast Turkey

1 turkey
Stuffings (see Stuffings Section, page 97)
50 to 100g / 2 to 4oz melted butter, depending on size of bird
Salt and pepper

Accompaniments
Same as for Roast Chicken (page 80) but include Cranberry Sauce (page 134)

1 If turkey is frozen, thaw completely and remove giblet pack
2 Wash fresh or thawed bird well. Dry thoroughly with soft kitchen paper
3 Fill crop cavity with 2 different stuffings
4 Stand bird in roasting tin. Brush heavily with melted butter. Pour remaining butter into tin
5 Cover bird loosely with aluminium foil. Put into centre of hot oven (230°C / 450°F or Gas No 8)
6 Immediately reduce temperature to moderate (160°C / 325°F or Gas No 3). Continue to roast for required length of time (see Roasting time page 85)
7 Uncover half way through cooking time and baste well
8 Sprinkle with salt and pepper. Replace foil. Return to oven to continue roasting
9 Remove foil for last 30 minutes (45 minutes if turkey is medium sized or large) to brown bird
10 Leave 5 minutes before carving (meat will be less crumbly and easier to slice)
11 Serve with accompaniments

Turkey Fritters

1 recipe Savoury Fritter Batter (page 146)
250g / 8oz cooked minced turkey
1 level teaspoon finely grated lemon rind
1 level teaspoon curry powder
Deep fat or oil for frying
50g / 2oz grated Wensleydale cheese

1 Make Fritter Batter as directed but stir in turkey, lemon rind and curry powder before folding in egg whites
2 Drop spoonfuls of mixture into hot fat or oil
3 Fry until well puffed and golden
4 Remove from pan and drain on soft kitchen paper
5 Transfer to paper-lined serving dish and sprinkle with cheese
6 Serve hot. **Serves 4**

Turkey & Walnut Fritters

1 Follow recipe and method for Turkey Fritters (above)
2 Include 25g / 1oz very finely chopped shelled walnut halves
3 Sprinkle with 50g / 2oz grated Leicester cheese instead of Wensleydale. **Serves 4**

Turkey in Paprika

1 large chopped onion
1 small chopped green pepper
40g / 1½oz butter
2 teaspoons olive or corn oil
1 level tablespoon flour
1½ level tablespoons paprika
1 level tablespoon tomato purée
1 level teaspoon caster sugar
300ml / ½ pint stock or water
½ level teaspoon salt
¼ level teaspoon caraway seeds (optional)
400g / 12oz cooked turkey
150g / 5oz carton natural yogurt

Accompaniments
Freshly boiled potatoes or rice

1 Fry onion and pepper in hot butter and oil until pale gold and soft
2 Remove from heat
3 Stir in flour, paprika, purée and sugar
4 Gradually blend in stock or water, salt and caraway seeds
5 Cook, stirring, until sauce comes to boil and thickens
6 Cover. Simmer gently for 15 minutes
7 Cut turkey into bite-size pieces. Add to pan with yogurt
8 Heat through for further 5 minutes without boiling
9 Accompany with potatoes or rice. **Serves 4**

Turkey Loaf

400g / 12oz cooked minced turkey
100g / 4oz fresh white breadcrumbs
½ level teaspoon dry mustard
1 small minced onion
75g / 3oz finely chopped mushrooms and stalks
½ level teaspoon celery salt
1 level teaspoon finely grated lemon rind
2 level tablespoons chopped parsley
2 large eggs, beaten
150ml / ¼ pint milk
1 teaspoon Worcestershire sauce
Seasoning to taste

1 Combine turkey, breadcrumbs, mustard, onion, mushrooms and stalks, celery salt, lemon rind and parsley
2 Stir in beaten eggs, milk and Worcestershire sauce
3 Season to taste with salt and pepper
4 Transfer to foil lined well-buttered 20cm × 13cm × 9cm / 2lb loaf tin
5 Smooth top with knife
6 Bake in centre of moderate oven (180°C / 350°F or Gas No 4) for 1 hour (or until firm)
7 Leave in tin for 5 minutes
8 Turn out on to serving dish
9 Serve hot or cold. **Serves 4 to 6**

Turkey & Almond Loaf

1 Follow recipe and method for Turkey Loaf (page 86)
2 Add 40g / 1½oz blanched, toasted and finely chopped almonds with parsley.
Serves 4 to 6

Turkey Flan

Nut Pastry made with 100g / 4oz flour (page 212)
1 recipe Mixed Cheese Dressing (page 123)
175g / 6oz cooked chopped turkey

Garnish
1 large sliced tomato
8 black or green olives

1 Roll out Pastry. Use to line 15cm/6in flan ring resting on lightly buttered baking tray
2 Prick well all over with fork
3 Line with aluminium foil to prevent pastry rising as it cooks
4 Bake towards top of hot oven (220°C / 425°F or Gas No 7) for 15 minutes
5 Remove foil. Continue to bake for further 7 to 10 minutes (or until pastry is pale gold)
6 Remove from oven. Lift off flan ring. Cool pastry case on wire rack
7 Combine Dressing with turkey
8 Spoon into cold pastry case
9 Garnish centre with slices of tomato and olives.
Serves 4 to 5

Cheese & Turkey Flan

1 recipe Cheese Pastry (page 212)
½ recipe Chantilly Mayonnaise (page 127)
175g / 6oz cooked chopped turkey
1 level tablespoon finely chopped watercress

Garnish
4 level tablespoons finely grated carrot
Watercress

1 Roll out Pastry. Use to line 15cm/6in flan ring resting on lightly buttered baking tray
2 Prick well all over
3 Line with aluminium foil to prevent Pastry from rising as it cooks
4 Bake towards top of hot oven (220°C / 425°F or Gas No 7) for 15 minutes
5 Remove foil. Continue to bake for further 7 to 10 minutes (or until Pastry is pale gold)
6 Remove from oven. Lift off flan ring. Cool pastry case on wire rack
7 Combine Mayonnaise with turkey and chopped watercress
8 Spoon into cold pastry case
9 Garnish edges with small mounds of grated carrot. Arrange watercress in centre.
Serves 4 to 5

Turkey Pilaf

1 large chopped onion
50g / 2oz butter
2 teaspoons olive or corn oil
225g / 8oz long-grain rice
600ml / 1 pint water
1 level teaspoon salt
250g / 8oz cooked turkey, cut into bite-size pieces
50g / 2oz seedless raisins
½ level teaspoon finely grated orange rind
100g / 4oz skinned and chopped tomatoes
25g / 1oz blanched, toasted and chopped almonds
1 level tablespoon finely chopped parsley

1 Fry onion in hot butter and oil until pale gold
2 Add rice. Fry further minute, turning all the time
3 Pour in water and salt. Bring to boil
4 Cover pan. Lower heat. Simmer for 15 minutes
5 Add all remaining ingredients
6 Continue simmering for further 7 to 10 minutes (or until rice grains have absorbed all the liquid)
7 Serve immediately.
Serves 4

Turkey & Mushroom Toasties

250g / 8oz cold cooked turkey, cut into bite-size pieces
1 recipe Mushroom Coating Sauce (page 130)
4 slices hot buttered toast

Garnish
Watercress

1 Add turkey to Sauce. Heat through gently
2 Stand toast on 4 serving plates
3 Top with equal amounts of turkey mixture
4 Garnish with watercress
5 Serve immediately. **Serves 4**

Turkey & Bacon Toasties

100g / 4oz cold cooked turkey, cut into bite-size pieces
100g / 4oz boiled bacon, chopped
1 recipe Mustard Coating Sauce (page 130)
4 slices hot buttered toast

Garnish
4 grilled tomato slices

1 Add turkey and bacon to Sauce. Heat through gently
2 Stand toast on 4 serving plates
3 Top with equal amounts of turkey mixture
4 Garnish each with slices of tomato
5 Serve immediately.
Serves 4

Game

Raised Game Pie (page 89)

F Hang, pluck, draw and clean inside with damp kitchen paper before freezing. Always ensure that Game is **completely** thawed before cooking. Storage time – 4 to 6 months.

Broadly speaking, game is in season during the autumn and winter months. There is no close season for rabbit, hare or pigeon, but the sale of hare is prohibited between March and July. Neither hare nor rabbit should be eaten when in kindle.

Game is generally hung to improve the flavour and make the flesh more tender. Whether or not to hang game at all is very much a matter of personal taste; there are no hard-and-fast rules. Hanging time is affected by the weather and length of time the game has been dead. It is always wise to ask the advice of the poulterer or butcher when the game is bought.

The table is a guide to the seasons and **approximate** hanging times.

Game	Season	Hanging time
Partridge	Sep 1 – Feb 1	Up to 8 days
Pheasant	Oct 1 – Feb 1	Up to 8 days
Grouse	Aug 12 – Dec 10	4 – 5 days
Pigeon	No Close Season	2 – 3 days
Woodcock	Oct 1 – Jan 31	4 – 5 days
Snipe	Aug 12 – Jan 31	5 – 8 days
Hare	No Close Season, but sale prohibited between March and July	7 – 8 days
Rabbit	No Close Season	4 – 5 days

Water Game	Season	Hanging time
Mallard	Sep 1 – Feb 20 (but inland season ends Jan 21)	2 – 3 days
Teal		
Widgeon		

Raised Game Pie

1 recipe Hot Water Crust Pastry (page 213)
250g/8oz pork sausage meat
500g/1lb raw game (pheasant, partridge, pigeon
or mixture)
400g/12oz rump steak
100g/4oz lean bacon
2 pickled walnuts
1 small peeled onion
½ level teaspoon mixed herbs
300ml/½ pint stock
Beaten egg for brushing
2 level teaspoons gelatine

1 Roll out two-thirds of Pastry. Use to line raised
pie mould or 18cm/7in loose-bottomed cake tin
2 Cover base neatly with sausage meat
3 Cut game into neat pieces. Discard bones, skin
and gristle
4 Cut steak into dice. Chop bacon and pickled
walnuts. Grate onion
5 Put game, steak, bacon, walnuts and onion into
bowl
6 Add herbs and mix well
7 Put into pie mould or cake tin. Pour in 150ml/
¼ pint stock
8 Roll out remaining Pastry into lid. Moisten
edges with water and cover pie
9 Press edges of lining Pastry and lid well
together to seal. Trim away any surplus
10 Brush top with egg
11 Decorate with pastry leaves (cut from trimmings). Brush with more egg
12 Make hole in top to allow steam to escape.
Stand on baking tray
13 Transfer to centre of moderately hot oven
200°C/400°F or Gas No 6). Bake for 30 minutes
14 Reduce temperature to moderate (180°C/
350°F or Gas No 4). Bake further 1¾ to 2 hours.
Cover top with greaseproof paper during last
¼ hour to prevent the pastry from browning too
much
15 Remove pie from oven
16 Heat remaining stock. Shower in gelatine and
stir until dissolved
17 Pour into pie through hole in top
18 Leave Pie in cool for 12 hours. Remove cake
tin or mould just before serving. **Serves 6 to 8**

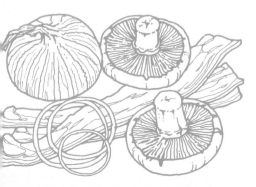

Grilled Wild Duck

2 young wild ducks
50g/2oz butter, melted
Pepper and salt
Maître d'Hôtel Butter (page 95)

Garnish
Watercress

1 Halve ducks
2 Stand in grill pan, skin sides down
3 Brush thickly with some of the butter
4 Sprinkle with salt and pepper
5 Grill for 5 minutes. Turn over
6 Brush with more butter
7 Sprinkle with salt and pepper
8 Grill for total of 20 to 25 minutes, turning
frequently and brushing with rest of melted butter
9 Transfer to a warm platter
10 Top each portion with piece of Maître d'Hôtel
Butter
11 Garnish with watercress. **Serves 4**

Fricassée of Rabbit

1 rabbit (young for preference), jointed
300ml/½ pint stock or water
300ml/½ pint milk
100g/4oz streaky bacon, chopped
4 cloves
1 large onion
1 blade mace
¼ level teaspoon mixed herbs
50g/2oz chopped mushrooms
½ level teaspoon salt
25g/1oz butter
25g/1oz flour

Garnish
2 slices toast
1 level tablespoon chopped parsley
2 lemon wedges

1 Put rabbit joints into saucepan
2 Pour in stock (or water) and milk
3 Add bacon
4 Press cloves into onion. Add to saucepan with
mace, herbs, mushrooms and salt
5 Bring to boil and remove scum
6 Lower heat and cover pan. Simmer very gently
for 1½ to 1¾ hours (or until rabbit is tender)
7 Strain liquor and reserve. Transfer rabbit to
warm platter and keep hot
8 Melt butter in clean saucepan. Add flour and
cook 2 minutes without browning
9 Gradually blend in rabbit liquor
10 Cook, stirring until sauce comes to boil and
thickens
11 Simmer 2 minutes and pour over rabbit
12 Cut toast into 8 triangles and arrange round
edge of dish
13 Sprinkle centre with parsley. Garnish with
lemon. **Serves 4**

Roast Pigeons

4 pigeons, plucked and drawn
Salt and pepper
100g/4oz butter
4 slices white bread
Extra butter

Garnish & Accompaniments
Watercress
Brown Sauce (page 133)
Very thin chips
Green Salad (see Salad Section, page 114)

1 Wipe insides of pigeons with clean damp kitchen paper. Sprinkle outsides with salt and pepper
2 Place 15g/½oz piece of butter inside each bird. Melt remaining butter
3 Stand birds in roasting tin and cover each with melted butter
4 Bake just above centre of moderately hot oven (200°C/400°F or Gas No 6) for 20 to 30 minutes, basting frequently with butter
5 About 5 minutes before pigeons are ready, fry bread in butter until crisp on both sides
6 Drain on soft kitchen paper. Transfer to warm serving plate
7 Serve Roast Pigeons on each slice. Garnish with watercress
8 Accompany with Brown Sauce, chips and green salad.
Serves at least 4

Stewed Pigeons

4 pigeons, plucked and drawn
50g/2oz butter
2 teaspoons olive or corn oil
300ml/½ pint Brown Sauce (page 133)
1 glass red wine
4 slices white bread
Extra butter

Accompaniments
Cooked peas
Cooked carrots
Boiled potatoes

1 Cut pigeons in half
2 Fry very gently in butter and oil until golden brown
3 Add Brown Sauce and wine to pan
4 Very slowly bring to boil. Cover pan and lower heat
5 Simmer pigeons gently for 35 to 45 minutes (or until tender)
6 About 5 minutes before pigeons are ready, fry bread in butter until crisp on both sides
7 Drain on soft kitchen paper. Transfer to large warm serving platter
8 Stand 2 pigeon halves on each slice. Coat with sauce from pan
9 Place mounds of peas, carrots and potatoes round edge of dish.
Serves at least 4

Jugged Hare

1 hare
50g/2oz butter
2 medium-sized onions
2 medium-sized carrots
1 medium-sized celery stalk
900ml/1½ pints water
1 level teaspoon salt
1 bay leaf
1 blade mace
6 peppercorns   **bouquet garni tied in muslin bag**
2 cloves
25g/1oz flour
2 extra tablespoons water
1 wine glass port
1 tablespoon redcurrant jelly

Garnish
100g/4oz fresh white breadcrumbs
50g/2oz finely shredded suet
1 level teaspoon mixed herbs
½ level teaspoon finely grated lemon rind
½ level teaspoon salt
Milk to bind
50g/2oz butter

Accompaniment
Extra redcurrant jelly

1 Joint hare (and reserve blood if liked)
2 Melt butter in large flameproof casserole. Add hare and fry until brown. Remove to plate
3 Slice vegetables. Add to pan and fry gently for 6 to 7 minutes
4 Replace hare
5 Add water, salt and bouquet garni
6 Cover casserole. Cook in centre of moderate oven (180°C/350°F or Gas No 4) for 2 to 3 hours (or until hare is tender)
7 Transfer joints of hare to warm serving dish and keep hot
8 Strain liquor from casserole. Pour into clean pan
9 Add flour, mixed to smooth paste with water, port and redcurrant jelly
10 Cook, stirring, until sauce comes to boil and thickens. Simmer 2 minutes
11 Remove from heat (and stir in reserved blood, if wanted)
12 To make Forcemeat Ball garnish, combine breadcrumbs with suet, herbs, lemon rind and salt and bind with milk
13 Shape into 12 small balls. Fry gently in butter until crisp and golden
14 Pour sauce over hare. Arrange Forcemeat Balls on top
15 Accompany with extra redcurrant jelly.
Serves 4

Pigeons in Cream Sauce

4 pigeons, plucked and drawn
Salt and pepper to taste
100g/4oz butter
150ml/¼ pint fresh double cream
1 tablespoon redcurrant jelly

Garnish & Accompaniment
Watercress
Boiled potatoes

1 Wipe insides of pigeons with clean damp kitchen paper. Sprinkle outsides with salt and pepper
2 Melt butter in large flameproof casserole
3 Add pigeons and fry gently until brown, turning frequently
4 Cover with lid and leave over very low heat for 45 minutes, turning birds once or twice
5 Transfer pigeons to warm serving dish and keep hot
6 Add cream and redcurrant jelly to remaining butter in casserole and heat through gently, without boiling, until jelly has melted
7 Season to taste and pour over the pigeons
8 Garnish with watercress and serve with potatoes. **Serves at least 4**

Milky Rabbit Casserole

4 rabbit joints
1 medium-sized onion
1 rasher lean bacon
2 medium-sized carrots
600ml/1 pint milk
½ teaspoon salt
Shake of pepper
¼ level teaspoon nutmeg
15g/½oz cornflour
2 extra tablespoons cold milk
15g/½ oz butter

Garnish
1 level tablespoon chopped parsley

1 Wash rabbit well. Wipe dry and arrange in 1 litre/2 pint heatproof dish
2 Chop onion and bacon. Slice carrot . Add to dish
3 Pour milk over rabbit. Sprinkle with salt, pepper and nutmeg
4 Cover with lid or aluminium foil. Cook in centre of moderate oven (180°C/350°F or Gas No 4) for 1¾ to 2 hours (or until rabbit is tender)
5 Transfer to warm serving dish and keep hot
6 Mix cornflour to smooth paste with 2 tablespoons cold milk. Combine with rabbit liquor left in dish
7 Pour into clean saucepan. Cook, stirring, until sauce comes to boil and thickens.
8 Add butter and simmer 3 minutes
9 Pour over rabbit and sprinkle with parsley.
Serves 4

Salmi of Pheasant

1 pheasant (young for preference) plucked, drawn and trussed
450ml/¾ pint Brown Sauce (page 133)
3 to 4 tablespoons port
2 teaspoons redcurrant jelly
175g/6oz button mushrooms
2 slices bread
Butter

1 Prepare the pheasant for roasting (see Roast Pheasant, page 92)
2 Roast for 20 minutes
3 Cut into neat joints and remove skin
4 Place in fairly large flameproof casserole
5 Add Brown Sauce, port and redcurrant jelly
6 Cover and simmer very gently for 30 minutes
7 Add mushrooms and continue to simmer for further 10 to 15 minutes (or until pheasant is tender)
8 Meanwhile, cut each slice of bread into 4 triangles. Fry gently in butter until crisp and golden
9 Uncover casserole and stand triangles of fried bread round edge of dish.
Serves 4

Salmi of Partridge

Follow recipe and method for Salmi of Pheasant (above) but use 2 partridges instead.
Serves 4

Salmi of Grouse

1 Follow recipe and method for Salmi of Pheasant (above) but use 2 grouse instead
2 Roast birds 15 minutes only.
Serves 4

Curried Game

400g/12oz cooked game
1 recipe Curry Sauce (page 134)

Accompaniment
350g/12oz freshly boiled long grain rice (about 175g/6oz raw)

Garnish
4 lemon wedges

1 Cut game into bite-sized pieces. Add to Curry Sauce
2 Heat through gently
3 Arrange rice in ring on warm serving dish. Fill centre with hot Curry Sauce and game
4 Garnish with lemon.
Serves 4

Roast Pheasant

1 pheasant (young for preference) plucked, drawn and trussed
50g / 2oz rump steak
4 rashers streaky bacon
75g / 3oz butter, melted
Plain flour

Garnish
Watercress
2 or 3 tail feathers (optional)

Accompaniments
50g / 2oz fresh breadcrumbs fried in 50g / 2oz butter
Bread Sauce (page 132)
Thin Gravy (page 133)
Thin chips
Green Salad (see Salad Section, page 114)

1 Stand pheasant in roasting tin. Place steak inside bird (this helps to keep it moist during cooking)
2 Cover pheasant breast with bacon rashers
3 Coat with melted butter
4 Roast just above centre of moderately hot oven (200°C / 400°F or Gas No 6) for 30 minutes, basting frequently
5 Remove from oven, lift off bacon and 'froth' the breast. (To do this, baste breast well with butter, dredge with flour and baste again.)
6 Return to oven for further 15 to 20 minutes (or until golden brown and frothy)
7 Transfer to warm serving platter. Remove trussing string. Garnish with watercress in the vent (and the feathers if used)
8 Accompany with small dish of fried breadcrumbs (for sprinkling over each portion), Bread Sauce, Gravy, chips and Salad. **Serves 4**

Roast Rabbit

1 whole rabbit (young for preference), skinned and cleaned
4 rashers streaky bacon
75g / 3oz butter, melted

Accompaniments
Gravy (page 133)
Cranberry Sauce (page 134)
Vegetables

1 Weigh rabbit and allow 15 minutes per 500g / 1lb roasting time and 15 minutes over
2 Stand in roasting tin. Top with bacon and coat with melted butter
3 Put into centre of hot oven (220°C / 425°F or Gas No 7) and roast for 15 minutes
4 Reduce temperature to moderate (180°C / 350°F or Gas No 4). Continue to roast for required amount of time, basting frequently with butter
5 Accompany with Gravy, Cranberry Sauce and vegetables. **Serves 4**

Roast Partridge

1 Follow recipe and method for Roast Pheasant (left)
2 Use 2 partridges
3 Put 25g / 1oz butter, instead of steak, inside each bird
4 Garnish with watercress but not feathers. The accompaniments remain the same as for Pheasant. **Serves 4**

Roast Grouse

1 Follow recipe and method for Roast Pheasant (left)
2 Use 2 plucked, drawn and trussed grouse instead of pheasant
3 Put 25g / 1oz butter, instead of steak, inside each bird and roast 30 to 35 minutes
4 Garnish with watercress but no feathers. The accompaniments remain the same as for Pheasant but Cranberry Sauce (page 134) should be included also. **Serves 4**

Rabbit Pie

1 rabbit, jointed
15g / ½oz butter
4 rashers chopped bacon
2 medium potatoes, peeled and sliced
2 medium leeks, sliced
2 medium carrots, sliced
1 tablespoon chopped parsley
¼ level teaspoon mixed herbs
Salt and pepper
Stock
200g / 8oz Shortcrust Pastry (page 211)

Glaze
Beaten egg

1 Wash the rabbit joints. Put in a pan with the butter to brown. Add chopped bacon
2 Slice the potatoes, leeks and carrots. Layer the pie dish alternately with rabbit, bacon and vegetables. Sprinkle each layer with parsley, herbs and seasoning
3 Half-fill the dish with stock. Cover with pastry. Make a hole in the centre to allow steam to escape. Decorate with pastry leaves and glaze with beaten egg
4 Bake in a hot oven (220°C / 425°F or Gas No 7) for 15-20 minutes, until pastry is set. Lower heat to moderate (160°C / 325°F or Gas No 3) and cook for about 1¼ hours

Marinades & Savoury Butters

Marinades

Marinades are used to tenderise uncooked foods and to improve their flavour and preserve their colour. Once raw foods have been coated with the chosen Marinade they should be covered, put into a cold larder or refrigerator and left for the required amount of time. As a general rule, cubed meat and fish should be marinated for 1 to 3 hours; large joints of meat and whole fish, overnight. As most Marinades contain an acid they, together with the food to be marinated, should be put into a glass, stainless steel or enamel dish or tray. Any turning or stirring should be done with a wooden spoon.

It is unnecessary to freeze Marinades but savoury butters can be useful if frozen in single portion pats, between freezer film. Storage time – 2 months.

Ingredients for Yogurt Marinade (below)

Yogurt Marinade

For cubes of lamb

150g / 5oz carton natural yogurt
1 tablespoon lemon juice
1 level tablespoon finely grated onion
½ level teaspoon salt

1 Combine ingredients well together
2 Add cubes of lamb. Toss until well coated
3 Cover and chill at least 3 hours, turning frequently

Wine Marinade

For large legs and shoulders of lamb and mutton; game

6 tablespoons dry red wine
3 tablespoons wine vinegar
3 tablespoons olive or corn oil
1 sprig *each* parsley and thyme
2 small bay leaves, crumbled
1 garlic clove, finely chopped
1 small onion, sliced
¼ level teaspoon nutmeg
1 level tablespoon caster sugar
Shake of Cayenne pepper

1 Combine ingredients well together
2 Pour over meat
3 Cover and refrigerate 8 to 12 hours, turning at least twice

Chicken Marinade

For portions of roasting chicken

3 tablespoons olive or corn oil
6 tablespoons dry white wine or cider
1 garlic clove, very finely chopped (optional)
1 small onion, very finely chopped
½ level teaspoon celery salt
Good shake pepper
¼ level teaspoon thyme or crushed rosemary

1 Gradually beat oil into wine or cider. Stir in rest of ingredients
2 Add chicken portions. Coat all over with Marinade mixture
3 Cover and chill 2 to 3 hours, turning at least twice

Lemon Marinade

For cubes or small fillets of fish; cubes or cutlets of lamb

2 tablespoons lemon juice
3 tablespoons olive or corn oil
½ to 1 level teaspoon salt
Freshly milled pepper

1 Combine ingredients well together
2 Add fish or meat. Coat all over with Marinade mixture
3 Cover and chill at least 3 hours, turning frequently

Spice Marinade

For cubes or small fillets of fish; cubes or cutlets of lamb

½ level teaspoon finely grated lemon rind
½ level teaspoon turmeric
½ level teaspoon ginger
1 small garlic clove, very finely chopped
1 tablespoon lemon juice
½ level teaspoon salt

1 Combine ingredients well together
2 Add fish or meat. Coat all over with Marinade mixture
3 Cover and chill 5 hours, turning frequently

Sweet-Sour Marinade

For cubes of pork and pork fillet; cubes or cutlets of lamb

4 tablespoons pineapple juice
2 teaspoons soy sauce
2 teaspoons lemon juice
1 small garlic clove, very finely chopped
¼ level teaspoon salt

1 Combine ingredients well together
2 Add meat. Coat all over with Marinade mixture
3 Cover and chill 2 hours, turning frequently

Beer Marinade

For joints of beef and thick steaks

6 tablespoons olive or corn oil
300ml / ½ pint beer
1 garlic clove, finely chopped
2 tablespoons lemon juice
1 level tablespoon caster sugar
½ to 1 level teaspoon salt

1 Gradually beat oil into beer then stir in remaining ingredients Pour over meat
2 Cover and refrigerate 4 to 5 hours, turning at least twice

Fiery Marinade

For pork fillet and chops

1 level teaspoon Cayenne pepper
2 tablespoons lemon juice
1 small onion, finely grated
¼ level teaspoon dry mustard
2 teaspoons Worcestershire sauce
½ level teaspoon salt

1 Combine ingredients well together
2 Add meat. Coat all over with Marinade mixture
3 Cover and chill 2 to 3 hours, turning frequently

Savoury Butters

These are highly-seasoned butters which add piquancy and flavour to grilled or fried meat and fish. After making, they should be well chilled, cut into small round pats of ½cm / ¼in thickness, and put on to the hot food immediately before serving.
All quantities are for 4

Tuna Butter

For veal and fish

50g / 2oz butter
50g / 2oz canned, drained tuna, very finely mashed
1 level teaspoon very finely chopped parsley
1 teaspoon lemon juice
Freshly milled black pepper to taste

1 Cream butter until soft
2 Gradually beat in tuna, parsley and lemon juice
3 Season with pepper
4 Chill

Anchovy Butter

For fish or steak

50g / 2oz butter
1 teaspoon anchovy essence
½ teaspoon lemon juice

1 Cream butter until soft
2 Beat in essence and lemon juice
3 Chill

Devilled Butter

For shellfish, ham, bacon and pork

50g / 2oz butter
½ level teaspoon dry mustard
1 teaspoon Worcestershire sauce
1 teaspoon lemon juice
Pinch Cayenne pepper

1 Cream butter until soft
2 Beat in remaining ingredients
3 Chill

Maître d'Hôtel Butter (below)

Curry Butter

For shellfish and lamb

50g/2oz butter
1 level teaspoon curry powder
¼ level teaspoon turmeric
1 teaspoon lemon juice

1 Cream butter until soft
2 Beat in remaining ingredients
3 Chill

Chive Butter

For steaks and chicken

50g/2oz butter
2 teaspoons very finely chopped chives
1 teaspoon lemon juice

1 Cream butter until soft
2 Gradually beat in chives and lemon juice
3 Chill

Lemon Butter

For fish, veal and chicken

50g/2oz butter
1 level teaspoon finely grated lemon rind
1 teaspoon lemon juice

1 Cream butter until soft
2 Gradually beat in lemon rind and juice
3 Chill

Maître d'Hôtel Butter

For fish and meat

50g/2oz butter
1 level teaspoon very finely chopped parsley
2 teaspoons lemon juice
Shake of pepper

1 Cream butter until soft
2 Gradually beat in remaining ingredients
3 Chill

Garlic Butter

For steaks

2 garlic cloves
50g / 2oz butter

1 Peel garlic cloves and boil in a little water for about 5 minutes
2 Drain and chop very finely
3 Cream butter until soft
4 Gradually beat in garlic
5 Chill

Green Butter

For fish

1 level teaspoon fresh tarragon
1 level teaspoon fresh chervil
1 level teaspoon fresh parsley
2 small spinach leaves
50g / 2oz butter
1 level teaspoon finely grated onion

1 Put tarragon, chervil, parsley and spinach into bowl
2 Cover with boiling water and leave 5 minutes
3 Drain
4 Cover with cold water, drain and dry in tea-towel
5 Chop finely
6 Cream butter until soft
7 Gradually beat in chopped herbs and onion
8 Chill

Smoked Cod's Roe Butter

For fish

50g / 2oz butter
25g / 1oz smoked cod's roe
1 teaspoon lemon juice
Freshly milled black pepper to taste

1 Cream butter until soft
2 Gradually beat in cod's roe and lemon juice
3 Season well with pepper
4 Chill

Herring Roe Butter

For fish

50g / 2oz butter
50g / 2oz canned soft herring roes
¼ level teaspoon made mustard
1 teaspoon lemon juice

1 Cream butter until soft
2 Gradually beat in small pieces of roe. Continue beating until smooth
3 Work in mustard and lemon juice
4 Chill

Mustard Butter

For beef, lamb, bacon, ham, shellfish, herrings and mackerel

50g / 2oz butter
1 level teaspoon made mustard (or 2 level teaspoons French mustard)

1 Cream butter untii soft
2 Gradually beat in mustard
3 Chill

Paprika Butter

For veal, bacon, ham and shellfish

50g / 2oz butter
1 level teaspoon paprika
¼ level teaspoon onion salt
Good shake pepper

1 Cream butter until soft
2 Gradually beat in remaining ingredients
3 Chill

Prawn Butter

For fish

50g / 2oz butter
50g / 2oz shelled prawns, very finely chopped
1 teaspoon lemon juice
¼ level teaspoon made mustard

1 Cream butter until soft
2 Gradually beat in remaining ingredients
3 Chill

Tomato Butter

For veal, lamb, bacon, ham and shellfish

50g / 2oz butter
2 level teaspoons tomato purée
¼ level teaspoon caster sugar
¼ teaspoon Worcestershire sauce

1 Cream butter until soft
2 Gradually beat in remaining ingredients
3 Chill

Horseradish Butter

For beef, herrings and mackerel

50g / 2oz butter
2 level teaspoons grated horseradish

1 Cream butter until soft
2 Gradually beat in horseradish
3 Chill

Stuffings

Ingredients for Stuffings

Stuffings should not be made over-wet by the addition of too much milk, egg, water or stock, etc. For best results, the stuffing should be fairly loose and crumbly but at the same time be firm enough to hold its shape when gathered together either with fork, spoon or fingertips. When stuffing a bird only place stuffing in crop end, not throughout the bird unless it is boned. Do **not** stuff poultry, meat, fish, etc, until just before it is to be cooked

F Do **not** freeze stuffed foods, eg, chicken, etc. Freeze stuffings separately. Storage time – 1 month. A good supply of frozen breadcrumbs is useful for making up stuffings at a future date.

Bacon Stuffing

For chicken, turkey and veal

100g / 4oz lean bacon
100g / 4oz fresh white breadcrumbs
½ level teaspoon dry mustard
¼ level teaspoon salt
½ level teaspoon mixed herbs
25g / 1oz butter, melted
Milk

1 Chop bacon fairly finely. Combine with breadcrumbs, mustard, salt and herbs
2 Bind loosely with butter and milk

Prawn Stuffing

For fish and tomatoes

100g / 4oz fresh white breadcrumbs
2 level teaspoons finely chopped parsley
½ level teaspoon finely grated lemon rind
50g / 2oz peeled prawns, coarsely chopped
½ level teaspoon salt
25g / 1oz butter, melted
Milk

1 Combine breadcrumbs with parsley, lemon rind, prawns and salt
2 Bind loosely with butter and milk

Ham & Pineapple Stuffing

For pork, lamb, chicken and duck

100g / 4oz fresh white breadcrumbs
50g / 2oz finely chopped lean ham
2 level tablespoons finely chopped canned
  pineapple
2 level teaspoons finely grated onion
¼ level teaspoon salt
25g / 1oz butter, melted
Milk

1 Combine breadcrumbs with ham, pineapple, onion and salt
2 Bind loosely with butter and milk

Celery & Tomato Stuffing

For lamb, veal, poultry, turkey and whole fish

100g / 4oz fresh white breadcrumbs
2 level tablespoons finely chopped celery
2 skinned and finely chopped tomatoes
½ level teaspoon salt
25g / 1oz butter, melted
Milk

1 Combine breadcrumbs and celery. Stir in tomatoes and salt
2 Bind loosely with butter and milk

Pork Sausage Stuffing

For chicken, turkey, veal and beef

250g / 8oz pork sausage meat
100g / 4oz fresh white breadcrumbs
½ level teaspoon thyme
¼ level teaspoon nutmeg
2 level teaspoons finely chopped parsley
½ level teaspoon salt
3 tablespoons milk

1 Put all ingredients into bowl
2 Knead well together

Chestnut Cream Stuffing

For chicken and turkey

100g / 4oz dried chestnuts, soaked overnight
100g / 4oz fresh white breadcrumbs
2 level teaspoons very finely grated onion
½ level teaspoon salt
¼ level teaspoon grated nutmeg
Good shake white pepper
50g / 2oz butter, melted
Fresh single cream

1 Drain chestnuts. Cook in boiling, salted water until tender, 20 to 30 minutes
2 Mince finely. Combine with breadcrumbs, onion, salt, nutmeg and pepper
3 Bind with melted butter and fresh single cream

If preferred, use 250g / 8oz fresh chestnuts instead of dried

Sage & Onion Stuffing

For pork, duck and goose

250g / 8oz onions
100g / 4oz fresh white breadcrumbs
½ level teaspoon sage
½ level teaspoon salt
Shake of white pepper
25g / 1oz butter, melted
Milk

1 Quarter onions. Cook in boiling, salted water until tender
2 Drain and chop finely
3 Combine with breadcrumbs. Add sage and salt and pepper
4 Bind loosely with melted butter and milk

Mushroom & Lemon Stuffing

For poultry, whole fish, tomatoes and marrow

1 small onion
100g / 4oz washed mushrooms and stalks
25g / 1oz butter
100g / 4oz fresh white breadcrumbs
½ level teaspoon finely grated lemon rind
1 teaspoon lemon juice
¼ to ½ level teaspoon salt
Shake of white pepper
2 level teaspoons finely chopped parsley
1 tablespoon milk

1 Finely chop onion and mushrooms and stalks. Fry very gently in butter 5 minutes
2 Remove from heat and stir in crumbs, lemon rind and juice, salt, pepper and parsley
3 If necessary, bind loosely with milk

If liquidiser is used to make breadcrumbs, include the parsley with the bread, to save chopping

Lemon, Parsley & Thyme Stuffing

For veal, poultry and fish

100g / 4oz fresh white breadcrumbs
1 level tablespoon finely chopped parsley
½ level teaspoon finely grated lemon rind
½ level teaspoon thyme
½ level teaspoon salt
Shake of white pepper
25g / 1oz butter, melted
Milk

1 Combine breadcrumbs with parsley, lemon rind, thyme and salt and pepper
2 Bind loosely with melted butter and milk

Liver & Onion Stuffing

For chicken and turkey

100g / 4oz chicken or calves' liver
1 small onion
40g / 1½oz butter
100g / 4oz fresh white breadcrumbs
½ level teaspoon finely grated lemon rind
1 teaspoon lemon juice
2 level teaspoons finely chopped parsley
½ level teaspoon paprika
½ level teaspoon salt
Milk

1 Cut liver into small dice. Chop onion finely
2 Fry both gently in butter 5 minutes
3 Remove from heat. Stir in breadcrumbs, lemon rind and juice, parsley, paprika and salt
4 Bind loosely with milk

Sweetcorn & Onion Stuffing

For lamb, veal, poultry and whole fish

100g / 4oz fresh white breadcrumbs
350g / 12oz can sweetcorn kernels, drained
1 level teaspoon finely grated onion
½ level teaspoon salt
Shake of pepper
25g / 1oz butter, melted
Milk

1 Combine breadcrumbs with corn and onion
2 Season with salt and pepper. Bind loosely with butter and milk

Apple & Walnut Stuffing

For pork, lamb, duck, goose, bacon joints and rabbit

500g / 1lb cooking apples
1 level tablespoon granulated sugar
100g / 4oz fresh white breadcrumbs
25g / 1oz finely chopped shelled walnut halves
2 level teaspoons finely grated onion (optional)
1 level teaspoon salt
Freshly milled pepper
50g / 2oz butter, melted
Beaten egg

1 Peel, core and coarsely chop apples
2 Combine with sugar, breadcrumbs, walnuts and onion, if used
3 Season with salt and pepper. Combine loosely with butter (and beaten egg if necessary)

Orange & Parsley Stuffing

For lamb, mutton, duck and whole fish

1 small onion
25g / 1oz butter
100g / 4oz fresh white breadcrumbs
Finely grated rind and juice of 1 medium-sized orange
2 level tablespoons finely chopped parsley
½ level teaspoon salt
Milk

1 Chop onion finely. Fry in butter very gently until pale gold
2 Remove from heat. Stir in breadcrumbs, orange rind and juice, parsley and salt
3 If necessary, bind loosely with milk

Savoury Rice Stuffing

For chicken and turkey

1 medium-sized onion
25g / 1oz butter
100g / 4oz long grain rice
300ml / ½ pint water
½ level teaspoon salt
1 level teaspoon crushed rosemary

1 Chop onion finely. Fry very gently in butter until pale gold
2 Add rice. Cook further minute
3 Pour in water and add salt and rosemary. Bring to boil, stirring
4 Lower heat and cover pan. Simmer 20 minutes (or until rice grains have absorbed all the liquid and are dry and separate)
5 Leave until cold before using

If preferred, ½ level teaspoon mixed herbs can be used instead of rosemary

Stuffed Potatoes with Bacon (below)

Fresh vegetables suitable for freezing should be washed and prepared and then blanched in rapidly boiling water to which 2 teaspoons salt per litre / 2 pints water is added. Blanching preserves colour, flavour and texture. Cool rapidly in iced water, dry and pack in handy sizes for the freezer. Salad stuff, eg, lettuce, watercress, etc, does not freeze successfully except when made into soups. Storage time – 10 to 12 months

Creamed Potatoes

750g / 1lb 8oz potatoes, peeled and washed
40g / 1½oz butter
3 tablespoons fresh cream or milk

Garnish
About 1 level tablespoon finely chopped parsley (optional)

1 Cook potatoes in boiling salted water until tender. Drain
2 Mash finely with fork or potato masher (or rub through sieve)
3 Return to saucepan
4 Add butter and fresh cream or milk
5 Beat over low heat until light and creamy
6 Pile into warm dish
7 Sprinkle with parsley if used. **Serves 4**

100

Stuffed Baked Potatoes

4 large potatoes
Salad oil
25g / 1oz butter
4 tablespoons milk
1 level teaspoon made mustard
100g / 4oz grated Cheddar cheese or crumbled Lancashire cheese
Salt and pepper to taste

1 Prepare potatoes and bake exactly as for Jacket Potatoes with Butter (page 102)
2 When tender, remove from oven and cut each in half lengthwise
3 Spoon insides into bowl. Mash finely with butter, milk and mustard
4 Add cheese and mix well. Season to taste with salt and pepper
5 Return mixture to potato cases
6 Re-heat towards top of hot oven (220°C / 425°F or Gas No 7) for 10 to 15 minutes. **Serves 4**

Stuffed Potatoes with Bacon

1 Follow recipe and method for Stuffed Baked Potatoes (above)
2 Use 175g / 6oz finely chopped fried bacon instead of cheese. **Serves 4**

Stuffed Potatoes with Ham & Cheese

1 Follow recipe and method for Stuffed Baked Potatoes (page 100)
2 Use 75g/3oz grated Derby cheese instead of Cheddar cheese or Lancashire cheese
3 Add 50g/2oz finely chopped ham to potato mixture. **Serves 4**

Stuffed Potatoes with Cheese & Parsley

1 Follow recipe and method for Stuffed Baked Potatoes (page 100)
2 Use 100g/4oz grated Double Gloucester cheese instead of Cheddar cheese or Lancashire cheese
3 Add 1 or 2 level tablespoons finely chopped parsley to potato mixture. **Serves 4**

Stuffed Potatoes with Smoked Haddock

1 Follow recipe and method for Stuffed Baked Potatoes (page 100)
2 Use 100g/4oz cooked and flaked smoked haddock instead of cheese. **Serves 4**

Stewed Potatoes

750g/1lb 8oz potatoes, peeled and washed
300ml/½ pint Basic White Pouring Sauce (page 128)

Garnish
1 level tablespoon snipped chives or green part of leek, chopped

1 Cut potatoes into ½cm/¼in thick slices
2 Put into saucepan with Sauce
3 Cover pan. Simmer gently until potatoes are tender (15 to 25 minutes, depending on type of potato)
4 Transfer to warm serving dish
5 Sprinkle with chives or chopped leek. **Serves 4**

Stewed Potatoes with Cheese

1 Follow recipe and method for Stewed Potatoes (above)
2 Omit chives or leek
3 After turning into warm serving dish, sprinkle top with 50g/2oz crumbled Lancashire cheese and brown under hot grill. **Serves 4**

Duchesse Potatoes

500g/1lb potatoes, peeled and washed
25g/1oz butter
Yolks of two small eggs
2 teaspoons hot milk
A little egg white

1 Cook potatoes in boiling salted water until tender. Drain
2 Mash with fork
3 Rub through fine sieve and return to saucepan
4 Stand over low heat
5 Add butter, egg yolks and milk
6 Beat until smooth
7 Transfer to forcing bag fitted with large star-shaped icing pipe
8 Pipe fairly small mounds or whirls on to buttered baking tray
9 Leave until cold
10 Brush with egg white
11 Bake just above centre of hot oven (220°C/425°F or Gas No 7) for 15 minutes (or until golden)
12 Serve hot. **Serves 4**

Snow (or Mousseline) Potatoes

500g/1lb potatoes, peeled and washed
25g/1oz butter
150ml/¼ pint hot milk

1 Cook potatoes in boiling salted water until tender. Drain
2 Mash very finely with fork or potato masher (or rub through fine sieve)
3 Return to saucepan. Stand over low heat
4 Add butter
5 Gradually beat in hot milk
6 Continue beating until potatoes are very light (the consistency of softly whipped cream)
7 Serve immediately. **Serves 4**

Sauté Potatoes

750g/1lb 8oz potatoes, peeled and washed
50g/2oz butter
2 tablespoons olive or corn oil
Salt and pepper

Garnish
1 level tablespoon finely chopped parsley

1 Cook potatoes in boiling salted water for 5 to 7 minutes. Drain and cool
2 Cut into ½cm/¼in thick slices
3 Heat butter and oil in large heavy frying pan. Add potato slices
4 Fry until golden-brown on both sides, turning occasionally
5 Transfer to warm serving dish
6 Sprinkle with salt, pepper and parsley. **Serves 4**

Buttered Roast Potatoes

**500 to 750g/1lb to 1lb 8oz potatoes, peeled and
washed**
50g/2oz butter
2 teaspoons olive or corn oil

1 Cut potatoes into quarters or leave whole if new
2 Cook in boiling salted water for 5 to 7 minutes.
Drain
3 Heat butter and oil in roasting tin
4 Add potatoes and turn in tin until well coated
with butter and oil
5 Roast towards top of moderately hot oven
(200°C/400°F or Gas No 6) for $\frac{3}{4}$ hour (or until
crisp and golden), basting at least twice.
Serves 4

Buttered and Minted New Potatoes

750g/1lb 8oz new potatoes, peeled and washed
40g/1$\frac{1}{2}$oz butter
3 fresh mint leaves

Garnish
**1 level tablespoon finely chopped parsley
(optional)**

1 Cook potatoes in boiling salted water until
tender. Drain
2 Stand saucepan of potatoes over low heat
3 Add butter and mint
4 Cover with lid
5 Leave over low heat for 2 to 3 minutes, shaking
pan frequently
6 Remove mint
7 Transfer potatoes to warm serving dish
8 Sprinkle with parsley if used.
Serves 4

Jacket Potatoes with Butter

4 large potatoes
Salad oil
50 to 75g/2 to 3oz butter

1 Wash, scrub and dry potatoes
2 Prick well all over with fork or make small slits in
each with sharp knife (to prevent potatoes from
bursting in oven)
3 Brush with salad oil. Stand on baking tray
4 Bake just above centre of moderately hot oven
(190°C/375°F or Gas No 5) for 1$\frac{1}{2}$ to 2 hours
(or until potatoes feel tender when gently
pressed)
5 Remove from oven. Cut a large cross on top of
each
6 Holding potato in clean tea towel, squeeze base
firmly to enlarge cut
7 Put a large piece of butter on to each
8 Serve immediately.
Serves 4

Jacket Potatoes with Cream & Chives

1 Follow recipe and method for Jacket Potatoes
with Butter (left)
2 Instead of butter, top each potato with 1 or 2
tablespoons fresh double cream and sprinkle
thickly with snipped chives. **Serves 4**

Potatoes Lyonnaise

1 Follow recipe and method for Sauté Potatoes
(page 101)
2 When Potatoes in pan are golden brown, add
250g/8oz sliced onions, fried in 50g/2oz butter
until golden. Mix well
3 Transfer to warm serving dish
4 Sprinkle with parsley. **Serves 4**

Casseroled Potatoes

750g/1lb 8oz potatoes, peeled and washed
Salt and pepper
50g/2oz butter
300ml/$\frac{1}{2}$ pint milk

1 Cut potatoes into thin slices
2 Dry well in clean tea towel
3 Fill 1 litre/2 pint buttered pie dish with layers of
potato slices, sprinkling salt and pepper between
layers
4 Melt 40g/1$\frac{1}{2}$oz butter and combine with milk
5 Pour into pie dish
6 Cover top with rest of butter, cut into thin flakes
7 Put into centre of moderately hot oven
(190°C/375°F or Gas No 5)
8 Bake, uncovered, for 1 hour (or until potatoes
are tender). **Serves 4**

Casseroled Potatoes with Parsley

1 Follow recipe and method for Casseroled
Potatoes (above)
2 Sprinkle 2 level tablespoons finely chopped
parsley between layers with salt and pepper.
Serves 4

Casseroled Potatoes with Cheese

1 Follow recipe and method for Casseroled
Potatoes (above)
2 Sprinkle 50 to 75g/2 to 3oz finely grated
Cheddar cheese or crumbled Lancashire cheese
between layers with salt and pepper. **Serves 4**

Potatoes Anna

750g / 1lb 8oz potatoes, washed and peeled
75g / 3oz butter, melted
Salt and pepper

1 Slice potatoes very thinly
2 Dry well in clean tea-towel
3 Brush $\frac{3}{4}$ to 1 litre / 1$\frac{1}{2}$ to 2 pint pie dish with butter. Fill with layers of potato slices arranged in overlapping circles
4 Brush each layer thickly with butter. Sprinkle with salt and pepper
5 Brush top layer with butter
6 Cover dish with buttered aluminium foil
7 Bake in centre of moderately hot oven (190°C / 375°F or Gas No 5) for 1$\frac{1}{4}$ hours
8 Turn out on to warm heatproof plate (potatoes should stay moulded in pie-dish shape)
9 Return to oven for further 20 to 30 minutes (or until outside is golden brown). **Serves 4**

Pease Pudding

500g / 1lb split peas
$\frac{1}{2}$ level teaspoon salt
15g / $\frac{1}{2}$oz butter, melted
Yolk of 1 standard egg
Seasoning to taste

1 Soak peas overnight. Drain
2 Put into saucepan. Cover with water
3 Add salt and bring slowly to boil
4 Reduce heat and cover pan
5 Simmer gently for 1$\frac{3}{4}$ to 2 hours, stirring occasionally
6 Add a little extra boiling water if peas begin to get dry'
7 Rub through sieve
8 Add butter and egg yolk. Mix well
9 Season to taste with pepper and salt if needed
10 Transfer to $\frac{1}{2}$ litre / 1 pint buttered heatproof dish
11 Re-heat in centre of moderate oven (180°C / 350°F or Gas No 4) for 30 minutes. **Serves 4 to 6**

Buttered Corn on the Cob

4 corn on the cob
50 to 75g / 2 to 3oz butter
Salt and pepper

1 Remove husks and silk from corn
2 Put into large frying pan, half full of gently boiling water
3 Boil for 4 to 5 minutes only, turning corn over once if water is insufficiently deep to cover them
4 Drain and serve with butter, allowing at least 15g / $\frac{1}{2}$oz per person
5 Pass salt and pepper separately. **Serves 4**

Buttered Peas

400 to 500g / 12oz to 1lb shelled peas (or 1 large packet frozen peas)
$\frac{1}{2}$ level teaspoon salt
2 fresh mint leaves
$\frac{1}{2}$ level teaspoon caster sugar
15g / $\frac{1}{2}$oz butter

1 Put peas into saucepan
2 Cover with boiling water
3 Add salt and mint
4 Cover pan. Simmer for 10 to 15 minutes (or until tender)
5 Drain and add sugar and butter
6 Cover pan
7 Toss peas gently
8 Remove mint and serve. **Serves 4**

Swiss Peas with Rice

400g / 12oz shelled peas (or 1 large packet frozen peas)
$\frac{1}{2}$ level teaspoon salt
175g / 6oz cooked rice (about 75g / 3oz raw)
1 small chopped onion
1 small chopped garlic clove (optional)
50g / 2oz butter
50g / 2oz sliced stuffed olives
2 level tablespoons finely chopped parsley

1 Put peas into saucepan
2 Cover with boiling water
3 Add salt
4 Cover pan and simmer for 10 to 15 minutes (or until peas are tender)
5 Drain and combine with rice
6 Fry onion and garlic, if used, in butter until pale gold
7 Add rice, peas, olives and parsley. Mix well
8 Heat through, gently, for about 5 to 7 minutes. Stir frequently
9 Transfer to warm serving dish. **Serves 4**

French-style Peas

400 to 500g / 12oz to 1lb shelled peas (or 1 large packet frozen peas)
6 large lettuce leaves, shredded
50g / 2oz butter
2 level teaspoons finely grated onion
$\frac{1}{4}$ level teaspoon salt
$\frac{1}{2}$ level teaspoon caster sugar
5 tablespoons water

1 Put all ingredients into saucepan
2 Slowly bring to boil
3 Lower heat and cover pan
4 Simmer very gently for 15 to 20 minutes (or until peas are tender)
5 Add a little extra water if peas become dry. **Serves 4**

Corn Fritters

100g / 4oz self-raising flour
Pinch nutmeg
½ level teaspoon salt
¼ level teaspoon dry mustard
2 standard eggs, beaten
2 tablespoons milk
250g / 8oz cooked sweetcorn, frozen or canned
Deep fat or oil for frying

1 Sift together flour, nutmeg, salt and mustard
2 Whisk egg and milk well together
3 Gradually beat into dry ingredients
4 When smooth and creamy, stir in corn
5 Drop about 16 spoonfuls of mixture into hot fat or oil
6 Fry for about 5 minutes (or until well puffed and golden)
7 Drain on soft kitchen paper.
Serves 4

Corn with Almonds

50g / 2oz blanched almonds
75g / 3oz butter
350g / 12oz can sweetcorn

1 Cut almonds into strips
2 Fry slowly in butter until pale gold
3 Add drained corn. Heat through gently
4 Transfer to warm serving dish.
Serves 4

Sweet-Sour Red Cabbage

1 medium-sized red cabbage (1 to 1¼kg / 2 to 2lb 8oz)
50g / 2oz butter
3 level tablespoons soft brown sugar
1 level teaspoon caraway seeds
3 cloves
500g / 1lb cooking apples
1 level tablespoon cornflour
4 tablespoons vinegar
300ml / ½ pint water
Salt and pepper to taste

1 Wash cabbage and cut into fine shreds
2 Melt butter in large saucepan. Add cabbage and fry briskly 5 minutes, shaking pan frequently
3 Stir in sugar, caraway seeds and cloves. Leave over low heat
4 Peel, core and chop apples. Add to pan
5 Mix cornflour to thin paste with vinegar. Add water and pour over cabbage
6 Cook, stirring, until mixture comes to boil and thickens. Season to taste
7 Reduce heat. Cover pan and simmer very slowly for 1½ hours
8 Stir occasionally. Serve hot with any meat or poultry dish. **Serves 4 to 6**

Savoury Cabbage

750g / 1lb 8oz young cabbage
50g / 2oz butter
1 medium-sized grated onion
2 rashers chopped streaky bacon
Pinch of grated nutmeg

1 Wash cabbage and shred finely, discarding hard stalks
2 Heat butter in large saucepan
3 Add all remaining ingredients
4 Cover pan
5 Cook very gently for 20 to 30 minutes (or until cabbage is just tender), shaking pan frequently.
Serves 4

Sweet-Sour White Cabbage

1 head white cabbage (750g to 1kg / 1lb 8oz to 2lb)
50g / 2oz butter
2 tablespoons water
2 tablespoons vinegar
Pinch of mixed spice
2 level teaspoons soft brown sugar
¼ level teaspoon salt

1 Wash cabbage. Shred finely
2 Put into saucepan with all remaining ingredients
3 Cover. Cook over low heat for 15 to 20 minutes (or until cabbage is just tender but still slightly crisp)
4 Shake pan frequently while cabbage is cooking
5 Uncover and cook fairly briskly until no liquid remains (about 5 minutes). **Serves 4**

Crisp Boiled Cabbage

750g to 1kg / 1lb 8oz to 2lb young cabbage
50g / 2oz butter

1 Wash cabbage and shred finely, discarding hard stalks
2 Plunge into 5 to 8cm / 2 to 3in of rapidly boiling salted water (in saucepan)
3 Cover pan and lower heat
4 Boil 6 to 8 minutes
5 Tip into colander and drain well
6 Return to pan and add butter
7 Cover. Stand over low heat for further 5 minutes, shaking pan frequently
8 Serve immediately. **Serves 4**

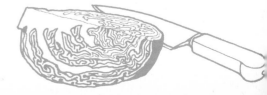

Corn with Almond (page 104) Haricot Beans with Tomatoes (below) Crisp Boiled Cabbage (page 104)

Baked Cabbage with Cream

500g / 1lb cabbage
150ml / ¼ pint fresh single cream
1 level teaspoon caster sugar
½ level teaspoon salt
½ level teaspoon paprika
4 level tablespoons toasted breadcrumbs
75g / 3oz grated Cheddar cheese

1 Wash cabbage and shred finely, discarding hard stalks
2 Transfer to large buttered heatproof dish
3 Cover with cream mixed with sugar, salt and paprika
4 Sprinkle breadcrumbs over top. Cover dish
5 Bake in centre of moderate oven (160°C / 325°F or Gas No 3) for 45 minutes
6 Remove from oven and cover with cheese
7 Brown under hot grill.
Serves 4

Haricot Beans with Tomatoes

400g / 12oz haricot beans, soaked overnight
1 level teaspoon salt
250g / 8oz skinned tomatoes
100g / 4oz lean bacon
1 medium-sized onion
75g / 3oz crumbled Lancashire cheese

1 Drain beans
2 Transfer to saucepan and cover with water
3 Add salt
4 Bring slowly to boil. Lower heat and cover pan
5 Simmer gently until tender
6 Meanwhile chop tomatoes, bacon and onion. Combine with drained cooked beans
7 Transfer to 1 litre / 2 pint heatproof dish
8 Sprinkle with cheese
9 Bake towards top of moderately hot oven (190°C / 375°F or Gas No 5) for 30 minutes.
Serves 4

Chinese-style Green Beans

500g / 1lb runner beans
4 rashers lean bacon
1 small grated onion
½ chopped garlic clove
40g / 1½oz butter
2 tablespoons soy sauce

1 Top and tail beans. Remove stringy sides
2 Slice beans diagonally into thin strips
3 Cook in boiling salted water for 15 to 20 minutes (or until tender)
4 Meanwhile chop bacon. Fry with onion and garlic in butter until pale gold
5 Drain beans and return to pan
6 Add bacon, onion and garlic and any remaining butter from pan
7 Pour in soy sauce
8 Heat through gently, shaking pan frequently. **Serves 4**

Creamed Green Beans

500g / 1lb French or runner beans
50g / 2oz sliced mushrooms and stalks
25g / 1oz butter
150ml / ¼ pint fresh double cream

1 Top and tail beans. Remove stringy sides if necessary
2 Slice runner beans diagonally into thin strips
3 Cook in boiling salted water for 15 to 20 minutes (or until tender)
4 Meanwhile fry mushrooms in butter and keep warm
5 Drain beans in colander
6 Return to pan
7 Add mushrooms and pan juices with cream
8 Mix well. Re-heat gently. **Serves 4**

Creamed Broad Beans

1 Follow recipe and method for Creamed Green Beans (above)
2 Use 500g / 1lb shelled broad beans instead of French or runner beans
3 If preferred, serve cooked, drained beans with 300ml / ½ pint Basic White Coating Sauce (page 129). **Serves 4**

Carrots in Parsley Sauce

500g / 1lb new carrots
300ml / ½ pint Parsley Coating Sauce (page 129)

1 Cook whole carrots in boiling salted water until tender. Drain
2 Transfer to warm serving dish
3 Coat with hot Sauce. **Serves 4**

Baked Buttered Carrots

1 medium-sized onion
50g / 2oz butter
500g / 1lb carrots, coarsely grated
½ level teaspoon salt
5 tablespoons water

1 Chop onion finely. Fry gently in butter until pale gold
2 Add grated carrots and salt. Mix well
3 Transfer to ½ litre / 1 pint heatproof dish
4 Add water
5 Cover dish and bake in centre of moderate oven (180°C / 350°F or Gas No 4) for 35 to 45 minutes (or until carrots are tender). **Serves 4**

Vichy Carrots

500g / 1lb carrots
50g / 2oz butter
1 level teaspoon caster sugar
¼ level teaspoon salt
1 teaspoon lemon juice

Garnish
1 level tablespoon finely chopped parsley

1 Slice carrots thinly
2 Put into saucepan with water to cover, butter, sugar, salt and lemon juice
3 Cover. Simmer gently for 15 to 20 minutes (or until tender)
4 Turn into warm serving dish
5 Sprinkle with parsley. **Serves 4**

Poached Asparagus

24 asparagus spears
Hollandaise Sauce (page 131) or Brown Butter Sauce (page 135)

1 Wash asparagus well and trim
2 Put into large fairly shallow saucepan or frying pan
3 Half-fill with unsalted water
4 Bring slowly to boil
5 Lower heat
6 Cover pan. Simmer for 12 to 15 minutes (or until tender)
7 Drain and serve with Sauce. **Serves 4**

Cold Globe Artichokes

4 medium-sized globe artichokes
1 tablespoon vinegar or lemon juice
French Dressing (page 123)

1 To clean artichokes, hold by stem end (at base) and plunge heads in and out of a large deep bowl of cold water
2 Cut off stems
3 Pull away bottom row of leaves from each (these are tough)
4 With kitchen scissors, trim off tips of remaining leaves
5 Stand grill pan rack in large saucepan containing 5cm / 2in boiling water
6 Add vinegar or lemon juice
7 Place artichokes, upright, on grid
8 Bring water to boil. Cover pan
9 Lower heat. Cook artichokes gently for 45 minutes to 1 hour
10 Drain thoroughly. Chill
11 Serve with Dressing. **Serves 4**

To eat artichokes, pull off leaves with fingers one at a time. Dip base of each leaf (the edible part) in Dressing and pass between teeth. Discard rest of leaf. Continue until you come to a pale cone of leaves. Lift these off and discard. Discard also the fuzzy centre underneath. Eat remaining heart with dressing.

Artichokes may be served hot, immediately after draining. Accompany with either melted butter or Hollandaise Sauce (page 131)

Artichokes Mornay

500g / 1lb Jerusalem artichokes
$\frac{1}{2}$ level teaspoon salt
2 teaspoons lemon juice
1 recipe Mornay Sauce (page 131)
50g / 2oz grated Cheddar cheese

1 Put peeled artichokes into saucepan
2 Cover with cold water
3 Add salt and lemon juice
4 Bring to boil and lower heat. Cover pan
5 Simmer for 20 minutes. Drain
6 Transfer to warm serving dish
7 Coat with Sauce
8 Sprinkle with cheese
9 Brown under hot grill. **Serves 4**

Ratatouille

1 large onion
1 garlic clove
50g / 2oz butter
2 tablespoons olive oil or corn oil
2 medium-sized aubergines
250g / 8oz courgettes or young marrow
1 medium-sized green pepper
250g / 8oz skinned tomatoes
$\frac{1}{2}$ level teaspoon salt
2 level tablespoons finely chopped parsley

1 Thinly slice onion. Chop garlic
2 Fry both gently in hot butter and oil (in saucepan) for 3 to 4 minutes
3 Slice unpeeled aubergines and courgettes or marrow fairly thinly
4 Chop de-seeded green pepper and tomatoes
5 Add to saucepan with salt and parsley
6 Cover pan. Simmer gently for 1 hour
7 Serve hot or cold. **Serves 4**

Braised Celery

1 medium-sized head of celery
Juice of 1 medium-sized lemon
$\frac{1}{2}$ level teaspoon salt
5 tablespoons water
50g / 2oz butter, melted
2 level teaspoons cornflour
2 tablespoons milk

1 Remove leaves from celery
2 Cut sticks into 7 to 10cm / 3 to 4in lengths. Wash thoroughly
3 Transfer to saucepan
4 Sprinkle with lemon juice and salt
5 Pour in water and melted butter
6 Cover with lid. Simmer gently for 25 minutes (or until tender)
7 Transfer celery to warm serving dish. Keep hot
8 Reduce liquor left in pan, by boiling briskly, to about 150ml / $\frac{1}{4}$ pint
9 Mix cornflour to smooth paste with milk
10 Add to celery liquor in pan
11 Cook, stirring, until mixture comes to boil and thickens
12 Simmer for 1 minute. Pour over celery.
Serves 4

Beetroots in Yogurt

400g / 12oz cooked beetroots
6 tablespoons natural yogurt
1 level tablespoon snipped chives
2 level teaspoons finely grated onion
$\frac{1}{2}$ level teaspoon salt

1 Coarsely grate beetroots
2 Put into saucepan with remaining ingredients
3 Heat through gently. **Serves 4**

Stuffed Peppers with Rice & Meat

4 medium-sized green peppers
1 medium-sized grated onion
25g / 1oz butter
250g / 8oz raw minced beef
225g / 8oz freshly cooked rice (about 100g / 4oz raw)
1 teaspoon Worcestershire sauce
Salt and pepper to taste
5 tablespoons cold water
25g / 1oz butter

1 Cut tops off peppers. Remove inside seeds and fibres
2 Put peppers into saucepan. Cover with boiling salted water
3 Simmer for 2 minutes
4 Carefully lift out of pan. Stand upside down to drain on soft kitchen paper
5 Fry onion gently in butter until pale gold
6 Add beef. Fry for 7 minutes, turning frequently
7 Stir in rice and Worcestershire sauce
8 Season to taste with salt and pepper
9 Stand peppers in shallow heatproof dish
10 Fill with meat and rice mixture
11 Pour water into dish
12 Put 7g / $\frac{1}{4}$oz butter on top of each
13 Re-heat in centre of moderate oven (180°C / 350°F or Gas No 4) for 15 minutes.
Serves 4

Stuffed Peppers with Rice & Cheese

4 medium-sized green peppers
225g / 8oz freshly boiled rice (about 100g / 4oz raw)
100g / 4oz crumbled Lancashire or grated Cheddar cheese
$\frac{1}{2}$ level teaspoon made mustard
150ml / $\frac{1}{4}$ pint fresh single cream
Salt and pepper to taste
25g / 1oz butter

1 Cut tops off peppers. Remove inside seeds and fibres
2 Put peppers into saucepan. Cover with boiling salted water
3 Simmer for 2 minutes
4 Carefully lift out of pan. Stand upside down to drain on soft kitchen paper
5 Combine rice with cheese, mustard and cream
6 Season to taste with salt and pepper
7 Stand peppers in shallow heatproof dish
8 Fill with equal amounts of rice mixture
9 Put knob butter on top of each. Completely cover dish with aluminium foil
10 Re-heat in centre of moderate oven (180°C / 350°F or Gas No 4) for 15 minutes.
Serves 4

Creamed Swedes

500g / 1lb swedes
25g / 1oz butter
4 tablespoons fresh single cream
Large pinch of nutmeg
Seasoning to taste

Garnish
1 level tablespoon finely chopped parsley

1 Dice peeled swedes. Cook, uncovered, in boiling salted water for about 30 minutes (or until tender)
2 Drain and mash finely
3 Stand pan over low heat. Add butter, cream and nutmeg
4 Beat until smooth and creamy
5 Season to taste. Transfer to warm serving dish
6 Sprinkle with parsley. **Serves 4**

Creamed Turnips

1 Follow recipe and method for Creamed Swedes
2 Use 500g / 1lb young turnips instead of swedes.
Serves 4

Baked Parsnips

4 medium-sized parsnips
50g / 2oz butter, melted
$\frac{1}{2}$ level teaspoon salt
150ml / $\frac{1}{4}$ pint water

Garnish
1 level tablespoon finely chopped parsley

1 Halve parsnips. Arrange in heatproof dish
2 Coat with butter. Sprinkle with salt
3 Pour water into dish. Cover with lid or aluminium foil
4 Bake in centre of moderately hot oven (190°C / 375°F or Gas No 5) for 45 minutes (or until tender)
5 Uncover. Sprinkle with parsley. **Serves 4**

Broccoli Allemande

1kg / 2lb fresh broccoli
$\frac{1}{2}$ level teaspoon salt
1 recipe Allemande Sauce (page 132)

1 Soak broccoli in cold water for 10 minutes. Drain
2 Remove large leaves and cut away tough parts of stalks
3 Put into saucepan. Add 2cm / 1in boiling water
4 Cover pan and simmer steadily for 10 to 12 minutes
5 Drain thoroughly and sprinkle with salt
6 Transfer to warm dish
7 Coat with Sauce. **Serves 4**

Stuffed Peppers with Rice and Cheese (page 108)

Mushrooms with Cream

400g / 12oz mushrooms and stalks
50g / 2oz butter
¼ level teaspoon salt
1 level tablespoon snipped chives
1 level tablespoon finely chopped parsley
150ml / ¼ pint fresh double cream

1 Slice mushrooms and stalks. Fry gently in butter for 5 minutes
2 Add all remaining ingredients
3 Heat through gently, without boiling
4 Transfer to warm serving dish. **Serves 4**

Mushroom Fritters

400g / 12oz button mushrooms
½ recipe Savoury Fritter Batter (page 146)
Deep fat or oil for frying

Garnish
1 level tablespoon finely chopped parsley

1 Trim ends of mushroom stalks
2 Wash mushrooms and dry thoroughly
3 Coat with Batter
4 Fry in deep hot fat or oil until golden
5 Drain on soft kitchen paper
6 Transfer to warm serving dish
7 Sprinkle with parsley. **Serves 4**

Fried Mushrooms

250 to 400g / 8 to 12oz mushrooms
50g / 2oz butter

1 Peel and wash mushrooms. Dry thoroughly
2 Remove stalks and trim. Cut each in half
3 Melt butter in saucepan
4 Add mushrooms and stalks. Toss until well coated with butter
5 Fry briskly, uncovered, for 5 minutes. Shake pan often
6 Serve immediately.
Serves 4

Grilled Mushrooms

250 to 400g / 8 to 12oz mushrooms
40 to 50g / 1½ to 2oz butter
Pepper and salt

1 Wipe mushrooms with dry cloth. Remove stalks
2 Stand mushrooms, brown sides down, in buttered grill pan
3 Grill for 2 to 2½ minutes, depending on size
4 Turn over. Put knob of butter on each
5 Sprinkle with salt and pepper
6 Grill for further 2 to 2½ minutes
7 Serve immediately.
Serves 4

Bacon-stuffed Onions

4 large onions
50g / 2oz fresh white breadcrumbs
100g / 4oz chopped lean bacon
Fresh single cream
Seasoning to taste
25g / 1oz butter

1 Cook onions in boiling salted water for
30 minutes. Drain and reserve 5 tablespoons
onion water
2 Cut slice off top of each onion
3 Carefully remove centres, leaving 1cm to
2cm / $\frac{1}{2}$in to $\frac{3}{4}$in thick onion shells
4 Chop onion centres finely. Mix with breadcrumbs and bacon
5 Bind with cream. Season to taste with salt and
pepper
6 Return mixture to onion shells
7 Stand filled onions in shallow heatproof dish.
Pour in onion water
8 Top each with knob of butter
9 Bake, uncovered, in centre of moderately hot
oven (190°C / 375°F or Gas No 5) until tender
(about 45 minutes)
10 Baste at least twice. **Serves 4**

Cheese & Parsley-stuffed Onions

1 Follow recipe and method for Bacon-stuffed
Onions (above)
2 Use 100g / 4oz grated Wensleydale or Derby
cheese instead of bacon
3 Add 1 level tablespoon finely chopped parsley.
Serves 4

Onions in Cheese Sauce

8 small onions
300ml / $\frac{1}{2}$ pint Cheese Coating Sauce (page 129)

Garnish
1 level tablespoon toasted breadcrumbs

1 Peel onions
2 Cook in boiling salted water for 25 to 40 minutes
(or until tender)
3 Drain. Transfer to warm serving dish
4 Coat with hot Sauce
5 Sprinkle with breadcrumbs. **Serves 4**

Buttered Boiled Onions

1 Follow recipe and method for Onions in Cheese
Sauce (above)
2 Coat with 50g / 2oz melted butter instead of
Cheese Sauce
3 Garnish by sprinkling lightly with nutmeg.
Serves 4

Fried Onions

3 medium-sized onions
50g / 2oz butter

1 Peel onions and cut into thin slices of even
thickness
2 Heat butter in frying pan
3 Add onion slices and fry until golden brown,
stirring frequently to prevent burning. **Serves 4**

Glazed & Sugared Onions

12 small onions
50g / 2oz butter
$\frac{1}{4}$ level teaspoon salt
1 level tablespoon soft brown sugar

1 Cook onions in boiling salted water for 25
minutes
2 Drain and dry
3 Melt butter in frying pan
4 Add salt and sugar
5 Heat for 1 minute
6 Add onions. Toss in butter mixture until well
coated
7 Cook over very low heat 15 minutes or until
glazed and golden. **Serves 4**

French-fried Onion Rings

4 medium-sized onions
Cold milk
Self-raising flour seasoned with salt and pepper
Deep fat or oil for frying

1 Slice onions thinly. Separate into rings
2 Dip in milk
3 Toss in seasoned flour
4 Fry in hot fat or oil until crisp and golden
5 Drain on soft kitchen paper
6 Serve immediately. **Serves 4**

Fried Aubergine

1 medium-sized aubergine
Salt
Milk
Flour
100g / 4oz butter
1 tablespoon corn or olive oil

1 Cut aubergine into $\frac{1}{2}$cm / $\frac{1}{4}$in thick slices
2 Sprinkle with salt and cover
3 Leave $\frac{1}{2}$ an hour
4 Drain thoroughly. Wipe each slice dry with
kitchen paper
5 Dip in milk. Toss in flour
6 Fry gently in hot butter and oil until crisp,
golden brown and tender (5 to 7 minutes). Drain
on soft kitchen paper. **Serves 4**

Stuffed Aubergines

2 medium-sized aubergines
1 large onion
4 rashers streaky bacon
1 small green pepper
500g / 1lb skinned tomatoes
50g / 2oz butter
100g / 4oz sliced mushrooms
100g / 4oz fresh white breadcrumbs
Seasoning to taste
100g / 4oz crumbled Lancashire cheese

1 Halve aubergine lengthwise
2 Scoop out pulp, leaving $\frac{1}{2}$cm / $\frac{1}{4}$in thick shells
3 Chop pulp and put into saucepan
4 Finely chop onion, bacon, green pepper and tomatoes
5 Add to aubergine pulp with butter
6 Simmer gently until pulp is tender
7 Remove from heat. Stir in mushrooms and sufficient breadcrumbs to thicken the mixture
8 Season to taste with salt and pepper
9 Pile back into aubergine shells
10 Sprinkle with cheese
11 Re-heat towards top of moderately hot oven (200°C / 400°F or Gas No 6) for 15 to 20 minutes.
Serves 4

Cauliflower with Cheese Sauce

1 medium-sized cauliflower
300ml / $\frac{1}{2}$ pint Cheese Coating Sauce (page 129)
75g / 3oz crumbled Lancashire or grated Cheddar cheese

1 Cook cauliflower in boiling salted water until tender (12 to 15 minutes)
2 Drain and divide into florets
3 Transfer to warm serving dish
4 Coat with hot Sauce
5 Sprinkle with cheese
6 Brown under hot grill. **Serves 4**

Cauliflower Sauté

1 medium-sized cauliflower
50g / 2oz butter
2 level teaspoons finely grated onion

Garnish
$\frac{1}{4}$ level teaspoon paprika

1 Cook cauliflower in boiling salted water until tender (12 to 15 minutes)
2 Drain and divide into florets
3 Melt butter in saucepan. Add onion and fry 2 minutes
4 Add cauliflower and fry gently, turning frequently, until golden
5 Transfer to warm serving dish
6 Sprinkle with paprika. **Serves 4**

Butter-baked Tomatoes

4 large tomatoes
25g / 1oz butter, melted
Salt and pepper

1 Stand tomatoes, stem sides down, in heatproof dish
2 Cut a shallow cross on top of each with sharp knife
3 Brush with butter. Sprinkle with salt and pepper
4 Bake in centre of moderately hot oven (200°C / 400°F or Gas No 6) for 15 minutes.
Serves 4

Stewed Tomatoes

1 medium-sized grated onion
25g / 1oz butter
500g / 1lb skinned tomatoes
$\frac{1}{2}$ level teaspoon salt
2 level teaspoons granulated sugar
50g / 2oz fresh white breadcrumbs
Pepper to taste

Garnish
1 level tablespoon finely chopped parsley or chives

1 Fry onion gently in butter for 3 minutes (in saucepan)
2 Cut tomatoes into quarters. Add with salt and sugar
3 Cover pan. Simmer gently for 15 minutes, stirring frequently
4 Add breadcrumbs. Heat through further minute
5 Season to taste with pepper
6 Transfer to warm serving dish
7 Sprinkle with parsley or chives. **Serves 4**

Fried Tomatoes with Cream

6 medium-sized tomatoes
Flour seasoned with salt and pepper
1 garlic clove
50g / 2oz butter
2 teaspoons olive or corn oil
150ml / $\frac{1}{4}$ pint fresh single cream
2 level teaspoons finely chopped parsley

1 Cut tomatoes into $\frac{1}{2}$cm / $\frac{1}{4}$in thick slices
2 Coat with seasoned flour
3 Rub cut clove of garlic round inside of frying pan
4 Add butter and oil. Heat
5 Add tomato slices. Fry on both sides until crisp and golden
6 Drain on soft kitchen paper. Transfer to hot dish
7 Stir cream and parsley into remaining butter in frying pan
8 Heat through gently. Do not allow to boil
9 Pour over tomato slices and serve immediately.
Serves 4

Marrow Provençale

1 medium-sized marrow
75g / 3oz butter
1 medium-sized grated onion
1 small chopped garlic clove (optional)
1 small chopped green pepper
250g / 8oz skinned and chopped tomatoes
100g / 4oz crumbled Lancashire or grated
**   Cheddar cheese**

1 Peel marrow. Cut into 2cm / 1in rings
2 Remove seeds from centres
3 Cut rings into 2cm / 1in cubes
4 Melt butter in large saucepan. Add marrow. Fry for 6 to 7 minutes (or until gold)
5 Transfer to plate
6 Add onion, garlic (if used) and green pepper to remaining butter in pan. Fry gently until pale gold
7 Add tomatoes and marrow. Mix well
8 Arrange half the mixture in fairly large heatproof dish
9 Cover with 50g / 2oz cheese
10 Add rest of marrow mixture
11 Sprinkle with remaining cheese
12 Bake, uncovered, in centre of moderately hot oven (190°C / 375°F or Gas No 5) for 30 minutes.
Serves 4

Spinach with Cream Sauce

750g / 1lb 8oz spinach
25g / 1oz butter
2 level teaspoons flour
150ml / ¼ pint fresh single cream
1 level teaspoon caster sugar
Seasoning to taste

1 Cut away tough stems from spinach
2 Wash leaves thoroughly under cold running water to remove grit
3 Tear into small pieces. Put into saucepan
4 Add 2cm / 1in boiling salted water
5 Cover. Cook for 7 to 8 minutes (or until tender). Drain well
6 Melt butter in second saucepan
7 Stir in flour. Cook for 2 minutes without browning
8 Gradually blend in cream
9 Cook, stirring, until sauce comes to boil and thickens
10 Add sugar and spinach
11 Season to taste
12 Heat through gently. **Serves 4**

Crumbed Brussels Sprouts

500g / 1lb Brussels sprouts
40g / 1½oz butter
2 level tablespoons breadcrumbs
¼ level teaspoon dry mustard

1 Remove outer leaves from sprouts if necessary
2 Make cross-cut in stem end of each
3 Soak for 10 minutes in cold salted water. Drain
4 Cook in boiling salted water for 10 minutes
5 Meanwhile melt butter in saucepan. Add crumbs and mustard. Fry gently until golden
6 Drain sprouts and transfer to warm serving dish
7 Coat with fried crumbs and any remaining butter from pan. **Serves 4**

Brussels Sprouts & Chestnuts

1 Prepare and boil sprouts as in recipe for Crumbed Brussels Sprouts (above)
2 Drain and return to pan. Add 175g / 6oz freshly cooked and halved chestnuts and 40g / 1½oz butter. Stand over low heat for 5 to 7 minutes, shaking pan frequently. **Serves 4**

Chicory au Beurre

4 heads of chicory
Juice of ½ lemon
1 level teaspoon granulated sugar
40g / 1½oz butter, melted

Garnish
1 level tablespoon chopped parsley

1 Cut thin slice off base of each head of chicory
2 Wash chicory under cold running water
3 Put into saucepan of boiling salted water. Add lemon juice and sugar
4 Simmer for 20 minutes
5 Drain and arrange in warm serving dish
6 Cover with melted butter
7 Sprinkle with parsley. **Serves 4**

Chicory Béchamel

1 Follow recipe and method for Chicory au Beurre (above)
2 Coat with 300ml / ½ pint hot Béchamel Sauce (page 129) instead of butter
3 Garnish with 1 level tablespoon toasted breadcrumbs instead of parsley. **Serves 4**

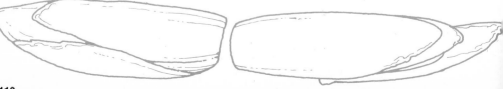

Chicory with Cream

1 Follow recipe and method for Chicory au Beurre (page 112)
2 Cover with 150ml / $\frac{1}{4}$ pint fresh single cream, heated through gently, instead of butter
3 Garnish with a light dusting of paprika instead of parsley. **Serves 4**

Stewed Mushrooms

250 to 400g / 8 to 12oz mushrooms
25g / 1oz butter
150ml / $\frac{1}{4}$ pint milk
$\frac{1}{4}$ level teaspoon salt
3 level teaspoons cornflour
3 teaspoons lemon juice

Garnish
1 level tablespoon chopped parsley

1 Wash and dry mushrooms and stalks
2 Fry gently in butter for 5 minutes
3 Pour in milk. Add salt
4 Cover pan. Simmer for 10 minutes
5 Mix cornflour to smooth paste with lemon juice
6 Add to pan
7 Cook, stirring, until mixture comes to boil and thickens
8 Simmer for 1 minute
9 Transfer to warm serving dish
10 Sprinkle with parsley. **Serves 4**

Leeks Aurore

4 medium-sized leeks
1 recipe Aurore Sauce (page 130)

1 Trim leeks. Remove all but 5 to 8cm / 2 to 3in of green leaves
2 Cut each leek in half lengthwise. Wash very thoroughly under cold running water to remove grit
3 Put into saucepan containing 5cm / 2in boiling salted water
4 Cover. Simmer for 15 to 20 minutes (or until tender)
5 Drain. Transfer to serving dish. Coat with hot Sauce. **Serves 4**

Leeks with White or Hollandaise Sauce

1 Follow recipe and method for Leeks Aurore (above)
2 Coat with 300ml / $\frac{1}{2}$ pint Basic White Coating Sauce (page 129) or Hollandaise Sauce (page 131) instead of Aurore Sauce. **Serves 4**

Salads

Side Salads

Tomato and Onion Salad (page 115) Dressed Green Salad (below) Winter Cole Slaw (below)

F Salad stuff, eg, lettuce, watercress, etc, does not freeze successfully except when made into soups.

Dressed Green Salad

1 Webb, Cos or round lettuce
1 clove garlic, peeled (optional)
1 recipe French Dressing (page 123)

1 Wash lettuce well and shake dry
2 Halve clove garlic. Press cut sides against base and sides of salad bowl
3 Tear lettuce into bite-size pieces and put into bowl
4 Just before serving, pour over dressing
5 With wooden spoon and fork, toss lettuce in dressing until every piece is coated
6 Serve with meat, poultry, offal, duck, turkey, fish, cheese or egg dishes. **Serves 4**

For mixed salad, add torn-up watercress and/or curly endive

For summer salad, add slices of cucumber, tomatoes, radishes, strips of red or green pepper and spring onions

Winter Cole Slaw

1 small or ½ medium-sized head of white cabbage (about 250g / 8oz)
2 eating apples
1 level tablespoon finely grated onion (optional)
2 heaped tablespoons finely chopped parsley
50g / 2oz grated Leicester cheese
150ml / 5fl oz carton soured cream
2 tablespoons milk
1 tablespoon lemon juice
2 teaspoons rose hip syrup
½ teaspoon Worcestershire sauce
½ level teaspoon salt

1 Shred or grate cabbage finely, wash well and drain
2 Peel apples and grate coarsely
3 Put cabbage and apples into large bowl
4 Add onion, parsley and cheese and mix well
5 Mix soured cream with milk, lemon juice, rose hip syrup, Worcestershire sauce and salt
6 Pour over cabbage mixture. Toss well with spoon and fork
7 Transfer to serving dish
8 Serve with meat, poultry, duck, turkey or fried fish dishes. **Serves 4**

Potato Cream Salad

500g / 1lb cold cooked potatoes
1 level teaspoon finely grated onion, or 2 spring onions, finely chopped (optional)
150ml / ¼ pint Mayonnaise (page 126)
5 tablespoons fresh double cream

Garnish
Snipped chives or paprika

1 Cut potatoes into small cubes
2 Put into a large bowl and mix in grated or chopped onion
3 Add Mayonnaise and cream and stir gently with spoon until potato cubes are thickly coated
4 Pile into a serving dish and sprinkle with chives or paprika
5 Serve with meat, poultry, duck, turkey, fish, cheese or egg dishes. **Serves 4**

Cucumber Salad

½ Cos or Webb lettuce
1 small cucumber
150g / 5oz carton natural yogurt
2 tablespoons Mayonnaise (page 126)
1 tablespoon lemon juice
¼ to ½ level teaspoon salt
Freshly milled pepper

1 Wash lettuce and shake dry
2 Tear leaves into bite-size pieces and put into serving dish
3 Add cucumber, peeled and cut into tiny dice, and mix well
4 Combine yogurt with Mayonnaise and lemon juice. Season to taste with salt and pepper
5 Pour over lettuce and cucumber and toss well
6 Serve with poultry, turkey, fish, cheese or egg dishes. **Serves 4**

Tomato & Onion Salad

500g / 1lb tomatoes
1 recipe French Dressing (page 123)
1 level teaspoon finely chopped onion
1 heaped tablespoon finely chopped parsley

1 Put tomatoes into bowl
2 Cover with boiling water, leave ½ a minute and drain
3 Slide off skins and discard
4 Return tomatoes to bowl and cover with very cold water
5 Leave 5 minutes and drain
6 Cut tomatoes into very thin slices
7 Arrange in large shallow serving dish
8 Pour over dressing and sprinkle with onion and parsley
9 Serve chilled with meat, poultry, duck, turkey, fish, shellfish, cheese or egg dishes. **Serves 4**

Tomato & Parsley Salad

6 large tomatoes
1 recipe Cream Cheese and Nut Dressing (page 123)

Garnish
4 level tablespoons finely chopped parsley

1 Put tomatoes into bowl
2 Cover with boiling water, leave ½ a minute and drain
3 Slide off skins and discard
4 Return tomatoes to bowl. Cover with very cold water
5 Leave 5 minutes and drain
6 Cut into thin slices and use to cover base of serving dish
7 Coat with dressing and garnish with rows of parsley
8 Serve with meat, offal, poultry, fish, shellfish and egg dishes.
Serves 4

Creamed Avocado Salad Slices

25g / 1oz Blue Stilton cheese
100g / 4oz cream cheese
2 level tablespoons finely chopped stuffed olives
2 level tablespoons toasted almonds
1 level tablespoon snipped chives
Finely grated rind and juice of 1 medium-sized lemon
2 teaspoons fresh single cream
¼ level teaspoon salt
1 level teaspoon paprika
Pinch of Cayenne pepper
1 large avocado pear
½ curly endive

Garnish
Strips of canned pimento

1 Crumble Stilton and mash finely with cream cheese. Stir in olives, almonds, chives, lemon rind and juice, cream, salt, paprika and pepper. Mix well
2 Cut avocado in half, peel and remove stone
3 Enlarge cavity in each half by scooping out some of the avocado flesh (which can be mashed and added to cheese mixture). Brush both halves – inside and out – with lemon juice to prevent discoloration
4 Pack cheese filling into cavities. Press both halves of avocado together
5 Immediately wrap in aluminium foil and chill
6 Before serving, wash endive, shake dry and use to cover base of serving platter
7 Unwrap avocado, cut into 4 slices and arrange on top of endive
8 Garnish each with strips of pimento
9 Serve with poultry, turkey, fish or egg dishes.
Serves 4

Creamed Cabbage & Caraway Salad

1 small or ½ medium-sized head of white
cabbage (about 250g / 8oz)
1 level tablespoon finely grated onion
1 level teaspoon caraway seeds
2 × 150ml / 5fl oz cartons soured cream
4 tablespoons lemon juice
2 level teaspoons soft brown sugar
Salt and pepper to taste

1 Shred or grate cabbage finely, wash well and
drain
2 Put into large bowl. Add onion and caraway
seeds and mix well
3 Combine soured cream with lemon juice, brown
sugar and salt and pepper to taste
4 Pour over cabbage mixture and toss well
5 Transfer to serving dish
6 Serve with Frankfurters or cold assorted sausages. **Serves 4**

Green Bean Salad

500g / 1lb young green beans
4 tablespoons olive oil
¼ level teaspoon salt
¼ level teaspoon dry mustard
¼ level teaspoon icing sugar
Freshly milled black pepper
1 clove garlic, very finely chopped (optional)
2 tablespoons wine vinegar
2 level tablespoons finely chopped parsley
2 level tablespoons snipped chives or green
part of leek
4 tablespoons fresh double cream

1 Trim beans and slice
2 Cook in boiling salted water until tender
3 Meanwhile, beat olive oil with salt, mustard,
sugar, freshly milled pepper to taste and the
garlic
4 Gradually beat in vinegar and continue beating
until dressing is thick
5 Stir in 1 tablespoon each parsley, chives or
finely chopped leek
6 Drain beans. While still hot, toss with dressing
7 Leave in cool for 2 hours. Just before serving,
stir in cream and sprinkle top with rest of parsley
and chives
8 Serve with meat, poultry, offal, duck, turkey,
fish, cheese or egg dishes. **Serves 4**

Apple & Walnut Salad

½ Cos or small Webb lettuce
6 celery stalks
3 large eating apples
75g / 3oz shelled walnut halves, coarsely
chopped
150ml / ¼ pint Mayonnaise (page 126)
5 tablespoons fresh double cream or soured
cream
1 tablespoon vinegar
Juice of 1 medium-sized lemon

1 Wash lettuce leaves and shake dry
2 Tear into bite-size pieces and use to cover base
of serving dish
3 Cut celery into thin slices and put into bowl
4 Peel and core 2 apples and cut into thin slices.
Add to celery, together with chopped nuts, and
mix well
5 Combine Mayonnaise with cream and vinegar
6 Pour over apple mixture and toss until ingredients are thickly coated
7 Arrange over lettuce
8 Cut third apple, unpeeled, into thin slices
9 Dip in lemon juice to prevent browning then
arrange on top of salad
10 Serve with meat, poultry, duck, or turkey
dishes. **Serves 4**

Stuffed Pepper Salad

2 medium-sized red or green peppers
100g / 4oz cream cheese
2 tablespoons fresh double cream
1 level teaspoon finely grated onion
3 level tablespoons very finely chopped ham or
chopped and salted cashew nuts
½ level teaspoon paprika
Seasoning to taste
½ round lettuce
1 large tomato

1 Wash peppers and wipe dry. Cut a slice from the
stem end of each. Remove all inside pips
2 Mix cream cheese with cream, onion, paprika
and ham or nuts. Season to taste
3 Stuff peppers with cheese mixture. Wrap in foil
and refrigerate overnight
4 Before serving, wash lettuce, shake leaves dry
and use to cover base of serving dish
5 Cut each pepper into 6 slices and arrange in a
ring on top of lettuce
6 Fill centre with wedges of tomato
7 Serve with lamb, poultry, fish, shellfish or egg
dishes. **Serves 4**

Brussels Sprouts & Celery Salad

400g/12oz Brussels sprouts
1 recipe Cream Cheese & Celery Dressing
  (page 123)

Garnish
1 finely grated carrot
8 shelled walnut halves

1 Trim and wash sprouts. Shred with sharp knife
2 Put into large bowl, add dressing and toss well
3 Transfer to serving dish. Garnish with mounds of grated carrot and nuts
4 Serve with meat, offal or egg dishes.
Serves 4

Russian Salad

1 lettuce heart
250g/8oz cooked potatoes
250g/8oz cooked carrots
100g/4oz cooked peas
100g/4oz cooked green beans
Mayonnaise (page 126)

Garnish
1 large hard-boiled egg
4 gherkins, sliced

1 Wash lettuce and shake leaves dry
2 Arrange in salad bowl
3 Cut potatoes and carrots into cubes
4 Put into large bowl
5 Add peas and beans and mix well
6 Combine gently with Mayonnaise, adding enough to coat vegetables fairly thickly
7 Pile on top of lettuce. Garnish with wedges of hard-boiled egg and slices of gherkin
8 Serve with meat, poultry, duck, turkey, fish, cheese or egg dishes. **Serves 4**

Tropicana Salad

2 large oranges
4 large tomatoes
2 large bananas
150ml/5fl oz carton soured cream
1 tablespoon lemon juice
1 level teaspoon grated horseradish
¼ level teaspoon salt

1 Peel oranges and remove all traces of pith. Cut into thin slices. Cut each slice into 4 and arrange over base of serving dish
2 Blanch and skin tomatoes, slice very thinly and place over oranges
3 Top with sliced bananas. Cover completely with the soured cream mixed with lemon juice, horseradish and salt
4 Serve with cold poultry, duck or turkey dishes.
Serves 4

Green Pepper & Onion Salad

½ curly endive
2 medium-sized green peppers
2 medium-sized onions
1 recipe Basic Cream Cheese Dressing
  (page 123)

Garnish
1 large hard-boiled egg
Paprika

1 Wash endive, shake dry and use to cover base of serving dish
2 Wash green peppers, de-seed and cut into thin strips
3 Peel and wash onions and slice thinly
4 Arrange pepper strips and onion slices on top of endive. Spoon dressing over
5 Garnish with slices of hard-boiled egg and paprika
6 Serve with veal, lamb, poultry, duck or egg dishes. **Serves 4**

Syrian Salad

½ Cos or Webb lettuce
100g/4oz *each* **cooked green beans, cooked peas and cooked diced carrot**
100g/4oz coarsely grated cucumber
150g/5oz carton natural yogurt
4 tablespoons fresh single cream
¼ to ½ level teaspoon salt

Garnish
Chopped fresh mint

1 Wash lettuce and shake leaves dry
2 Tear into bite-size pieces and use to cover bases of 4 individual plates
3 Arrange beans, peas, carrot and cucumber in separate piles on top
4 Mix yogurt with the cream and salt. Spoon over vegetables
5 Garnish with chopped mint
6 Serve with meat, offal, poultry, duck or egg dishes. **Serves 4**

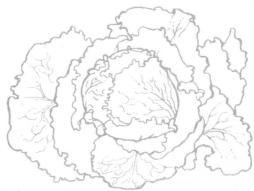

Main Course Salads

Prawn and Pineapple Salad (below)

Prawn & Pineapple Salad

1 Webb or Cos lettuce
1 medium-sized can pineapple cubes, well
  drained
175g/6oz fresh or frozen peeled prawns
175g/6oz Derby cheese, diced
1 recipe Soured Cream with Stilton Dressing
  (page 121)
2 tablespoons fresh single cream

Garnish
Paprika
Unpeeled cucumber slices

1 Wash lettuce and shake leaves dry
2 Tear into bite-size pieces and use to cover
4 individual plates
3 Mix pineapple cubes well together with the
prawns and cheese. Pile equal amounts on top of
lettuce
4 Pour over Dressing mixed with the cream.
Garnish lightly with paprika and cucumber slices.
Serves 4

Egg & Sardine Salad

1 round lettuce
1 can sardines in pure olive oil
2 large hard-boiled eggs
1 large stalk celery
1 recipe Soured Cream with Chives Dressing
  (page 122)

Garnish
Paprika
4 lemon wedges

1 Wash lettuce and shake leaves dry
2 Tear into bite-size pieces and use to cover 4
individual plates
3 Skin and bone sardines. Chop eggs finely
4 Wash celery and cut into thin slices
5 Put sardines into bowl and mash finely with
eggs
6 Add celery. Blend in Dressing
7 Pile equal amounts over lettuce. Sprinkle lightly
with paprika and top each with wedge of lemon.
Serves 4

Spinach & Cottage Cheese Salad

500g / 1lb fresh spinach
1 Webb or medium-sized Cos lettuce
250g / 8oz back bacon
150ml / ¼ pint olive or corn oil
1 level teaspoon dry mustard
1 level teaspoon salt
2 level teaspoons icing or caster sugar
1 level tablespoon very finely grated onion
4 tablespoons wine or cider vinegar
225g / 8oz Cottage cheese

1 Thoroughly wash and drain spinach
2 Repeat with lettuce
3 Tear spinach and lettuce leaves into bite-size pieces (discarding stems) and put into large salad bowl. Mix well
4 Coarsely chop bacon and fry in own fat until crisp. Drain on soft kitchen paper. Add to greens when cold
5 Mix oil with mustard, salt, sugar and onion. Beat in the vinegar
6 Pour half over salad greens and bacon and toss well
7 Mix Cottage cheese with remaining dressing. Add to greens in bowl
8 Toss again. **Serves 4**

Cheddar Cheese & Apple Salad

1 round lettuce
150ml / 5fl oz carton soured cream
3 tablespoons milk
1 teaspoon lemon juice
1 level teaspoon icing or caster sugar
1 level teaspoon salt
2 eating apples, peeled and cored
225g / 8oz Cheddar cheese
canned pineapple rings

Garnish
4 slices unpeeled orange
8 black olives

1 Wash lettuce and shake leaves dry
2 Tear into bite-size pieces and use to cover base of serving dish
3 Combine soured cream with milk, lemon juice, sugar and salt
4 Cut apples and cheese into small dice. Chop pineapple coarsely
5 Add to soured cream mixture and toss lightly together
6 Pile over lettuce
7 Garnish with orange slices and olives. **Serves 4**

Cottage Cheese Summer Salad

1 round lettuce
12 radishes
½ large cucumber, peeled
1 bunch spring onions
450g / 1lb Cottage cheese
150ml / 5fl oz carton soured cream
2 teaspoons lemon juice
½ level teaspoon salt
Good shake of pepper

Garnish
Paprika

1 Wash lettuce, shake leaves dry then tear into bite-size pieces
2 Slice radishes and cucumber thinly
3 Peel onions and coarsely chop
4 Put vegetables into bowl and mix well together
5 Arrange equal amounts on 4 individual plates. Place a mound of Cottage cheese in centre of each
6 Mix soured cream with lemon juice, salt and pepper and pour over salads
7 Sprinkle lightly with paprika. **Serves 4**

Tongue & Cucumber Salad

6 large lettuce leaves
175g / 6oz tongue
175g / 6oz Caerphilly cheese
½ medium-sized cucumber, peeled
150g / 5oz carton natural yogurt
2 tablespoons fresh single cream
1 level tablespoon snipped chives or green part of leek
¼ level teaspoon dry mustard
¼ level teaspoon salt
½ level teaspoon icing sugar
1 teaspoon lemon juice

Garnish
1 large tomato

1 Wash lettuce leaves and shake dry
2 Tear into bite-size pieces and use to cover base of serving dish
3 Cut tongue into thin strips. Cut cheese and cucumber into small dice. Put into bowl
4 Combine yogurt with cream, chives (or finely chopped leek), mustard, salt, sugar and lemon juice
5 Beat well then pour over tongue and cucumber
6 Toss thoroughly and arrange mounds over lettuce
7 Garnish with sliced tomato. **Serves 4**

Herring Salad

½ Cos lettuce
3 rollmops
150ml / 5fl oz carton soured cream
2 tablespoons milk
½ level teaspoon paprika
½ level teaspoon finely grated lemon rind
2 large hard-boiled eggs
1 small pickled cucumber

1 Wash lettuce and shake leaves dry
2 Tear into bite-size pieces and use to cover base of serving dish
3 Drain rollmops well and cut into wide strips. Put into a bowl and add soured cream, milk, paprika, lemon rind and chopped eggs
4 Mix well then pile over lettuce
5 Garnish with slices of pickled cucumber. Serve very cold. **Serves 4**

Tuna & Bacon Salad

250g / 8oz back bacon
½ Cos lettuce
1 level tablespoon finely chopped onion
200g / 7oz can middle-cut tuna
2 large hard-boiled eggs
Double recipe Watercress & Yogurt Dressing (page 124)

1 Chop bacon and fry in own fat until crisp
2 Drain on soft kitchen paper
3 Wash lettuce and shake leaves dry
4 Tear into bite-size pieces and put into a large bowl
5 Add bacon, onion, drained and flaked tuna, chopped eggs and dressing
6 Toss well and transfer to serving dish. **Serves 4**

Cottage Cheese & Peach Salad

½ Cos lettuce
½ recipe French Dressing (page 123)
350g / 12oz Cottage cheese
5 tablespoons Mayonnaise (page 126) or soured cream
100g / 4oz salted cashew nuts

Garnish
1 medium can peach slices
4 black olives or grapes

1 Wash lettuce and shake leaves dry
2 Tear into bite-size pieces and toss with French Dressing
3 Use to cover base of 4 individual serving plates
4 Put Cottage cheese into bowl. Combine with Mayonnaise or soured cream and the nuts
5 Pile equal amounts on to plates. Garnish with the peach slices (well drained) and olives or grapes. **Serves 4**

Ham, Cheese & Cabbage Toss

1 recipe Cream Cheese and Onion Dressing (page 123)
6 tablespoons Mayonnaise (page 126)
1 small green pepper
1 small head of white cabbage (about 250g / 8oz)
3 eating apples
175g / 6oz lean ham
175g / 6oz Wensleydale cheese
1 tablespoon lemon juice

1 Combine Dressing with Mayonnaise
2 Add washed, finely chopped and de-seeded green pepper. Chill thoroughly
3 Before serving, shred or grate cabbage finely, wash well and drain. Peel and core 2 apples and cut into dice. Cut ham into shreds and cheese into small cubes
4 Put cabbage, apples, ham and cheese into large bowl and add dressing
5 Toss well and transfer to serving dish
6 Garnish with third apple, unpeeled, cut into slices and dipped in the lemon juice to prevent browning. **Serves 4**

Sweet Corn & Chicken Salad

1 head of chicory
350g / 12 oz can sweet corn
250g / 8oz cooked chicken
100g / 4oz Cheshire cheese
1 recipe Banana Dressing (page 122)

Garnish
Canned pimento

1 Separate leaves of chicory, wash well and drain. Arrange on round platter, radiating from the centre
2 Drain sweet corn. Tip into a bowl
3 Cut chicken into bite-size pieces. Cut cheese into small cubes. Add to corn and mix well
4 Pour Dressing over corn mixture and toss
5 Pile on to centre of dish over chicory leaves. Garnish with trellis of pimento strips. **Serves 4**

Swedish Sausage Salad

1 round lettuce
400g / 12oz cold, cooked pork sausages
250g / 8oz cold cooked potatoes
1 recipe Swedish Mayonnaise (page 126)

Garnish
Parsley

1 Wash lettuce, shake leaves dry and use to cover base of a serving dish
2 Cut sausages into slices. Dice potatoes
3 Put both into bowl and add Dressing
4 Toss well together. Arrange over lettuce
5 Garnish with parsley. **Serves 4**

Salad Dressings

Ingredients for Salad Dressings

Salad dressings and mayonnaise do not freeze successfully as they tend to separate out

Many dressings in this section are ideal to serve with Meat Fondues

All quantities of dressings are sufficient for 4 to 6 servings

Basic Soured Cream Dressing

For green and mixed salads; potato salads; meat, poultry, fish, cheese and egg salads

150ml / 5fl oz carton soured cream
1 tablespoon milk
1 tablespoon lemon juice or vinegar
to 1 level teaspoon icing or caster sugar
level teaspoon salt
Shake of pepper

Beat soured cream well together with milk and lemon juice or vinegar
Stir in sugar. Season to taste with salt and pepper
If a thinner dressing is preferred, add a little extra milk
Leave 15 minutes in the cool before using

Soured Cream with Nuts Dressing

For poultry, fish and egg salads

1 Follow recipe and method for Basic Soured Cream Dressing (left)
2 Add 50g / 2oz finely chopped walnuts or finely chopped salted almonds before seasoning with salt and pepper

Soured Cream with Stilton Dressing

For all green and mixed salads

50g / 2oz Blue Stilton cheese
150ml / 5fl oz carton soured cream
2 tablespoons milk
¼ level teaspoon salt
Freshly milled pepper

1 Put Stilton into a bowl. Mash finely with a fork
2 Gradually blend in soured cream and milk
3 Season to taste with salt and pepper
4 Leave in cool 15 minutes before using
5 If thinner dressing is preferred, add a little more milk

Soured Cream with Dates Dressing

For winter vegetable salads

100g / 4oz stoned dates
3 tablespoons water
150ml / 5fl oz carton soured cream

1 Put dates and water into a pan. Bring slowly to the boil
2 Cover pan and simmer gently for 10 minutes
3 Cool dates, chop finely and beat into soured cream

Soured Cream with Parsley Dressing

For same salads as Basic Soured Cream Dressing

1 Follow recipe and method for Basic Soured Cream Dressing (page 121)
2 Stir in 1 heaped tablespoon finely chopped parsley before seasoning with salt and pepper

Soured Cream with Cucumber Dressing

For all poultry and fish salads

1 Follow recipe and method for Basic Soured Cream Dressing (page 121)
2 Stir in 4 level tablespoons very finely grated peeled cucumber before seasoning with salt and pepper

Soured Cream with Tomato Dressing

For vegetable, poultry, egg and fish salads

1 Follow recipe and method for Basic Soured Cream Dressing (page 121)
2 Stir in 2 teaspoons tomato purée and 1 finely chopped, skinned tomato before seasoning with salt and pepper

Soured Cream with Mustard Dressing

For beef, ham and tongue salads; salads made with canned fish

1 Follow recipe and method for Basic Soured Cream Dressing (page 121)
2 Add 1 level teaspoon made mustard with lemon juice or vinegar

Soured Cream with Lemon Dressing

For poultry, fish and egg salads

1 Follow recipe and method for Basic Soured Cream Dressing (page 121)
2 Stir in 1 level teaspoon finely grated lemon rind before seasoning with salt and pepper

Soured Cream with Paprika Dressing

For veal, poultry and egg salads

1 Follow recipe and method for Basic Soured Cream Dressing (page 121)
2 Stir in 2 level teaspoons paprika before seasoning with salt and pepper

Soured Cream with Chives Dressing

For same salads as Basic Soured Cream Dressing

1 Follow recipe and method for Basic Soured Cream Dressing (page 121)
2 Stir in 1 heaped tablespoon snipped chives before seasoning with salt and pepper

Soured Cream with Horseradish Dressing

For cold roast beef and salad

1 Follow recipe and method for Basic Soured Cream Dressing (page 121)
2 Stir in 2 level teaspoons grated horseradish before seasoning with salt and pepper

Banana Dressing

For winter vegetable salads

2 medium-sized bananas
2 tablespoons lemon juice
5 tablespoons Mayonnaise (page 126)
150g / 5oz carton natural yogurt
1 level teaspoon bottled horseradish sauce
½ level teaspoon icing or caster sugar
½ level teaspoon salt
Pinch of Cayenne pepper

1 Mash bananas finely
2 Beat in lemon juice, Mayonnaise, yogurt, horseradish sauce and sugar
3 Season to taste with salt and pepper
4 Use immediately

Cream Cheese & Nut Dressing

For green and mixed salads; combination salads of fruit and vegetables

225g/8oz cream cheese
4 tablespoons fresh single cream
1 tablespoon lemon juice
2 tablespoons salted cashew nuts, very finely chopped
50g/2oz finely grated Cheddar cheese
1 level teaspoon icing or caster sugar
Shake of pepper
¼ to ½ level teaspoon salt

1 Beat cream cheese, cream and lemon juice together until smooth
2 Stir in chopped nuts, grated cheese and sugar
3 Season to taste with pepper and salt
4 If thinner dressing is preferred, add a little more cream

Basic Cream Cheese Dressing

For green and mixed salads; salads with poultry, fish or eggs

100g/4oz cream cheese
1 tablespoon fresh single cream
¼ level teaspoon salt
1 level teaspoon icing or caster sugar
4 teaspoons lemon juice or vinegar

1 Put cream cheese into a bowl. Gradually blend in cream
2 Stir in remaining ingredients
3 Leave in cool 15 minutes before using
4 If thinner dressing is preferred, add a little more cream

Cream Cheese & Celery Dressing

For same dishes as Basic Cream Cheese Dressing

1 Follow recipe and method for Basic Cream Cheese Dressing (above)
2 Use ½ level teaspoon celery salt instead of plain salt

Cream Cheese & Onion Dressing

For beef, tongue and ham salads

1 Follow recipe and method for Basic Cream Cheese Dressing (above)
2 Add 1 level teaspoon very finely grated onion with the lemon juice or vinegar

Cream Cheese & Garlic Dressing

For green and tomato salads

1 Follow recipe and method for Basic Cream Cheese Dressing (left)
2 Use ¼ level teaspoon garlic salt instead of the plain salt

Cream Cheese & Apricot Dressing

For fresh fruit salads; canned fruits

100g/4oz cream cheese
6 level tablespoons apricot purée (made from canned or stewed apricots)
1 tablespoon lemon juice
3 tablespoons Mayonnaise (page 126)
Pinch of salt

1 Put cream cheese into bowl. Mash finely with fork. Beat in apricot purée
2 Add lemon juice, Mayonnaise and salt. Beat until smooth

Mixed Cheese Dressing

For green and mixed salads

50g/2oz Blue Stilton cheese
100g/4oz cream cheese
4 level tablespoons very finely grated Cheddar cheese
½ garlic clove, finely chopped (optional)
5 tablespoons milk
¼ level teaspoon salt
Good shake of pepper

1 Mash the Stilton and cream cheese together. Add Cheddar cheese and garlic (if used)
2 Gradually beat in milk. Season to taste with salt and pepper

French Dressing

For all tossed salads

4 tablespoons olive or corn oil or mixture
½ level teaspoon *each* salt, icing or caster sugar and dry mustard
¼ teaspoon Worcestershire sauce
2 tablespoons vinegar (wine for preference) or lemon juice

1 Put oil, salt, sugar, mustard and Worcestershire sauce into a basin
2 Beat until smooth
3 Gradually beat in vinegar or lemon juice. Continue beating until dressing thickens

Basic Yogurt Dressing

For green and mixed salads; potato salads; meat, poultry, fish, cheese and egg salads

150g / 5oz carton natural yogurt
2 tablespoons fresh single cream
3 teaspoons lemon juice
1 level teaspoon icing or caster sugar
¼ level teaspoon salt
Shake of pepper

1 Pour yogurt into a bowl. Beat in cream, lemon juice and sugar
2 Season to taste with salt and pepper
3 Leave 15 minutes in cool before using

Watercress & Yogurt Dressing

For poultry, fish and egg salads

1 Follow recipe and method for Basic Yogurt Dressing (above)
2 Stir in 2 or 3 level tablespoons very finely chopped watercress before seasoning with salt and pepper

Egg, Anchovy & Yogurt Dressing

For green and fish salads

1 Follow recipe and method for Basic Yogurt Dressing (above)
2 Add 2 finely chopped, large hard-boiled eggs and 25g / 1oz canned and finely chopped anchovy fillets before seasoning with salt

Curry Yogurt Dressing

For poultry, fish and egg salads

1 Follow recipe and method for Basic Yogurt Dressing (above)
2 Add 2 level teaspoons curry powder and 1 level tablespoon sweet pickle before seasoning with salt and pepper

Piquant Yogurt Dressing

For green and mixed salads; meat, poultry and egg salads

1 Follow recipe and method for Basic Yogurt Dressing (above)
2 Stir in 1 teaspoon Worcestershire Sauce, large pinch of Cayenne pepper, 1 level teaspoon paprika and ½ finely chopped clove of garlic

Fruity Yogurt Dressing

For fresh fruit salads; canned fruits

150g / 5oz carton natural yogurt
3 tablespoons fresh orange juice
1 tablespoon lemon juice
1 tablespoon rose hip syrup

1 Pour yogurt into a bowl. Beat in remaining ingredients
2 Chill at least 30 minutes before using

Tomato Yogurt Dressing

For all green and mixed salads

1 Beat French Dressing (page 123) into 1 can condensed tomato soup
2 Stir in 150g / 5oz carton natural yogurt, 1 teaspoon Worcestershire sauce and 2 level teaspoons finely grated onion
3 Pour into screw-top jar and refrigerate. This dressing keeps up to 2 weeks but should be shaken well before using

Whipped Cream Dressing

For cold poultry, fish and egg salads

150ml / ¼ pint fresh double cream
2 tablespoons milk
3 teaspoons lemon juice or wine vinegar
¼ level teaspoon salt
Shake of Cayenne pepper

1 Beat milk and cream together until thick
2 Gradually stir in lemon juice or vinegar
3 Season to taste with salt and pepper

Fluffy Whipped Cream Dressing

For cold poultry, fish and egg salads

1 Follow recipe and method for Whipped Cream Dressing (above)
2 Fold in one stiffly whisked egg white after seasoning with salt and pepper

Whipped Cream Horseradish Dressing

For cold roast beef and salad

1 Follow recipe and method for Whipped Cream Dressing (above)
2 Stir in 2 level tablespoons grated horseradish with the lemon juice or vinegar
3 Season to taste with salt, pepper and ½ to 1 level teaspoon icing sugar

Watercress and Yogurt Dressing (page 124) served with Egg Salad

Butter Dressing

For green and mixed salads; salads with poultry, turkey, fish or cheese

50g/2oz butter
2 standard eggs
150ml/5fl oz carton soured cream
3 tablespoons white vinegar
½ level teaspoon salt
Shake of pepper

1 Melt butter. Beat well with eggs and soured cream
2 Bring vinegar to boil and gradually beat into egg mixture
3 Pour into double saucepan (or basin standing over pan of gently simmering water)
4 Cook, stirring, until mixture thickens. On no account allow to boil
5 Remove from heat. Season and chill before using

Dairy Salad Dressing

For green and mixed salads; salads with white fish, poultry, eggs or cheese

4 tablespoons *each* milk, vinegar and salad oil
½ level teaspoon icing or caster sugar
¼ level teaspoon *each* made mustard and salt
Pepper

1 Beat milk, vinegar and oil together until smooth and well blended. Beat in sugar, mustard and salt
2 Season to taste with pepper

Cottage Cheese & Mint Dressing

For canned fruit; fresh fruit salads

100g/4oz Cottage cheese
2 to 3 level teaspoons mint jelly
Finely grated rind and juice of 1 medium-sized lemon
3 tablespoons fresh orange juice

1 Rub Cottage cheese through a fine sieve
2 Put into bowl. Beat in mint jelly, lemon rind and juice and orange juice
3 Chill before using

Cottage Cheese Salad Dressing

For green and mixed salads; salads with poultry, fish and eggs

225g/8oz Cottage cheese
3 tablespoons French Dressing (page 123)
2 tablespoons lemon juice
1 level tablespoon finely grated Cheddar cheese
Large pinch of garlic salt (optional)
¼ level teaspoon salt
Shake of pepper

1 Put Cottage cheese, French Dressing, lemon juice, Cheddar cheese and garlic salt (if used) into bowl. Beat with whisk until smooth
2 Season to taste with salt and pepper
3 Leave 15 minutes to cool before using
4 For an even smoother dressing, sieve cottage cheese first

Ravigotte

For cold meat salads

1 Add to French Dressing (page 123): 1 level tablespoon finely grated onion, 2 level teaspoons finely chopped capers, 1 heaped tablespoon finely chopped parsley and ½ level teaspoon **each** finely chopped fresh chervil and tarragon
2 Mix well

Blue Stilton Dressing

For all green and mixed salads

Gradually beat French Dressing (page 123) into 25 to 50g / 1 to 2oz finely mashed Blue Stilton

Creamed Onion Dressing

For all green and mixed salads; salads with poultry and eggs

1 Gradually beat French Dressing (page 123) into 75 to 100g / 3 to 4oz cream cheese
2 Add 1 level teaspoon finely grated onion and 1 level tablespoon very finely chopped parsley

Mustard Dressing

For meat fondues or cold meats

1 level tablespoon flour
Pinch cayenne pepper
1¼ level tablespoons sugar
1 level teaspoon dry mustard
½ level teaspoon salt
150ml / ¼ pint milk
2 egg yolks, beaten
4 tablespoons vinegar

1 Mix the dry ingredients with a little cold milk until smooth
2 Heat the remainder of the milk and when boiling stir into the blended ingredients. Return the mixture to the pan and bring to the boil, stirring continuously.
3 Cool slightly, stir in the egg yolks and return the pan to the heat
4 Cook gently until the mixture thickens, but do not allow to boil
5 When cool, stir in the vinegar
To obtain a rich dressing, stir in a little whipped cream before serving

Mayonnaise

Yolks of 2 standard eggs
½ level teaspoon *each* dry mustard, salt and caster sugar
¼ teaspoon Worcestershire sauce (optional)
Shake of pepper
300ml / ½ pint salad oil
2 tablespoons vinegar or lemon juice
1 tablespoon hot water

1 Put yolks, mustard, salt, sugar, Worcestershire sauce (if used) and pepper into a bowl. Beat until smooth
2 Beating more quickly, add 150ml / ¼ pint oil, **a drop at a time**, and continue beating until Mayonnaise is very thick
3 Stir in 1 tablespoon vinegar or lemon juice
4 Beat in rest of oil gradually, about 2 teaspoons at a time
5 When all the oil has been added, stir in last tablespoon of vinegar or lemon juice and the hot water. (The water helps to prevent separation.)
6 Adjust seasoning to taste. Transfer to covered container. Will keep in cool up to 2 weeks

Swedish Mayonnaise

For cold pork, lamb and mutton dishes; cold sausage platters

Add to Mayonnaise (above) after stirring in hot water: 150ml / ¼ pint thick and unsweetened apple purée, 1 or 2 level teaspoons grated horseradish and 5 tablespoons soured cream

Thousand Island Mayonnaise

For all green and egg salads

Add to Mayonnaise (above) after stirring in hot water: 4 tablespoons fresh double cream, 1½ tablespoons tomato ketchup, ½ level teaspoon bottled chilli sauce (or use all ketchup), 2 level tablespoons finely chopped stuffed olives, 2 level teaspoons finely grated onion, 1 level tablespoon finely chopped green pepper, 1 finely chopped small hard-boiled egg and 1 heaped tablespoon finely chopped parsley

Louis Mayonnaise

For cold shellfish and winter vegetable salads

Add to Mayonnaise (above) after stirring in hot water: 3 tablespoons fresh double cream, 1 to 2 teaspoons bottled chilli sauce, 1 teaspoon Worcestershire sauce, finely chopped ½ small green pepper, 1 level tablespoon finely grated onion and 2 tablespoons lemon juice.

Camilla Mayonnaise

For cold poultry, fish and egg salads

Stir 150ml / 5fl oz carton soured cream into Mayonnaise (page 126) before stirring in the hot water

Chantilly Mayonnaise

For cold poultry, fish and egg salads

Stir 150ml / ¼ pint fresh whipped double cream into Mayonnaise (page 126) before stirring in the hot water

Curry Mayonnaise

For cold poultry and egg salads

Add to Mayonnaise (page 126) after stirring in the hot water: 2 level teaspoons curry powder, 1 level teaspoon finely grated onion, pinch of Cayenne pepper and 1 level tablespoon sweet pickle

Rémoulade Mayonnaise

For cold fish and shellfish dishes; cold meat and poultry dishes

Add to mayonnaise (page 126) after stirring in hot water: 2 level teaspoons made mustard, 1 level teaspoon finely chopped parsley, 1 level tablespoon *each* finely chopped gherkins and capers, 1 level teaspoon *each* fresh chervil and tarragon and 1 level teaspoon anchovy essence

Russian Mayonnaise

For green and mixed salads; cold shellfish and egg dishes

Add to Mayonnaise (page 126) after stirring in hot water: 150ml / 5fl oz carton soured cream, 2 teaspoons bottled chilli sauce, 2 level tablespoons finely chopped canned pimento, 1 teaspoon vinegar, 1 level teaspoon paprika and 1 large chopped hard-boiled egg

Verte Mayonnaise

For cold salmon and salmon trout

1 Mince very finely a handful of parsley, 2 level tablespoons fresh tarragon and chives, 2 heaped tablespoons torn-up spinach leaves and 2 level tablespoons watercress
2 Add to Mayonnaise (page 126) after stirring in hot water

Aioli Mayonnaise

For all vegetable salads; salads with hard-boiled eggs, beef and lamb

Add one very finely chopped clove of garlic to Mayonnaise (page 126) after stirring in the hot water. Chill before using

Tartare Mayonnaise

For fried fish dishes

Add to Mayonnaise (page 126) after stirring in hot water: 1 level tablespoon *each* finely chopped capers and parsley and 2 tablespoons finely chopped gherkins

Green Dragon Mayonnaise

For all cold fish and shellfish dishes

1 Mince finely 1 garlic clove, 3 anchovy fillets, 2 tablespoons chives and handful of parsley
2 Add to the Mayonnaise (page 126) after stirring in hot water. Blend in 2 teaspoons tarragon vinegar and lemon juice and 150ml / 5fl oz carton soured cream
3 Adjust salt and pepper to taste

Spanish Mayonnaise

For green and egg salads

Add to Mayonnaise (page 126) after stirring in hot water: 2 level tablespoons tomato purée and 3 level tablespoons chopped canned pimento

Tivoli Mayonnaise

For poultry, tongue, ham, fish and egg salads

Add 150g / 5oz carton natural yogurt to Mayonnaise (page 126) before stirring in hot water

Cucumber and Soured Cream Mayonnaise

For meat fondues, meat or poultry

½ small cucumber
4 tablespoons soured cream
½ recipe Mayonnaise (page 126)
Salt and pepper
1 teaspoon lemon juice
1 tablespoon chopped chives

1 Chop cucumber and place in a bowl
2 Add all other ingredients and stir thoroughly.

Sauces

 Sauces may be frozen, but must be under-seasoned as freezing develops flavours. Stir continuously when reheating sauces which have been frozen and correct consistency. Storage time – 4 months.

Savoury Sauces

Simple White Pouring Sauce

15g / ½oz cornflour
300ml / ½ pint milk
Small knob of butter
¼ to ½ level teaspoon salt
Shake of pepper

1 Mix cornflour to smooth paste with a little cold milk
2 Warm remainder of milk. Pour on to paste and mix well
3 Return to pan
4 Cook, stirring, until Sauce comes to boil and thickens
5 Simmer for 2 minutes
6 Remove from heat and stir in butter
7 Season to taste with salt and pepper. **Serves 6**

Simple White Coating Sauce

1 Follow recipe and method for Simple White Pouring Sauce (above)
2 Increase cornflour to 20g / ⅔oz. **Serves 4**

Basic White Pouring Sauce

15g / ½oz butter
15g / ½oz flour
300ml / ½ pint milk
¼ to ½ level teaspoon salt
Shake of pepper

1 Melt butter in pan. Add flour and cook over low heat, stirring, for 2 minutes. Do not allow mixture (roux) to brown
2 Gradually blend in milk
3 Cook, stirring, until Sauce comes to boil and thickens
4 Simmer very gently for 3 minutes
5 Season to taste with salt and pepper. **Serves 6**

Cheese Sauce (page 129) served with Cauliflower

Basic White Coating Sauce

1 Follow recipe and method for Basic White Pouring Sauce (page 128)
2 Increase butter and flour to 25g/1oz each.
Serves 4

One-stage White Sauce

1 Follow recipe for Basic White Pouring Sauce (page 128)
2 Put butter, flour and milk into pan. Heat, whisking continuously, until Sauce thickens and is cooked
3 Season to taste with salt and pepper. **Serves 6**

Parsley Sauce

For bacon, ham and fish dishes; also boiled mutton

1 Follow recipe and method for either Basic White Pouring Sauce (page 128) or Basic White Coating Sauce (above)
2 After seasoning with salt and pepper stir in 1 or 2 level tablespoons finely chopped parsley.
Serves 4 to 6

Rich White Sauce (Béchamel)

For fish, poultry, egg and vegetable dishes

300ml/½ pint milk
1 small peeled onion
1 small peeled carrot
½ small celery stalk
2 cloves
6 white peppercorns
1 blade mace
1 sprig parsley
25g/1oz butter
25g/1oz flour
Seasoning to taste
2 tablespoons fresh double cream

1 Put milk into saucepan. Add quartered onion, thickly sliced carrot, sliced celery, cloves, peppercorns, mace and parsley
2 Slowly bring just up to boil
3 Remove from heat and cover
4 Leave ½ an hour. Strain, reserving milk liquor
5 Melt butter in pan. Add flour and cook over low heat, stirring, for 2 minutes. Do not allow mixture (or roux) to brown
6 Gradually blend in flavoured milk
7 Cook, stirring, until Sauce comes to boil and thickens. Simmer very gently for 3 minutes
8 Remove from heat and season to taste with salt and pepper. Stir in cream.
Serves 4

Onion Sauce

For tripe, lamb grills and roasts and boiled mutton

1 Follow recipe and method for either Basic White Pouring Sauce (page 128) or Basic White Coating Sauce (left)
2 Before seasoning with salt and pepper stir in 1 large onion, boiled and finely chopped
3 Re-heat gently before using. **Serves 4 to 6**

Cheese Sauce

For fish, poultry, ham, bacon, egg and vegetable dishes

1 Follow recipe and method for either Basic White Pouring Sauce (page 128) or Basic White Coating Sauce (left)
2 Before seasoning with salt and pepper, stir in 50g/2oz finely grated Cheddar or 50g/2oz crumbled Lancashire cheese, ½ to 1 level teaspoon made mustard and pinch of Cayenne pepper.
Serves 4 to 6

Lemon Sauce

For fish, poultry, egg and veal dishes

1 Follow recipe and method for either Basic White Pouring Sauce (page 128) or Basic White Coating Sauce (left)
2 Before seasoning with salt and pepper stir in finely grated rind of 1 small lemon and 1 tablespoon lemon juice
3 Re-heat gently before using. **Serves 4 to 6**

Béarnaise Sauce

For meat grills and roasts or grilled fish

2 tablespoons tarragon vinegar
3 tablespoons wine vinegar
1 level tablespoon finely chopped onion
Yolks of 2 standard eggs
2 teaspoons cold water
100g/4oz softened butter
Seasoning to taste

1 Put both vinegars and onion into saucepan. Boil gently until liquid is reduced by about one-third
2 Leave until cold and strain
3 Put egg yolks, reduced vinegar liquor and water into double saucepan (or basin standing over pan of simmering water). Whisk until thick and fluffy
4 Gradually add butter, a tiny piece at a time. Continue whisking until each piece has been absorbed by the Sauce and Sauce itself has thickened
5 Season to taste with salt and pepper. **Serves 4**

Maître d'Hôtel Sauce

For baked, grilled, poached or steamed fish

1 Follow recipe and method for either Basic White Pouring Sauce (page 128) or Basic White Coating Sauce (page 129)
2 Use 150ml / ¼ pint milk and 150ml / ¼ pint fish stock instead of all milk
3 Before seasoning with salt and pepper stir in juice of ½ medium-sized lemon, 2 level table-spoons finely chopped parsley and 2 tablespoons fresh double cream
4 Re-heat gently (without boiling) before using.
Serves 4 to 6

Mushroom Sauce

For fish, poultry, veal, egg and cheese dishes

1 Follow recipe and method for either Basic White Pouring Sauce (page 128) or Basic White Coating Sauce (page 129)
2 Before seasoning with salt and pepper stir in 50 to 75g / 2 to 3oz mushrooms–finely chopped and lightly fried in butter
3 Re-heat gently before using.
Serves 4 to 6

Anchovy Sauce

For grilled, baked, steamed, poached and fried fish dishes, and fried veal dishes

1 Follow recipe and method for either Basic White Pouring Sauce (page 128) or Basic White Coating Sauce (page 129)
2 Before seasoning with salt and pepper, stir in 2 level teaspoons anchovy essence and 1 teaspoon lemon juice. **Serves 4 to 6**

Cumberland Sauce

For ham and game dishes

150ml / ¼ pint red wine or port
4 tablespoons redcurrant jelly
Finely grated rind and juice of 1 medium-sized lemon and orange
2 level teaspoons finely grated onion
1 level teaspoon made mustard
¼ level teaspoon ground ginger
¼ level teaspoon salt
Shake of pepper

1 Put all ingredients into pan. Slowly bring just up to boil, stirring occasionally
2 Remove from heat. Cover and leave 10 minutes
3 Leave unstrained and serve hot or strain and serve cold.
Serves 4

Prawn or Shrimp Sauce

For fish dishes

1 Follow recipe and method for either Basic White Pouring Sauce (page 128) or Basic White Coating Sauce (page 129)
2 Before seasoning with salt and pepper, stir in 50g / 2oz finely chopped peeled prawns or 50g / 2oz peeled whole shrimps, ½ level teaspoon dry mustard mixed with 2 teaspoons lemon juice and ½ level teaspoon anchovy essence
3 Re-heat gently before using. **Serves 4 to 6**

Egg Sauce

For fish, poultry and veal dishes

1 Follow recipe and method for either Basic White Pouring Sauce (page 128) or Basic White Coating Sauce (page 129)
2 Before seasoning with salt and pepper, stir in 1 large, finely chopped hard-boiled egg
3 Re-heat gently before using.
Serves 4 to 6

Mustard Sauce

For herring, mackerel, cheese, ham and bacon dishes

1 Follow recipe and method for either Basic White Pouring Sauce (page 128) or Basic White Coating Sauce (page 129)
2 Before seasoning with salt and pepper, stir in 2 level teaspoons dry mustard mixed with 2 teaspoons vinegar
3 Re-heat gently before using. **Serves 4 to 6**

Aurore Sauce

For fish and egg dishes

1 Follow recipe and method for Béchamel Sauce (page 129)
2 Before seasoning with salt and pepper, stir in 2 level tablespoons tomato purée and ½ level teaspoon caster sugar
3 Re-heat gently before using. Do not allow to boil. **Serves 4**

Mousseline Sauce

For same dishes as Hollandaise Sauce

1 Follow recipe and method for Hollandaise Sauce (page 131)
2 Stir in 3 tablespoons lightly whipped fresh double cream just before serving. **Serves 6**

Chaud-Froid Sauce

For coating portions of cold chicken and whole skinned fish, or cutlets of fish such as salmon and salmon trout

1 Follow recipe and method for Béchamel Sauce (page 129)
2 Before seasoning with salt and pepper stir in
3 level teaspoons gelatine dissolved in 150ml/¼ pint hot water
3 Use when cold and just on setting point. **Serves 4**

Cucumber Sauce

For all fish dishes

1 Follow recipe and method for Béchamel Sauce (page 129)
2 Before seasoning with salt and pepper stir in
4 level tablespoons finely grated peeled cucumber and large pinch of nutmeg
3 Re-heat gently before using. Do not allow to boil. **Serves 4**

Hollandaise Sauce

For asparagus and broccoli, poached fish, egg and chicken dishes

1 teaspoon lemon juice
1 teaspoon wine vinegar
1 tablespoon cold water
3 white peppercorns
½ small bay leaf
Yolks of 4 standard eggs
225g/8oz softened butter
Seasoning to taste

1 Put lemon juice, vinegar, water, peppercorns and bay leaf into saucepan. Boil gently until liquor is reduced by half
2 Leave until cold and strain
3 Put egg yolks and reduced vinegar liquor into double saucepan (or basin standing over pan of gently simmering water)
4 Whisk until thick and foamy
5 Gradually add butter, a tiny piece at a time. Continue whisking until each piece has been absorbed by the Sauce and Sauce itself is consistency of Mayonnaise
6 Season to taste with salt and pepper. Serve immediately. **Serves 6**

Hot Horseradish Sauce

For beef roasts and grills; grilled or fried trout, mackerel and herrings

1 Follow recipe and method for Béchamel Sauce (page 129)
2 Before seasoning with salt and pepper, stir in 2 level tablespoons grated horseradish, ½ level teaspoon sugar and 1 teaspoon vinegar
3 Re-heat gently before using. Do not allow to boil. **Serves 4**

Mornay Sauce

For poultry, fish, shellfish and egg dishes

1 Follow recipe and method for Béchamel Sauce (page 129)
2 Before seasoning with salt and pepper, stir in yolk of standard egg mixed with 2 extra tablespoons fresh double cream and 50g/2oz very finely grated Cheddar cheese
3 Stand over low heat. Whisk until Sauce is smooth. Do not allow to boil. **Serves 4**

Mock Hollandaise Sauce

For poultry and steamed, poached or grilled fish dishes

1 Follow recipe and method for Béchamel Sauce (page 129)
2 Before seasoning with salt and pepper, stir in yolk of standard egg mixed with 2 extra tablespoons fresh double cream and 2 teaspoons lemon juice
3 Re-heat gently before using. Do not allow to boil. **Serves 4**

Hot Tartare Sauce

For all hot fish dishes

1 Follow recipe and method for Béchamel Sauce (page 129)
2 Before seasoning with salt and pepper, stir in yolk of standard egg mixed with 2 extra tablespoons fresh double cream, 1 tablespoon very finely chopped parsley, 2 teaspoons finely chopped gherkins and 2 teaspoons finely chopped capers
3 Re-heat gently before using. Do not allow to boil. **Serves 4**

Caper Sauce

For boiled mutton, fried or grilled mackerel and herrings

1 Follow recipe and method for either Basic White Pouring Sauce (page 128) or Basic White Coating Sauce (page 129)
2 Stir in 2 tablespoons chopped capers and 2 teaspoons caper vinegar from caper jar
3 Re-heat gently before using.
Serves 4 to 6

Velouté Sauce

For poultry and veal, or poached, grilled and steamed fish dishes

25g / 1oz butter
25g / 1oz finely chopped mushrooms
2 or 3 parsley sprigs
25g / 1oz flour
300ml / ½ pint poultry, veal or fish stock (depending on dish)
2 peppercorns
2 teaspoons lemon juice
4 tablespoons fresh double cream or soured cream
Seasoning to taste

1 Melt butter in saucepan. Add mushrooms and parsley and fry very gently for 5 minutes
2 Stir in flour. Gradually blend in stock. Add peppercorns
3 Cook, stirring, until Sauce comes to boil and thickens
4 Reduce heat, cover pan. Simmer very gently for 30 minutes
5 Strain, stir in lemon juice and cream. Season to taste with salt and pepper
6 Re-heat gently before using. Do not allow to boil.
Serves 4 to 6

Apple Sauce

For pork roasts and grills, duck and goose dishes

500g / 1lb cooking apples
3 tablespoons water
Large pinch of salt
2 level teaspoons caster sugar
15g / ½oz butter

1 Peel, core and slice apples. Put into pan with water
2 Cook gently until soft and pulpy. Either beat to a purée or rub through sieve or liquidise
3 Return to pan, add salt, sugar and butter
4 Re-heat gently
5 Serve hot or cold.
Serves 6

Suprême Sauce

For same dishes as Velouté Sauce

1 Follow recipe and method for Velouté Sauce (left)
2 After straining, stir in lemon juice, followed by the cream, mixed with yolk of standard egg
3 Season to taste with salt and pepper
4 Re-heat gently before using. Do not allow to boil. **Serves 4 to 6**

Allemande Sauce

For poached chicken and vegetable dishes

40g / 1½oz butter
25g / 1oz flour
300ml / ½ pint chicken stock
2 teaspoons lemon juice
Yolks of 2 standard eggs
2 tablespoons fresh single cream
Seasoning to taste

1 Melt 25g / 1oz butter in pan. Add flour and cook over low heat, stirring, for 2 minutes. Do not allow mixture (roux) to brown
2 Gradually blend in stock
3 Cook, stirring, until Sauce comes to boil and thickens
4 Lower heat. Cover pan and simmer very gently for 10 minutes
5 Remove from heat. Whisk in remaining butter, followed by lemon juice and egg yolks mixed with cream
6 Season to taste with salt and pepper
7 Re-heat gently before using. Do not allow to boil. **Serves 4 to 6**

Bread Sauce

For poultry

4 cloves
1 small peeled onion
6 white peppercorns
1 blade mace or large pinch nutmeg
½ small bay leaf
300ml / ½ pint milk
50g / 2oz fresh white breadcrumbs
25g / 1oz butter
2 tablespoons fresh single cream
Seasoning to taste

1 Press cloves into onion and put into saucepan
2 Add peppercorns, mace or nutmeg, bay leaf and milk
3 Slowly bring to boil. Reduce heat, cover pan and simmer 15 minutes
4 Strain. Combine hot milk with breadcrumbs, butter and cream
5 Season to taste with salt and pepper
6 Re-heat gently. **Serves 4 to 6**

Brown (or Espagnole) Sauce

25g / 1oz butter
1 teaspoon olive oil or corn oil
25g / 1oz chopped lean ham or bacon
½ small peeled onion
½ small celery stalk
25g / 1oz mushrooms and stalks
½ small peeled carrot
25g / 1oz flour
425ml / ¾ pint beef stock
2 level teaspoons tomato purée
 (or 1 small chopped tomato)
1 small bay leaf
2 sprigs parsley
Seasoning to taste

1 Put butter and oil into pan. Heat until both are sizzling
2 Add ham or bacon, chopped onion, celery, mushrooms with stalks and sliced carrot
3 Fry gently 7 to 10 minutes (or until golden)
4 Add flour and cook, stirring, until it turns light brown
5 Gradually blend in stock. Cook, stirring, until Sauce comes to boil and thickens
6 Add purée or chopped tomato, bay leaf and parsley. Cover pan
7 Simmer gently for 30 minutes
8 Strain, season to taste with salt and pepper
9 Re-heat before using.
Serves 4

Meat or Poultry Gravy

Meat or poultry dripping
1 level tablespoon cornflour
300ml / ½ pint stock or water
Seasoning to taste

1 Pour off all but 1 tablespoon dripping from roasting tin
2 Add cornflour and combine
3 Stand tin over very low heat. Gradually blend in stock or water
4 Cook, stirring, until gravy comes to boil and thickens
5 Lower heat. Simmer for 3 minutes
6 Season to taste with salt and pepper.
Serves 4 to 6

Bigarrade Sauce

For duck, goose and game dishes

1 Follow recipe and method for Brown Sauce (above)
2 After straining, stir in juice of 1 small lemon and orange and 2 tablespoons dry red wine
3 Season to taste with salt and pepper
4 Re-heat before serving. **Serves 4**

Brown Onion Sauce

For offal and beef dishes

1 Follow recipe and method for Brown Sauce (left)
2 After straining add 1 large onion, finely chopped and lightly fried in butter
3 Season to taste with salt and pepper
4 Re-heat before serving. **Serves 4**

Madeira Sauce

For tongue, game and beef roasts and grills

1 Follow recipe and method for Brown Sauce (left)
2 After straining, stir in 3 tablespoons Madeira wine. Season to taste with salt and pepper
3 Re-heat before serving. **Serves 4**

Réforme Sauce

For lamb grills, mutton cutlets and beef fillets

1 Follow recipe and method for Brown Sauce (left)
2 After straining, add 3 tablespoons dry red wine and 1 tablespoon redcurrant jelly
3 Simmer with lid off pan for 15 minutes
4 Season to taste with salt
5 Re-heat before using. **Serves 4**

Mint Sauce

For lamb and mutton roasts

4 level tablespoons finely chopped mint
3 tablespoons boiling water
3 level teaspoons caster sugar
¼ level teaspoon salt
3 tablespoons vinegar

1 Stir mint into boiling water. Add sugar and salt
2 Leave until cold
3 Add vinegar and mix well. **Serves 4 to 6**

Piquant Sauce

For pork grills and roasts, ham and bacon dishes and meat rissoles

1 Follow recipe and method for Brown Sauce (left)
2 After straining, add 2 level teaspoons *each*, finely chopped gherkins and capers, 1½ teaspoons Worcestershire sauce and 2 tablespoons vinegar
3 Simmer with lid off pan for 10 minutes
4 Season to taste with salt and pepper
5 Re-heat before using. **Serves 4**

Tomato Sauce

For meat, fried and baked fish, egg, cheese, spaghetti and macaroni dishes

50g / 2oz butter
2 teaspoons olive or corn oil
1 medium-sized sliced onion
1 clove finely chopped garlic (optional)
50g / 2oz chopped lean bacon or ham
25g / 1oz flour
250g / 8oz chopped tomatoes
1 level tablespoon tomato purée
300ml / ½ pint stock or water
1 bay leaf
1 blade of mace
6 white peppercorns
¼ level teaspoon basil or mixed herbs
1 level teaspoon brown sugar
2 teaspoons lemon juice
Seasoning to taste

1 Put butter and oil into pan and heat until both are sizzling
2 Add onion, garlic if used, and bacon or ham. Fry gently until pale gold
3 Stir in flour, tomatoes, purée, stock or water, bay leaf, mace, peppercorns, basil or mixed herbs and sugar
4 Bring to the boil, stirring. Reduce heat and cover pan
5 Simmer gently for 45 minutes
6 Strain. Add lemon juice. Season to taste with salt and pepper
7 Re-heat before using.
Serves 4 to 6

Curry Sauce

For pouring over hard-boiled eggs or combining with pieces of cooked fish, chicken, meat or vegetables

50g / 2oz butter
2 teaspoons olive or corn oil
2 large finely chopped onions
1 finely chopped garlic clove (optional)
2 level tablespoons curry powder
1 level tablespoon flour
2 cloves
1 level tablespoon tomato purée
¼ level teaspoon *each*, ground ginger and cinnamon
2 level tablespoons sweet pickle or chutney
1 tablespoon lemon juice
3 level teaspoons granulated sugar
425ml / ¾ pint stock or water
½ to 1 level teaspoon salt

1 Put butter and oil into pan. Heat until both are sizzling
2 Add onions and garlic (if used). Fry gently until pale gold
3 Stir in curry powder and flour. Add cloves, purée, ginger and cinnamon, sweet pickle or chutney, lemon juice and sugar
4 Gradually blend in stock or water. Slowly bring to the boil, stirring
5 Lower heat. Season with salt and cover pan
6 Simmer slowly ¾ to 1 hour
7 Sauce may be strained and re-heated before using. **Serves 4**

Cranberry Sauce

For poultry, duck, goose, game, turkey, lamb and mutton dishes

300ml / ½ pint water
175g / 6oz granulated sugar
250g / 8oz cranberries

1 Put water and sugar into saucepan. Heat slowly until sugar dissolves
2 Add cranberries. Cook fairly quickly for 2 to 3 minutes (or until skins pop open)
3 Reduce heat. Simmer very gently for 10 minutes
4 Serve hot or cold.
Serves 6

Quick Cream Sauce

For veal, poultry, fish, egg and cheese dishes

1 can condensed cream soup (flavour to taste)
4 tablespoons fresh cream or milk

1 Put soup and cream or milk into saucepan
2 Heat through gently, stirring. **Serves 4 to 6**

Sweet and Sour Sauce

For meat fondues, meats or poultry

50g / 2oz butter
2 medium-sized finely chopped onions
2 rashers chopped lean bacon
2 tablespoons tomato purée
300ml / ½ pint cider
150ml / ¼ pint water
1 tablespoon demerara sugar
Salt and pepper
2 tablespoons Worcestershire sauce
2 tablespoons mango chutney
3 teaspoons arrowroot

1 Melt butter in a pan and fry onions and bacon until soft but not brown
2 Add all remaining ingredients except arrowroot
3 Bring to the boil, stirring, and simmer for 15-20 minutes uncovered
4 Blend arrowroot with 2 tablespoons water, add to the pan and cook, stirring, for 1 minute. Serve hot or cold. **Serves 4 to 6**

Savoury Butter Sauces

These consist of melted butter with one or two simple additions. To keep the butter a good colour and prevent dark speckles and bitterness, the butter should be clarified first. The method for doing this is as follows:
Put required amount of butter into pan and melt over very low heat. Leave to stand a few minutes then strain through fine muslin into clean basin. Butter will now be clear and free of milky solids.

Brown Butter Sauce

For hot asparagus and broccoli

75g/3oz clarified butter

1 Put butter into saucepan. Cook very slowly until it turns light brown
2 Serve immediately. **Serves 4**

Black Butter Sauce

For poached and steamed fish, egg and vegetable dishes

75g/3oz clarified butter
1 teaspoon vinegar

1 Put butter into saucepan. Cook very slowly until it turns dark brown
2 Stir in vinegar at once. Serve immediately.
Serves 4

Black Butter Sauce with Capers

For poached or steamed fish and brain dishes

75g/3oz clarified butter
1 teaspoon vinegar
1 level tablespoon chopped capers

1 Put butter into saucepan. Cook very slowly until it turns dark brown
2 At once stir in vinegar and capers. Serve immediately. **Serves 4**

Lemon Butter Sauce

For poached and steamed fish dishes

75g/3oz clarified butter
1 level tablespoon finely chopped parsley
1 teaspoon lemon juice
Shake of pepper

1 Put butter into saucepan. Cook very slowly until it turns light brown
2 Stir in remaining ingredients. Serve immediately.
Serves 4

Barbecue Sauces

These are brushed on to foods during cooking. Use them on meat or fish and vegetables on skewers (Kebabs), chops, steaks and portions of poultry in a rotisserie, under the grill or over a barbecue pit. They should be brushed on to the foods during the latter part of cooking: prolonged heating would make the spices bitter

Mild Barbecue Sauce

For meat, poultry or fish

300ml/½ pint tomato ketchup
25g/1oz butter
3 tablespoons vinegar
¼ level teaspoon chilli powder
1 level teaspoon brown sugar
½ level teaspoon celery salt
½ level teaspoon mixed herbs

1 Put all ingredients into pan
2 Bring slowly to the boil, stirring
3 Cover pan and simmer gently for 15 minutes

Poultry Barbecue Sauce

For poultry and duck

300ml/½ pint dry cider, apple juice or white wine
1 level teaspoon crushed rosemary
1 finely chopped garlic clove (optional)
1 small onion, finely grated
2 teaspoons Worcestershire sauce
75g/3oz butter
2 level teaspoons paprika
½ level teaspoon salt

1 Put all ingredients into pan
2 Bring slowly to the boil, stirring
3 Cover pan. Simmer gently for 15 minutes

Meat Barbecue Sauce

For all types of meat

25g/1oz butter
1 teaspoon olive or corn oil
1 medium-sized onion, finely chopped
3 tablespoons water
2 tablespoons vinegar
1 tablespoon Worcestershire sauce
2 tablespoons lemon juice
2 level teaspoons soft brown sugar
2 level teaspoons made mustard
½ level teaspoon salt
½ level teaspoon paprika
¼ level teaspoon chilli powder

1 Put butter and oil into saucepan. Heat until both are sizzling
2 Add onion. Fry gently until pale gold
3 Add all remaining ingredients. Bring slowly to boil, stirring
4 Reduce heat. Cover pan and simmer gently 30 minutes

Curried Barbecue Sauce

For meat fondues, meats or poultry

1 recipe Mayonnaise (page 126)
4 tablespoons tomato ketchup
1 teaspoon lemon juice
1 teaspoon Worcestershire sauce
1 teaspoon grated onion
1 teaspoon curry powder
3 drops Tabasco sauce

1 Mix ingredients thoroughly together in a bowl. Serve hot or cold

Sweet Sauces

Red Jam Sauce

For steamed and baked puddings

2 level teaspoons arrowroot or cornflour
150ml / ¼ pint cold water
4 level tablespoons raspberry, strawberry, plum or blackcurrant jam
2 teaspoons lemon juice
1 level tablespoon caster sugar

1 Mix arrowroot or cornflour to smooth paste with a little of the cold water
2 Put rest of water into pan. Add jam, lemon juice and sugar
3 Heat gently, stirring, until sugar is dissolved. Combine with arrowroot or cornflour paste
4 Return to pan. Cook, stirring, until Sauce comes to boil and both thickens and clears
5 Simmer for 2 minutes. **Serves 4 to 6**

Apricot Jam Sauce

For steamed and baked puddings

1 Follow recipe and method for Red Jam Sauce (above)
2 Use apricot jam instead of red jam. **Serves 4 to 6**

Fudge Sauce

For ice cream, steamed and baked puddings

25g / 1oz plain chocolate
15g / ½oz butter
2 tablespoons warm milk
100g / 4oz soft brown sugar
3 level teaspoons golden syrup
½ teapoon vanilla essence

1 Break up chocolate. Put into basin standing over saucepan of hot water. Add butter
2 Leave until chocolate and butter have melted, stirring once or twice
3 Blend in milk. Transfer to saucepan. Add sugar and golden syrup
4 Stand over low heat. Stir until sugar has dissolved
5 Bring to the boil. Boil steadily without stirring for 5 minutes
6 Remove from heat. Add vanilla and mix well. Serve hot. **Serves 4**

For a Sauce that hardens quickly over ice cream, boil an extra 2 to 3 minutes. If there is any Sauce left over, it can be re-heated in a basin over a pan of simmering water

Brandy Sauce (below)

Sweet White Sauce

For steamed and baked puddings

15g / ½oz cornflour
300ml / ½ pint milk
Knob butter
1 level tablespoon caster sugar

1 Mix cornflour to smooth paste with a little of the cold milk
2 Warm remainder. Pour on to paste and mix well
3 Return to pan
4 Cook, stirring, until Sauce comes to boil and thickens
5 Simmer for 2 minutes
6 Remove from heat. Stir in butter and sugar.
Serves 4 to 6

Brandy Sauce

For Christmas Puddings, baked and steamed fruit puddings

1 Follow recipe and method for Sweet White Sauce (left)
2 Add 1 to 2 tablespoons brandy with the butter and sugar. **Serves 4 to 6**

Vanilla Sauce

For steamed and baked puddings

1 Follow recipe and method for Sweet White Sauce (left)
2 Add ½ to 1 teaspoon vanilla essence with butter and sugar. **Serves 4 to 6**

Rum Hard Sauce

For same dishes as Brandy Hard Sauce

1 Follow recipe and method for Brandy Hard
Sauce (right)
2 Use rum instead of brandy
3 Sprinkle Sauce lightly with mixed spice instead
of cinnamon. **Serves 6 to 8**

Coffee Cream Sauce

For ice cream, hot gingerbread, Christmas Pudding, mince pies

2 standard eggs
6 tablespoons hot strong coffee
50g / 2oz caster sugar
Pinch of salt
150ml / ¼ pint fresh double cream

1 Beat eggs well. Gradually beat in coffee
2 Put into double saucepan (or basin standing
over pan of simmering water)
3 Add sugar and salt. Cook, without boiling, until
Sauce is thick enough to coat back of spoon. Stir
frequently
4 Remove from heat and chill
5 Just before serving, whip cream until thick.
Gently stir in Coffee Sauce. **Serves 4 to 6**

Whipped Sherry Sauce

For steamed and baked puddings, ice cream,
stewed fruit and fruit pies

Yolks of 2 standard eggs
2 level tablespoons sifted icing sugar
4 tablespoons sweet sherry

1 Put all ingredients into basin standing over pan
of simmering water
2 Whisk until thick, light and foamy
3 Serve at once. **Serves 4**

Golden Syrup Sauce

For steamed and baked puddings

2 level teaspoons arrowroot or cornflour
4 tablespoons cold water
4 level tablespoons golden syrup
Finely grated rind and juice of 1 small lemon

1 Mix arrowroot or cornflour to smooth paste with
cold water
2 Put into saucepan with syrup and grated rind
and juice
3 Heat gently, stirring, until Sauce comes to boil
and both thickens and clears
4 Simmer for 2 minutes.
Serves 4 to 6

Rum or Brandy Fudge Sauce

For same dishes as Fudge Sauce

1 Follow recipe and method for Fudge Sauce
(page 136)
2 Add 2 teaspoons rum or brandy instead of
vanilla essence. **Serves 4**

Coffee Fudge Sauce

For same dishes as Fudge Sauce

1 Follow recipe and method for Fudge Sauce
(page 136)
2 Add 1 level teaspoon instant coffee powder with
the butter. **Serves 4**

Brandy Hard Sauce

For Christmas Puddings, baked and steamed fruit
puddings

100g / 4oz softened butter
100g / 4oz sifted icing sugar
100g / 4oz caster sugar
1 tablespoon milk
1 tablespoon brandy
50g / 2oz ground almonds
Cinnamon

1 Beat butter until creamy
2 Gradually beat in icing and caster sugars
alternately with milk and brandy. Cream until light
and fluffy
3 Add almonds and mix well
4 Pile into small dish. Sprinkle lightly with cinnamon. **Serves 6 to 8**

Chocolate Sauce

For steamed and baked puddings

1 level tablespoon cornflour
300ml / ½ pint milk
50g / 2oz grated plain chocolate
½ teaspoon vanilla essence
15g / ½oz butter
1 to 1½ level tablespoons caster sugar

1 Mix cornflour to smooth paste with a little of the
cold milk
2 Put remainder of milk into saucepan and add
chocolate. Heat very slowly until chocolate melts
3 Pour on to cornflour paste and mix well. Return
to pan
4 Cook, stirring, until Sauce comes to boil and
thickens
5 Add vanilla, butter and sugar. Simmer 3
minutes. **Serves 4 to 6**

Quick Chocolate Sauce

For ice cream, steamed and baked puddings, Profiteroles

75g / 3oz caster sugar
75g / 3oz soft brown sugar
75g / 3oz cocoa powder
300ml / ½ pint milk
1 teaspoon vanilla essence
25g / 1oz butter

1 Put all ingredients into saucepan. Stand over low heat
2 Stir until sugar has dissolved. Slowly bring to boil
3 Boil briskly, without stirring, for 2 minutes (or until Sauce coats back of spoon). **Serves 4 to 6**

If a more fudge-like Sauce is preferred, boil an extra 2 to 3 minutes

Butterscotch Sauce

For steamed and baked puddings, for serving over sliced bananas, for ice cream

1 level tablespoon cornflour
150ml / ¼ pint milk
25g / 1oz butter
100g / 4oz soft brown sugar
½ to 1 teaspoon vanilla essence

1 Mix cornflour to smooth paste with a little of the cold milk
2 Pour rest of milk into saucepan. Add butter and sugar
3 Stand over low heat. Stir until sugar dissolves
4 Pour on to cornflour paste and return to pan
5 Cook, stirring, until Sauce comes to boil and thickens. Add vanilla
6 Simmer 3 minutes. **Serves 4 to 6**

Orange or Lemon Butterscotch Sauce

For steamed and baked puddings, for serving over sliced bananas, for ice cream

1 Follow recipe and method for Butterscotch Sauce (above)
2 Add ½ level teaspoon finely grated orange or lemon rind to cornflour paste
3 Omit vanilla. **Serves 4 to 6**

Marmalade Sauce

For steamed and baked puddings

1 Follow recipe and method for Red Jam Sauce (page 136)
2 Use orange marmalade instead of the red jam. **Serves 4 to 6**

Custard Sauce

For steamed and baked puddings, fruit and mince pies, stewed fruit

2 standard eggs
2 level teaspoons caster sugar
300ml / ½ pint milk
¼ teaspoon vanilla essence (optional)

1 Beat eggs with sugar and 3 tablespoons milk
2 Heat rest of milk to lukewarm
3 Beat into eggs. Pour into double saucepan (or basin standing over pan of simmering water)
4 Cook, without boiling, until custard thickens enough to coat back of spoon thinly. Stir frequently. Pour into cold jug and stir in vanilla
5 Serve hot or cold. **Serves 4 to 6**

Sauce thickens up slightly on cooling

Coffee Custard Sauce

For steamed and baked puddings

1 Follow recipe and method for Custard Sauce (above)
2 Add 1 or 2 level teaspoons instant coffee powder to the milk while it is warming
3 Omit vanilla. **Serves 4 to 6**

Chocolate Custard Sauce

For steamed and baked puddings

1 Follow recipe and method for Custard Sauce (above)
2 Melt 25g / 1oz grated plain chocolate in the milk while it is warming. **Serves 4 to 6**

Orange Custard Sauce

For same dishes as Lemon Custard Sauce

1 Follow recipe and method for Custard Sauce (above)
2 Add ½ level teaspoon finely grated orange rind to the milk while it is warming
3 Omit vanilla. **Serves 4 to 6**

Lemon Custard Sauce

For steamed and baked puddings, fruit pies and stewed fruit

1 Follow recipe and method for Custard Sauce (above)
2 Add ½ level teaspoon finely grated lemon rind to the milk while it is warming. Omit vanilla.
Serves 4 to 6

Batters

Lemon and Apricot Pancakes (page 141)

 Batters freeze uncooked. Pancakes freeze successfully unfilled – with freezer film between each.
Storage time – 2 to 3 months

It has for many years been accepted that batter is improved by standing; but modern research has shown that this is not so. Long beating of batter is unnecessary. The batter will rise satisfactorily if the egg and the first half of the milk are beaten in briskly for a short time

To keep Pancakes warm as they are being made, stack one on top of the other on large plate. Stand over pan of gently simmering water. Cover with large lid or second plate

To store cooked Pancakes, stack in airtight tin with greaseproof paper between each. Leave in a cold larder or refrigerator for 1 or 2 days. To re-heat, fry about $\frac{1}{2}$ minute per side in pan lightly brushed with butter

Pancake Batter

100g / 4oz plain or self-raising flour
Large pinch salt
1 standard egg
250ml / $\frac{1}{2}$ pint milk
1 tablespoon melted butter

1 Sift flour and salt into bowl
2 Beat to smooth creamy batter with unbeaten egg, half the milk and melted butter
3 Stir in remaining milk and use as required

Pancakes

Melted butter for frying
1 recipe Pancake Batter (left)

1 Lightly brush base of 20 or 22cm / 8 or 9in frying pan with melted butter. Stand over medium heat
2 When pan and butter are hot, pour in 2 or 3 tablespoons of batter mixture (just enough to coat base of pan thinly and evenly)
3 Fry until golden brown. Turn over with fish slice or spatula, or toss
4 Cook second side until golden and mottled
5 Repeat with rest of batter mixture.
Makes 8 Pancakes

Sweet Pancakes

Lemon or Orange Pancakes

1 Make Pancakes (page 140)
2 Sprinkle with caster sugar and either lemon or orange juice
3 Roll up by sliding nearest edge of Pancake between prongs of fork and turning fork over and over
4 Remove fork. Serve Pancakes as soon as possible after rolling
5 Accompany with wedges of lemon or orange. **Serves 4**

Lemon & Apricot Pancakes

1 Make Pancakes (page 140)
2 Spread with 5 to 6 tablespoons apricot jam, melted and warmed with 1 to 2 tablespoons lemon juice and 1 level teaspoon finely grated lemon rind
3 Roll up. **Serves 4**

Spiced Apple Pancakes

1 Make Pancakes (page 140)
2 Spread with hot thick apple purée (made from about 500g/1lb apples), flavoured with cinnamon and sweetened to taste with sugar
3 Roll up
4 Top each with a spoonful of fresh double cream. **Serves 4**

Banana Cream Pancakes

1 Make Pancakes (page 140)
2 Spread with 4 large mashed bananas, combined with 150ml/¼ pint lightly whipped fresh double cream, ½ level teaspoon nutmeg and sifted icing sugar to taste
3 Roll up. **Serves 4**

Mandarin Cream Pancakes

1 Make Pancakes (page 140)
2 Spread with can of mandarin oranges (well drained), combined with 150ml/¼ pint stiffly whipped fresh double cream
3 Roll up
4 Accompany with syrup from can of mandarins warmed through with 1 to 2 tablespoons sherry. **Serves 4**

Raspberry or Strawberry Pancakes

1 Make Pancakes (page 140)
2 Spread with 5 to 6 tablespoons melted and warmed raspberry or strawberry jam
3 Roll up. **Serves 4**

Golden Syrup & Orange Pancakes

1 Make Pancakes (page 140)
2 Spread with 5 to 6 tablespoons golden syrup, melted and warmed, with 1 level teaspoon finely grated orange rind
3 Roll up. **Serves 4**

Coconut & Apricot Pancakes

1 Make up Pancake Batter (page 140)
2 Stir in 2 level tablespoons desiccated coconut before making Pancakes
3 Spread evenly with 3 to 4 tablespoons melted apricot jam
4 Fill with canned drained apricot halves
5 Roll up
6 Dust evenly with caster or sifted icing sugar
7 Top each with heaped tablespoon stiffly whipped fresh double cream. **Serves 4**

Party Layer Pancakes

6 tablespoons apricot jam
1 tablespoon lemon juice
8 freshly made Pancakes (page 140)
1 recipe Meringue Topping (page 227)
8 halved glacé cherries

1 Put jam and lemon juice into saucepan. Stand over low heat until warm
2 Place first Pancake on large heatproof plate
3 Spread with jam and lemon juice. Add second Pancake. Spread with more jam and lemon juice
4 Repeat with rest of Pancakes
5 Swirl Meringue mixture over the top
6 Stud with halved cherries
7 Flash bake in hot oven (230°C/450°F or Gas No 8) for 1 to 2 minutes (or until pale gold)
8 Cut into wedges like a cake. Serve immediately. **Serves 8**

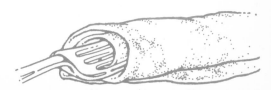

Cottage Cheese Blintzes

1 recipe Pancake Batter (page 140)
350g / 12oz Cottage cheese
Yolk of 1 standard egg
4 level tablespoons caster sugar
1 teaspoon vanilla essence
About 50g / 2oz butter
1 level teaspoon cinnamon
150ml / 5fl oz soured cream or natural yogurt

1 Cook 8 Pancakes on **one side only**. Turn out on to clean tea-towel
2 Mix Cottage cheese well together with egg yolk, 2 tablespoons caster sugar and vanilla
3 Put equal amounts on to centres of *cooked* sides of Pancakes
4 Fold edges of Pancakes over filling, envelope style
5 Melt butter in large pan. Leave until hot and sizzling
6 Put in 4 Blintzes, with joins underneath. Fry on both sides until golden
7 Remove from pan. Drain on kitchen paper. Keep hot
8 Add more butter to pan if necessary. Fry remaining Blintzes until golden
9 Sprinkle with sugar and cinnamon
10 Serve immediately
11 Serve soured cream or yogurt separately.
Serves 4

Cottage Cheese & Raisin Blintzes

1 Follow recipe and method for Cottage Cheese Blintzes (above)
2 Omit vanilla
3 Add 50 to 75g / 2 to 3oz seedless raisins and 1 level teaspoon finely grated lemon or orange rind to Cottage cheese with yolk and sugar.
Serves 4

Cottage Cheese & Banana Blintzes

1 Follow recipe and method for Cottage Cheese Blintzes (above)
2 Add 3 medium-sized, mashed bananas to Cottage cheese with yolk, sugar and vanilla.
Serves 4

Cottage Cheese & Peach Blintzes

1 Follow recipe and method for Cottage Cheese Blintzes (above)
2 Add 4 to 5 heaped tablespoons canned peach slices (well drained) to Cottage cheese with yolk and sugar. **Serves 4**

Cottage Cheese & Strawberry Blintzes

1 Follow recipe and method for Cottage Cheese Blintzes (left)
2 Instead of sprinkling fried Blintzes with sugar and cinnamon, arrange on warm serving platter and cover with 5 to 6 tablespoons melted and warmed strawberry jam. **Serves 4**

Crêpes Suzettes

8 cooked Pancakes (page 140)
100g / 4oz butter
25g / 1oz caster sugar
½ level teaspoon finely grated lemon rind
½ level teaspoon finely grated orange rind
4 tablespoons Cointreau, Curaçao or Grand Marnier
2 tablespoons Brandy

1 Fold Pancakes like envelopes
2 Melt butter in pan. Add sugar, lemon and orange rind, and Cointreau, Curaçao or Grand Marnier
3 Bring to boil. Add Pancakes
4 Heat through, turning twice
5 Pour Brandy into pan. Put lighted match to sauce and allow it to flame
6 Serve Pancakes as soon as flames have subsided. **Serves 4**

Mock Crêpes Suzettes

8 cooked Pancakes (page 140)
50g / 2oz butter
50g / 2oz caster sugar
Finely grated rind and juice of 1 large orange
3 tablespoons sweet sherry or white wine

1 Fold Pancakes like envelopes
2 Melt butter in pan. Add sugar, orange rind and juice and sherry, or wine
3 Bring to boil. Add Pancakes
4 Heat through, turning twice
5 Serve immediately. **Serves 4**

Cottage Cheese & Pineapple Pancakes

1 Make Pancakes (page 140)
2 Spread with 225g / 8oz Cottage cheese combined with 4 to 5 tablespoons canned, drained and chopped pineapple and caster or sifted icing sugar to taste
3 Roll up
4 Sprinkle each with sifted icing sugar. **Serves 4**

Savoury Pancakes

Brittany Pancakes

1 Make Pancakes (page 140)
2 Stuff with 225g/8oz cooked minced beef moistened with 1 or 2 tablespoons Gravy (page 133), 1 tablespoon tomato ketchup and dash of Worcestershire sauce
3 Roll up. Arrange in heatproof dish
4 Coat with 300g/10½oz can condensed cream soup (flavour to taste)
5 Re-heat in centre of moderate oven (180°C/350°F or Gas No 4) for 20 minutes. **Serves 4**

Country Pancakes

1 Make Pancakes (page 140)
2 Fry 100g/4oz chopped mushrooms and stalks and 4 large skinned and chopped tomatoes in 25g/1oz butter. Use to stuff Pancakes
3 Roll up. Arrange in heatproof dish
4 Coat with 300ml/½ pint Cheese Coating Sauce (page 129 combined with 150g/5oz carton natural yogurt
5 Sprinkle with 25g/1oz crumbled Lancashire cheese. Brown under hot grill
6 Serve immediately.
Serves 4

Creamed Smoked Haddock Pancakes

1 Make Pancakes (page 140)
2 Combine 500g/1lb flaked smoked haddock (cooked in milk) with 150ml/5fl oz carton soured cream or 150ml/¼ pint fresh double cream. Use to stuff Pancakes
3 Roll up. Arrange in heatproof dish
4 Coat with freshly made Mock Hollandaise Sauce (page 131). Sprinkle with 25g/1oz crumbled Lancashire cheese
5 Brown under hot grill
6 Garnish with parsley and lemon wedges.
Serves 4

Kidney Pancakes

1 Make Pancakes (page 140)
2 Fill with 350g/12oz cooked, chopped kidney, combined with 150ml/¼ pint Brown Sauce (page 133)
3 Roll up. Serve immediately.
Serves 4

Creamed Chicken Pancakes

1 Make Pancakes (page 140)
2 Combine 350g/12oz cooked minced chicken with 300ml/½ pint Béchamel Sauce (page 129)
3 Add 2 tablespoons dry sherry or white wine. Season well. Use to stuff Pancakes
4 Roll up. Transfer to heatproof dish
5 Coat with 50g/2oz melted butter mixed with 2 tablespoons dry sherry or white wine. Cover dish with lid or aluminium foil
6 Re-heat just above centre of moderately hot oven (190°C/375°F or Gas No 5) for 15 to 20 minutes. **Serves 4**

Miniature Party Pancakes

1 Follow recipe and method for Pancakes (page 140) but pour only 1 tablespoon batter, for each Pancake, into lightly buttered and heated small frying pan
2 Fry on both sides
3 Stack on clean tea-towel. Spread with Cottage cheese
4 Roll up. Spear on to cocktail sticks.
Makes about 25 Pancakes

Party Pancake Kebabs

1 Make 25 Miniature Party Pancakes (above)
2 Wrap round cooked cocktail sausages, sections of grilled tomatoes, rolls of grilled bacon, whole grilled mushrooms and pieces of cooked kidney
3 Spear on to cocktail sticks. If liked, sticks can be pressed into a grapefruit or small green cabbage.
Makes 25 Kebabs

Prawn & Lemon Pancakes

1 Make Pancakes (page 140)
2 Fill with 225g/8oz peeled prawns, combined with 150ml/¼ pint Basic White Coating Sauce (page 129)
3 Roll up. Arrange in heatproof dish
4 Coat with Black Butter Sauce (page 135). Cover with lid or aluminium foil
5 Re-heat in centre of moderate oven (180°C/350°F or Gas No 4) for 20 minutes
6 Garnish with lemon wedges. **Serves 4**

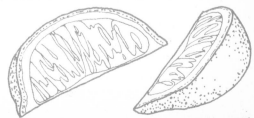

Toreador Pancakes (below)

Tuna & Cucumber Pancakes

1 Make Pancakes (page 140)
2 Fill with 200g / 7oz can drained tuna, finely mashed with 4 tablespoons natural yogurt
3 Roll up. Arrange in heatproof dish
4 Coat with 300ml / ½ pint Cucumber Coating Sauce (page 131). Sprinkle lightly with toasted breadcrumbs
5 Re-heat in centre of moderate oven (180°C / 350°F or Gas No 4) for 20 minutes.
Serves 4

Bacon & Parsley Pancakes

1 Make Pancakes (page 140)
2 Stuff with 350g / 12oz chopped fried bacon combined with 150ml / ¼ pint Parsley Coating Sauce (page 129)
3 Roll up. Arrange in heatproof dish
4 Top each with pat of Mustard Butter (page 96). Cover with lid or aluminium foil
5 Re-heat in centre of moderate oven (180°C / 350°F or Gas No 4) for 20 minutes.
Serves 4

Ham & Cheese Pancakes

1 Make Pancakes (page 140)
2 Stuff with 225g / 8oz chopped lean ham, combined with 150ml / ¼ pint Mornay Sauce (page 131)
3 Roll up. Arrange in heatproof dish
4 Top each with pat of Devilled Butter (page 94). Cover with lid or aluminium foil
5 Re-heat in centre of moderate oven (180°C / 350°F or Gas No 4) for 2 minutes.
Serves 4

Toreador Pancakes

1 Make Pancakes (page 140)
2 Chop 1 small onion. Fry in 25g / 1oz butter until golden
3 Add 225g / 8oz chopped corned beef. Fry further 2 minutes. Use to stuff Pancakes
4 Roll up. Arrange in heatproof dish
5 Coat with 300g / 10½oz can condensed tomato soup. Sprinkle with crushed potato crisps or toasted breadcrumbs
6 Re-heat in centre of moderately hot oven (190°C / 375°F or Gas No 5) for 15 to 20 minutes.
Serves 4

American Pancakes

1 Make Pancakes (page 140)
2 Stuff with hot, grilled bacon rashers, allowing 2 rashers per Pancake
3 Roll up
4 Top each with half a canned pineapple ring and sprig of watercress. **Serves 4**

Yorkshire Pudding

50g / 2oz butter or meat dripping
1 recipe Pancake Batter (page 140)

1 Pre-heat oven to hot (220°C / 425°F or Gas No 7)
2 Put butter or dripping (or use mixture of both) into 25cm × 30cm / 10in × 12in baking tin. Heat in oven until faint haze just appears
3 Pour in batter
4 Bake just above centre of oven 30 minutes
5 Reduce temperature to moderately hot (200°C / 400°F or Gas No 6)
6 Bake for further 15 to 20 minutes. **Serves 6 to 8**

Small Yorkshire Pudding

1 Follow recipe and method for Yorkshire Pudding (page 144)
2 Use half quantity of Pancake Batter
3 Pour into 23cm×18cm / 9in×7in baking tin
4 Bake for same length of time as large Pudding.
Serves 3 to 4

Savoury Batter Puddings

Toad-in-the-Hole

1 Arrange 500g / 1lb pork sausages in 25cm×30cm / 10in×12in baking tin
2 Bake just above centre of hot oven (220°C / 425°F or Gas No 7) for 10 minutes
3 Remove from oven. Pour in 1 recipe Pancake Batter (page 140)
4 Bake as for Yorkshire Pudding. **Serves 4 to 6**

Most sausages can be cooked in their own fat. Other sausages however–especially thin or skinless ones–might need the addition of 25 to 50g / 1 to 2oz butter

Bacon Batter Pudding

1 Follow recipe and method for Yorkshire Pudding (page 144)
2 After pouring batter into tin add 225 to 350g / 8 to 12oz chopped lean bacon
3 Bake as for Yorkshire Pudding. **Serves 4 to 6**

Meat Ball Batter Pudding

1 Follow recipe and method for Yorkshire Pudding (page 144)
2 After pouring batter into tin add 500g / 1lb lean minced beef, well seasoned and shaped into small balls
3 Bake as for Yorkshire Pudding. **Serves 4 to 6**

Corned Beef Batter Pudding

1 Follow recipe and method for Yorkshire Pudding (page 144)
2 After pouring batter into tin add 225 to 350g / 8 to 12oz corned beef, cut into 2cm / 1in cubes
3 Bake as for Yorkshire Pudding. **Serves 4 to 6**

Sweet Batter Puddings

Apple Batter Pudding

1 Follow recipe and method for Yorkshire Pudding (page 144)
2 Add 500g / 1lb peeled, cored and thickly sliced apples to hot butter in tin
3 Sprinkle with 100g / 4 oz caster sugar and 1 level teaspoon cinnamon
4 Pour in Pancake Batter
5 Bake as for Yorkshire Pudding. **Serves 4 to 6**

Rhubarb Batter Pudding

1 Follow recipe and method for Yorkshire Pudding (page 144)
2 Add 500g / 1lb rhubarb, cut into 2cm / 1in lengths, to hot butter in tin
3 Sprinkle with 100g / 4oz caster sugar and 1 level teaspoon powdered ginger
4 Pour in Pancake Batter
5 Bake as for Yorkshire Pudding. **Serves 4 to 6**

Dried Fruit Batter Pudding

1 Follow recipe and method for Yorkshire Pudding (page 144)
2 Add 100g / 4oz mixed dried fruit to hot butter in tin
3 Sprinkle with 50g / 2oz caster sugar and 1 level teaspoon finely grated lemon rind
4 Pour in Pancake Batter
5 Bake as for Yorkshire Pudding. **Serves 4 to 6**

Plum Batter Pudding

1 Follow recipe and method for Yorkshire Pudding (page 144)
2 Add 500g / 1lb halved and stoned cooking plums to hot butter in tin
3 Sprinkle with 100g / 4 oz caster sugar and 1 level teaspoon mixed spice
4 Pour in Pancake Batter
5 Bake as for Yorkshire Pudding. **Serves 4 to 6**

145

Popovers

50g / 2oz plain flour
Pinch of salt
1 small egg
125ml / ¼ pint milk
40g / 1½oz melted butter

1 Pre-heat oven to hot (220°C / 425°F or Gas No 7)
2 Sift flour and salt into bowl. Beat to smooth creamy batter with unbeaten egg and milk
3 Pour a little melted butter into 12 deep bun tins
4 Heat in oven for 3 minutes. Spoon about 1 tablespoon batter into each
5 Bake for 20 minutes
6 Serve hot with any roast joint or with bacon or gammon. **Serves 4**

Fruit Popovers

1 Follow recipe and method for Popovers (above)
2 Add 6 level teaspoons currants to hot butter in tins before spooning in batter
3 Bake as for Popovers. Serve hot with syrup or honey and butter. **Serves 4**

Fritter & Coating Batters

Sweet Fritter Batter

For coating fruit such as bananas and pineapple

50g / 2oz plain flour
Pinch of salt
1 level teaspoon sifted icing sugar
4 tablespoons lukewarm water
2 teaspoons melted butter
White of 1 standard egg

1 Sift flour and salt into bowl. Add sugar
2 Gradually mix to thick smooth batter with water and butter
3 Whisk egg white to stiff snow
4 Fold into flour mixture. Use as required

Spicy Fritter Batter

1 Follow recipe and method for Sweet Fritter Batter (above)
2 Sift ½ level teaspoon mixed spice or cinnamon with flour and salt

Orange or Lemon Fritter Batter

1 Follow recipe and method for Sweet Fritter Batter (left)
2 Add ½ level teaspoon finely grated orange or lemon rind with water and butter

Almond Fritter Batter

1 Follow recipe and method for Sweet Fritter Batter (left)
2 Add ½ teaspoon almond essence with water and butter

Savoury Fritter Batter

For coating fish, meat, poultry and vegetables

100g / 4oz plain flour
½ level teaspoon salt
Shake of pepper
125ml to 150ml / ¼ pint lukewarm water
1 tablespoon melted butter
Whites of 2 standard eggs

1 Sift flour and salt into bowl. Add pepper
2 Gradually mix to thick smooth batter with water and butter
3 Whisk egg whites to stiff snow
4 Fold into flour mixture. Use as required

Mustard Fritter Batter

1 Follow recipe and method for Savoury Fritter Batter (above)
2 Sift 1 level teaspoon dry mustard with flour and salt

Curry Fritter Batter

1 Follow recipe and method for Savoury Fritter Batter (above)
2 Sift 3 level teaspoons curry powder with flour and salt

Coating Batter

For coating fish, meat and vegetables

100g / 4oz plain or self-raising flour
¼ level teaspoon salt
1 standard egg
1 tablespoon melted butter
125ml / ¼ pint milk

1 Sift flour and salt into bowl
2 Beat to smooth creamy batter with unbeaten egg, butter and milk. Use as required

Hot Puddings

Bread and Butter Pudding (below) Chocolate Semolina Pudding (page 148)

F Steamed puddings and hot milk puddings do not freeze successfully. Individual pies and tartlets may be frozen filled. Storage time–3 to 4 months.

Bread & Butter Pudding

6 thin slices white bread
About 50g / 2oz butter
50g / 2oz currants or sultanas (or mixture)
40g / 1½oz caster sugar
2 large eggs
600ml / 1 pint milk

1 Remove crusts from bread. Spread slices thickly with butter. Cut into fingers or small squares
2 Put half fingers or squares into 1 litre / 2 pint buttered heatproof dish
3 Sprinkle with all the fruit and half the sugar
4 Top with remaining bread fingers or squares, buttered sides uppermost. Sprinkle with rest of sugar
5 Beat eggs and milk well together. Strain into dish over bread
6 Leave to stand ½ an hour (so that bread absorbs some of the liquid). Bake in centre of moderate oven (160°C / 325°F or Gas No 3) for ¾ to 1 hour (or until Pudding is set and the top is crisp and golden). **Serves 4**

Semolina Pudding

600ml / 1 pint milk
40g / 1½oz semolina
25g / 1oz caster sugar
15g / ½oz butter

1 Put milk into pan and heat to lukewarm
2 Sprinkle in semolina. Cook slowly, stirring, until mixture comes to boil and thickens
3 Add sugar and butter. Cook very gently further 5 to 7 minutes, stirring often. **Serves 4**

Alternatively, turn the Pudding into ½ litre / 1 pint buttered heatproof dish as soon as it has come to the boil and thickened. Sprinkle with nutmeg and bake in centre of moderate oven (160°C / 325°F or Gas No 3) for 30 minutes.
To make Semolina Pudding with egg, cook Pudding gently for 5 minutes only, after adding sugar and butter. Cool 7 to 10 minutes. Stir in 1 standard egg, well beaten. Re-heat gently, **without boiling,** further 2 to 3 minutes

Sago Pudding

1 Follow recipe and method for Semolina Pudding (above)
2 Use Sago instead of Semolina. **Serves 4**

Lemon Semolina (or Sago) Pudding

1 Follow recipe and method for Semolina Pudding (page 147) or Sago Pudding (page 147)
2 Add 1 level teaspoon finely grated lemon rind with sugar. **Serves 4**

Orange Semolina (or Sago) Pudding

1 Follow recipe and method for Semolina Pudding (page 147) or Sago Pudding (page 147)
2 Add 1 level teaspoon finely grated orange rind with the sugar. **Serves 4**

Chocolate Semolina (or Sago) Pudding

1 Follow recipe and method for Semolina Pudding (page 147) or Sago Pudding (page 147)
2 Melt 25g / 1oz grated plain chocolate in the milk while it is warming.
Serves 4

Fruit Semolina (or Sago) Pudding

1 Follow recipe and method for Semolina Pudding (page 147) or Sago Pudding (page 147)
2 Add 50g / 2oz seedless raisins with the sugar.
Serves 4

Cabinet Pudding

6 trifle sponge cakes
50g / 2oz glacé cherries
25g / 1oz caster sugar
2 large eggs
600ml / 1 pint milk
1 teaspoon vanilla essence

1 Cut each cake into 6 cubes
2 Chop cherries coarsely. Put cake cubes and cherries into basin. Add sugar and toss lightly together to mix
3 Beat eggs, milk and vanilla well together. Gently stir into cake cube mixture
4 Leave to stand for 30 minutes. Turn into $\frac{3}{4}$ litre / 1$\frac{1}{2}$ pint well-buttered pudding basin. Cover securely with buttered greaseproof paper or buttered aluminium foil
5 Steam very gently for 1 hour. Turn out carefully on to warm plate. Accompany with fresh double cream. **Serves 4**

Baked Rice Pudding (or Barley, Tapioca or Macaroni)

50g / 2oz pudding rice (or flaked rice, barley, tapioca or broken macaroni)
600ml / 1 pint milk
25g / 1oz caster sugar
1 strip of lemon rind
Grated nutmeg
15g / $\frac{1}{2}$oz butter

1 Wash rice and drain well. Put into $\frac{3}{4}$ litre / 1$\frac{1}{2}$ pint, buttered heatproof dish and stir in milk
2 Leave rice to soak and soften for 30 minutes. Add sugar and lemon rind and stir well
3 Sprinkle top with grated nutmeg. Dot with butter
4 Put into centre of slow oven (150°C / 300°F or Gas No 2) and bake 2 to 2$\frac{1}{2}$ hours. Stir in skin 2 or 3 times during first hour of cooking to increase creaminess.
Serves 4

To make a Rice Pudding with egg, remove Pudding from oven after 1$\frac{1}{2}$ or 2 hours. Cool for 10 minutes. Stir in 1 standard egg well beaten, and return to oven. Continue to bake for recommended cooking time

Vanilla Rice Pudding (or Barley, Tapioca or Macaroni)

1 Follow recipe and method for Baked Rice Pudding (above).
2 Add $\frac{1}{2}$ teaspoon vanilla with the sugar instead of strip of lemon rind.
Serves 4

Orange Rice Pudding (or Barley, Tapioca or Macaroni)

1 Follow recipe and method for Baked Rice Pudding (above).
2 Add 1 level teaspoon finely grated orange rind with sugar.
Serves 4

Chocolate Rice Pudding (or Barley, Tapioca or Macaroni)

1 Follow recipe and method for Baked Rice Pudding (above).
2 Melt 40 to 50g / 1$\frac{1}{2}$ to 2oz grated plain chocolate in the milk before stirring into the rice
3 Omit strip of lemon rind and nutmeg
4 If liked, add $\frac{1}{2}$ teaspoon vanilla essence with the sugar.
Serves 4

Fruit Rice Pudding (or Barley, Tapioca or Macaroni)

1 Follow recipe and method for baked Rice Pudding (page 148).
2 Add 50g / 2oz seedless raisins with the sugar. **Serves 4**

Sponge Pudding

100g / 4oz self-raising flour
Pinch of salt
100g / 4oz butter
100g / 4oz caster sugar
2 large eggs
4 tablespoons cold milk

1 Sift flour and salt into bowl
2 Cream butter and sugar until light and fluffy. Beat in eggs, singly, adding tablespoon of flour with each
3 Fold in remaining flour alternately with milk. Transfer to buttered $\frac{3}{4}$ litre / 1$\frac{1}{2}$ pint pudding basin
4 Cover securely with buttered greaseproof paper or aluminium foil. Steam steadily 1$\frac{1}{2}$ to 2 hours (or until well risen and firm)
5 Turn out on to warm plate. Serve with fresh double cream or sweet sauce to taste (see Sauce Section, page 136). **Serves 4**
To bake Pudding Turn mixture into $\frac{3}{4}$ to 1 litre / 1$\frac{1}{2}$ to 2 pint buttered pie dish. Bake in centre of moderate oven (180°C / 350°F or Gas No 4) for $\frac{3}{4}$ to 1 hour (or until wooden cocktail stick, inserted into centre, comes out clean)

Chocolate Sponge Pudding

1 Follow recipe and method for Sponge Pudding (above) but use 75g / 3oz self-raising flour only
2 Sift into bowl with salt **plus** 15g / $\frac{1}{2}$oz cornflour and 15g / $\frac{1}{2}$oz cocoa powder
3 Cream butter and sugar with $\frac{1}{2}$ teaspoon vanilla essence. **Serves 4**

Fruit Sponge Pudding

1 Follow recipe and method for Sponge Pudding (above)
2 Stir in 50g / 2oz currants, sultanas or seedless raisins after beating in eggs. **Serves 4**

Jam Sponge Pudding

1 Follow recipe and method for Sponge Pudding (above)
2 Put 2 level tablespoons jam into bottom of buttered basin before adding Pudding mixture. **Serves 4**

Baked Egg Custard

3 large eggs or yolks of 4 standard eggs
600ml / 1 pint milk
25g / 1oz caster sugar
Grated nutmeg

1 Beat whole eggs or egg yolks with milk. Strain into $\frac{3}{4}$ litre / 1$\frac{1}{2}$ pint buttered heatproof dish then stir in sugar
2 Sprinkle top lightly with nutmeg. Stand in roasting tin containing enough water to come about half way up the sides of the dish
3 Bake in centre of moderate oven (160°C / 325°F or Gas No 3) for 45 minutes to 1 hour (or until firm). **Serves 4**

Coconut Egg Custard

1 Follow recipe and method for Baked Egg Custard (above)
2 Add 2 level tablespoons desiccated coconut with sugar. **Serves 4**

Lemon Egg Custard

1 Follow recipe and method for Baked Egg Custard (above)
2 Add 1 level teaspoon finely grated lemon rind with sugar. **Serves 4**

Orange Egg Custard

1 Follow recipe and method for Baked Egg Custard (above)
2 Add 1 level teaspoon finely grated orange rind with sugar.
Serves 4

Apple Charlotte

500g / 1lb cooking apples
100g / 4oz caster sugar
100g / 4oz fresh white breadcrumbs
Finely grated rind of 1 medium-sized lemon
75g / 3oz butter, melted

1 Peel, core and slice apples
2 Combine sugar, breadcrumbs and lemon rind
3 Fill buttered 1 litre / 2 pint heatproof dish with alternate layers of breadcrumb mixture and apples. Begin and end with breadcrumb mixture and sprinkle melted butter between layers
4 Put into centre of moderately hot oven (190°C / 375°F or Gas No 5). Bake for 45 minutes to 1 hour (or until apples are tender and top is golden brown)
5 Serve with fresh double cream, soured cream or custard. **Serves 4**

Double Crust Fruit Pie (page 151)

Plain Family Pudding

150g / 6oz self-raising flour
Pinch of salt
75g / 3oz butter
75g / 3oz caster sugar
1 large beaten egg
5 to 6 tablespoons cold milk for mixing

1 Sift flour and salt into bowl.
2 Rub in butter finely
3 Add sugar. Mix to fairly soft consistency with egg and milk
4 Stir briskly until well combined. Transfer to $\frac{3}{4}$ to 1 litre / $1\frac{1}{2}$ to 2 pint buttered pudding basin
5 Cover securely with buttered greaseproof paper or aluminium foil. Steam steadily for $1\frac{1}{2}$ to 2 hours (or until Pudding is well risen and firm)
6 Turn out on to warm plate. Serve with fresh double cream or sweet sauce to taste (see Sauce Section page 136). **Serves 4**

To bake Pudding Turn mixture into $\frac{3}{4}$ to 1 litre / $1\frac{1}{2}$ to 2 pint buttered pie dish. Put into centre of moderately hot oven (190°C / 375°F or Gas No 5) and bake 15 minutes. Reduce temperature to moderate (160°C / 325°F or Gas No 3) and bake a further 35 to 40 minutes (or until wooden cocktail stick inserted into centre of pudding comes out clean). Remove from oven and turn out on to warm plate

Chocolate Pudding

1 Follow recipe and method for Plain Family Pudding (left) but use 125g / 5oz self-raising flour only
2 Sift into bowl with the salt **plus** 15g / $\frac{1}{2}$oz corn-flour and 15g / $\frac{1}{2}$oz cocoa powder.
Serves 4

Coconut Pudding

1 Follow recipe and method for Plain Family Pudding (left) but add 40 to 50g / $1\frac{1}{2}$ to 2oz desiccated coconut with the sugar
2 Add 1 teaspoon vanilla essence with egg and milk.
Serves 4

Date & Walnut Pudding

1 Follow recipe and method for Plain Family Pudding (left)
2 Add 50g / 2oz chopped dates and 25g / 1oz finely chopped walnuts with sugar.
Serves 4

Double Crust Fruit Pie

500g / 1lb apples, rhubarb, gooseberries, plums, damsons, fresh apricots, cooking cherries, blackberries or mixture of fruits
100 to 150g / 4 to 5oz granulated sugar
1 recipe Short Crust Pastry (page 211)
Beaten egg or milk for brushing

1 Prepare fruit according to type
2 Cut Pastry into 2 equal pieces
3 Roll out half and use to line 20cm / 8in lightly buttered flat heatproof plate (or shallow heat-proof pie plate). Cover Pastry – to within 2cm / 1in of edges – with alternate layers of fruit and sugar, beginning and ending with fruit
4 Moisten edges of Pastry with water. Cover with lid, rolled and shaped from rest of Pastry
5 Press edges well together to seal
6 Flake edges by cutting lightly with back of knife then 'ridge' with fork all round
7 Brush with beaten egg or milk. Make 2 slits in top to allow steam to escape then stand Pie on baking tray
8 Bake just above centre of hot oven (220°C / 425°F or Gas No 7) for 20 minutes. Reduce heat to moderate (180°C / 350°F or Gas No 4). Bake further 30 to 45 minutes
9 Remove from oven. Sprinkle top lightly with caster sugar
10 Serve with fresh single or double cream, soured cream, natural yogurt, ice cream or custard. **Serves 4 to 5**

Fruit Crumble

500g / 1lb either cooking apples, rhubarb, gooseberries, damsons, plums, blackberries or red or blackcurrants
100 to 175g / 4 to 6oz granulated sugar, depending on sharpness of fruit

Crumble Topping
150g / 6oz plain flour
75g / 3oz butter
50 to 75g / 2 to 3oz caster sugar

1 Prepare fruit according to type. Put into ¾ to 1 litre / 1½ to 2 pint heatproof dish in layers with granulated sugar
2 Sift flour into bowl and rub in butter finely. Add sugar, then toss ingredients lightly together to mix
3 Sprinkle Crumble thickly and evenly over fruit. Press down lightly with palm of hand then smooth top with knife
4 Put into centre of moderately hot oven (190°C / 375°F or Gas No 5) and bake 15 minutes
5 Reduce temperature to moderate (180°C / 350°F or Gas No 4). Bake further 45 minutes or until top is lightly brown
6 Serve with fresh double cream, soured cream or custard. **Serves 4**

Fruit Pie

1kg / 2lb apples, rhubarb, gooseberries, plums, damsons, fresh apricots, cooking cherries, blackberries or mixture of fruits
175 to 225g / 6 to 8oz granulated sugar, depending on sharpness of fruit
1 recipe Short Crust (page 211), Rough Puff (page 213) or Flaky Pastry (page 214)
Beaten egg or milk for brushing

1 Prepare fruit according to type
2 Fill 1 litre / 2 pint pie dish with alternate layers of fruit and sugar. Begin and end with fruit. Dome fruit in centre so that it supports Pastry
3 Roll out Pastry. Cut into oval or round 4cm / 1½in wider than top of dish
4 Moisten edges of dish with water. Line with strip of Pastry cut from trimmings
5 Moisten strip with water then cover with Pastry lid, pressing edges well together to seal
6 Flake edges by cutting lightly with back of knife then 'ridge' with fork all way round
7 Brush with beaten egg or milk. Make 2 slits in top to allow steam to escape
8 Bake just above centre of hot oven (220°C / 425°F or Gas No 7) for 15 minutes. Reduce temperature to moderate (180°C / 350°F or Gas No 4). Bake further 30 to 45 minutes
9 Remove from oven. Sprinkle top lightly with caster sugar
10 Serve with fresh single or double cream, soured cream, natural yogurt or custard.
Serves 4 to 6

Fresh Fruit Suet Pudding

750g / 1lb 8oz cooking apples, rhubarb, plums, damsons, blackberries, gooseberries, black or redcurrants or mixture of fruits
1 recipe Suet Crust Pastry (page 212)
1 level tablespoon fresh white breadcrumbs
100 to 150g / 4 to 5oz granulated or soft brown sugar
1 tablespoon water

1 Prepare fruit according to type
2 Roll out two-thirds of Pastry and use to line buttered 1 litre / 2 pint pudding basin
3 Fill with alternate layers of breadcrumbs, sugar and fruit, beginning and ending with breadcrumbs
4 Pour in water
5 Moisten edges of lining Pastry with water. Cover with lid rolled from rest of Pastry
6 Press edges of lining and Pastry lid well together to seal
7 Cover securely with buttered greaseproof paper or aluminium foil. Steam steadily for 2½ to 3 hours
8 Serve from basin, with clean table napkin round it.
Serves 4

Coffee Fudge Cream Pie

Short Crust Pastry (page 211) made with
   150g / 6oz flour
2 level tablespoons apricot jam
75g / 3oz butter
75g / 3oz caster sugar
1 standard egg
40g / 1½oz finely chopped shelled walnut halves
100g / 4oz sifted self-raising flour
4 teaspoons liquid coffee essence
2 teaspoons cold milk
150ml / 5fl oz carton soured cream

1 Roll out Pastry. Use to line 20cm / 8in plain or fluted flan ring resting on lightly buttered baking tray
2 Spread base with apricot jam
3 Cream butter and sugar together until light and fluffy. Beat in egg and walnuts
4 Fold in flour alternately with coffee essence and milk. Transfer to pastry case
5 Smooth top with knife. Put into centre of hot oven (220°C / 425°F or Gas No 7) and bake 15 minutes
6 Reduce temperature to moderate (160°C / 325°F or Gas No 3). Bake further 25 to 30 minutes (or until wooden cocktail stick, inserted into centre, comes out clean)
7 Remove from oven. Cover top with soured cream then return to oven for further 2 minutes.
Serves 4 to 6

Steamed Suet Pudding

100g / 4oz plain flour
¼ level teaspoon salt
1½ level teaspoons baking powder
100g / 4oz fresh white breadcrumbs
75g / 3oz caster sugar
75g / 3oz finely shredded suet
1 large egg, beaten
6 to 8 tablespoons cold milk to mix

1 Sift flour, salt and baking powder into bowl
2 Add breadcrumbs, sugar and suet. Mix to soft batter with beaten egg and milk
3 Turn into buttered 1 litre / 2 pint pudding basin and cover securely with buttered greaseproof paper or aluminium foil. Steam steadily for 2½ to 3 hours
4 Turn out on to warm plate. Serve with sweet sauce to taste (see Sauce Section, page 136).
Serves 4

Fair Lady Pudding

1 Follow recipe and method for Steamed Suet Pudding (above)
2 Add finely grated rind of 1 medium-sized orange or lemon with sugar. **Serves 4**

Four-fruit Pudding

1 Follow recipe and method for Steamed Suet Pudding (left)
2 Add 25g / 1oz *each* dates, figs and prunes – all chopped – and 25g / 1oz mixed chopped peel with sugar. **Serves 4**

College Pudding

1 Follow recipe and method for Steamed Suet Pudding (left)
2 Sift 1 level teaspoon mixed spice with flour
3 Add 100g / 4oz mixed dried fruit with sugar (use ½ caster sugar and ½ soft brown). **Serves 4**

Marmalade Pudding

1 Follow recipe and method for Steamed Suet Pudding (left)
2 Put 2 level tablespoons marmalade into bottom of buttered basin before adding pudding mixture.
Serves 4

Syrup or Treacle Pudding

1 Follow recipe and method for Steamed Suet Pudding (left)
2 Put 2 level tablespoons golden syrup or treacle into bottom of buttered basin before adding pudding mixture. **Serves 4**

Spotted Dick

1 Follow recipe and method for Steamed Suet Pudding (left)
2 Add 75g / 3oz currants and 25g / 1oz mixed chopped peel with sugar.
Serves 4

Apple Fritters

3 medium-sized cooking apples
1 recipe Sweet Fritter Batter (page 146)
Deep fat or oil for frying
Sifted icing sugar

1 Peel and core apples. Cut each into ½cm / ¼in thick rings
2 Coat with Fritter Batter. Fry in deep hot fat or oil for 2 to 3 minutes (or until golden)
3 Remove from pan and drain on soft kitchen paper. Dredge thickly with sifted icing sugar. Accompany with fresh single cream, soured cream or natural yogurt.
Serves 4

Apple Turnovers

1 recipe Rough Puff (page 213), Flaky (page 214),
   Cream Cheese Pastry (page 214) or Milk 'Puff'
   Pastry (page 214)
250g/8oz cooking apples
50g/2oz caster sugar
A little lightly beaten egg white
Extra caster sugar

1 Roll out Pastry and cut into six 10cm/4in
squares
2 Peel, core and thinly slice apples. Mix with
sugar. Put equal amounts on to centres of each
square
3 Moisten edges of Pastry with cold water. Fold
each in half to form a triangle, completely enclosing fruit
4 Press edges together to seal. Flake by cutting
lightly with back of knife then 'ridge' with fork
5 Transfer Turnovers to buttered baking tray.
Brush with egg white and sprinkle with sugar
6 Bake towards top of hot oven (220°C/425°F or
Gas No 7) for 20 minutes. Reduce temperature to
moderate (180°C/350°F or Gas No 4). Bake
further 20 minutes
7 Serve with fresh single or double cream or
custard. **Serves 6**

Baked Apple Dumplings

4 medium-sized cooking apples
40g/1½oz granulated sugar
1 level teaspoon finely grated lemon rind or
   1 level teaspoon cinnamon
1 recipe Short Crust Pastry (page 211) or Rich
   Short Crust Pastry (page 212)
Milk for brushing
Sifted icing sugar

1 Peel apples thinly. Remove cores two-thirds of
the way down each apple. (If cut right through,
filling will fall out and make pastry soggy)
2 Mix sugar with lemon rind or cinnamon. Put
equal amounts into apple cavities
3 Cut Pastry into 4 pieces. Roll each out into
circle about 4cm/1½in larger all the way round
than the apples
4 Place apples on centre of each Pastry round.
Moisten edges with water. Wrap Pastry closely
round each apple, pressing joins well together to
seal
5 Stand on lightly buttered baking tray with joins
underneath. Brush with milk. Make a slit in top of
each to allow steam to escape
6 Bake in centre of hot oven (220°C/425°F or
Gas No 7) for 15 minutes. Reduce temperature to
moderate (180°C/350°F or Gas No 4). Bake
further 30 minutes
7 Remove from oven, dredge with sifted icing
sugar and serve with fresh single or double
cream, soured cream, natural yogurt or custard.
Serves 4

Baked Apples with Syrup & Lemon

4 Bramley apples (or other cooking apples)
1 level tablespoon golden syrup
¼ level teaspoon finely grated lemon rind
25g/1oz butter
3 tablespoons warm water

1 Wash apples and wipe dry. Remove cores
two-thirds of the way down each
2 With sharp knife, score line round each apple,
about a third of the way down from top
3 Stand apples in heatproof dish
4 Mix syrup and lemon rind well together. Spoon
equal amounts into apple cavities
5 Top each with large knob of butter. Pour the
warm water into dish
6 Bake just above centre of moderate oven
(180°C/350°F or Gas No 4) for 45 minutes to
1 hour (or until apples puff up and are tender).
Baste at least twice while apples are cooking.
Serve with fresh single or double cream, soured
cream, natural yogurt or custard. **Serves 4**

Pineapple & Lemon Upside-down Pudding

Base
50g/2oz butter
50g/2oz soft brown sugar
1 medium-sized can pineapple rings

Pudding Mixture
200g/8oz self-raising flour
¼ level teaspoon salt
100g/4oz butter
100g/4oz caster sugar
Finely grated rind of 1 medium-sized lemon
2 large eggs
4 to 5 tablespoons cold milk to mix

1 For base, melt butter and stir in sugar. Use to
cover bottom of 1 litre/2 pint buttered pie dish.
Arrange pineapple rings – well drained – over base
and sides
2 For pudding, sift flour and salt into bowl and rub
in butter finely
3 Add sugar and lemon rind. Toss ingredients
lightly together. Mix to fairly soft batter with eggs
and milk
4 Transfer to prepared dish and bake in centre of
moderately hot oven (190°C/375°F or Gas No 5)
for 30 minutes. Reduce temperature to moderate
(180°C/350°F or Gas No 4). Bake further 35 to
45 minutes (or until wooden cocktail stick,
inserted into centre of pudding, comes out clean)
5 Leave in dish 5 minutes. Turn out on to warm
plate
6 Serve with fresh double cream or with
pineapple syrup from can, warmed through
gently.
Serves 4 to 6

Treacle Tart (below) Mince Pies (page 155)

Custard Tart

**Short Crust Pastry (page 211) made with
    150g/6oz flour**
1 level tablespoon fresh white breadcrumbs
300ml/½ pint lukewarm milk
2 standard eggs
Yolk of 1 standard egg
25g/1oz caster sugar
Grated nutmeg

1 Roll out Pastry. Use to line 20 to 23cm/8 to 9in
heatproof buttered pie plate
2 Sprinkle base of Pastry with breadcrumbs.
Stand plate on baking tray
3 Beat milk with eggs, egg yolk and sugar. Strain
into Pastry-lined pie plate
4 Sprinkle top with nutmeg. Put into centre of
moderately hot oven (200°C/400°F or Gas No 6)
5 Bake 15 minutes. Reduce temperature to moderate (160°C/325°F or Gas No 3). Bake further
30 to 45 minutes (or until custard is set)
6 Serve warm. **Serves 4 to 6**

Treacle Tart

**Short Crust Pastry (page 211) made with
    150g/6oz flour**
2 level tablespoons fresh white breadcrumbs
2 level tablespoons black treacle
1 level tablespoon golden syrup
½ level teaspoon finely grated lemon rind
2 teaspoons lemon juice

1 Roll out Pastry. Use to line 20cm/8in heatproof
buttered plate. Trim surplus from edges
2 Mix breadcrumbs with treacle, syrup, lemon
rind and juice. Spread over Pastry to within
2cm/1in of edges. Moisten edges with cold water
3 Cut remaining Pastry into thin strips. Arrange in
criss-cross design over treacle filling
4 Press strips well on to Pastry edges and put
plate on to baking tray. Bake just above centre of
moderately hot oven (200°C/400°F or Gas No 6)
for 30 minutes (or until Pastry is golden). Serve
with fresh single or double cream, soured cream,
natural yogurt or custard. **Serves 4**

Syrup Tart

Follow recipe and method for Treacle Tart
(page 154) but instead of treacle and syrup use
level tablespoons syrup. **Serves 4**

Jam Tart

Follow recipe and method for Treacle Tart
(page 154) but instead of treacle and syrup use
level tablespoons jam
Omit lemon rind and juice. **Serves 4**

Mince Tart

recipe Short Crust (page 211) or Rich Short
  Crust Pastry (page 212)
50g / 1lb mincemeat
Beaten egg
sifted icing sugar

Cut Pastry into 2 equal portions
Roll out one half. Use to line 18 to 20cm / 7 to 8in
flat heatproof plate, lightly buttered
Spread mincemeat over Pastry to within
cm / ½ in of edges. Moisten edges of Pastry with
water
Cover with lid, rolled and shaped from rest of
Pastry. Press edges well together to seal
Flake edges by cutting lightly with the back of a
knife. 'Ridge' with fork all way round
Brush with beaten egg and stand plate on
baking tray. Bake just above centre of hot oven
220°C / 425°F or Gas No 7) for 15 minutes
Reduce temperature to moderately hot
200°C / 400°F or Gas No 6). Bake further 30
minutes
Remove from oven, dredge thickly with icing-
sugar and serve warm with fresh single or double
cream or custard. **Serves 6**

Mince Pies

recipe Short Crust (page 211) or Rich Short
  Crust Pastry (page 212)
50g / 12oz mincemeat
eaten egg for brushing
sifted icing sugar

Roll out Pastry. From it cut 12 rounds with
cm / 3½in plain or fluted biscuit cutter and 12
rounds with 6cm / 2½in biscuit cutter
Use larger rounds to line 12 deep bun tins
Put equal amounts of mincemeat into each. Top
with remaining rounds. Brush with beaten egg
Bake in centre of hot oven (220°C / 425°F or Gas
No 7) for 20 to 25 minutes (or until golden brown)
Remove from tins and dredge thickly with sifted
icing sugar
Serve warm with lightly whipped fresh double
cream or custard. **Serves 4 to 6**

Christmas Pudding

100g / 4oz plain flour
½ level teaspoon mixed spice
¼ level teaspoon grated nutmeg
225g / 8oz fresh white breadcrumbs
275g / 10oz finely shredded suet
225g / 8oz soft brown sugar
350g / 12oz *each* seedless raisins and sultanas
50g / 2oz mixed chopped peel
**50g / 2oz shelled walnut halves or blanched
  almonds**
Finely grated rind of 1 small orange
4 large eggs, beaten
½ wine glass brandy or dry sherry
½ teaspoon almond essence
150ml / ¼ pint milk

1 Sift flour, spice and nutmeg into large bowl. Add
breadcrumbs, suet, sugar, raisins, sultanas, peel,
finely chopped walnuts or almonds and grated
orange rind
2 Toss well together
3 Combine with beaten eggs, brandy or sherry,
almond essence and milk. Mix well
4 Leave overnight in cool. Divide between two
buttered 1 litre / 2 pint basins
5 Cover securely with buttered greaseproof paper
or aluminium foil. Steam steadily for 6 hours,
replenishing water as it boils away
6 Cool 15 minutes in basins. Turn out and leave
until completely cold
7 Wrap in greaseproof paper and then aluminium
foil. Store in cool dry cupboard until needed
8 To serve, unwrap Pudding or Puddings, return
to buttered basin or basins, cover and steam a
further 2 hours. Turn out on to warm dish. Serve
with sweet sauce to taste (see Sauce Section,
page 136) or fresh double cream.
Each Pudding serves 6 to 7

If preferred, puddings may be stored in the basins
in which they are cooked

Eve's or Apple Pudding

500g / 1lb cooking apples
75 to 100g / 3 to 4oz caster sugar
1 recipe Sponge Pudding (page 149)

1 Peel, core and thinly slice apples. Arrange, in
layers, in 1¼ litre / 2½ pint buttered pie dish,
sprinkling sugar between layers
2 Cover with Sponge Pudding mixture
3 Bake in centre of moderate oven (180°C / 350°F
or Gas No 4) for 1 to 1¼ hours (or until wooden
cocktail stick, inserted into centre of sponge
mixture, comes out clean). Accompany with fresh
double cream. **Serves 4 to 5**

If preferred, gooseberries, rhubarb, apple mixed
with blackberries, plums or damsons may be used
instead of apples

Baked Jam Roll

1 recipe Short Crust Pastry (page 211)
225g / 8oz jam
Milk for brushing
Caster sugar

1 Roll out Pastry into 25cm×20cm / 10in×8in rectangle
2 Spread with jam to within 1cm / ½in of edges. Moisten edges with cold water
3 Roll up like Swiss roll, starting from one of the longer sides. Press edges well together to seal
4 Transfer to buttered baking tray, with join underneath. Brush with milk. Sprinkle with caster sugar
5 Bake just above centre of hot oven (220°C / 425°F or Gas No 7) for 20 minutes. Lower heat to moderately hot (190°C / 375°F or Gas No 5). Bake further 20 minutes
6 Serve with fresh single or double cream, natural yogurt or custard. **Serves 4**

Queen of Puddings

75g / 3oz fresh white breadcrumbs
25g / 1oz caster sugar
1 level teaspoon finely grated lemon rind
450ml / ¾ pint cold milk
25g / 1oz butter
Yolks of 2 standard eggs
2 level tablespoons warmed raspberry jam
1 recipe Meringue Topping (page 227)

1 Put breadcrumbs, sugar and lemon rind into basin. Toss lightly together to mix
2 Pour milk into pan. Add butter and heat gently until butter melts
3 Pour on to breadcrumb mixture. Stir well and leave to stand for 30 minutes. Beat in egg yolks
4 Spread into ¾ litre / 1½ pint buttered heatproof dish
5 Put into centre of moderate oven (160°C / 325°F or Gas No 3) and bake 30 minutes (or until firm and set)
6 Remove from oven and spread with jam. Cover with whirls of Meringue
7 Return to oven and bake further 30 to 40 minutes (or until Meringue is pale gold). Accompany with fresh double cream. **Serves 4**

Roly-Poly Pudding

1 recipe Suet Crust Pastry (page 212)
3 to 4 level tablespoons golden syrup, treacle, marmalade or jam
1 level teaspoon finely grated lemon rind

1 Roll out Pastry into 25cm×20cm / 10in×8in rectangle
2 Spread with syrup, treacle, marmalade or jam to within 2cm / 1in of edges. Sprinkle with lemon rind

Apple Amber

500g / 1lb cooking apples
1 tablespoon water
25g / 1oz butter
50 to 75g / 2 to 3oz caster sugar
3 level tablespoons stale cake crumbs (plain cake is best)
1 level teaspoon cinnamon
Yolks of 2 standard eggs
Meringue Topping (page 227)

1 Peel, core and slice apples. Put into pan with water and butter
2 Cook until soft and pulpy. Beat until smooth
3 Add sugar, cake crumbs, cinnamon and egg yolks. Mix well
4 Transfer to ½ litre / 1 pint heatproof dish and top with Meringue
5 Put into centre of slow oven (150°C / 300°F or Gas No 2). Bake 30 minutes (or until Meringue is light gold). Accompany with fresh double cream. **Serves 4**

Baked Banana Sponge

75g / 3oz self-raising flour
Pinch of salt
75g / 3oz butter
75g / 3oz caster sugar
½ level teaspoon finely grated lemon rind
2 small eggs
2 small bananas

1 Sift flour and salt into bowl
2 Cream butter, sugar and lemon rind until light and fluffy. Beat in eggs, singly, adding tablespoon of flour with each
3 Slice in bananas (slices should be about 1cm / ½in thick). Mix well, then gently fold in remaining flour
4 Transfer to well-buttered 20cm×10cm×6cm / 1lb loaf tin. Bake in centre of moderate oven (180°C / 350°F or Gas No 4) for 20 minutes. Reduce temperature (160°C / 325°F or Gas No 3) and bake further 20 to 25 minutes (or until wooden cocktail stick, inserted into centre, comes out clean)
5 Turn out on to warm dish and serve with fresh single cream or custard. **Serves 4**

3 Moisten edges of Pastry with cold water. Roll up loosely like Swiss roll, starting from one of the shorter sides
4 Press edges and join underneath well together to seal. Wrap loosely in buttered aluminium foil
5 Twist ends of foil so that they stay closed. Steam Pudding for 2½ to 3 hours
5 Unwrap and serve with sweet sauce to taste (see Sauce Section, page 136). **Serves 4**

Cold Desserts

Orange and Strawberry Chantilly (below)

Pastry and meringue bases and choux bases should be frozen unfilled. Fresh fruit in season may be puréed and frozen for fruit fools, whips, snows and mousses. Storage time—3 months. Cheese cakes may be frozen made-up. Storage time—4 to 6 months.

Orange & Strawberry Chantilly

3 large oranges
400g / 12oz strawberries
2 to 3 tablespoons sweet white wine (or brandy)
300ml / ½ pint fresh double cream
2 tablespoons milk
50g / 2oz sifted icing sugar
White of 1 standard egg

1 Put oranges into large bowl, cover with boiling water and leave 10 minutes. (This makes the skin and pith easier to remove)
2 Drain oranges, peel and chill.
3 Halve strawberries and put into shallow serving dish
4 Slice oranges thinly, arrange on top of strawberries, sprinkle with the wine or brandy. Chill at least 1 hour
5 Just before serving, whip cream and milk together until thick. Stir in sugar and egg white, beaten to a stiff snow
6 Pile over fruit mixture and serve immediately. Serves 4 to 6

Pineapple Romanoff

1 large fresh pineapple
3 tablespoons Curaçao
250g / 8oz fresh strawberries
300ml / ½ pint fresh double cream
75g / 3oz sifted icing sugar
Finely grated rind and juice of ½ lemon

1 Cut pineapple in half lengthwise, cutting through leafy crown as well. (Each half should have own crown)
2 Remove and discard core. Gently scoop out flesh and cut into neat cubes
3 Put pineapple cubes into a bowl, mix with the Curaçao and chill for at least 2 hours
4 About 1 hour before serving, slice all but 4 strawberries. Whip the cream thick then stir in sugar, grated lemon rind and juice, pineapple cubes and juices and sliced strawberries
5 Mix well, spoon into pineapple halves and chill at least ½ an hour
6 Just before serving, decorate with remaining 4 whole strawberries. Serves 4

Gooseberry Whip

250g/8oz gooseberries
3 tablespoons water
25 to 50g/1 to 2oz granulated sugar
2 level teaspoons gelatine
4 tablespoons hot water
¼ level teaspoon finely grated lemon rind
4 tablespoons fresh double cream
2 teaspoons milk
White of 1 standard egg
Green food colouring

Decoration
4 tablespoons fresh double cream, whipped
Leaves cut from angelica

1 Top and tail gooseberries. Put into pan with 3 tablespoons water
2 Bring slowly to the boil. Cover pan with lid and simmer until fruit is soft
3 Remove from heat. Sweeten to taste with sugar. Either rub through sieve or liquidise
4 Put gelatine and hot water in a basin. Stir until dissolved, over pan of boiling water
5 Add to gooseberry mixture with lemon rind. Leave in the cold until just beginning to thicken
6 Whip cream and milk together until lightly stiff. Gradually stir in fruit mixture then gently fold in egg white, beaten to stiff snow
7 Tint pale green with colouring. Turn into large serving bowl and chill until firm and set
8 Just before serving, decorate with whipped cream and angelica. **Serves 4**

Frosted Fruit Mould

1 lemon-flavoured jelly
5 tablespoons boiling water
150ml/¼ pint fairly thick apricot purée, made from stewed or canned fruit
2 level teaspoons finely grated lemon rind
150g/5oz carton natural yogurt

Decoration
16 black grapes, in pairs
White of 1 small egg, lightly beaten
2 to 3 level tablespoons caster sugar

1 Put jelly and 5 tablespoons boiling water into a saucepan and stand over very low heat until jelly dissolves
2 Pour into a measuring jug and make up to 300ml/½ pint with cold water. Stir in the fruit purée and lemon rind
3 Leave until cold but still liquid, then gradually beat into the yogurt
4 When evenly combined, transfer to ½ litre/1 pint fancy mould, first rinsed with cold water
5 Chill for at least 2 hours
6 Before serving, frost grapes by dipping in the beaten egg white then tossing in the caster sugar
7 Turn mould out on to a plate and surround with grapes. **Serves 4**

Summer Pudding

6 large slices stale bread
100g/4oz granulated sugar
5 tablespoons water
750g/1lb 8oz soft summer fruits (either rhubarb, raspberries, strawberries, gooseberries, stoned cherries, black or redcurrants, or mixture of fruits)
150ml/¼ pint fresh double cream
1 tablespoon milk

1 Remove crusts from bread. Cut slices into neat fingers
2 Put sugar and water into pan and heat slowly until sugar melts, stirring
3 Add fruit and simmer gently for about 7 to 10 minutes (gooseberries, blackcurrants may take a few minutes longer)
4 Line base and sides of 1 litre/2 pint pudding basin with bread fingers. Add half the hot fruit mixture. Cover with more bread fingers
5 Pour in rest of fruit mixture and top with remaining bread fingers
6 Cover with saucer or plate. Put a heavy weight on top
7 Refrigerate or leave in cold pantry overnight
8 Turn out on to plate. Serve with the cream, whipped with the milk until lightly stiff.
Serves 4 to 6

Rich Fruit Fool

500g/1lb either gooseberries, apples, black or redcurrants, rhubarb, blackberries or rasp-berries
3 tablespoons water
75 to 175g/3 to 6oz caster sugar to sweeten, depending on sharpness of fruit
300ml/½ pint fresh double cream
2 tablespoons milk
Red or green food colouring

Decoration
4 tablespoons fresh double cream, whipped
About 25g/1oz finely chopped, shelled walnut halves or finely chopped toasted almonds

1 Prepare fruit according to type. Put into pan with the water
2 Bring slowly to the boil, cover with lid and simmer until fruit is soft
3 Remove from heat. Add sugar to taste. Either rub through sieve or liquidise. Leave until completely cold
4 Whip cream and milk together until lightly stiff then gradually fold in the fruit purée
5 If Fool is pale (which it will be if made from apples or gooseberries) tint pale pink or green
6 Transfer to 4 sundae glasses and chill
7 Before serving, whip cream until thick, pipe whirls on top of each Fool, then sprinkle with nuts. **Serves 4**

Custard Cream Fruit Fool

1 Follow recipe and method for Rich Fruit Fool (page 158) but use half the cream and milk and 150ml / $\frac{1}{4}$ pint cold custard
2 Mix the custard with the fruit purée then fold into the whipped cream and milk. **Serves 4**

Custard Fruit Fool

Follow recipe and method for Rich Fruit Fool (page 158) but instead of cream and milk, combine 300ml / $\frac{1}{2}$ pint fairly thick cold custard with the fruit purée. **Serves 4**

Lemon Milk Jelly

4 level teaspoons gelatine
3 tablespoons hot water
50g / 2oz caster sugar
1 level teaspoon finely grated lemon rind
600ml / 1 pint milk
Yellow food colouring

1 Put gelatine and hot water in a basin. Stir until dissolved, over pan of boiling water
2 Put sugar, lemon rind and milk into saucepan. Stand over very low heat until sugar dissolves
3 When gelatine and milk are both lukewarm, combine by pouring milk gently on to the gelatine
4 Stir well and tint pale yellow with colouring
5 Pour into a $\frac{3}{4}$ litre / $1\frac{1}{2}$ pint mould, first rinsed with cold water
6 Leave in cool place until set. Turn out on to a serving plate. **Serves 4**

Orange Milk Jelly

1 Follow recipe and method for Lemon Milk Jelly (above) but use grated orange rind instead of lemon rind
2 Colour pale orange wth orange food colouring. **Serves 4**

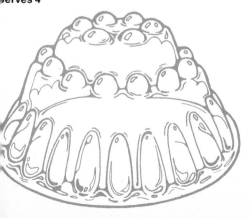

Chocolate Milk Jelly

1 Follow recipe and method for Lemon Milk Jelly (left) but omit lemon rind and colouring
2 Dissolve 50g / 2oz plain chocolate with the sugar in the milk
3 Stir in 1 teaspoon vanilla essence. **Serves 4**

Coffee Milk Jelly

1 Follow recipe and method for Lemon Milk Jelly (left) but omit lemon rind and colouring
2 Instead, add 2 to 3 level teaspoons instant coffee powder to the milk. **Serves 4**

Vanilla Milk Jelly

1 Follow recipe and method for Lemon Milk Jelly (left) but use 1 or 2 teaspoons vanilla essence instead of lemon rind
2 Colour pale pink or green with red or green food colouring. **Serves 4**

Raspberry Cream Ring

1 lemon-flavoured jelly
5 tablespoons boiling water
450ml / $\frac{3}{4}$ pint milk
Finely grated rind and juice of 1 large lemon
1 level tablespoon caster sugar
40g / 1$\frac{1}{2}$oz semolina
300ml / $\frac{1}{2}$ pint fresh double cream
Whites of 2 standard eggs

Decoration
250 to 400g / 8 to 12oz fresh raspberries

1 Put jelly and 5 tablespoons boiling water into a saucepan. Stand over very low heat until jelly dissolves
2 Pour into measuring jug and make up to 300ml / $\frac{1}{2}$ pint with cold water. Leave on one side
3 Put milk, grated lemon rind and sugar into a saucepan. Heat to lukewarm
4 Sprinkle in semolina and cook slowly, stirring, until mixture comes to the boil and thickens
5 Simmer gently for 3 minutes. Remove from heat then stir in the melted jelly and lemon juice
6 Leave in cold until just beginning to thicken and set
7 Whip cream until lightly stiff. Beat egg whites to stiff snow
8 Fold cream and beaten egg whites alternately into cooled jelly and semolina mixture. Transfer to 1 litre / 2 pint ring mould, first rinsed with cold water
9 Chill until firm and set. Turn out on to plate and fill centre with raspberries.
Serves 4

Blancmange

3 level tablespoons cornflour
600ml / 1 pint milk
40g / 1½oz caster sugar
1 teaspoon vanilla essence
15g / ½oz butter

1 Mix cornflour to smooth paste with a little of the cold milk
2 Warm remainder, combine with cornflour paste, then return to pan
3 Cook, stirring, until mixture comes to boil and thickens. Reduce heat to low and simmer 3 minutes
4 Remove from heat and stir in remaining ingredients
5 Pour into ½ litre / 1 pint mould, first rinsed with cold water, then cool
6 Refrigerate until cold and firm. Turn out on to plate
7 Serve with stewed or canned fruit.
Serves 4

Lemon Blancmange

Follow recipe and method for Blancmange (above) but add 1 level teaspoon finely grated lemon rind and a few drops of yellow colouring to the milk while it is warming. **Serves 4**

Orange Blancmange

Follow recipe and method for Blancmange (above) but add 1 level teaspoon finely grated orange rind and a few drops of orange colouring to the milk while it is warming. **Serves 4**

Coffee Blancmange

Follow recipe and method for Blancmange (above) but add 2 to 3 level teaspoons instant coffee powder to the milk while it is warming. **Serves 4**

Honey Blancmange

Follow recipe and method for Blancmange (above) but use 1 tablespoon honey instead of the sugar. **Serves 4**

Extra Creamy Blancmange

Follow recipe and method for Blancmange (above) but use either 600ml / 1 pint Channel Island milk or 300ml / ½ pint of your usual milk and 300ml / ½ pint fresh single cream. **Serves 4**

Spiced Apple Whip

175g / 6oz cooking apples, weighed after peeling and coring
1 clove
¼ level teaspoon mixed spice
½ level teaspoon finely grated lemon rind
3 tablespoons cold water
25 to 40g / 1 to 1½oz granulated sugar
2 level teaspoons gelatine
4 tablespoons hot water
4 tablespoons fresh double cream
2 teaspoons milk
White of 1 standard egg
Red food colouring

Decoration
4 tablespoons fresh double cream, whipped
8 glacé cherries

1 Slice apples thinly and put into a saucepan with the clove, spice, lemon rind and cold water
2 Bring slowly to the boil, cover pan with lid and simmer until fruit is soft
3 Remove from heat. Remove clove. Sweeten to taste with sugar. Either rub through sieve or liquidise
4 Put gelatine and hot water in a basin. Stir until dissolved, over a pan of boiling water
5 Add to apple mixture and leave in cold until just beginning to thicken and set
6 Whip cream and milk together until lightly stiff. Gradually stir in fruit mixture then gently fold in egg white, beaten to a stiff snow
7 Tint pale pink. Turn into serving bowl and chill until firm and set
8 Just before serving, decorate with whipped cream and whole cherries. **Serves 4**

Orange Snow Creams

1 orange-flavoured jelly
5 tablespoons boiling water
150ml / ¼ pint fresh double cream
Whites of 2 standard eggs

Decoration
Fresh mint leaves or glacé cherries

1 Put jelly and 5 tablespoons boiling water into a saucepan. Stand over a very low heat until jelly dissolves
2 Pour into a measuring jug and make up to 450ml / ¾ pint with cold water. Leave in cool place until just beginning to thicken and set
3 Whip cream until lightly stiff. Beat egg whites to stiff snow
4 Turn jelly into large bowl and whisk until foamy. Fold in whipped cream alternately with beaten egg whites
5 When smooth and well blended, transfer to 4 sundae glasses and chill until firm
6 Just before serving, decorate with mint leaves or halved glacé cherries. **Serves 4**

Pots-au-Chocolat (below)

Pots-au-Chocolat

75g / 3oz plain chocolate
25g / 1oz butter
Yolks and whites of 3 standard eggs
1 tablespoon warm water
150ml / ¼ pint fresh double cream

1 Break up chocolate and put into basin standing over saucepan of hot water. Add butter and leave until both have melted, stirring once or twice
2 Beat in egg yolks. When mixture is smooth, remove from heat and stir in warm water
3 Beat egg whites to stiff snow and gently fold into chocolate mixture
4 Transfer to 4 individual dishes or sundae glasses and chill
5 Just before serving, decorate each with the cream, whipped until lightly stiff. **Serves 4**

Pots-au-Chocolat with Coffee

Follow recipe and method for Pots-au-Chocolat (left) but add 2 level teaspoons instant coffee powder with the butter.
Serves 4

Pots-au-Chocolat with Sherry, Brandy or Rum

Follow recipe and method for Pots-au-Chocolat (left) but omit water. Use instead
1 tablespoon lukewarm sherry, brandy or rum.
Serves 4

Peach Sherbet

3 level teaspoons gelatine
6 tablespoons hot water
1 level tablespoon granulated sugar
150ml / ¼ pint peach purée, made from canned
** peaches**
2 tablespoons lemon juice
Whites of 2 standard eggs

Decoration
150ml / ¼ pint fresh double cream, whipped
Cinnamon or blanched and chopped pistachio
** nuts or chopped almonds or toasted coconut**

1 Put gelatine and hot water in a basin. Stir until
dissolved, over a pan of boiling water.
2 Add sugar. Stir in peach purée and lemon juice
3 When cold and just beginning to thicken and
set, fold in egg whites, beaten to stiff snow
4 Pile into 4 sundae glasses and chill until set
5 Just before serving, decorate each with whipped
cream. Dust cream with cinnamon or sprinkle
with nuts or coconut. **Serves 4**

Apricot Sherbet

1 Follow recipe and method for Peach Sherbet
(above) but use apricot purée instead of peach
2 Decorate with cream and sprinkle with chopped
nuts, coconut or chopped glacé cherries.
Serves 4

Junket

600ml / 1 pint ordinary Pasteurised (or Channel
** Island) milk**
2 level teaspoons caster sugar
1 teaspoon essence of rennet

1 Put milk and sugar into saucepan and warm to
blood heat. The temperature should be no more
than 36°C / 98°F. (To test this, dip the tip of the
little finger in the milk. It should strike neither hot
nor cold but should feel comfortably warm.)
2 Pour milk into serving dish, stir in rennet and
leave for 1½ to 2 hours at room temperature
3 After junket has set, it can be refrigerated and
served very cold. **Serves 4 to 6**

Sterilised milk and UHT are **not** suitable for
junket making since the junkets will not set
satisfactorily; homogenised milk can be used if a
softer dessert is preferred.

Coffee Junket

Follow recipe and method for Junket (above) but
stir in 2 level teaspoons instant coffee powder
with sugar. **Serves 4 to 6**

Fresh Lemon Junket

1 Follow recipe and method for Junket (left) but
stir in 1 level teaspoon finely grated lemon rind
with the sugar
2 Colour pale yellow with food colouring before
adding rennet. **Serves 4 to 6**

Fresh Orange Junket

1 Follow recipe and method for Junket (left) but
stir in 1 level teaspoon finely grated orange rind
with the sugar
2 Colour pale orange with food colouring before
adding rennet. **Serves 4 to 6**

Vanilla Honeycomb Mould

4 level teaspoons gelatine
4 tablespoons hot water
Yolks and whites of 2 standard eggs
50g / 2oz caster sugar
600ml / 1 pint milk
1 teaspoon vanilla essence

1 Put gelatine and hot water in a basin. Stir until
dissolved, over a pan of boiling water.
2 Beat egg yolks and sugar together until thick.
Transfer to double saucepan (or basin standing
over saucepan of simmering water)
3 Add milk. Cook, stirring, until custard thickens
and coats back of spoon thinly. (Do not boil or
mixture will curdle.)
4 Remove from heat and add vanilla and dissolve
gelatine
5 Whisk egg whites to stiff snow and fold into
custard mixture
6 Pour into ¾ to 1 litre / 1½ to 2 pint mould, first
rinsed with cold water
7 Chill until firm and set. Turn out on to plate.
Serves 4 to 6

If separate layers are preferred, bring mixture just
up to boil after egg whites have been added and
pour into the mould straight away. Cool and chill.

Lemon Honeycomb Mould

Follow recipe and method for Vanilla Honeycomb
Mould (above) but use 1 level teaspoon finely
grated lemon rind instead of vanilla. **Serves 4 to 6**

Orange Honeycomb Mould

Follow recipe and method for Vanilla Honeycomb
Mould (above) but use 1 level teaspoon finely
grated orange rind instead of vanilla.
Serves 4 to 6

Crème Café

150ml / ¼ pint strong black coffee
3 level teaspoons gelatine
450ml / ¾ pint milk
50g / 2oz semolina
75g / 3oz caster sugar
Yolks and whites of 2 standard eggs
150ml / ¼ pint fresh double cream

Decoration
About 50g / 2oz grated plain chocolate

1 Bring coffee to boil, remove from heat and add gelatine. Stir briskly until dissolved. Leave to cool
2 Put milk into pan, heat to lukewarm, then sprinkle in the semolina. Cook, stirring all the time, until the mixture comes to boil and thickens
3 Lower heat and simmer for 3 minutes
4 Remove from heat and beat in sugar, egg yolks and dissolved gelatine and coffee. Leave in the cool until just beginning to thicken and set
5 Beat cream until lightly stiff. Whisk egg whites to stiff snow
6 Fold cream and beaten whites alternately into semolina mixture. When evenly combined, transfer to serving dish
7 Chill until lightly set. Just before serving, sprinkle with grated chocolate. **Serves 4 to 6**

Crème Caramel

50g / 2oz granulated sugar
2 tablespoons cold water
2 teaspoons boiling water
3 large eggs
300ml / ½ pint milk
25g / 1oz caster sugar
½ teaspoon vanilla essence
150ml / ¼ pint fresh single cream

1 Brush ½ litre / 1 pint heatproof dish with melted butter
2 Put granulated sugar and cold water into a small heavy-based pan. Stand over low heat and stir until sugar dissolves
3 Bring to boil, then boil more briskly – without stirring – until syrup turns a deep gold. Remove from heat and stir in boiling water. Pour into heatproof dish
4 Tilt dish quickly so that base is completely covered with caramel
5 Beat eggs and milk well together. Add sugar and vanilla and mix well
6 Strain into dish (any sugar remaining in strainer should be rubbed through). Stand dish in roasting tin containing enough cold water to come halfway up the sides of the dish
7 Put into centre of moderate oven (160°C / 325°F or Gas No 3) and cook for ¾ to 1 hour
8 Remove from oven and cool. Turn out on to serving dish when completely cold. Serve chilled
9 Serve single cream separately. **Serves 4**

Crème Orange

1 Follow recipe and method for Crème Café (left) but use 150ml / ¼ pint fresh orange juice instead of the coffee
2 Beat in 1 level teaspoon finely grated orange rind with the sugar. **Serves 4 to 6**

Crème Brulée ('Burnt' Cream)

Yolks of 4 standard eggs
300ml / ½ pint fresh double cream
3 level tablespoons sifted icing sugar
1 teaspoon vanilla essence
Caster sugar

1 Beat egg yolks thoroughly
2 Heat cream until hot in double saucepan (or basin standing over saucepan of simmering water)
3 Pour hot cream on to yolks, beating all the time
4 Return mixture to saucepan or basin. Add icing sugar and vanilla
5 Cook without boiling, stirring all the time, until mixture thickens and coats back of spoon heavily
6 Remove from heat, pour into ½ litre / 1 pint buttered baking dish and chill overnight
7 About 1 hour before serving, sprinkle ½cm / ¼in thick layer of caster sugar over the top
8 Stand under hot grill and leave until sugar starts to turn deep gold and caramelise
9 Remove from heat and chill again
10 Can be accompanied with cold stewed apricots or gooseberries. **Serves 4**

Small Crèmes Caramel

1 Follow recipe and method for Crème Caramel (left). Very carefully spoon equal amounts of hot caramel into 4 individual, well-buttered metal moulds
2 Strain in custard mixture then bake for ½ an hour
3 Leave until completely cold before unmoulding. **Serves 4**

Lemon Cheesecake (below) Fresh Grape Flan (page 165)

Chocolate Hazelnut Flan

1 Follow recipe and method for Almond and Apricot Flan (page 170) but use raspberry jam instead of apricot and ground hazelnuts instead of almonds
2 Cover top of cold flan with 150ml / $\frac{1}{4}$ pint fresh double cream, whipped until stiff with 1 tablespoon milk and sweetened to taste with sifted icing sugar
3 Decorate by sprinkling grated plain chocolate thickly over the top. **Serve 4 to 6**

Lemon Cheesecake

150g / 6oz digestive biscuits
75g / 3oz butter, melted
225g / 8oz Cottage cheese
150ml / $\frac{1}{4}$ pint fresh double cream
50g / 2oz caster sugar
Grated rind and juice of 1 lemon

1 Crush biscuits. Mix with melted butter and use half to cover base of 18cm / 7in flan case. Chill
2 Rub Cottage cheese through sieve. Whip cream until thick
3 Fold Cottage cheese, sugar, lemon rind and juice into cream
4 Spread mixture over crumbs. Top with a lattice of remaining crumbs. Chill for 1 hour before serving. **Serves 6**

Pineapple Cheesecake

1 Follow recipe and method for Lemon Cheesecake (left) but use 1 small can drained crushed pineapple, instead of lemon rind and juice and only 25g / 1oz caster sugar.
Serves 6

Almond and Orange Cheesecake

1 Follow recipe and method for Lemon Cheesecake (left) but add $\frac{1}{2}$ to 1 teaspoon almond essence to biscuit crumb mixture
2 Instead of lemon rind and juice add 1 teaspoon finely grated orange rind and 2 tablespoons natural yogurt to cream
3 Decorate with a lattice of remaining crumbs and 1 thinly sliced orange. **Serves 6**

Cherry Cheesecake

1 Follow recipe and method for Lemon Cheesecake (left) but use only 75g / 3oz digestive biscuits and 40g / 1$\frac{1}{2}$ oz butter for base and omit lattice of crumbs
2 Chill Cheesecake until firm. Just before serving, spread top with $\frac{1}{2}$ can cherry pie filling. **Serves 6**

Berry Flan

This flan has a layer of French Custard Filling underneath the fruit to prevent the pastry from becoming wet and soggy.

1 recipe Sweet Flan Pastry (page 214)
Yolk of 1 standard egg
25g / 1oz caster sugar
15g / ½oz flour
½ teaspoon vanilla essence
150ml / ¼ pint milk
500g / 1lb raspberries, strawberries or logan-
berries
2 tablespoons redcurrant jelly
150ml / ¼ pint fresh double cream
1 tablespoon milk
1 level tablespoon sifted icing sugar
2 teaspoons orange juice or sherry

1 Roll out pastry. Use it to line a 15 to 18cm / 6 to 7in fluted flan ring resting on lightly buttered baking tray. Prick well all over. Line with aluminium foil (to prevent pastry rising as it cooks). Bake just above centre of moderate oven (200°C / 400°F or Gas No 6) for 15 minutes
2 Remove foil. Return flan to oven. Bake further 15 minutes (or until crisp and golden). Remove and cool
3 Beat egg yolk and sugar together until thick and light. Stir in flour and vanilla and gradually blend in milk
4 Pour into small saucepan and cook, stirring, until mixture comes to boil and thickens. Simmer 3 minutes. Remove from heat and cool
5 When completely cold, spread over base of flan case, cover with berries and brush with melted redcurrant jelly
6 Beat cream and milk together until thick. Stir in sugar and either orange juice or sherry
7 Pipe or spoon mixture over fruit filling. Chill for a good ½ hour before serving.
Serves 6

Peach or Apricot Flan

1 Follow recipe and method for Berry Flan (above) but use well-drained peach slices or apricot halves instead of berry fruit
2 Brush with melted apricot jam instead of red-currant jelly.
Serves 6

Fresh Grape Flan

1 Follow recipe and method for Berry Flan (above) but cover filling with alternate rows of halved and seeded black and green grapes instead of berry fruit
2 Brush with melted apricot jam instead of red-currant jelly. **Serves 6**

Glazed Apple Flan

1 Follow recipe and method for Berry Flan (left) but cover filling with thin slices of peeled apple, poached in syrup (made from 100g / 4oz granulated sugar and 4 tablespoons water) and then drained
2 Sprinkle apples with caster sugar
3 Put under hot grill until sugar just starts turning golden
4 Chill before decorating with cream mixture.
Serves 6

Peaches Mistral

4 canned peach halves
100g / 4oz strawberries
25g / 1oz sifted icing sugar
150ml / ¼ pint fresh double cream
1 tablespoon milk
12 blanched and toasted almonds

1 Drain peach halves thoroughly and put on to 4 individual plates, cut sides uppermost
2 Slice strawberries, mix with icing sugar then spoon equal amounts into peach cavities
3 Whip cream and milk together until thick. Pipe whirls over each peach half
4 Decorate with whole almonds. Chill at least ½ an hour before serving. **Serves 4**

Loganberry Meringue Basket

1 Meringue Basket (page 226)
300ml / ½ pint double cream
3 tablespoons milk
2 teaspoons Grand Marnier or Cointreau
75 to 100g / 3 to 4oz sifted icing sugar
500g / 1lb fresh loganberries

1 Put Meringue Basket on serving dish
2 Whip cream and milk together until thick. Gently stir in liqueur, sugar to taste and half of the loganberries
3 Pile into Basket and stud top with remaining berries
4 Chill thoroughly before serving.
Serves 4 to 6

Strawberry or Raspberry Meringue Basket

1 Follow recipe and method for Loganberry Meringue Basket (above), but use strawberries or raspberries instead of the loganberries
2 Cut half the strawberries into slices or use half of the whole raspberries and stir into the cream. Stud the top with whole berries.
Serves 4 to 6

Fruit Salad Meringue Basket

1 Follow recipe and method for Loganberry Meringue Basket (page 165) but omit berry fruit
2 Pile cream into Basket. Cover top with rings of sliced bananas (first dipped in lemon juice to prevent browning), cubes of pineapple, halved black and green grapes (with seeds removed), halved and pitted canned red cherries, drained canned peach slices and drained mandarin oranges
4 Brush fruit with melted apricot jam just before serving **Serves 4 to 6**

Crème Monte Carlo

1 can mandarin oranges
300ml / ½ pint fresh double cream
2 tablespoons milk
2 level tablespoons sifted icing sugar
1 level teaspoon finely grated tangerine rind (optional)
6 meringue halves, bought or home made

1 Reserve 8 mandarin segments for decoration
2 Divide remainder, with syrup, between 4 sundae glasses
3 Whip cream and milk together until mixture stands in soft peaks then stir in sugar and tangerine rind if used
4 Break up meringues into small pieces and fold into cream mixture
5 Pile over fruit in glasses. Decorate each with 2 mandarin segments
6 Chill well before serving. **Serves 4**

Strawberry Choux Ring

1 recipe Choux Pastry (page 214)
300ml / ½ pint fresh double cream
2 tablespoons milk
1 level teaspoon vanilla essence
100g / 4oz sifted icing sugar
400g / 12oz fresh strawberries, sliced

1 Using a forcing bag and 1cm / ½in plain icing tube, pipe a thick 18cm / 7in ring on a buttered baking tray
2 Put into centre of moderately hot oven (200°C / 400°F or Gas No 6) and bake 15 minutes
3 Reduce temperature to moderate (180°C / 350°F or Gas No 4). Bake further 30 minutes (or until well puffed and golden)
4 Cool on wire rack
5 About 1 hour before serving, cut ring in half horizontally. Beat cream and milk together until thick. Gently stir in vanilla, 75g / 3oz icing sugar and sliced strawberries
6 Pile mixture into bottom half of ring. Replace top and dredge with remaining icing sugar
7 Chill and serve. **Serves 5 to 6**

Charlotte Mocha

4 level teaspoons gelatine
4 tablespoons hot water
Yolks and whites of 2 standard eggs
2 level tablespoons caster sugar
300ml / ½ pint milk
100g / 4oz plain chocolate
150ml / ¼ pint strong black coffee
About 20 Boudoir biscuits

Decoration
150ml / ¼ pint fresh double cream, whipped

1 Put gelatine and hot water in a basin. Stir until dissolved, over a pan of boiling water
2 Put egg yolks and sugar into double saucepan (or basin standing over pan of simmering water). Beat until very thick and pale in colour
3 Heat milk to lukewarm. Combine with beaten yolks and sugar. Cook, stirring, until custard thickens slightly
4 Remove from heat, add dissolved gelatine and mix well
5 Cover base of 15cm / 6in soufflé dish, Charlotte mould or cake tin with 5 tablespoons custard. Chill
6 Break up chocolate and put into basin standing over pan of hot water. Leave until melted, stirring once or twice
7 Add coffee. Mix thoroughly and combine with remaining custard. Fold in egg whites, whipped until stiff
8 Arrange biscuits close together round sides of dish, mould or cake tin. Fill with custard mixture
9 Chill until firm and set
10 Just before serving, trim biscuits level with filling then turn out on to a plate
11 Decorate with whipped cream. **Serves 5 to 6**

Chocolate Apricot Trifle

1 cream-filled chocolate Swiss roll
1 medium-sized can apricot halves
2 tablespoons orange squash or brandy
150ml / ¼ pint fresh double cream
1 tablespoon milk
2 level tablespoons sifted icing sugar
White of 1 standard egg

Decoration
50g / 2oz grated plain chocolate

1 Cut Swiss roll into about 10 slices. Arrange over base of shallow serving dish, overlapping if necessary
2 Moisten with 4 tablespoons syrup from apricots mixed with squash or brandy. Arrange apricots on top
3 Whip cream and milk together until thick. Stir in sugar then fold in the egg white, beaten until stiff
4 Pile over apricots and chill
5 Just before serving, sprinkle with grated chocolate. **Serves 4 to 6**

Strawberry Mousse

400g / 12oz strawberries
1 tablespoon orange juice (or sherry, Cointreau
or Grand Marnier)
50 to 75g / 2 to 3oz sifted icing sugar
300ml / ½ pint fresh double cream
Whites of 2 standard eggs

Decoration
12 extra strawberries

1 Either crush strawberries finely or rub through a
sieve or liquidise
2 Add orange juice or alternative, then sweeten to
taste with icing sugar
3 Whip cream until lightly stiff. Beat egg whites to
stiff snow
4 Fold cream and beaten whites alternately into
fruit mixture. Pile into 4 sundae glasses
5 Chill well. Just before serving, decorate each
with whole strawberries. **Serves 4**

Raspberry Mousse

Follow recipe and method for Strawberry Mousse
(above) but use 400g / 12oz fresh raspberries
instead of the strawberries. **Serves 4**

Pear Condé

600ml / 1 pint milk
25g / 1oz caster sugar
75g / 3oz washed pudding rice
Strip of lemon rind
150ml / ¼ pint fresh double cream
8 canned pear halves
4 to 5 level tablespoons apricot jam

Decoration
8 glacé cherries
16 leaves cut from angelica

1 Put milk, sugar, rice and lemon rind into double
saucepan. Cook very slowly, stirring occasionally,
until rice is tender and swollen and most of milk
has been absorbed (about 1½ to 2 hours)
2 Remove strip of lemon rind. Spread rice into
shallow serving dish
3 Leave until cold and then chill
4 Just before serving, whip cream until thick.
Arrange pear halves, cut side down, on chilled
rice then brush with melted apricot jam
5 Decorate with the whipped cream, halved
cherries and angelica. **Serves 4**

Peach Condé

Follow recipe and method for Pear Condé (above)
but use 8 canned peach halves instead of the
pears. **Serves 4**

Syllabub (below)

Syllabub

150ml / ¼ pint white wine
2 tablespoons lemon juice
2 level teaspoons finely grated lemon rind
75g / 3oz caster sugar
300ml / ½ pint fresh double cream

1 Put wine, lemon juice, rind and sugar into bowl.
Leave for minimum of 3 hours
2 Add cream and whip until mixture stands in soft
peaks
3 Transfer to 6 sundae glasses. Leave in a cool
place for several hours before serving. **Serves 6**

Lemon Meringue Pie

Short Crust Pastry, made with 150g / 6oz flour (page 211)
2 level tablespoons cornflour
50g / 2oz caster sugar
Finely grated rind and juice of 2 large lemons
150ml / ¼ pint water
Yolks of 2 standard eggs
15g / ½oz butter
1 recipe Meringue Topping (page 227)

1 Roll out pastry. Use it to line a 15 to 18cm / 7 to 8in fluted flan ring resting on lightly buttered baking tray. Prick well all over, line with aluminium foil (to prevent pastry rising as it cooks). Bake just above centre of a moderate oven (200°C / 400°F or Gas No 6) for 15 minutes
2 Remove foil. Return flan to oven. Bake further 15 minutes (or until crisp and golden). Remove from oven
3 To make filling, put cornflour, sugar and lemon rind into a basin. Mix to smooth paste with a little of the cold water
4 Heat rest of water with the lemon juice. Combine with paste then return to pan
5 Cook, stirring, until mixture comes to boil and thickens. Simmer 3 minutes
6 Beat in yolks and butter. Cook gently for further minute then pour into flan case
7 Pile meringue on top. Bake as directed for Meringue Topping (page 227)
8 Serve very cold.
Serves 4 to 6

Oeufs à la Neige (Snow Eggs)

Yolks and whites of 3 standard eggs
100g / 4oz caster sugar
450ml / ¾ pint milk
1 teaspoon vanilla essence or ½ level teaspoon finely grated lemon rind

1 Beat egg whites to a stiff snow
2 Add 50g / 2oz sugar and continue beating until mixture is shiny and stands in firm peaks
3 Put milk into saucepan. Heat slowly until bubbles just start appearing (it must never boil)
4 Reduce heat and drop small mounds of egg white mixture, from a tablespoon, into the milk
5 Poach gently for 4 minutes turning once
6 Lift out carefully with draining spoon and stand on clean, folded tea-towel
7 Pour warm milk on to egg yolks and whisk lightly
8 Transfer to a double saucepan (or basin standing over saucepan of simmering water). Add remaining sugar and cook, stirring all the time, until custard thickens. Do not allow to boil
9 Remove from heat, add vanilla or lemon rind, and cool
10 Pour into serving dish, arrange poached meringues on the top and chill. **Serves 4**

Orange Chiffon Pie

Short Crust Pastry made with 150g / 6oz flour (page 211)
1 orange flavour jelly
150ml / ¼ pint boiling water
Yolks and whites of 2 standard eggs
75g / 3oz caster sugar

Decoration
150ml / ¼ pint fresh double cream, whipped
50 to 75g / 2 to 3oz green or black grapes

1 Roll out pastry. Use it to line an 18 to 20cm / 7 to 8in fluted flan ring resting on lightly buttered baking tray. Prick well all over. Line with aluminium foil (to prevent pastry rising as it cooks).
2 Bake just above centre of hot oven (220°C / 425°F or Gas No 7) for 15 minutes
3 Remove foil and return flan to oven. Bake further 15 minutes (or until crisp and golden). Remove from oven and cool
4 To make filling, put jelly and water into saucepan. Stand over very low heat until jelly dissolves, stirring all the time
5 Remove from heat. Leave in cool until just beginning to thicken and set
6 Beat egg yolks and sugar together until very thick and pale in colour. Gradually whisk in cooled jelly
7 Beat egg whites to stiff snow. Gently fold in jelly and egg yolk mixture
8 Pile into baked pastry case and chill
9 Before serving, decorate with whipped cream and halved and seeded grapes.
Serves 4 to 6

Trifle Alexandra

Stale sponge or Madeira cake
1 medium-sized can peach halves
150ml / ¼ pint fresh double cream
1 tablespoon milk
1 level tablespoon sifted icing sugar
White of 1 standard egg
100g / 4oz fresh or frozen strawberries
Extra sifted icing sugar

1 Line base of fairly small serving dish with cake. Moisten with 4 to 5 tablespoons syrup from peaches
2 Arrange peach halves on top
3 Whip cream and milk together until thick. Stir in sugar then fold in egg white, beaten to a stiff snow
4 Pile over peaches and chill
5 Just before serving, crush strawberries finely, sweeten to taste with icing sugar and trickle gently over the cream.
Serves 4 to 5

Gâteau St. Honoré

1 recipe Sweet Flan Pastry (page 214)
1 recipe Choux Pastry (page 214)
300ml / $\frac{1}{2}$ pint fresh double cream
2 tablespoons milk
4 level tablespoons sifted icing sugar
4 level tablespoons apricot jam
10 glacé cherries

1 Pre-heat oven to hot (220°C / 425°F or Gas No 7)
2 Roll out Sweet Flan Pastry into a round
19 to 20cm / $7\frac{1}{2}$ to 8in across. Stand on a buttered baking tray. Prick all over with a fork. Moisten 1cm / $\frac{1}{2}$in wide band round the edge with water
3 With a forcing bag and 1cm / $\frac{1}{2}$in plain icing tube, pipe fairly thin circle of Choux Pastry on top of moistened edge
4 Pipe rest of Choux Pastry into 10 small mounds on second buttered baking tray
5 Stand Sweet Flan round towards top of oven; the tray of small Choux mounds in the centre
6 Bake for 15 minutes. Reduce temperature to moderately hot (190°C / 375°F or Gas No 5), reverse position of trays and bake a further 20 minutes
7 Remove both trays from oven. Transfer pastry round and baked puffs to cooling rack. Make small slits in both the Choux ring and puffs to allow steam to escape
8 When pastry is completely cold, whip cream and milk together until thick. Stir in the sugar. Halve puffs and fill with whipped cream. Pile remaining cream into centre of pastry round
9 Brush Choux ring heavily with melted apricot jam and stand filled puffs on top
10 Brush puffs with rest of melted jam. Top each with a whole cherry
11 Chill $\frac{1}{2}$ an hour before serving. **Serving 8 to 10**

Profiteroles with Chocolate Sauce (below)

Basic Cream Mould

3 tablespoons water
1 level tablespoon granulated sugar
3 level teaspoons gelatine
300ml / $\frac{1}{2}$ pint fresh double cream
300ml / $\frac{1}{2}$ pint sweetened cold custard (made
   with custard powder)
1 teaspoon vanilla essence

1 Put water, sugar and gelatine in a basin. Stir until dissolved, over a pan of boiling water. Leave until cool
2 Whip cream until lightly stiff. Remove skin from custard, whisk until completely smooth, then whisk in cooled gelatine mixture and vanilla
3 Fold in whipped cream then leave in the cool until mixture just begins to thicken and set, stirring occasionally
4 Transfer to $\frac{3}{4}$ litre / $1\frac{1}{2}$ pint mould, first rinsed with cold water. Chill until firm and set
5 Turn out on to plate and serve with stewed or canned fruit. **Serves 4 to 5**

Profiteroles

1 recipe Choux Pastry (page 214)
300ml / $\frac{1}{2}$ pint fresh double cream
2 tablespoons milk
3 to 4 level tablespoons sifted icing sugar
Quick Chocolate Sauce (page 139)

1 Pipe or spoon 20 equal amounts of Choux Pastry – well apart – on large buttered baking tray. Put into centre of hot oven (220°C / 425°F or Gas No 7). Bake 25 minutes (or until golden and well puffed)
2 Remove from oven. Make a small slit in the side of each. Return to oven (with heat switched off) for a further 5 minutes for puffs to dry out. Cool on a wire rack
3 About 1 hour before serving, whip cream and milk together until thick. Stir in sugar
4 Halve puffs and fill with the cream. Pile in a pyramid shape in shallow serving dish
5 Pour over lukewarm Quick Chocolate Sauce. Chill a good $\frac{1}{2}$ hour before serving. **Serves 4**

Coffee Cream Mould

Follow recipe and method for Basic Cream Mould (page 169) but stir 2 to 3 level teaspoons instant coffee powder into hot gelatine mixture and omit vanilla. **Serves 4 to 5**

Chocolate Cream Mould

Follow recipe and method for Basic Cream Mould (page 169) but melt 75g/3oz plain, grated chocolate in the water with the sugar and gelatine. **Serves 4 to 5**

Cherry Cream Mould

1 Follow recipe and method for Basic Cream Mould (page 169) but use almond essence instead of vanilla
2 Just before moulding, stir in 50 to 75g/2 to 3oz finely chopped glacé cherries. **Serves 4 to 5**

Basic Fruit & Cream Mould

4 tablespoons water
1 level tablespoon granulated sugar
3 level teaspoons gelatine
150ml/¼ pint fresh double cream
150ml/¼ pint sweetened, cold custard (made from custard powder)
150ml/¼ pint sweetened gooseberry purée, made from canned or stewed fruit
Green food colouring

Decoration
Whole gooseberries

1 Put water, sugar and gelatine in a basin. Stir until dissolved, over a pan of boiling water. Leave on one side until cool
2 Whip cream until lightly stiff. Remove skin from custard, whisk until completely smooth, then whisk in fruit purée and cooled gelatine mixture
3 Fold in whipped cream and colour pale green. Leave in cool until just beginning to thicken and set
4 Transfer to ¾ litre/1½ pint mould, first rinsed with cold water, and chill until firm
5 Turn out on to a plate. Decorate lower edge of mould with a border of whole gooseberries.
Serves 4 to 6

Banana Snow

6 medium-sized bananas
3 tablespoons lemon juice
2×150g/5oz cartons natural or banana yogurt
4 level tablespoons caster sugar
150ml/¼ pint fresh double cream
Whites of 2 standard eggs

Decoration
About 25g/1oz grated plain chocolate

1 Mash bananas to a purée with the lemon juice. Stir in yogurt and sugar and mix well
2 Whip cream until lightly stiff. Beat egg whites to stiff snow
3 Fold cream and beaten whites alternately into banana mixture. Pile into a serving dish
4 Chill thoroughly. Just before serving, sprinkle with grated chocolate. **Serves 4 to 6**

Almond & Apricot Flan

Short Crust Pastry made with 100g/4oz flour (page 211)
2 level tablespoons apricot jam
75g/3oz butter
75g/3oz caster sugar
1 large egg
25g/1oz cake crumbs (from plain cake)
50g/2oz ground almonds
25g/1oz self-raising flour
1 tablespoon milk
1 medium-sized can apricot halves

Decoration
150ml/¼ pint fresh double cream, whipped
6 glacé cherries

1 Roll out pastry. Use to line a 15 to 18cm/6 to 7in fluted flan ring resting on lightly buttered baking tray
2 Spread base with jam
3 Cream butter with sugar until light and fluffy, then beat in whole egg
4 Stir in cake crumbs and almonds. Fold in flour alternately with milk
5 Transfer to pastry case and smooth top with a knife
6 Bake just above centre of a hot oven (220°C/425°F or Gas No 7) for 15 minutes. Reduce temperature to moderate (180°C/350°F or Gas No 4) and bake a further 30 minutes
7 Remove flan ring and cool flan
8 Just before serving, cover top of cold flan with well-drained apricot halves. Decorate with whipped cream and halved cherries. **Serves 4 to 6**

Frozen Desserts

Dairy Cream Ice (below)

 All freeze successfully.
Storage time – 2 to 3 months.
The fast freeze compartment of the freezer may be used instead of the refrigerator to make up recipes.

Dairy Cream Ice

300ml / $\frac{1}{2}$ pint fresh double cream
2 tablespoons milk
5 level tablespoons sifted icing sugar
1 teaspoon vanilla essence

1 Turn refrigerator to coldest setting at least 1 hour before making Cream Ice
2 Pour cream and milk into well-chilled bowl and beat both together until lightly stiff
3 Stir in icing sugar and essence. Pour into ice cube tray
4 Put tray in freezing compartment of refrigerator. Freeze for 45 minutes or until Cream Ice has frozen about 1cm / $\frac{1}{2}$in round sides of tray
5 Pour into chilled bowl, break up with fork and stir gently until smooth
6 Return to washed and dried tray. Freeze 2 hours or until firm. **Serves 4**

Almond Dairy Cream Ice

1 Follow recipe and method for Dairy Cream Ice (left) but add 1 teaspoon almond essence instead of vanilla
2 Before second freezing, stir in 25g / 1oz toasted, finely chopped almonds. **Serves 4**

Coffee Dairy Cream Ice

Follow recipe and method for Dairy Cream Ice (left) but add 2 to 3 level teaspoons instant coffee powder mixed with 2 teaspoons hot water (then left to get cold) instead of vanilla. **Serves 4**

Pistachio Dairy Cream Ice

1 Follow recipe and method for Dairy Cream Ice (left) but omit vanilla
2 Stir in 25g / 1oz very finely chopped blanched Pistachio nuts before second freezing
3 Cream Ice can be tinted pale green with food colouring. **Serves 4**

Preserved Ginger Dairy Cream Ice

1 Follow recipe and method for Dairy Cream Ice (page 171) but reduce sugar by 1 tablespoon and omit vanilla
2 Before second freezing, stir in 25 to 40g/ 1 to 1½oz very finely chopped preserved ginger and 1 tablespoon ginger syrup. **Serves 4**

Chocolate Dairy Cream Ice

1 Follow recipe and method for Dairy Cream Ice (page 171)
2 While mixture is freezing for first time, mix 2 level tablespoons cocoa powder to a smooth paste with 3 tablespoons boiling water
3 Leave until cold then beat into Cream Ice before second freezing. **Serves 4**

Chocolate Brandy Dairy Cream Ice

Follow recipe and method for Chocolate Dairy Cream Ice (above) but stir in 3 teaspoons brandy with cocoa mixture.
Serves 4

Chocolate Hazelnut Dairy Cream Ice

Follow recipe and method for Chocolate Dairy Cream Ice (above) but stir in 40g/1½oz very finely chopped hazelnuts with cocoa mixture.
Serves 4

Chocolate Rum Dairy Cream Ice

Follow recipe and method for Chocolate Dairy Cream Ice (above) but stir in 2 teaspoons rum with cocoa mixture.
Serves 4

Maraschino Dairy Cream Ice

1 Follow recipe and method for Dairy Cream Ice (page 171) but reduce sugar by 1 tablespoon and omit vanilla
2 Before second freezing, stir in 2 to 3 table-spoons coarsely chopped Maraschino-flavoured cherries and 1 tablespoon Maraschino-flavoured syrup. **Serves 4**

Orange Dairy Cream Ice

1 Follow recipe and method for Dairy Cream Ice (page 171) but reduce sugar by 1 tablespoon and omit vanilla
2 Before second freezing, add 1 level teaspoon finely grated orange rind and 1 tablespoon Cointreau. **Serves 4**

Lemon Dairy Cream Ice

1 Follow recipe and method for Dairy Cream Ice (page 171) but omit vanilla
2 Before second freezing, stir in 2 level teaspoons finely grated lemon rind. **Serves 4**

Lemon Cream Snow

1 Follow recipe and method for Dairy Cream Ice (page 171) but omit vanilla
2 Before second freezing, fold in 1 stiffly beaten white of standard egg and 2 level teaspoons finely grated lemon rind. **Serves 4**

Praline Dairy Cream Ice

1 Follow recipe and method for Dairy Cream Ice (page 171) but omit vanilla
2 Before second freezing, stir in 50g/2oz finely crushed nut brittle. **Serves 4**

Rich Chocolate Cream Ice

50g/2oz plain chocolate
1 standard egg
25g/1oz icing or caster sugar
2 teaspoons vanilla essence
150ml/¼ pint fresh double cream

1 Turn refrigerator to coldest setting at least 1 hour before making Cream Ice
2 Break up chocolate. Melt in basin standing over a saucepan of hot water. Cool
3 Put egg and sugar into a double saucepan (or basin standing over saucepan of hot water). Whisk until thick and creamy
4 Remove from heat. Continue whisking until mixture is cool
5 Stir in cooled chocolate and vanilla. Fold in cream, beaten until lightly stiff
6 Pour into ice cube tray. Put into freezing compartment of refrigerator and freeze for 45 minutes (or until Cream Ice has frozen 1cm/½in round sides of tray)
7 Turn into chilled bowl, break up with a fork then stir until smooth
8 Return to washed and dried tray. Freeze for 1½ to 2 hours or until firm. **Serves 4**

Banana Splits (below)

Chocolate Chip Dairy Cream Ice

Follow recipe and method for Dairy Cream Ice (page 171) but stir in 50g/2oz coarsely grated plain chocolate before second freezing. **Serves 4**

Peach Dairy Cream Ice

1 Follow recipe and method for Dairy Cream Ice (page 171) but reduce sugar by 2 tablespoons and omit vanilla
2 Before second freezing, stir in 2 tablespoons rose hip syrup, 1 level teaspoon finely grated lemon rind and 4 drained, coarsely chopped, canned peach halves. **Serves 4**

Apricot Dairy Cream Ice

1 Follow recipe and method for Dairy Cream Ice (page 171) but reduce sugar by 2 tablespoons and omit vanilla
2 Before second freezing, stir in 2 tablespoons rose hip syrup, 1 level teaspoon finely grated orange rind and 8 drained, coarsely chopped, canned apricot halves. **Serves 4**

Tutti-Frutti Dairy Cream Ice

1 Follow recipe and method for Dairy Cream Ice (page 171)
2 Before second freezing, stir in 2 drained and finely chopped, canned pineapple rings, 2 tablespoons drained and coarsely chopped, canned mandarin oranges and 1 small sliced banana. **Serves 4**

Banana Splits

150ml / $\frac{1}{4}$ pint fresh double cream
4 large bananas
1 recipe French Custard Ice Cream (page 174)
25g / 1oz finely chopped shelled walnut halves
4 glacé cherries
Hot Chocolate Sauce (page 138) or hot Fudge Sauce (page 136)

1 Whip cream until lightly stiff
2 Split bananas lengthwise and quickly sandwich together with spoonfuls of the Cream Ice
3 Stand on 4 individual plates then top with the whipped cream
4 Sprinkle with nuts and put whole cherry in centre of each
5 Serve immediately. Serve Chocolate or Fudge Sauce separately. **Serves 4**

173

French Custard Ice Cream

300ml / ½ pint fresh single cream
2 large beaten eggs
3 level tablespoons granulated sugar
2 teaspoons vanilla essence

1 Turn refrigerator to coldest setting at least 1 hour before making Ice Cream
2 Put cream, eggs and sugar into double saucepan (or basin standing over saucepan of gently simmering water)
3 Cook, stirring all the time, until custard is thick enough to coat thinly the back of the spoon. Do not allow to boil
4 Pour into a bowl, stir in vanilla and leave until cold
5 Pour into ice cube tray and transfer to freezing compartment of refrigerator
6 Freeze for 1 hour or until Ice Cream has frozen about 1 cm / ½ in round sides of tray
7 Turn into a chilled bowl and whisk until smooth
8 Return to washed and dried tray and freeze 1½ to 2 hours or until firm. **Serves 4**

French Custard Dairy Ice

1 Follow recipe and method for French Custard Ice Cream (above) but increase sugar by 1 level tablespoon and vanilla by 1 teaspoon
2 After beating Ice Cream until smooth, fold in 150ml / ¼ pint very cold, fresh double cream, whipped until lightly stiff
3 Return to tray, or trays, depending on size, and freeze for 1½ to 2 hours or until firm. **Serves 4 to 6**

Ice Cream Gâteau

300ml / ½ pint fresh double cream
4 tablespoons milk
2 to 3 level tablespoons sifted icing sugar
2 Victoria Sandwich Cakes (page 228)
2 tablespoons sweet sherry
2 tablespoons apricot jam
1 recipe Dairy Cream Ice (page 171),
**   Maraschino Dairy Cream Ice (page 172)**
**   or Rich Chocolate Cream Ice (page 172)**

Decoration
Fresh berry fruits (strawberries or raspberries)
**   or pieces of glacé fruits**

1 Put cream and milk into a bowl and whip until thick
2 Sweeten with the icing sugar
3 Sprinkle each sandwich cake with sherry then spread with apricot jam
4 Sandwich together with spoonfuls of Cream Ice and stand on a serving dish
5 Quickly swirl whipped cream over top and sides with a knife then decorate with fruit
6 Serve immediately. **Serves 6**

Crushed Fruit Ice Cream

150ml / ¼ pint fresh double cream
3 tablespoons sweetened fruit purée (made
**   from choice of strawberries, raspberries,**
**   canned peaches or canned apricots)**
2 level tablespoons sifted icing sugar
2 level tablespoons sliced strawberries, whole
**   raspberries or coarsely chopped peaches or**
**   apricots**

1 Turn refrigerator to coldest setting at least 1 hour before making Ice Cream
2 Whip cream and fruit purée until thick
3 Stir in sugar then pour in ice cube tray
4 Put into freezing compartment of refrigerator. Freeze for 45 minutes (or until Ice Cream has frozen about 1 cm / ½ in round sides of tray)
5 Turn into a chilled bowl, break up gently with a fork and stir until smooth
6 Add pieces of fruit. Mix well. Return to washed and dried tray
7 Freeze for 1½ to 2 hours or until firm. **Serves 4**

Italian Cream Ice

Yolks of 2 standard eggs
50g / 2oz sifted icing sugar
2 teaspoons vanilla essence
300ml / ½ pint fresh double cream
2 tablespoons milk

1 Turn refrigerator to coldest setting at least 1 hour before making Cream Ice
2 Put egg yolks and sugar into a double saucepan (or basin standing over saucepan of gently simmering water). Beat until thick and creamy
3 Remove from heat. Continue beating until cool, then stir in vanilla
4 Pour cream and milk into chilled bowl and beat until lightly stiff
5 Gently fold in beaten yolks and sugar then transfer to 1 or 2 ice cube trays, depending on size. Put into freezing compartment of refrigerator
6 Freeze for 45 minutes (or until Cream Ice has frozen about 1 cm / ½ in round sides of tray)
7 Turn into chilled bowl, break up gently with a fork then stir until smooth
8 Return to washed and dried tray, or trays. Freeze for 1½ to 2 hours or until firm.
Serves 4

Strawberry or Raspberry Dairy Cream Ice

1 Follow recipe and method for Dairy Cream Ice (page 171)
2 Before second freezing, stir in 75 to 100g / 3 to 4oz sliced strawberries or the same amount of whole raspberries. **Serves 4**

Frozen Raspberry Mousse

**150ml / ¼ pint sweetened raspberry purée, made
from fresh, frozen or canned fruit**
2 teaspoons lemon juice
**25 to 75g / 1 to 3oz sifted icing sugar, depending
on sharpness of fruit**
150ml / ¼ pint fresh double cream
1 tablespoon milk
Whites of 2 standard eggs

1 Turn refrigerator control to coldest setting at
least 1 hour before making Mousse
2 Put purée into basin. Add lemon juice and sugar
to taste. (Freezing tends to reduce sweetness so it
is better to over-sweeten)
3 Whip cream and milk together until lightly stiff.
Beat egg whites to stiff snow
4 Fold cream and egg whites alternately into fruit
mixture. Transfer to 1 or 2 ice cube trays
5 Put into freezing compartment of refrigerator
and freeze until firm
6 To serve, spoon into small glass dishes.
Serves 4

Frozen Strawberry Mousse

Follow recipe and method for Frozen Raspberry
Mousse (above) but use strawberry purée instead
of the raspberry. **Serves 4**

Pineapple & Lemon Sundae

1 Soak 1 medium-sized can of pineapple cubes in
Maraschino-flavoured syrup
2 Divide between 4 to 6 sundae glasses. Top each
with scoop of Lemon Dairy Cream Ice (page 172).
Serves 4 to 6

Coffee Cream Sundae

1 Scoop Coffee Dairy Cream Ice (page 171) into 6
sundae glasses
2 Top with lightly whipped fresh double cream,
flavoured to taste with liquid coffee essence or
Tia Maria liqueur.
Serves 6

Cherry Cream Sundae

1 Scoop Dairy Cream Ice (page 171), French
Custard Dairy Ice (page 174) or Italian Cream Ice
(page 174) into 6 sundae glasses
2 Add stewed red cherries to each then decorate
with lightly whipped fresh double cream
3 Top each with 2 whole raspberries.
Serves 6

Pineapple & Strawberry Sundae

1 Put 1 pineapple ring into 4 or 6 sundae glasses
2 Top with scoops of Dairy Cream Ice (page 171),
French Custard Dairy Ice (page 174) or Italian
Cream Ice (page 174)
3 Decorate with whipped fresh double cream and
whole strawberries. **Serves 4 to 6**

Chestnut Cream Sundae

1 Scoop French Custard Ice Cream (page 174)
into 4 sundae glasses
2 Pipe canned chestnut purée over top of each to
resemble vermicelli
3 Put mound of lightly whipped, fresh double
cream on to the centre of each
4 Top with 2 Maraschino-flavoured cherries.
Serves 4

Pineapple & Coffee Sundae

1 Soak 1 medium-sized can of pineapple cubes in
a little rum
2 Divide between 4 to 6 sundae glasses then top
with scoops of Coffee Dairy Cream Ice (page 171)
3 Pipe stiffly whipped, fresh double cream over
each. Sprinkle **lightly** with ground coffee.
Serves 4 to 6

Redcurrant Sundae

1 Put scoops of Dairy Cream Ice (page 171),
French Custard Dairy Ice (page 174) or Italian
Cream Ice (page 174) into 4 to 6 sundae glasses
2 Cover with fresh redcurrants (stems removed)
3 Top with softly whipped fresh double cream.
Serves 4 to 6.

Fruit Cocktail & Strawberry Sundae

1 Divide a medium-sized can of fruit cocktail
between 4 to 6 sundae glasses
2 Sprinkle with Kirsch, if liked. Top with scoops of
Strawberry Dairy Cream Ice (page 174).
Serves 4 to 6

Peach Melba

1 Put scoops of French Custard Ice Cream
(page 174) into 4 sundae glasses
2 Top each with canned peach half
3 Spoon over raspberry purée made by crushing
175 to 225g/6 to 8oz fresh raspberries with sifted
icing sugar to taste
4 If fresh peaches are preferred, skin them,
cut in half and poach gently in a syrup made by
dissolving 100g/4oz granulated sugar in
4 tablespoons water.
Serves 4

Canteloupe Cups

2 small Cantaloupe melons
1 recipe Lemon Cream Snow (page 172)
150ml/¼ pint fresh double cream
100g/4oz whole strawberries

1 Chill melons for at least 1 hour before using
2 Cut each in half, remove pips and put on to
4 plates
3 Fill cavities with scoops of Lemon Cream Snow.
Decorate with stiffly whipped cream and strawberries
4 Serve immediately.
Serves 4

Tutti-Frutti Basket

150ml/¼ pint fresh double cream
1 tablespoon milk
1 recipe Tutti-Frutti Dairy Cream Ice (page 173)
1 Meringue Basket (page 226)
Chocolate Sauce (page 138)

1 Whip cream and milk together until thick
2 Spoon Tutti-Frutti Dairy Cream Ice neatly into
Meringue Basket
3 Quickly pipe trellis of cream over the top
4 Serve immediately
5 Serve hot Chocolate Sauce separately.
Serves 4 to 6

Mandarin & Lemon Sundae

1 Mix a can of mandarin oranges with sweet
sherry or Grand Marnier to taste and reserve
4 to 6 segments for decoration
2 Divide fruit between 4 to 6 sundae glasses. Top
with scoops of Lemon Dairy Cream Ice (page 172)
3 Put heaped tablespoon of lightly whipped fresh
double cream on to each
4 Decorate with mandarins and fresh mint leaves
if available.
Serves 4 to 6

Tangy Fruit Sorbet

175g/6oz granulated sugar
6 mint leaves or ½ teaspoon dried mint
Juice of 1 small lemon
Finely grated rind and strained juice of
    1 medium-sized orange
4 tablespoons rose hip syrup
White of 1 standard egg
25g/1oz caster sugar

Decoration
Mint leaves or fresh strawberries or raspberries

1 Turn refrigerator to coldest setting at least
1 hour before making Sorbet
2 Put granulated sugar, 150ml/¼ pint water and
mint into a pan
3 Stand pan over low heat and stir until sugar
dissolves
4 Remove from heat and strain. Stir in
300ml/½ pint water, lemon juice, orange rind,
orange juice and rose hip syrup
5 Mix well. Pour into 2 ice cube trays
6 Put into freezing compartment of refrigerator.
Freeze for 1 hour or until mixture has half frozen
7 Beat egg white to stiff snow. Add caster sugar.
Continue whisking until white is very stiff and
shiny
8 Pour fruit mixture into chilled bowl. Whisk until
smooth. Gently stir in beaten egg white. Return to
washed and dried ice cube trays. Chill 45 minutes
and re-whisk
9 Pour back into trays. Freeze 1½ to 2 hours or
until firm
10 Spoon into small dishes and top with more
mint leaves or fresh strawberries or raspberries
11 Serve immediately.
Serves 6

Midsummer Glories

300ml/½ pint strawberry or raspberry jelly,
    already set
150ml/¼ pint fresh double cream
1 recipe Dairy Cream Ice (page 171), French
    Custard Dairy Ice (page 174) or Italian Cream
    Ice (page 174)
1 medium-sized can peach slices
250g/8oz fresh strawberries (small for prefer-
    ence) or raspberries
4 glacé cherries

1 Turn jelly out on to a sheet of damp greaseproof
paper and chop coarsely with knife dipped in and
out of cold water
2 Whip cream until stiff
3 Quickly fill tall glasses with alternate layers of
jelly, Cream Ice and fruit
4 Put 1 or 2 tablespoons of cream on to each. Top
with a whole cherry
5 Serve immediately.
Serves 4

Omelette Soufflé Surprise (Baked Alaska) (below)

Frozen Crunch Flan

200g/8oz plain chocolate digestive biscuits
75g/3oz butter
150ml/¼ pint fresh double cream
1 recipe Almond Dairy Cream Ice (page 171) or
    Preserved Ginger Dairy Cream Ice (page 172)

Decoration
Peach slices and glacé cherries

1 To make flan case, crush biscuits finely
2 Melt butter in pan and stir in the crumbs
3 Stand 18cm/7in plain flan ring on a baking tray.
Press crumbs thickly and evenly over base and
sides
4 Refrigerate until firm
5 Just before serving, whip cream until lightly stiff
6 Remove flan from refrigerator, gently lift off ring
and transfer case to serving plate
7 Fill with tablespoons of the Cream Ice then
cover with the whipped cream
8 Decorate with peach slices (well drained) and
cherries
9 Serve immediately. **Serves 6**

Omelette Soufflé Surprise (Baked Alaska)

1 single layer sponge or sandwich cake
    18cm/7in (at least 1 day old)
1 or 2 tablespoons brandy or sherry
Meringue Topping, made with 3 egg whites
    (page 227)
1 recipe Dairy Cream Ice (page 171), French
    Custard Dairy Ice (page 174) or Italian Cream
    Ice (page 174)
Pieces of Glacé fruits (optional)

1 Put cake on to a heatproof plate and moisten
with brandy or sherry
2 Make Meringue Topping
3 Put tablespoons of Cream Ice in mound on top
of cake
4 Swirl Meringue completely over cake and
Cream Ice or pipe it over with a large star-shaped
tube and forcing bag
5 Stud with fruits (if used) then flash bake (see
baking of Meringue Topping page 227)
6 Serve immediately. **Serves 4 to 6**

Soufflés

Lemon Soufflé (below)

 Open freeze cold sweet soufflés in freezer-proof soufflé dish. Pack in a rigid polythene container. Storage time – 3 months. Hot soufflés do not freeze successfully.

Cold Sweet Soufflés

Lemon Soufflé

3 level teaspoons gelatine
3 tablespoons hot water
Yolks and whites of 2 large eggs
50g / 2oz caster sugar
Finely grated rind and juice of 1 medium-sized lemon
150ml / ¼ pint fresh double cream

Decoration
About 40g / 1½oz finely chopped, shelled walnut halves or blanched and toasted almonds
4 tablespoons fresh double cream, whipped
Leaves of angelica or crystallised violet petals

1 Prepare dish first. Put 10cm / 4in strip of folded greaseproof paper round ½ litre / 1 pint soufflé dish, making sure paper stands 4 to 5 cm / 1½ to 2in above edge of dish. Tie on securely. Brush inside of strip with salad oil

2 Put gelatine and hot water in a basin. Stir until dissolved, over a pan of boiling water
3 Whisk egg yolks and sugar together in a bowl over a pan of hot water until very thick and pale. Remove bowl from hot water and continue whisking until mixture is cool. Gently whisk in dissolved gelatine, lemon rind and juice
4 Leave in cold until just beginning to thicken and set
5 Whisk cream until lightly stiff. Beat egg whites to stiff snow
6 Gently fold lemon mixture into cream. Fold in beaten whites
7 Pour into prepared soufflé dish (mixture should reach almost to top of paper). Chill until firm and set
8 Just before serving, ease paper away from mixture with a knife dipped in hot water. Gently press chopped nuts against sides of Soufflé
9 Decorate top with whipped cream and either angelica or crystallised violets. **Serves 4**

Chocolate Soufflé

3 level teaspoons gelatine
3 tablespoons hot water
50g / 2oz plain chocolate
1 tablespoon milk
1 teaspoon vanilla essence
Yolks and whites of 2 large eggs
50g / 2oz caster sugar
150ml / ¼ pint fresh double cream

Decoration
About 40g / 1½oz finely chopped shelled walnut
  halves, blanched toasted almonds or
  hazelnuts
4 tablespoons fresh double cream, whipped
Chocolate buttons or small pieces preserved
  ginger

1 Prepare dish as for Cold Lemon Soufflé
(page 178)
2 Put gelatine and hot water in a basin. Stir until
dissolved, over a pan of boiling water
3 Break up chocolate and put into basin standing
over pan of hot water. Leave until melted, stirring
once or twice. Blend in milk and vanilla
4 Beat egg yolks and sugar together in a bowl
over a pan of hot water until very thick and pale.
Remove bowl from hot water and continue whisking until mixture is cool. Whisk in dissolved
gelatine and melted chocolate and milk. Leave in
cool until just beginning to thicken and set
5 Whip cream until lightly stiff. Beat egg whites to
a stiff snow
6 Gently fold chocolate mixture into cream. Fold
in beaten whites
7 Pour into prepared soufflé dish (mixture should
reach almost to top of paper). Chill until firm and
set
8 Just before serving, ease paper away from
mixture with a knife dipped in hot water. Gently
press chopped nuts against sides of Soufflé
9 Decorate top with whipped cream and either
chocolate buttons or ginger.
Serves 4

Mocha Soufflé

1 Follow recipe and method for Chocolate Soufflé
(above) but add 2 to 3 level teaspoons instant
coffee powder to the chocolate in the basin
2 Press chopped hazelnuts against sides of
Soufflé
3 Decorate top with whipped cream and whole
hazelnuts. Serves 4

Coffee Soufflé

1 Follow recipe and method for Chocolate Soufflé
(left) but omit chocolate and vanilla
2 Warm tablespoon of milk. Stir in 2 to 3 level
teaspoons instant coffee powder. Whisk into
beaten yolks and sugar with dissolved gelatine
3 Press chopped walnuts against sides of Soufflé
4 Decorate with whipped cream and shelled
walnut halves. Serves 4

Strawberry Soufflé

3 level teaspoons gelatine
3 tablespoons hot water
150ml / ¼ pint strawberry purée (made from
  canned, frozen or fresh berries)
2 teaspoons lemon juice
25 to 75g / 1 to 3oz sifted icing sugar
150ml / ¼ pint fresh double cream
Whites of 2 large eggs

Decoration
4 tablespoons fresh double cream, whipped
Small whole strawberries

1 Prepare dish as for cold Lemon Soufflé
(page178)
2 Put gelatine and hot water in a basin. Stir until
dissolved, over a pan of boiling water
3 Combine strawberry purée with lemon juice.
Stir in dissolved gelatine
4 Sweeten to taste with icing sugar. Leave in the
cool until just beginning to thicken and set
5 Whip cream until lightly stiff. Beat egg whites to
stiff snow
6 Gently fold fruit mixture into cream. Lastly, fold
in beaten egg whites
7 Pour into prepared soufflé dish (mixture should
reach almost to top of paper). Chill until firm and
set
8 Just before serving ease paper away from
mixture with a knife dipped in hot water. Decorate
top with whipped cream and whole berries.
Serves 4

Raspberry Soufflé

1 Follow recipe and method for Strawberry
Soufflé (above)
2 Use 150ml / ¼ pint raspberry purée instead of the
strawberry
3 Decorate top with whipped cream and whole
raspberries. Serves 4

Hot Sweet Soufflés

Vanilla Soufflé

50g/2oz butter
50g/2oz plain flour
300ml/½ pint lukewarm milk
50g/2oz caster sugar
1 teaspoon vanilla essence
Yolks of 3 large eggs
Whites of 3 or 4 large eggs

1 Melt butter in saucepan and add flour. Cook 2 minutes without browning, stirring all the time
2 Gradually whisk in warm milk (with a whisk, not a spoon). Continue whisking gently until sauce comes to boil and thickens
3 Simmer about 2 minutes. Sauce should be very thick and leave sides of pan clean
4 Remove from heat and cool slightly. Beat in sugar, vanilla and egg yolks
5 Beat egg whites to stiff snow. Gently fold into sauce mixture with large metal spoon
6 Transfer to well-buttered 1 to 1¼ litre/2 to 2½ pint soufflé dish (or similar straight-sided, heatproof dish). Put into centre of moderately hot oven (190°C/375°F or Gas No 5)
7 Bake 45 minutes when Soufflé should be well-risen with a high, golden crown
8 Remove from oven and serve immediately with Red Jam Sauce (page 136).
Serves 4

It is **vital** not to open the oven door while the Soufflé is baking or it will fall

Almond Soufflé

1 Follow recipe and method for Vanilla Soufflé (above) but use almond essence instead of vanilla
2 Add 75g/3oz ground almonds before beating in egg yolks
3 Serve with fresh single cream or Red Jam Sauce (page 136). **Serves 4**

Apricot Soufflé

1 Follow recipe and method for Vanilla Soufflé (above) but use ½ teaspoon almond essence instead of vanilla
2 Before beating in egg yolks add 4 tablespoons thick apricot purée (made from canned or fresh stewed apricots)
3 Serve with fresh single cream.
Serves 4

Banana Soufflé

1 Follow recipe and method for Vanilla Soufflé (left) but omit vanilla
2 Before beating in egg yolks add 2 small, finely mashed bananas and 2 teaspoons lemon juice
3 Serve with fresh single cream.
Serves 4

Chocolate Soufflé

1 Follow recipe and method for Vanilla Soufflé (left) but melt 50g/2oz grated plain chocolate in the milk
2 Serve with fresh single cream.
Serves 4

Coffee Soufflé

1 Follow recipe and method for Vanilla Soufflé (left) but omit vanilla
2 Add 2 to 3 level teaspoons instant coffee powder to warm milk
3 Serve with fresh single cream or Chocolate Sauce (page 138).
Serves 4

Orange or Lemon Soufflé

1 Follow recipe and method for Vanilla Soufflé (left) but omit vanilla
2 Before beating in egg yolks add 2 level teaspoons finely grated orange or lemon rind
3 Serve with fresh single cream.
Serves 4

Walnut or Hazelnut Soufflé

1 Follow recipe and method for Vanilla Soufflé (left) but before beating in egg yolks add 75g/3oz very finely chopped, shelled walnut halves or hazelnuts
2 Serve with fresh single cream or Chocolate Sauce (page 138).
Serves 4

Pineapple Soufflé

1 Follow recipe and method for Vanilla Soufflé (left) but before beating in egg yolks add 4 level tablespoons finely chopped canned pineapple (well drained)
2 Serve with fresh single cream.
Serves 4

Hot Savoury Soufflés

Cheese Soufflé

50g / 2oz butter
50g / 2oz plain flour
300ml / ½ pint lukewarm milk
100g / 4oz very finely grated Cheddar cheese
  (stale for preference)
1 level teaspoon made mustard
½ level teaspoon salt
¼ teaspoon Worcestershire sauce
Yolks of 3 large eggs
Whites of 3 or 4 large eggs

1 Melt butter in saucepan and add flour. Cook
2 minutes without browning, stirring all the time
2 Gradually whisk in warm milk (with a whisk, not
a spoon). Continue whisking gently until sauce
comes to boil and thickens
3 Simmer about 2 minutes. Sauce should be quite
thick and leave sides of pan clean
4 Remove from heat and cool slightly. Beat in
cheese, mustard, salt, Worcestershire sauce and
egg yolks
5 Beat egg whites to stiff snow. Gently fold into
sauce mixture with large metal spoon
6 Transfer to well-buttered 1 to 1¼ litre / 2 to 2½ pint
soufflé dish (or similar straight-sided, heatproof
dish). Put into centre of moderately hot oven
(190°C / 375°F or Gas No 5)
7 Bake 45 minutes. The Soufflé should be well-
risen with a high, golden crown
8 Remove from oven and serve immediately.
Serves 4

It is **vital** not to open the oven door while the
Soufflé is baking or it will fall

Bacon Soufflé

1 Follow recipe and method for Cheese Soufflé
(above) but omit cheese
2 Before beating in egg yolks add 100g / 4oz very
finely chopped, fried bacon. **Serves 4**

Crab Soufflé

1 Follow recipe and method for Cheese Soufflé
(above) but omit cheese
2 Before beating in egg yolks add 1 teaspoon
lemon juice, 2 teaspoons tomato ketchup, 1 level
tablespoon finely chopped parsley and 100 to
175g / 4 to 6oz finely chopped crab meat.
Serves 4

Ham Soufflé

1 Follow recipe and method for Cheese Soufflé
(left) but omit cheese
2 Before beating in egg yolks add 100 to 175g /
4 to 6oz minced ham. **Serves 4**

Asparagus Soufflé

1 Follow recipe and method for Cheese Soufflé
(left) but omit cheese and Worcestershire sauce
2 Before beating in egg yolks add 100g / 4oz very
finely chopped asparagus. **Serves 4**

Mushroom Soufflé

1 Follow recipe and method for Cheese Soufflé
(left) but omit cheese and Worcestershire sauce
2 Before beating in egg yolks add 100g / 4oz finely
chopped, fried mushrooms. **Serves 4**

Onion Soufflé

1 Follow recipe and method for Cheese Soufflé
(left) but omit cheese and Worcestershire sauce
2 Before beating in egg yolks add 100g / 4oz very
finely chopped, boiled onions.
Serves 4

Tongue Soufflé

1 Follow recipe and method for Cheese Soufflé
(left) but omit cheese
2 Before beating in egg yolks add 100g / 4oz
minced tongue. **Serves 4**

Smoked Haddock Soufflé

1 Follow recipe and method for Cheese Soufflé
(left) but halve quantity of salt
2 Before beating in egg yolks add 100 to 175g /
4 to 6oz finely flaked, cooked smoked haddock.
Serves 4

Turkey Soufflé

1 Follow recipe and method for Cheese Soufflé
(left) but omit cheese
2 Before beating in egg yolks add 1 level tablespoon very finely chopped parsley and 100g / 4oz
cooked, minced turkey. **Serves 4**

Cheese Omelette (page 183)

Ideally, omelettes should be made in a special omelette pan (kept only for omelette-making), or in a non-stick frying pan. If you have neither of these, and want to make omelettes in your ordinary frying pan, you can achieve better results by 'proving' the pan first. This will prevent the egg mixture from sticking and can be done very simply

To 'prove' a pan quickly, first melt a knob of butter in the pan, then sprinkle the base liberally with cooking salt. Heat together slowly for a few minutes until hot, then rub clean with soft kitchen paper. You should **not** attempt to 'prove' non-stick pans

If you are considering buying a special omelette pan, make sure it has a heavy base, curved sides,

and is fairly shallow. It is important to 'prove' this pan well before use. After use just wipe the inside clean with soft kitchen paper. **Don't** wash, or it will need reproving

One point to remember is that a 15cm / 6in pan is ideal for a 2 large or 3 standard egg omelette and an 18cm / 7in one ideal for a 3 large or 4 standard egg omelette

Omelettes are not suitable for freezing. Eggs may be successfully frozen, separated or whole, if 2 or 3 are slightly beaten, together with salt or sugar. Savoury dishes – 1 teaspoon salt to 2 eggs. Sweet dishes – 2 teaspoons sugar to 2 eggs. Storage time – 9 months

Savoury Omelettes

Plain or French Omelette (Unfilled)

3 large or 4 standard eggs
4 teaspoons cold water
Seasoning to taste
25g / 1oz butter

Garnish
Parsley

1 Beat eggs and water lightly together. Season to taste with salt and pepper
2 Put butter into omelette pan. Heat until sizzling but not brown
3 Pour in beaten eggs
4 After about 5 seconds, move edges of setting omelette to centre of pan with fork, knife or spatula. At same time tilt pan quickly in all directions with other hand so that uncooked egg flows to edges
5 Cook further $\frac{1}{2}$ to 1 minute (or until underneath is set and top is slightly moist)
6 Remove from heat. Fold in half in pan and slide out on to a warm plate
7 Garnish with parsley and serve immediately.
Serves 2

Parsley Omelette

Add 1 level tablespoon finely chopped fresh parsley to beaten eggs just before making Plain Omelette (above). **Serves 2**

Ham & Potato Omelette

1 Lightly fry 1 rounded tablespoon diced ham and 1 rounded tablespoon diced potatoes in a little butter
2 Add to beaten eggs just before making Plain Omelette (above).
Serves 2

Fried Onion Omelette

1 Lightly fry about 1 level tablespoon finely chopped onion in a little butter
2 Add to beaten eggs just before making Plain Omelette (above).
Serves 2

Bacon, Mushroom & Onion Omelette

1 Fry gently in a little butter 1 level tablespoon **each** finely chopped lean bacon, mushrooms and onion
2 Add to beaten eggs just before making Plain Omelette (left). **Serves 2**

Leek & Mushroom Omelette

1 Fry gently in a little butter 1 level tablespoon **each** finely chopped leek, mushrooms and onion
2 Add to beaten eggs just before making Plain Omelette (left). **Serves 2**

Cheese Omelette

Add 40 to 50g / $1\frac{1}{2}$ to 2oz very finely grated Cheddar cheese to beaten eggs just before making Plain Omelette (left)
Serves 2

Chive Omelette

Add 2 level tablespoons very finely chopped chives to beaten eggs just before making Plain Omelette (left). **Serves 2**

Watercress Omelette

Add 1 level tablespoon very finely chopped watercress to beaten eggs just before making Plain Omelette (left). **Serves 2**

Fluffy Savoury Omelette

Yolks and whites of 3 large or 4 standard eggs
4 teaspoons water
Salt and pepper
25g / 1oz butter

1 Beat egg yolks and water lightly together. Season to taste with salt and pepper
2 Beat egg whites to stiff, peaky snow. Gently fold egg yolks into them
3 Melt butter in large omelette pan. When hot and sizzling, pour in egg mixture
4 Cook, without moving, for 2 to $2\frac{1}{2}$ minutes or until base is set. Stand below pre-heated hot grill. Leave 2 to 3 minutes (or until top is well puffed and golden)
5 Slide out on to warmed plate. Cut into 2 or 3 portions. Serve immediately.
Serves 2 or 3

Filled French or Plain Omelettes

Cover half the made Plain Omelette (page 183) – while still in the pan – with chosen filling. Fold other half over then slide Omelette on to plate

Asparagus Omelette

Fill Plain Omelette (page 183) with 100g/4oz cooked asparagus tips warmed through in a little butter. **Serves 2**

Bacon Omelette

Fill Plain Omelette (page 183) with 100g/4oz coarsely chopped, lean bacon, lightly fried in a little butter. **Serves 2**

Croûton Omelette

1 Fill Plain Omelette (page 183) with 3 rounded tablespoons $\frac{1}{2}$cm/$\frac{1}{4}$in bread cubes fried until crisp and golden in a little butter
2 Sprinkle with onion, garlic, or celery salt.
Serves 2

Chicken Omelette

Fill Plain Omelette (page 183) with diced cooked chicken (about 100g/4oz) warmed through with a little Aurore Sauce (page 130) or Mushroom Sauce (page 130).
Serves 2

Tomato Omelette

Fill Plain Omelette (page 183) with 100g/4oz skinned and coarsely chopped tomatoes, fried gently in a little butter.
Serves 2

Crab Omelette

Fill Plain Omelette (page 183) with 100g/4oz flaked crab meat warmed through with a little Lemon Sauce (page 129).
Serves 2

Ham Omelette

Fill Plain Omelette (page 183) with 100g/4oz lean ham, lightly fried in a little butter.
Serves 2

Kidney Omelette

Fill Plain Omelette (page 183) with 100g/4oz thinly sliced kidneys, fried in a little butter.
Serves 2

Mushroom Omelette

Fill Plain Omelette (page 183) with 100g/4oz sliced mushrooms lightly fried in a little butter.
Serves 2

Onion Omelette

Fill Plain Omelette (page 183) with 100g/4oz thinly sliced onions, fried until pale gold in a little butter.
Serves 2

Spanish Omelette

1 large onion
1 large boiled potato
100 to 175g/4 to 6oz tomatoes
50g/2oz fresh red or green peppers or canned red peppers
25g/1oz butter
2 teaspoons olive or corn oil
3 large or 4 standard eggs
2 teaspoons cold water
Salt and pepper

1 Cut onion into very thin rings
2 Dice potato. Blanch, skin and chop tomatoes. Chop pepper
3 Put butter and oil into a 20 to 23cm/8 to 9in frying pan. When hot and sizzling, add onions and potato dice
4 Fry gently until both are pale gold, turning fairly often. Add tomatoes and peppers. Fry a further 2 to 3 minutes
5 Beat eggs lightly with water. Season to taste with salt and pepper then pour into pan over vegetables
6 Cook gently until base is firm. Stand below pre-heated hot grill. Leave 1 or 2 minutes (or until top is just set)
7 Slide flat, unfolded Omelette on to warm platter. Cut into 2 portions
8 Serve immediately.
Serves 2

Sweet Omelettes

Sweet Soufflé Omelette

Yolks and whites of 3 large or 4 standard eggs
25g / 1oz caster sugar
½ teaspoon vanilla essence
25g / 1oz butter
About 4 teaspoons sifted icing sugar

1 Beat egg yolks with caster sugar and vanilla until very thick and pale in colour
2 Beat egg whites to stiff, peaky snow. Gently fold egg yolk mixture into them
3 Melt butter in large omelette pan. When hot and sizzling, pour in egg mixture
4 Cook without moving for 2 to 2½ minutes or until base is set. Stand below pre-heated hot grill. Leave 2 to 3 minutes (or until top is well puffed and golden)
5 Remove from grill and turn out on to sheet of greaseproof paper dusted with icing sugar
6 Score line down centre, fold in half and serve immediately. **Serves 4**

Lemon Soufflé Omelette

1 Follow recipe and method for Sweet Soufflé Omelette (above)
2 Add 1 level teaspoon finely grated lemon rind to beaten yolks. **Serves 4**

Orange Soufflé Omelette

1 Follow recipe and method for Sweet Soufflé Omelette (above)
2 Add 1 level teaspoon finely grated orange rind to beaten yolks. **Serves 4**

Raspberry Soufflé Omelette

1 Follow recipe and method for Sweet Soufflè Omelette (left)
2 After turning out on to sheet of greaseproof paper, score line down centre
3 Cover half with 3 level tablespoons warmed raspberry jam
4 Fold in half and serve immediately. **Serves 4**

Apricot Soufflé Omelette

1 Follow recipe and method for Sweet Soufflé Omelette (left)
2 After turning out on to sheet of greaseproof paper, score line down centre
3 Cover half with 3 level tablespoons warmed apricot jam
4 Fold in half and serve immediately. **Serves 4**

Strawberry Soufflé Omelette

1 Follow recipe and method for Sweet Soufflé Omelette (left)
2 After turning out on to sheet of greaseproof paper, score line down centre
3 Cover half with 50 to 75g / 2 to 3oz crushed strawberries mixed with a little orange juice or sweet sherry.
4 Fold in half and serve immediately.
Serves 4

Apple Soufflé Omelette

1 Follow recipe and method for Sweet Soufflé Omelette (left)
2 After turning out on to sheet of greaseproof paper, score line down centre
3 Cover half with 2 to 3 tablespoons warmed, sweetened apple purée flavoured with a little cinnamon.
4 Fold in half and serve immediately.
Serves 4

For alternate method of serving, do not fold omelette but cut into 4 portions on sugared paper. Transfer to warm plates and spoon jam or fruit – where used – over each

Chicory au Gratin et Jambon (below)

Belgium

Chicory au Gratin et Jambon (Chicory with Cheese and Ham)

8 heads chicory
Juice of ½ lemon
25g / 1oz butter
25g / 1oz flour
150ml / ¼ pint milk
Grated nutmeg
50g / 2oz grated Cheddar cheese
Salt and pepper to taste
8 slices cooked ham
Fresh breadcrumbs

1 Wash and clean the chicory, place in boiling salted water with the juice of ½ lemon (this keeps them white). Boil for 25 minutes

2 Strain chicory, reserving 150ml / ¼ pint of the cooking liquor
3 Melt butter in a pan. Add flour and cook over a low heat, stirring, for 2 minutes. Do not allow the mixture (roux) to brown. Gradually blend in the milk and chicory liquor
4 Cook, stirring, until the sauce comes to the boil and thickens. Add nutmeg, grated cheese and season to taste
5 Wrap each head of chicory in a slice of ham, then place in a heatproof dish. Pour sauce over, and top with breadcrumbs
6 Place under a pre-heated grill to brown. Serve hot. **Serves 4**

France

Coquilles St-Jacques

4 scallops
4 tablespoons white wine
100g / 4oz sliced mushrooms
1 recipe Mornay Sauce (page 131)
25g / 1oz grated Cheddar cheese
25g / 1oz fresh breadcrumbs
450g / 1lb potatoes, boiled and mashed
25g / 1oz butter

Garnish
Lemon slices
Parsley

1 Remove scallops from their shells. Discard
darker intestine. Wash thoroughly. Place in a
saucepan with wine and mushrooms. Poach for
10 minutes
2 Make Mornay Sauce (page 131). Drain scallops
and add wine and mushrooms to the sauce
3 Place scallops back in their shells. Pour sauce
over
4 Sprinkle with grated cheese and breadcrumbs,
mixed together
5 Cream the potatoes with butter, pipe a border
around the edge of each scallop shell
6 Place scallops under a pre-heated grill to brown
7 Serve hot, garnished with lemon slices and
parsley.
Serves 4

Pâté Maison

100g / 4oz lean bacon, thinly sliced
3 tablespoons brandy
450g / 1lb calves' liver, minced
100g / 4oz belly pork, minced
1 egg
2 tablespoons fresh cream
2 tablespoons lemon juice
1 clove of garlic, crushed
Salt and pepper to taste
50g / 2oz chicken livers, coarsely chopped

1 Remove rinds from bacon and line a $\frac{1}{2}$ litre /
1 pint heatproof dish with bacon. Sprinkle with
brandy.
2 Mix together liver, belly pork, eggs, cream,
lemon juice, garlic, salt and pepper to taste. Place
half of this mixture in the lined dish, then a layer
of the chopped chicken liver, followed by the
remaining meat mixture
3 Stand dish in a shallow pan of hot water and
place in the centre of a slow oven (150°C / 300°F or
Gas No 2) for about 2 hours. Cover with foil if the
Pâté becomes too brown
4 Place a weight on top of the cooked Pâté and
chill overnight in a refrigerator. Turn out of mould
and serve with fingers of hot, buttered toast.
Serves 6 to 8

Denmark

Bondepige Med Slør
(Danish Peasant Girl with a Veil)

750g / 1lb 8oz cooking apples, peeled and sliced
75g / 3oz caster sugar
50g / 2oz butter
100g / 4oz fresh white breadcrumbs
25g / 1oz brown sugar
150ml / $\frac{1}{4}$ pint fresh double cream

1 Cook the apples with sugar and a little water,
until pulpy. Sieve or liquidise to a purée. Cool
2 Melt the butter in a frying pan, add breadcrumbs
and brown sugar. Heat gently, stirring until the
breadcrumbs are browned. Cool
3 Arrange alternate layers of apple purée and
breadcrumbs in a glass dish, finishing with a layer
of breadcrumbs
4 Whip the cream slightly, and pour over the top
of the pudding, to almost cover the breadcrumbs.
Serve chilled. **Serves 4 to 6**

Bornholm Herrings

2 rollmops or pickled herrings
2 × 150g / 5oz cartons natural yogurt
$\frac{1}{4}$ to $\frac{1}{2}$ level teaspoon salt
Shake of pepper
2 level teaspoons finely grated onion
Large pinch grated nutmeg

Garnish
Paprika and snipped chives

1 Cut each rollmop or pickled herring into
8 pieces
2 Arrange in shallow serving dish
3 Combine yogurt with salt, pepper, onion and
nutmeg. Pour over the fish
4 Chill
5 Just before serving, sprinkle with paprika and
chives
6 Accompany with brown bread and butter.
Serves 4

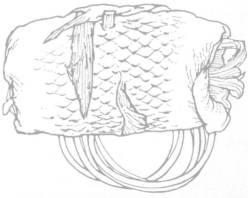

Germany

Schwarzwälder Kirschtorte
(Black Forest Gâteau)

125g/5oz butter, melted
6 eggs
¼ teaspoon vanilla essence
225g/8oz caster sugar
50g/2oz plain flour, sifted twice
50g/2oz cocoa powder

Syrup
150g/6oz sugar
6 tablespoons cold water
4 tablespoons Kirsch

Decoration
600ml/1 pint fresh double cream
50g/2oz sifted icing sugar
3 tablespoons Kirsch
150g/6oz fresh or canned red cherries, stoned
Grated chocolate or chocolate vermicelli

1 Grease and flour the bases and sides of three 18cm/7in sandwich tins
2 Strain melted butter through muslin to clarify. Whisk together eggs, vanilla essence and sugar, over a saucepan of hand-hot water, until mixture is thick and the texture of softly whipped cream (about 8 to 10 minutes)
3 Remove bowl from saucepan, continue whisking for a further 5 minutes
4 Gently fold in the flour, cocoa powder and clarified butter, using a metal spoon. Divide mixture between the prepared tins
5 Place in the centre of a moderate oven (180°C/350°F or Gas No 4) for 10 to 15 minutes. Remove from oven and cool for 5 minutes in the tins, then remove on to a rack to cool thoroughly
6 Meanwhile, place the sugar and water for the syrup in a saucepan. Heat gently for about 5 minutes, then cool and add Kirsch
7 Whip the cream until thick, then stir in the sifted icing sugar and Kirsch
8 Prick the cooled sponge cakes all over with a skewer. Soak the cooled syrup into the cakes. Allow to rest for 5 minutes
9 Sandwich the cakes together with whipped cream and halved cherries
10 Spread the top and sides with cream. Toss the remaining cherries, roughly chopped, over the top surface of the cake
11 Gently press grated chocolate or chocolate vermicelli over the entire surface. Serve at once.
Serves 8 to 10

Biersuppe mit Milch
(Beer Soup with Milk)

300ml/½ pint German beer
Juice of ½ lemon
Small piece of cinnamon stick
600ml/1 pint milk
2 egg yolks
Sugar
Salt

Garnish
Croûtons of fried bread

1 Place beer, lemon juice and cinnamon in a saucepan
2 Heat the milk, pour over the egg yolks, stir well. Add to the hot beer
3 Season with sugar and salt
4 Serve, garnished with croûtons of fried bread.
Serves 4

Holland

Erwtensoep (Pea Soup)

450g/1lb dried or split peas
3 litres/6 pints water
450g/1lb ham or boiling bacon
1 marrow bone
450g/1lb potatoes, peeled and sliced
600ml/1 pint milk
Salt and pepper to taste
3 sliced leeks
3 sticks chopped celery

Garnish
Chopped parsley

1 Wash the peas and soak overnight in 1½ litres/3 pints water. Drain
2 The following day, simmer the ham and marrow bone in 1½ litres/3 pints water for 1 hour. Then add peas and cook until soft for a further hour
3 Add potatoes about 40 minutes before serving
4 Remove the marrow bone and ham, scrape out marrow and return this to the soup. Slice ham and keep hot
5 Sieve the soup or place in a liquidiser, add the milk, salt and pepper. Add leeks and celery and cook for a further 20 minutes, stirring occasionally
6 Serve hot, sprinkled with chopped parsley.
Serves 4 to 6

This is a traditional Dutch soup, served more as a main course, in huge bowls with the ham on a smaller side plate served separately

Boter Koek (Buttercake)

225g / 8oz butter
225g / 8oz soft brown sugar
1 level teaspoon finely grated lemon rind
1 standard egg
225g / 8oz plain flour
50g / 2oz chopped crystallised ginger or
  50g / 2oz blanched and chopped almonds

1 Cream butter, sugar and lemon rind until light and fluffy
2 Beat in egg. Gently fold in flour and ginger
3 Spread into Swiss roll tin (approximately 20cm×30cm / 8in×12in) and scatter almonds over top
4 Bake in centre of moderate oven (180°C / 350°F or Gas No 4) for 45-50 minutes (or until golden)
5 Remove from oven. Cool slightly and cut into squares or fingers
6 Store in an airtight tin when cold.
About 24 pieces

Jachtschotel (Hunter's Dish)

225g / 8oz onions
50g / 2oz butter
225g / 8oz cooked meat, minced
300ml / ½ pint stock
Pinch of ground cloves
Salt and pepper to taste
1 cooking apple, peeled and chopped
450g / 1lb potatoes, boiled and mashed
Fresh breadcrumbs
15g / ½oz butter

1 Slice the onions and fry them in the butter until soft and lightly browned
2 Add minced meat, stock, seasonings, chopped apple and potato, simmer gently for ½ hour
3 Pour the mixture into a 1 litre / 2 pint greased heatproof dish. Sprinkle breadcrumbs on top, dot with butter and brown in a hot oven (230°C / 450°F or Gas No 8) for 10 minutes
4 Serve hot. **Serves 4**

Italy

Lasagne Verdi

1 recipe Spaghetti Bolognaise (page 203)
225g / 8oz lasagne verdi
1 recipe Mornay Sauce (page 131)
50g / 2oz grated Cheddar cheese

1 Make Spaghetti Bolognaise Sauce (page 203). Omit spaghetti, but instead cook lasagne verdi in the same way
2 Make Mornay Sauce (page 131)
3 Arrange layers of cooked lasagne, Bolognaise Sauce and Mornay Sauce in a 1 litre / 2 pint heatproof dish, finishing with a layer of lasagne topped with Mornay Sauce
4 Sprinkle with grated cheese
5 Place in the centre of a moderate oven (180°C / 350°F or Gas No 4) for 45 minutes to 1 hour. Serve hot. **Serves 4**

Fritto Misto

100g / 4oz plain flour
Salt
3 tablespoons melted butter
150ml / ¼ pint tepid milk
Deep fat for frying
1 chicken breast
100g / 4oz chicken livers
100g / 4oz Cheddar cheese
Few florets of cauliflower
225g / 8oz courgettes
100g / 4oz button mushrooms
100g / 4oz peeled prawns
1 egg white

Garnish
Lemon wedges

1 Mix the flour and salt with the melted butter. Blend in the tepid milk to make a smooth coating batter
2 Cut the chicken breast, livers, cheese, cauliflower and courgettes into bite-size pieces. Leave the mushrooms and prawns on one side temporarily
3 Whisk the egg white until stiff and fold into the batter
4 Coat the prepared foods in batter, including mushrooms and prawns, then deep fry them until crisp and golden. Remove from pan and drain on crumpled paper towel
5 Place the Fritto Misto on to individual plates and garnish with lemon wedges. **Serves 4**

Irish Stew (page 191)

Risotto Milanese

1 small finely chopped onion
50g / 2oz butter
350g / 12oz long grain rice
900ml / 1½ pints hot chicken stock or water
Salt and pepper
25g / 1oz extra butter

Accompaniment
75g / 3oz finely grated Cheddar cheese

1 Fry onion gently in butter until pale gold
2 Add rice. Fry further minute, turning it over all
the time. Gradually pour in hot stock or water
3 Cover pan. Simmer for 20-30 minutes (or until
rice grains have swollen and absorbed most of
the liquid). Stir frequently with fork
4 Add seasoning with extra 25g / 1oz butter and
25g / 1oz cheese. Stir gently.
Serves 4

Ireland

Irish Potato Scones

450g / 1lb potatoes, peeled
2 level teaspoons salt
50g / 2oz butter
100g / 4oz flour

1 Cook potatoes in boiling, salted water for about
20 minutes, until soft. Drain and mash well
2 Add salt and butter, then work in the flour, to
make a stiff mixture
3 Turn onto a floured board, knead lightly, then
roll out to ½cm / ¼in thickness
4 Cut into circles with a cutter, about 4cm / 2in
5 Cook on a greased hot girdle or thick based
frying pan, for 4 to 5 minutes, on each side, until
golden brown
6 Serve hot, spread with butter.
Makes about 10 Scones

Irish Stew

1kg/2lb potatoes
250g/8oz onions
1¼kg/2lb 8oz middle neck of lamb
450ml/¾ pint stock or water
1 level teaspoon salt
Pepper
3 level tablespoons finely chopped parsley

1 Thinly slice potatoes and onions
2 Divide lamb into neat pieces. Cut away surplus fat
3 Put vegetables and lamb into saucepan
4 Pour in stock. Season with salt and pepper
5 Bring to boil and lower heat
6 Cover pan. Simmer gently for 1½ hours (or until meat is tender)
7 Transfer to warm dish and sprinkle thickly with parsley.
Serves 4

Luxembourg

Trout Riesling

4 medium trout
25g/1oz flour
Salt and pepper
50g/2oz butter
1 tablespoon salad oil
1 tablespoon finely chopped parsley
1 tablespoon finely chopped chives
3 shallots
Pinch chervil
1 twig tarragon
200ml/⅓ pint dry Riesling
300ml/½ pint fresh single cream
Paprika
Salt and pepper

Accompaniments
Boiled potatoes

1 Clean, wash and dry the trout with kitchen paper. Coat them in seasoned flour
2 Heat butter and oil in a pan and fry the fish gently for 2-3 minutes on each side
3 Remove the fish and transfer to a greased casserole dish
4 Fry the finely chopped herbs in the pan. Stir in the Riesling wine and pour mixture onto the fish
5 Add the fresh cream, paprika and seasoning to taste
6 Cover and bake in a moderately hot oven (200°C/400°F or Gas No 6) for 15-20 minutes. Baste the trout occasionally with the sauce
7 Remove the trout and keep warm. Pour sauce into pan and boil gently until thick, whisking continuously. Cover the fish with the sauce and serve with potatoes.
Serves 4

Langues de Chat (Cat's Tongues)

50g/2oz butter
50g/2oz caster sugar
1 egg
50g/2oz self-raising flour
½ recipe Vanilla Butter Cream Frosting (page 244)
50g/2oz plain chocolate, melted

1 Grease a baking tray
2 Cream together the butter and sugar until light and fluffy. Beat in the egg
3 Work in the flour to make a mixture of a consistency which can be piped
4 Place mixture in a piping bag, fitted with a large star-shaped nozzle
5 Pipe fingers 10cm/4in long on baking tray, spacing them out to allow room for spreading
6 Place in the oven (220°C/425°F or Gas No 7) for about 5 minutes. Cool
7 Sandwich the biscuits together with Butter Cream Frosting, then dip the ends into melted chocolate. **Makes about 12**

Pot au Feu

425g/15oz can tomatoes
300ml/½ pint stock
2 chopped carrots
½ small shredded white cabbage
2 chopped onions
1 chopped leek
2 sticks chopped celery
1 small chopped cauliflower
Salt and pepper
100g/4oz grated Cheddar cheese
Chopped parsley

1 Place all the ingredients, except cheese and parsley, in a large saucepan. Simmer for 35 to 40 minutes
2 Serve the soup sprinkled with cheese and parsley. Check seasoning. **Serves 4 to 6**

Pot au Feu is a traditional country recipe of Luxembourg which is continually allowed to simmer on the hot-plate, and so is immediately ready for serving when required
It is suitable for serving as a meal in itself and can be varied by using different vegetables according to those in season

Pinwheel Sandwich (page 195) Asparagus Rolls (page 194) Pork and Apple Sandwich (page 193) Lettuce, Beef and Horseradish Sandwich (page 195)

Use fresh, but not very new, bread. Make sure that the slices are not too thick

Allow 175g/6oz softened and well-creamed butter for every 24 large bread slices

Make sure that the butter completely covers the bread slices. It acts as a waterproof barrier, preventing moisture from fillings seeping through into the bread and making it soggy

Prepare all fillings beforehand and check to see that they are really well seasoned. If using soft fillings, such as chopped hard-boiled eggs combined with natural yogurt, have something crisp – lettuce or chopped celery for example – to go with it. Contrast of texture adds interest

Allow 225g/8oz of sliced meat, cheese or smoked fish to fill about 8 sandwiches

Number of sandwiches to allow per person will depend on appetite and type of fillings used. As a general guide, allow 1½ to 2 full rounds or 8 to 10 small sandwiches for each person. A round is two slices of bread

If sandwiches are made in advance at night for a packed lunch the next day wrap them in aluminium foil or in a polythene bag and keep in a cold larder or refrigerator overnight

Crust removal is a matter of choice. Large sandwiches keep better if the crusts are left on. Dainty afternoon sandwiches, made from very thin bread, look more attractive and less clumsy if the crusts are removed

Sandwiches can be frozen, but do not include salad vegetables, hard-boiled eggs and mayonnaise in the fillings. Avoid using rather wet fillings as they make sandwiches soggy when thawed. Freeze sandwiches uncut, interleaved with film or greaseproof paper between each one. Storage time – 1 month.

Basic Sandwiches

Lettuce, Cottage Cheese & Pineapple Sandwich

12 large slices white or brown bread
Butter
Shredded lettuce
225g/8oz Cottage cheese
4 tablespoons chopped canned pineapple

1 Spread bread thickly with butter
2 Sandwich slices together, in pairs, with lettuce followed by Cottage cheese mixed with pineapple
3 Cut each sandwich into 2 or 4 pieces. **Serves 4**

Cheese & Celery Sandwich

12 large slices brown bread
Butter
175g/6oz thinly sliced Cheshire cheese
3 tablespoons chopped celery
4 tablespoons fresh double cream

1 Spread bread thickly with butter
2 Sandwich slices together, in pairs, with cheese followed by celery well mixed with double cream
3 Cut each sandwich into 2 or 4 pieces. **Serves 4**

Stilton, Lettuce & Ham Sandwich

12 large slices white or brown bread
Butter
175g/6oz Blue Stilton cheese
6 slices lean ham (approximately 175g/6oz)
Shredded lettuce

1 Spread bread thickly with butter
2 Sandwich slices together, in pairs, with cheese, ham and shredded lettuce
3 Cut each sandwich into 2 or 4 pieces. **Serves 4**

Pork & Apple Sandwich

12 large slices white or brown bread
Butter
6 large slices cold roast pork
1 large unpeeled and grated eating apple
4 tablespoons natural yogurt

1 Spread bread thickly with butter
2 Sandwich slices together, in pairs, with slices of pork followed by apple mixed with yogurt
3 Cut each sandwich into 2 or 4 pieces.
Serves 4

Bacon & Banana Sandwich

12 large slices white or brown bread
Butter
3 medium-sized mashed bananas
12 rashers grilled bacon

1 Spread bread thickly with butter
2 Sandwich slices together, in pairs, with mashed bananas and bacon rashers
3 Cut each sandwich into 2 or 4 pieces.
Serves 4

Smoked Roe & Cucumber Sandwich

12 large slices brown bread
Butter
Smoked cod's roe
Cucumber slices, peeled if preferred

1 Spread bread thickly with butter
2 Sandwich slices together, in pairs, with a thin spread of cod's roe and slices of cucumber
3 Cut each sandwich into 2 or 4 pieces.
Serves 4

Cheese, Apple & Leek Sandwich

12 large slices brown bread
Butter
175g/6oz thinly sliced Derby or Wensleydale cheese
3 level tablespoons grated unpeeled eating apple
3 level tablespoons chopped raw leek
4 to 5 tablespoons natural yogurt

1 Spread bread thickly with butter
2 Sandwich slices together, in pairs, with cheese followed by apple and leek, well mixed with yogurt
3 Cut each sandwich into 2 or 4 pieces. **Serves 4**

Cress, Cheese & Carrot Sandwich

12 large slices brown bread
Butter
Mustard and cress
175g/6oz thinly sliced Double Gloucester cheese
6 level tablespoons grated carrot
4 tablespoons soured cream or natural yogurt

1 Spread bread thickly with butter
2 Sandwich slices together, in pairs, with mustard and cress and cheese, followed by grated carrot mixed with soured cream or yogurt
3 Cut each sandwich into 2 or 4 pieces. **Serves 4**

Asparagus Rolls

1 Remove crusts from very thin, very fresh, slices of white or brown bread
2 Stand on damp tea towel (this helps to prevent bread from cracking)
3 Spread with well-creamed butter
4 Put 2 asparagus tips, with points facing outwards, on to each slice
5 Roll up and hold in place with wooden cocktail sticks
6 Stand on plate or small tray
7 Cover with aluminium foil or sheet of polythene
8 Chill thoroughly
9 Remove sticks just before serving.
Allow 2 to 3 per person

Watercress & Creamed Fish Sandwich

12 large slices brown bread
Butter
About 6 tablespoons chopped watercress
175g/6oz flaked white fish, cooked
50g/2oz peeled prawns
½ level teaspoon finely grated lemon rind
4 to 5 tablespoons salad cream

1 Spread bread thickly with butter
2 Sandwich slices together, in pairs, with watercress followed by fish, prawns and lemon rind mixed with salad cream
3 Cut each sandwich into 2 or 4 pieces. **Serves 4**

Tomato, Cress & Sardine Sandwich

12 slices white or brown bread
Butter
4 large tomatoes, skinned if preferred, and sliced
Mustard and cress
1 can (approximately 125g/4½oz) drained sardines
4 tablespoons natural yogurt
2 teaspoons lemon juice

1 Spread bread thickly with butter
2 Sandwich slices together, in pairs, with tomato slices and mustard and cress followed by sardines, mashed with yogurt and lemon juice
3 Cut each sandwich into 2 or 4 pieces. **Serves 4**

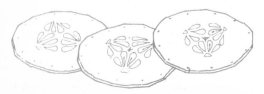

Cheese, Onion & Tomato Sandwich

12 large slices white bread
Butter
175g/6oz sliced Cheddar cheese
1 medium-sized thinly sliced raw onion
4 large tomatoes, skinned if preferred, and sliced

1 Spread bread thickly with butter
2 Sandwich slices together, in pairs, with cheese, raw onion rings and slices of tomato
3 Cut each sandwich into 2 or 4 pieces. **Serves 4**

Cream Cheese, Gherkin & Tomato Sandwich

12 large slices brown bread
Butter
100 to 175g/4 to 6oz cream cheese
3 to 4 level tablespoons finely chopped gherkins
4 large tomatoes, skinned if preferred, and sliced

1 Spread bread thickly with butter
2 Sandwich together, in pairs, with cream cheese, gherkins and slices of tomato
3 Cut each sandwich into 2 or 4 pieces. **Serves 4**

Salmon & Lettuce Sandwich

12 large slices white or brown bread
Butter
Shredded lettuce
1 can (approximately 225g/8oz) red salmon
1 level teaspoon finely grated lemon rind
2 level teaspoons finely grated onion
3 to 4 tablespoons natural yogurt

1 Spread bread thickly with butter
2 Sandwich slices together, in pairs, with lettuce followed by well-drained salmon mashed with lemon rind, grated onion and yogurt
3 Cut each sandwich into 2 or 4 pieces. **Serves 4**

Afternoon Tea Sandwiches

1 Spread very thin slices of white or brown bread with well-creamed butter
2 Sandwich together with choice of finely chopped hard-boiled egg mixed with salad cream, thin slices of peeled cucumber, smoked salmon, well-seasoned cream cheese or fish or meat paste
3 Remove crusts and cut each sandwich into 4 squares or triangles
4 Arrange attractively on serving plate
5 Sprinkle with mustard and cress.
Allow 8 to 10 squares or triangles per person

Pin Wheel Sandwiches

1 Remove crusts from very thin, very fresh, slices of white or brown bread
2 Stand on damp tea towel (this helps to prevent bread from cracking)
3 Spread with well-creamed butter
4 Cover with choice of well-seasoned cream cheese, smoked cod's roe, smoked salmon, soft liver sausage, pâté, fish or meat paste
5 Roll up and hold in place with wooden cocktail sticks
6 Stand on plate or small serving tray
7 Cover with aluminium foil or sheet of polythene
8 Chill thoroughly
9 Just before serving, remove sticks and cut each roll into thin slices.
Allow about 8 to 12 Pin Wheels per person

Egg & Creamed Salad Sandwich

12 large slices white or brown bread
Butter
4 large sliced hard-boiled eggs
4 level tablespoons grated cabbage
2 level tablespoons grated carrot
4 chopped spring onions
4 tablespoons fresh double cream

1 Spread bread thickly with butter
2 Sandwich slices together, in pairs, with slices of egg followed by cabbage, carrot and onions mixed with cream
3 Cut each sandwich into 2 or 4 pieces.
Serves 4

Fried Sandwiches

4 large slices white bread
Butter
75 to 100g/3 to 4oz Cheddar cheese or sliced cooked meat or 2 sliced hard-boiled eggs
Ketchup or pickles
1 standard egg
4 tablespoons milk
Extra 50g/2oz butter
2 teaspoons olive or corn oil

1 Spread bread with butter
2 Sandwich slices together, in pairs, with choice of cheese, meat or eggs and ketchup or pickles to taste
3 Press firmly together and cut each sandwich into 2 triangles or squares
4 Soak a few minutes in egg beaten with milk
5 Fry in 50g/2oz hot butter and oil until golden brown on both sides
6 Drain on soft kitchen paper
7 Serve immediately.
Serves 2

Tongue & Cucumber Sandwich

12 large slices white or brown bread
Butter
6 large slices tongue
4 level tablespoons cucumber, peeled if preferred, and chopped
4 to 5 tablespoons fresh double or soured cream

1 Spread bread thickly with butter
2 Sandwich slices together, in pairs, with tongue followed by cucumber mixed with cream
3 Cut each sandwich into 2 or 4 pieces. **Serves 4**

Lettuce, Cheese & Walnut Sandwich

12 large slices white or brown bread
Butter
Shredded lettuce
175 to 225g/6 to 8oz grated Leicester cheese
25g/1oz finely chopped shelled walnut halves
3 tablespoons natural yogurt

1 Spread bread thickly with butter
2 Sandwich slices together, in pairs, with lettuce then cheese well mixed with walnuts and yogurt
3 Cut each sandwich into 2 or 4 pieces. **Serves 4**

Avocado & Onion Sandwich

12 slices white or brown bread
Butter
1 large thinly sliced onion
1 medium-sized avocado pear
1 tablespoon lemon juice
2 tablespoons fresh double cream
½ level teaspoon paprika

1 Spread bread thickly with butter
2 Sandwich slices together, in pairs, with onion rings followed by avocado pulp, finely mashed with lemon juice, cream and paprika
3 Cut each sandwich into 2 or 4 pieces. **Serves 4**

Lettuce, Beef & Horseradish Sandwich

12 large slices white or brown bread
Butter
6 large slices beef or corned beef
Shredded lettuce
4 tablespoons natural yogurt
½ to 1 level teaspoon grated horseradish

1 Spread bread thickly with butter
2 Sandwich slices together, in pairs, with beef or corned beef and lettuce then yogurt mixed with horseradish. Cut each into 2 or 4 pieces. **Serves 4**

Toasted Sandwiches

Toasted Bean and Bacon Sandwich

8 large slices white or brown bread
Butter
445g / 15½oz can baked beans
150g / 6oz bacon
Made mustard

Garnish
Watercress or parsley

1 Spread bread thickly with butter
2 Fry the bacon until crisp, then crumble it and mix with beans and mustard
3 Sandwich bread together, in pairs with bean and bacon mixture
4 Toast each sandwich lightly on both sides
5 Press down firmly and cut into 2 triangles
6 Garnish with watercress or parsley
7 Serve immediately. **Serves 3 to 4**

Toasted Beef & Tomato Sandwich

8 large slices white or brown bread
Butter
100 to 175g / 4 to 6oz cold roast beef, sliced
Made mustard
4 medium-sized sliced tomatoes

Garnish
Watercress or parsley

1 Spread bread thickly with butter
2 Sandwich together, in pairs, with beef, spread with mustard and cover with tomato slices
3 Toast each sandwich lightly on both sides
4 Press down firmly and cut into 2 triangles
5 Garnish with watercress or parsley
6 Serve immediately. **Serves 3 to 4**

Toasted Hamburger and Stilton Sandwich

1 Follow recipe and method for Toasted Beef and Tomato Sandwich (above)
2 Fill each with slices of Stilton cheese (100 to 175g / 4 to 6oz) and top with a grilled hamburger and some mustard pickle.
Serves 4

Toasted Lancashire Cheese and Apple Sandwich

1 Follow recipe and method for Toasted Beef and Tomato Sandwich (left)
2 Fill each with crumbled Lancashire cheese (100 to 175g / 4 to 6oz) and 2 peeled, cored and diced eating apples.
Serves 4

Toasted Cheese & Pickle Sandwich

1 Follow recipe and method for Toasted Beef and Tomato Sandwich (left)
2 Fill each with slices of Cheddar cheese (100 to 175g / 4 to 6oz) and mustard pickle. **Serves 4**

Toasted Bacon & Mushroom Sandwich

1 Follow recipe and method for Toasted Beef and Tomato Sandwich (left)
2 Fill sandwiches with 225g / 8oz grilled bacon rashers and 100g / 4oz sliced and fried or grilled mushrooms.
Serves 4

Toasted Egg & Haddock Sandwich

8 large slices white or brown bread
Butter
4 large eggs
100g / 4oz cooked flaked smoked haddock
2 tablespoons milk
Extra 15g / ½oz butter
1 level tablespoon finely chopped parsley
Seasoning to taste

Garnish
Watercress or parsley

1 Spread bread thickly with butter
2 Scramble eggs lightly with smoked haddock, milk, 15g / ½oz butter, parsley and seasoning to taste
3 Sandwich buttered bread slices together, in pairs, with egg mixture
4 Toast each sandwich lightly on both sides
5 Press down firmly and cut into 2 triangles
6 Garnish with watercress or parsley
7 Serve immediately. **Serves 3 to 4**

Hawaiian Club Sandwich (below)

Club Sandwiches

These are hearty-sized tasty sandwiches made from 3 slices white or brown bread layered with a variety of fillings. They are very useful for a quick lunch or supper

Hawaiian Club Sandwich

3 large slices freshly made white or brown toast
Butter
4 small crisp lettuce leaves
1 large canned pineapple ring, well drained
About 50g / 2oz sliced Derby cheese
Mild mustard

Garnish
2 stuffed olives or gherkins

1 Spread first slice of toast with butter
2 Cover with lettuce leaves and pineapple ring
3 Top with second slice of toast
4 Spread with more butter
5 Cover with cheese. Spread cheese with a little mild mustard
6 Butter third slice of toast. Put on top of cheese, buttered side down
7 Cut into 2 triangles
8 Garnish with olives or gherkins speared on to cocktail sticks. **Serves 1**

Sausage & Chutney Club Sandwich

1 Follow recipe and method for Hawaiian Club Sandwich (left)
2 For first layer, use crisp lettuce leaves topped with slices of cold cooked pork sausages
3 For second layer, use 2 or 3 slices of Wensleydale cheese covered with sweet pickle or chutney. **Serves 1**

Egg & Cheese Club Sandwich

1 Follow recipe and method for Hawaiian Club Sandwich (left)
2 For first layer, use crisp lettuce leaves topped with slices of hard-boiled egg and hot Mornay Sauce (page 131)
3 For second layer, use 2 slices of Caerphilly cheese covered with skinned tomato slices. **Serves 1**

Ham Club Sandwich

1 Follow recipe and method for Hawaiian Club Sandwich (left)
2 For first layer, use crisp lettuce leaves topped with about 2 tablespoons Cottage cheese
3 For second layer, use slices of ham covered with thin raw onion rings. **Serves 1**

Danish-style Open Sandwiches

There are four pointers to success when making these
1 Whether you are using white, brown, rye bread or pumpernickel, make sure the slices are covered thickly with butter
2 See that the butter comes right to the edges of every slice
3 Be generous with toppings and garnishes
4 Provide knives and forks

Prawn & Mayonnaise Open Sandwich

1 Cover slice of buttered bread with lettuce leaves
2 Arrange mound of peeled prawns or shrimps in centre
3 Top with heaped tablespoon Mayonnaise (page 126)
4 Sprinkle lightly with paprika
5 Garnish with parsley. **Serves 1**

Egg & Tomato Open Sandwich

1 Arrange slices of tomatoes, skinned if preferred, down one edge of buttered bread slice
2 Arrange hard-boiled egg slices down the other edge of slice
3 Cover centre join with spoons of Mayonnaise (page 126)
4 Sprinkle with chopped chives. **Serves 1**

Boiled Beef & Carrot Open Sandwich

1 Cover slice of buttered bread with slices of boiled beef
2 Put a mound of natural yogurt in centre
3 Surround with ring of cooked carrot slices
4 Top with half a pickled onion. **Serves 1**

Liver Sausage & Potato Salad Open Sandwich

1 Cover slice of buttered bread with rounds of liver sausage
2 Arrange a cross of potato salad on top
3 Sprinkle lightly with paprika
4 Garnish with one gherkin. **Serves 1**

Rollmop & Yogurt Open Sandwich

1 Stand crisp lettuce leaf on corner of buttered bread slice
2 Cover rest of slice with large pieces of rollmop
3 Put 2 heaped teaspoons natural yogurt in centre
4 Sprinkle with paprika
5 Garnish with slices of pickled cucumber.
Serves 1

Scrambled Egg & Salmon Open Sandwich

1 Cover slice of buttered bread with lettuce leaves or watercress
2 Top with 1 or 2 cold scrambled eggs and strips of smoked salmon
3 Garnish with 1 or 2 black olives.
Serves 1

Ham, Cheese & Pineapple Open Sandwich

1 Cover slice of buttered bread with large slice of ham
2 Top with 1 canned pineapple ring, well drained
3 Fill centre with mound of cottage cheese
4 Garnish with strips of red or green pepper.
Serves 1

Lettuce & Tongue Open Sandwich

1 Cover slice of buttered bread with shredded lettuce
2 Top with slice of tongue
3 Arrange line of skinned tomato slices down centre
4 Sprinkle with chopped parsley
5 Garnish by piping with Mustard Butter (page 96).
Serves 1

Cheese, Peach & Olive Open Sandwich

1 Cover slice of buttered bread with crisp lettuce leaves
2 Top with layer of Cottage cheese
3 Stand line of well-drained peach slices down centre
4 Garnish with black olives.
Serves 1

Danish Open Sandwiches. Cheese, Peach and Olive, Prawn and Mayonnaise, Liver Sausage and Potato (page 198), Salami and Cheese, Pork and Orange (below) Rollmop and Yogurt (page 198)

Caviare, Egg Yolk & Onion Open Sandwich

1 Cover slice of buttered bread with lettuce leaves
2 Top with ring of caviare or Danish-style caviare (Lump fish)
3 Fill centre with raw egg yolk
4 Sprinkle with finely grated onion. **Serves 1**

Pork & Orange Open Sandwich

1 Cover slice of buttered bread with crisp lettuce leaves
2 Top with slices of cold roast pork
3 Put heaped teaspoon of Curry Yogurt Dressing (page 124) in centre
4 Garnish with slice of orange, shaped into twist, and watercress. **Serves 1**

Salami & Cheese Open Sandwich

1 Cover slice of buttered bread with crisp lettuce leaves
2 Top with ring of salami slices
3 Fill centre with Cottage cheese
4 Garnish with wedge of tomato. **Serves 1**

Cheese & Date Open Sandwich

1 Cover slice of buttered bread with crisp lettuce leaves or watercress
2 Top with slice of Cheshire cheese
3 Put heaped teaspoon of Soured Cream with Dates Dressing (page 122) in centre
4 Garnish with orange slice, shaped into twist. **Serves 1**

Corned Beef and Vegetable Tart (page 201)

Corned Beef Pie

175g / 6oz corned beef
50g / 2oz fresh white breadcrumbs
50g / 2oz finely grated Caerphilly cheese
2 level tablespoons finely chopped parsley
2 level teaspoons finely grated onion
½ teaspoon Worcestershire sauce
3 tablespoons milk
¼ level teaspoon salt
Shake of pepper
1 recipe Short Crust Pastry (page 211)
Milk for brushing

1 Chop beef. Combine with breadcrumbs, cheese, parsley, onion, Worcestershire sauce, milk, salt and pepper
2 Cut Pastry into 2 equal-sized pieces
3 Roll out one half and use to line 20cm / 8in buttered heatproof plate
4 Pile filling in centre. Moisten edges of Pastry with water
5 Cover with rest of Pastry, rolled into lid
6 Press edges well together to seal. Ridge with fork or press into flutes
7 Brush with milk
8 Bake towards top of moderately hot oven (200°C / 400°F or Gas No 6) for 45 minutes
9 Serve hot or cold. **Serves 4 to 6**

Flaky Cheese & Onion Pasties

1 recipe Flaky Pastry (page 214)
175g / 6oz finely grated Wensleydale cheese
1 level tablespoon finely grated onion
Beaten egg to bind
Salt and pepper
Milk for brushing

1 Roll out Pastry into 40cm×20cm / 16in×8in rectangle
2 Cut into eight 10cm / 4in squares
3 Combine cheese with onion. Bind fairly stiffly with egg. Season to taste with salt and pepper
4 Put equal amounts of cheese mixture on to centres of Pastry squares
5 Moisten edges of Pastry with water. Fold squares in half to form triangles
6 Press edges well together to seal. Flake by cutting with back of knife
7 Make 2 or 3 snips across top of each Pasty with scissors. Transfer to damp baking tray
8 Leave for 30 minutes
9 Brush with milk. Bake towards top of hot oven (220°C / 425°F or Gas No 7) for 10 minutes
10 Reduce temperature to moderately hot (200°C / 400°F or Gas No 6). Bake further 10 to 15 minutes (or until well puffed and brown)
11 Serve hot. **Serves 4**

Corned Beef & Vegetable Tarts F

Short Crust Pastry (page 211) made with
175g / 6oz flour
100g / 4oz corned beef
50g / 2oz cooked diced potato
50g / 2oz cooked peas
15g / ½oz butter
15g / ½oz flour
4 tablespoons milk
1 standard egg, beaten
Salt and pepper

1 Roll out Pastry. Cut into 12 rounds with 8cm / 3in biscuit cutter
2 Use to line 12 lightly buttered bun tins
3 Chop corned beef. Combine with potatoes and peas
4 Melt butter in pan. Stir in flour and cook 2 minutes without browning. Gradually blend in milk. Cook, stirring, until mixture thickens
5 Remove from heat. Stir in beef, potatoes, peas and beaten egg. Season to taste
6 Spoon equal amounts into Pastry-lined tins
7 Bake just above centre of moderately hot oven (200°C / 400°F or Gas No 6) for 10 minutes
8 Reduce temperature to 190°C / 375°F or Gas No 5 and bake for further 12 to 15 minutes
9 Remove from tins. Serve hot or cold.
Serves 4

Cheese & Parsley Pudding

Yolks and whites of 2 standard eggs
300ml / ½ pint lukewarm milk
75g / 3oz grated Derby or Cheshire cheese
50g / 2oz fresh white breadcrumbs
½ level teaspoon dry mustard
½ level teaspoon salt
2 level tablespoons finely chopped parsley

Garnish
Watercress

1 Beat egg yolks with milk and cheese
2 Combine crumbs with mustard, salt and parsley
3 Gradually stir in warm milk mixture and mix well
4 Leave to stand 30 minutes. Fold in egg whites, beaten to stiff snow
5 Transfer to ½ litre / 1 pint buttered heatproof dish. Bake towards top of moderately hot oven (200°C / 400°F or Gas No 6) for 25 to 30 minutes (or until golden)
6 Garnish with watercress. **Serves 4**

Cheese & Ham Pudding

1 Follow recipe and method for Cheese and Parsley Pudding (above)
2 Add 25 to 50g / 1 to 2oz finely chopped ham instead of parsley. **Serves 4**

Cheese & Sultana Pie

300ml / ½ pint Basic White Coating Sauce (page 129)
100g / 4oz finely grated Derby or Cheddar cheese
1 standard egg, beaten
175g / 6oz sultanas
1 recipe Short Crust Pastry (page 211)
Milk for brushing

1 Warm sauce, add cheese and stir until melted
2 Remove from heat and cool to lukewarm. Beat in egg and sultanas
3 Cut Pastry into 2 equal-sized pieces
4 Roll out one half and use to line 20cm / 8in buttered heatproof pie plate
5 Fill with cheese mixture. Moisten edges of Pastry with cold water
6 Cover with lid rolled from rest of Pastry
7 Press Pastry edges well together to seal. Make 2 slits in top with knife
8 Transfer pie to baking tray and brush with milk
9 Bake towards top of moderately hot oven (200°C / 400°F or Gas No 6) for 40 minutes
10 Serve hot or cold. **Serves 4**

Cheese & Sausage Pie

1 Follow recipe and method for Cheese and Sultana Pie (above)
2 Use 175g / 6oz thinly sliced, cooked pork sausages instead of sultanas.
Serves 4

Savoury Cheese & Onion Casserole

6 large slices white bread
175g / 6oz grated Double Gloucester cheese
3 standard eggs
¼ level teaspoon salt
½ small onion, finely grated
450ml / ¾ pint lukewarm milk
Shake of pepper

1 Trim crusts off bread. Cut each slice into 2 triangles
2 Arrange half the triangles over base of fairly shallow buttered ¾ to 1 litre / 1½ to 2 pint heatproof dish
3 Sprinkle bread layer with 100g / 4oz cheese. Cover with remaining bread triangles
4 Beat eggs with salt, onion, warm milk and pepper. Pour into dish over bread and cheese
5 Leave to stand for 30 minutes
6 Sprinkle with rest of cheese
7 Bake in centre of moderate oven (180°C / 350°F or Gas No 4) for 50 minutes to 1 hour (or until well browned)
8 Serve immediately. **Serves 4**

Cheese & Walnut Buns

150g / 6oz self-raising flour
¼ level teaspoon baking powder
¼ level teaspoon salt
½ level teaspoon dry mustard
75g / 3oz butter
40g / 1½oz very finely grated Derby cheese
25g / 1oz finely chopped shelled walnut halves
1 standard egg, beaten
5 to 6 tablespoons cold milk

1 Sift flour, baking powder, salt and mustard into bowl. Rub in butter finely
2 Add cheese and walnuts. Toss lightly together
3 Mix to fairly soft batter with egg and milk, stirring briskly. Transfer to 12 buttered bun tins
4 Bake just above centre of moderately hot oven (200°C / 400°F or Gas No 6) for 20 minutes (or until well risen and golden)
5 Serve hot with butter. **Serves 4**

Cheese & Ham Buns

1 Follow recipe and method for Cheese and Walnut Buns (above)
2 Use 25g / 1oz finely chopped ham instead of walnuts. **Serves 4**

Cheese & Raisin Buns

1 Follow recipe and method for Cheese and Walnut Buns (above)
2 Use 25g / 1oz chopped seedless raisins instead of walnuts. **Serves 4**

Cheese & Prawn Buns

1 Follow recipe and method for Cheese and Walnut Buns (above)
2 Use 50g / 2oz finely chopped peeled prawns instead of walnuts. **Serves 4**

Spaghetti Neapolitan

350g / 12oz spaghetti
1 recipe freshly made Tomato Sauce (page 134)

Accompaniment
100g / 4oz finely grated Cheddar cheese

1 Cook spaghetti in boiling salted water until tender (about 20 minutes), stirring often to prevent sticking
2 Drain well. Transfer equal amounts to 4 warm serving plates
3 Pour Tomato Sauce over each. Serve hot. Serve cheese separately. **Serves 4**

Cheese Roll Puffs

50g / 2oz luncheon meat
1 large hard-boiled egg
1 small celery stalk
2 tablespoons sweet pickle
4 tablespoons fresh double cream
Salt and pepper to taste
4 large soft rolls
175g / 6oz grated Wensleydale or Cheddar cheese
1 standard egg, beaten
1 level teaspoon made mustard

1 Chop luncheon meat, egg and celery
2 Combine with pickle and 2 tablespoons cream. Season to taste with salt and pepper
3 Cut rolls in half. Spread with meat mixture
4 Arrange on lightly buttered baking tray
5 Mix cheese with beaten egg, rest of cream and mustard
6 Spoon over roll halves. Bake just above centre of moderately hot oven (200°C / 400°F or Gas No 6) for 10 to 15 minutes (or until golden and fluffy)
7 Serve immediately.
Serves 4

Macaroni Cheese

75g / 3oz broken macaroni
20g / ¾oz butter
20g / ¾oz flour
½ level teaspoon dry mustard
300ml / ½ pint milk
175g / 6oz crumbled Lancashire or grated Cheddar cheese
Salt and pepper to taste

Garnish
Parsley

1 Cook macaroni in about 1 litre / 2 pints boiling salted water until tender (15 to 20 minutes)
2 After 10 minutes, melt butter in saucepan, add flour and mustard and cook slowly for 2 minutes. Stir often and do not allow mixture to brown
3 Gradually blend in milk. Cook, stirring until sauce comes to boil and thickens
4 Simmer for 2 minutes and remove from heat
5 Stir in 100g / 4oz cheese. Season to taste with salt and pepper
6 Drain macaroni, add to sauce and mix well
7 Transfer to ¾ litre / 1½ pint buttered heatproof dish
8 Sprinkle rest of cheese on top and brown under hot grill
9 Garnish with parsley.
Serves 4

If Macaroni Cheese is prepared in advance, re-heat towards top of moderately hot oven (200°C / 400°F or Gas No 6) 15 to 20 minutes

Macaroni Cheese with Bacon

1 Follow recipe and method for Macaroni Cheese (page 202)
2 Add 100g/4oz chopped and lightly fried bacon to sauce with macaroni. **Serves 4**

Macaroni Cheese with Smoked Haddock

1 Follow recipe and method for Macaroni Cheese (page 202)
2 Add 100g/4oz cooked and flaked smoked haddock to sauce with macaroni. **Serves 4**

Spaghetti Bolognese

1 medium-sized onion
40g/1½oz butter
2 teaspoons olive or corn oil
250g/8oz lean minced beef
1 garlic clove (optional)
100g/4oz mushrooms
300ml/½ pint water
1 bay leaf
150g/5oz can tomato purée
2 level teaspoons sugar
½ level teaspoon basil or mixed herbs
Salt and pepper
350g/12oz spaghetti

Accompaniment
75 to 100g/3 to 4oz finely grated Cheddar cheese

1 Chop onion finely. Fry slowly in butter and oil until pale gold
2 Add beef. Fry further 3 to 4 minutes, breaking it up and stirring all the time
3 Chop garlic (if used). Wash mushrooms and stalks
4 Add to saucepan with water, bay leaf, purée, sugar, basil or mixed herbs and salt and pepper to taste
5 Bring slowly to boil, stirring. Cover pan and lower heat
6 Simmer gently for 30 minutes and uncover
7 Continue to cook for further 20 to 30 minutes (or until sauce is thick and creamy and about half the liquid has evaporated). Stir frequently
8 Meanwhile, cook spaghetti in boiling salted water until tender (about 20 minutes), stirring often to prevent sticking
9 Drain well. Transfer equal amounts to 4 warm serving plates
10 Pour sauce over each. Serve immediately
11 Serve cheese separately.
Serves 4

Ingredients for Spaghetti Bolognese (above)

Pizza Neapolitan (below)

Pizza Neapolitan

Dough Base
225g / 8oz plain flour
1 level teaspoon salt
15g / ½oz butter
7g / ¼oz fresh yeast or 1 level teaspoon dried yeast
4 tablespoons lukewarm water
4 tablespoons lukewarm milk
¼ level teaspoon sugar (only if using dried yeast)
About 25g / 1oz butter, melted

Filling
225g / 8oz grated Cheddar cheese
100g / 4oz grated Caerphilly cheese
500g / 1lb skinned and sliced tomatoes
1 level teaspoon marjoram, basil or thyme
Salt and pepper
Anchovy fillets
Black olives

1 Sift flour and salt into bowl
2 Rub in butter
3 Blend yeast to smooth cream with water. Stir in milk. If using dried yeast, dissolve sugar in water and sprinkle yeast on top. Leave 10 to 15 minutes (or until frothy). Stir in milk
4 Mix dry ingredients to dough with yeast liquid, adding extra flour if needed, until dough leaves sides of bowl clean
5 Turn out and knead thoroughly 5 to 10 minutes (or until dough feels smooth and elastic)
6 Cover and leave until doubled in size
7 Turn out on to floured board. Roll into long strip. Brush with melted butter and roll up like Swiss roll. Repeat 3 times
8 Divide dough into 4 equal-sized pieces. Shape each into 15cm / 6in round
9 Place on large buttered baking tray
10 Cover with alternate layers of cheese and tomatoes, sprinkling herbs and salt and pepper between layers
11 Finish with layer of cheese. Decorate tops with lattice of anchovy fillets
12 Stud with olives. Leave in cool for ½ an hour
13 Bake towards top of hot oven (230°C / 450°F or Gas No 8) for 25 to 30 minutes
14 Serve hot or cold. **Serves 4**

Pizza with Mushrooms & Ham

1 Follow recipe and method for Pizza Neapolitan (page 204)
2 Instead of garnishing with anchovies and olives, use 50g/2oz sliced mushrooms, lightly fried in a little butter, 50g/2oz ham cut into strips and 2 small skinned tomatoes, cut into wedges.
Serves 4

Cheese, Egg & Noodle Ring

175g/6oz flat noodles
300ml/½ pint Basic White Coating Sauce (page 129)
225g/8oz finely grated Cheddar cheese
225g/8oz cooked sliced green beans or peas
Salt and pepper to taste
4 large hard-boiled eggs
1 level tablespoon finely chopped parsley

1 Cook noodles in boiling salted water until tender
2 Drain and arrange in ring on warm serving dish. Keep hot
3 Warm sauce and stir in 175g/6oz cheese and beans or peas. Season to taste
4 Halve eggs, add to sauce and heat through gently
5 Pour into noodle ring
6 Sprinkle with remaining cheese mixed with parsley
7 Serve immediately. **Serves 4**

Welsh Rarebit

4 large slices white or brown bread
25g/1oz softened butter
1 level teaspoon made mustard
¼ level teaspoon salt
Shake Cayenne pepper
¼ teaspoon Worcestershire sauce
175g/6oz crumbled Lancashire or grated Cheddar cheese
2 tablespoons milk

1 Toast bread on one side only
2 Cream butter well. Stir in mustard, salt, Cayenne pepper, Worcestershire sauce, cheese and milk
3 Spread equal amounts thickly over untoasted sides of bread
4 Brown under hot grill.
Serves 4

Buck Rarebit

1 Follow recipe and method for Welsh Rarebit (above)
2 Serve each with poached egg on top.
Serves 4

Bacon Rarebit

1 Follow recipe and method for Welsh Rarebit (left)
2 Serve each with 2 slices grilled or fried streaky bacon on top. **Serves 4**

Tomato Rarebit

1 Follow recipe and method for Welsh Rarebit (left)
2 Serve each with 2 or 3 grilled or fried tomato slices on top.
Serves 4

Creamed Corn & Ham Scramble

6 standard eggs
4 tablespoons fresh single cream
15g/½oz butter
1 can sweetcorn kernels (about 225g/8oz)
100g/4oz finely chopped lean ham
Large pinch of grated nutmeg
Salt and pepper
4 slices hot buttered toast

Garnish
1 level tablespoon finely chopped parsley

1 Beat eggs and cream well together
2 Pour into frying pan. Add butter, drained sweetcorn, ham, grated nutmeg and salt and pepper to taste
3 Scramble over low heat until creamy
4 Pile equal amounts on to buttered toast and sprinkle with parsley.
Serves 4

Cheese & Crab Ramekins

4 large hard-boiled eggs
150ml/¼ pint Cheese Coating Sauce (page 129)
100g/4oz cooked crab meat
25g/1oz butter
25g/1oz grated Leicester cheese

Garnish
Watercress

Accompaniment
4 slices hot buttered toast

1 Chop eggs coarsely
2 Add to sauce with crab meat and butter
3 Heat through gently. Do not allow to boil
4 Transfer equal amounts to 4 buttered Ramekin dishes or individual heatproof dishes
5 Sprinkle tops with cheese. Brown under hot grill. Garnish with watercress
6 Serve at once with hot buttered toast.
Serves 4

Creamed Roes on Toast

400g / 12oz soft herring roes
150ml / ¼ pint milk
3 level teaspoons flour
1 tablespoon fresh cream
Salt and pepper
4 slices hot buttered toast

Garnish
Paprika
4 lemon wedges
Parsley

1 Rinse roes in cold water
2 Put into saucepan. Add 150ml / ¼ pint milk
3 Cover pan and simmer for 7 minutes
4 Mash with fork. Stir in flour blended with fresh cream
5 Cook, stirring, until mixture comes to boil and thickens. Simmer gently for 5 minutes
6 Season to taste with salt and pepper
7 Transfer equal amounts to buttered toast
8 Sprinkle with paprika. Garnish with lemon and parsley. **Serves 4**

Quiche Lorraine

Short Crust Pastry made with 150g / 6oz flour
(page 211)
100g / 4oz streaky bacon
150ml / ¼ pint milk
150ml / ¼ pint fresh single cream
3 standard eggs, beaten
Large pinch grated nutmeg
Salt and pepper

1 Roll out Pastry. Use to line 20cm / 8in flan ring resting on lightly buttered baking tray
2 Cut bacon into strips. Fry lightly in its own fat until soft but not crisp
3 Drain thoroughly on soft kitchen paper. Use to line base of pastry case
4 Heat milk and cream to just below boiling point. Combine with beaten eggs
5 Season with grated nutmeg and salt and pepper to taste. Pour into pastry case
6 Bake in centre of moderately hot oven (200°C / 400°F or Gas No 6) for 10 minutes. Reduce temperature to moderate (160°C / 325°F or Gas No 3). Bake for further 35 to 45 minutes (or until filling is set)
7 Serve hot. **Serves 4 to 5**

Marrow Cheese

1 medium-sized marrow
2 large onions
100g / 4oz crumbled Lancashire cheese
300ml / ½ pint Basic White Coating Sauce
(page 129)
2 level tablespoons toasted breadcrumbs
25g / 1oz butter

1 Peel marrow. Cut into 2cm / 1in thick slices
2 Remove centres. Cut rings into cubes
3 Steam over boiling water until just tender
4 Peel onions, cut into rings and cook in boiling salted water until soft. Drain
5 Arrange half steamed marrow over base of 1 to 1¼ litre / 2 to 2½ pint buttered heatproof dish
6 Cover with onions. Sprinkle with 75g / 3oz of cheese. Top with rest of marrow
7 Coat with Sauce. Sprinkle with remaining cheese and breadcrumbs
8 Dot with butter. Re-heat towards top of hot oven (220°C / 425°F or Gas No 7) for 15 minutes (or until top is light brown). Serve with baked jacket potatoes and butter. **Serves 4**

Potato Cheese & Parsley Pie

750g / 1lb 8oz potatoes
4 tablespoons milk
1 standard egg, beaten
1 level teaspoon dry mustard
175g / 6oz grated Double-Gloucester cheese
3 level tablespoons finely chopped parsley
½ level teaspoon yeast extract
Seasoning to taste

1 Cook potatoes in boiling salted water until tender. Drain
2 Mash finely with milk, egg, mustard, 100g / 4oz cheese, parsley and yeast extract
3 Season to taste with salt and pepper
4 Transfer to buttered 1 litre / 2 pint heatproof dish. Sprinkle remaining cheese over top
5 Re-heat towards top of hot oven (220°C / 425°F or Gas No 7) for 15 minutes (or until top is light brown). Serve with baked tomatoes. **Serves 4**

Potato Cheese & Onion Pie

1 Follow recipe and method for Potato Cheese and Parsley Pie (above)
2 Add 1 medium-sized finely chopped boiled onion with parsley. **Serves 4**

Vegetarian Dishes

Cheese and Noodle Hot Pot (below)

Cheese & Noodle Hot Pot

225g / 8oz flat noodles
1 medium-sized onion
25g / 1oz butter
300ml / $\frac{1}{2}$ pint Basic White Coating Sauce
 (page 129)
2 level tablespoons tomato purée
50g / 2oz chopped hazelnuts
225g / 8oz Cottage cheese
Salt and pepper
50g / 2oz crumbled Lancashire cheese

Garnish
1 sliced tomato
Parsley

1 Cook noodles in boiling salted water until
tender. Drain
2 Chop onion. Fry gently in butter until golden
3 Stir cooked noodles and fried onion into Sauce
4 Add purée, hazelnuts and Cottage cheese
5 Mix thoroughly. Season to taste with salt and
pepper
6 Transfer to 1 litre / 2 pint buttered heatproof
dish and sprinkle with cheese
7 Re-heat just above centre of moderately hot
oven (190°C / 375°F or Gas No 5) for 20 to 25
minutes (or until top is golden)
8 Garnish with tomato slices and parsley
9 Serve with a green vegetable. **Serves 4**

Gloucester Pie

8 slices bread (day old for preference)
Butter
100g / 4oz Double Gloucester cheese
250g / 8oz skinned tomatoes
150ml / $\frac{1}{4}$ pint milk
1 standard egg
1 level teaspoon made mustard
$\frac{1}{4}$ level teaspoon salt
Shake of pepper
Extra 25g / 1oz butter

1 Cut crusts from slices of bread. Butter slices
thickly
2 Sandwich together, in pairs, with thinly sliced
cheese and slices of tomato
3 Cut each sandwich into 4 triangles. Arrange in
buttered shallow heatproof dish
4 Beat milk with egg, mustard and salt and pepper
to taste
5 Pour into dish over sandwiches
6 Leave to stand for $\frac{1}{2}$ an hour (or until bread has
absorbed all the liquid). Dot top with pieces of
extra butter
7 Bake just above centre of moderately hot oven
(190°C / 375°F or Gas No 5) for 25 to 30 minutes
(or until top is crisp and golden)
8 Serve with a green vegetable or green salad.
Serves 4

Cheese & Rice Hot Pot

1 Follow recipe and method for Cheese and Noodle Hot Pot (page 207)
2 Use 225 to 350g/8 to 12oz rice instead of noodles. **Serves 4**

Almond Rissoles

100g/4oz ground almonds
175g/6oz fresh white breadcrumbs
1 small onion, finely grated
3 level tablespoons finely chopped parsley
½ level teaspoon mixed herbs
1 standard egg, beaten
25g/1oz butter, melted
Salt and pepper
Cold milk to mix

Coating
1 small egg, beaten
About 25g/1oz toasted breadcrumbs
50g/2oz butter
2 teaspoons olive or corn oil

1 Put almonds and breadcrumbs into bowl
2 Finely grate onion and add to breadcrumb mixture with parsley and herbs
3 Work in egg and butter. Season to taste
4 Mix to stiff paste with milk. Shape into 8 rissoles
5 Coat with beaten egg and crumbs
6 Fry in hot butter and oil until crisp and golden, allowing about 4 to 5 minutes per side
7 Drain on soft kitchen paper and serve hot with mixed vegetables or cold with salad. **Serves 4**

Hazelnut Rissoles

1 Follow recipe and method for Almond Rissoles (above)
2 Use ground hazelnuts instead of almonds, and fresh brown breadcrumbs instead of white. **Serves 4**

Cashew Nut Rissoles

1 Follow recipe and method for Almond Rissoles (above)
2 Use ground cashew nuts instead of almonds
3 Add 1 level teaspoon finely grated lemon rind with mixed herbs. **Serves 4**

Egg & Mushroom Savoury

250g/8oz mushrooms
2 tablespoons milk
6 standard eggs
2 level tablespoons finely chopped parsley
½ level teaspoon salt
2 large skinned tomatoes
75g/3oz crumbled Lancashire cheese

1 Peel mushrooms. Arrange in frying pan and pour in milk
2 Bring just up to boil. Remove from heat
3 Transfer mushrooms to ½ litre/1 pint buttered heatproof dish
4 Beat eggs with mushroom liquor
5 Add parsley and salt
6 Scramble lightly until creamy
7 Spoon over mushrooms. Top with slices of tomato
8 Sprinkle thickly with crumbled cheese
9 Brown under hot grill
10 Serve with fried potatoes. **Serves 4**

Vegetable Curry with Cheese

½ medium-sized cauliflower
250g/8oz carrots
250g/8oz potatoes
4 large celery stalks
1 recipe Curry Sauce (page 134)
350g/12oz freshly boiled rice (about 175g/6oz raw)

Accompaniment
175g/6oz grated Derby or crumbled Lancashire cheese

1 Divide cauliflower into florets. Slice carrots and potatoes thinly. Chop celery
2 Cook all vegetables in boiling salted water until tender. Drain
3 Add to Curry Sauce. Heat through gently
4 Cover base of warm serving dish with rice
5 Arrange curried vegetables on top
6 Serve cheese separately. **Serves 4**

Haricot Bean & Cheese Curry

1 Follow recipe and method for Vegetable Curry with Cheese (above)
2 Instead of vegetables, add 350g/12oz haricot beans, soaked overnight and cooked in boiling salted water until tender. **Serves 4**

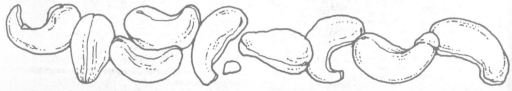

Egg and Mushroom Savoury (page 208)

Peanut Mince

1 large onion
100g / 4oz mushrooms
1 medium-sized celery stalk
1 large carrot
40g / 1½oz butter
¼ level teaspoon yeast extract
225g / 8oz coarsely chopped peanuts
150ml / ¼ pint milk
150ml / ¼ pint water
4 heaped tablespoons rolled oats
Salt and pepper
2 level tablespoons finely chopped parsley

1 Chop onion, mushrooms and celery
2 Grate carrot
3 Fry gently in butter until pale gold. Stir in yeast extract, peanuts, milk and water
4 Slowly bring to boil. Cover pan. Simmer gently until vegetables are tender
5 Add oats. Continue to simmer, uncovered, until mince is thick. Stir frequently
6 Season to taste with salt and pepper. Add parsley
7 Serve with creamy mashed potato and green vegetables.
Serves 4

Nut & Macaroni Curry

350g / 12oz broken macaroni
175g / 6oz cashew nuts
1 recipe Curry Sauce (page 134)

Accompaniments
½ fresh cucumber, peeled and sliced
4 large sliced tomatoes
Finely chopped parsley
½ bunch watercress

1 Cook macaroni in boiling salted water until tender
2 Drain. Add, with nuts, to Curry Sauce. Heat through gently
3 Pile on to warm plates
4 Accompany with separate bowls of cucumber slices, sliced tomatoes sprinkled with parsley and watercress. **Serves 4**

Egg & Macaroni Curry

1 Follow recipe and method for Nut and Macaroni Curry (above)
2 Add 4 large chopped hard-boiled eggs instead of nuts. **Serves 4**

Cottage Cheese & Parsley Tart

Short Crust Pastry made with 150g / 6oz flour
  (page 211)
1 large onion
25g / 1oz butter
450g / 1lb Cottage cheese
4 level tablespoons finely chopped parsley
2 standard eggs, beaten
Salt and pepper

Garnish
Watercress
Grated carrot

1 Roll out Pastry. Use to line 20cm / 8in plain flan ring resting on lightly buttered baking tray
2 Chop onion finely. Fry gently in butter until golden
3 Rub Cottage cheese through fine sieve. Combine with fried onion, parsley and beaten eggs
4 Season to taste with salt and pepper. Beat well. Pour into Pastry case
5 Bake just above centre of moderately hot oven (190°C / 375°F or Gas No 5) for 15 minutes
6 Reduce temperature to moderate (160°C / 325°F or Gas No 3). Continue to bake further 45 minutes (or until filling is set and top is golden)
7 Carefully lift off flan ring. Transfer tart to warm serving dish
8 Garnish with watercress and mounds of grated carrot. **Serves 4 to 5**

Cottage Cheese & Walnut Tart

1 Follow recipe and method for Cottage Cheese and Parsley Tart (above)
2 Add only 1 level tablespoon parsley and 50g / 2oz finely chopped shelled walnut halves. **Serves 4 to 5**

Parsnip Roast

750g / 1lb 8oz parsnips
50g / 2oz butter
4 tablespoons fresh double cream
75g / 3oz grated Cheddar cheese
Salt and pepper

1 Slice parsnips. Cook in boiling salted water until tender. Drain
2 Mash finely. Beat in butter, cream and 50g / 2oz cheese
3 Season well to taste with salt and pepper
4 Transfer to 1 litre / 1½ pint buttered heatproof dish
5 Cover with remaining cheese
6 Brown towards top of hot oven (220°C / 425°F or Gas No 7) for 10 to 15 minutes (or until top is golden)
7 Serve with a crisp green salad and baked jacket potatoes. **Serves 4**

Parsnip Cakes

500g / 1lb parsnips
50g / 2oz fresh brown breadcrumbs
1 level tablespoon fine oatmeal
1 level teaspoon grated onion
Salt and pepper to taste
Milk to bind

Coating
Beaten egg
About 25g / 1oz toasted breadcrumbs
50g / 2oz butter
2 teaspoons olive or corn oil

1 Cook parsnips in boiling salted water until tender. Drain
2 Mash finely. Combine with breadcrumbs, oatmeal and onion
3 Season to taste with salt and pepper. Bind with milk
4 Leave until cold. Shape into 8 cakes
5 Coat with beaten egg and crumbs
6 Fry in hot butter and oil until crisp and golden, allowing 2 to 3 minutes per side
7 Drain on soft kitchen paper
8 Serve hot with Parsley Coating Sauce (page 129) and a green vegetable. **Serves 4**

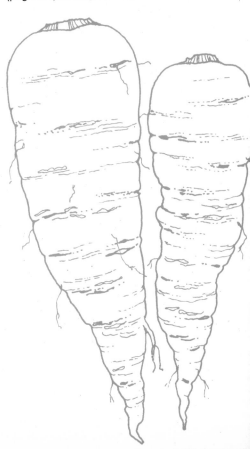

Pastry

Ingredients for Short Crust Pastry (below)

Home-made Pastry When a recipe calls for a certain weight of pastry, the weight refers to the amount of flour used and not to the total amount of pastry. For example, if a recipe says you need 100g/4oz Short Crust Pastry, it means you start off with 100g/4oz flour and then add all the other ingredients

Bought Pastry When a recipe calls for a certain weight of bought pastry, this **does** refer to total weight. Thus if a recipe says you need 225g/8oz Puff Pastry, you should buy 225g/8oz Puff Pastry

Pastry freezes well, baked or unbaked, except Hot Water Crust and Suet Crust Pastry.
Flan cases should be stored in a box to prevent breakages.
Pies may be frozen, with the cooked filling or separately.
Storage time – baked 6 months, unbaked 3 months.

Short Crust Pastry

For sweet and savoury flans, pies, tarts and tartlets, pasties, patties, turnovers etc

200g/8oz plain flour
¼ level teaspoon salt
100g/4oz butter
Cold water to mix; allow between 1 to 1½ teaspoons per 25g/1oz of flour

1 Sift flour and salt into bowl
2 Add butter. Cut into flour with a knife then rub in with fingertips. When rubbed in sufficiently, the mixture should look like fine breadcrumbs
3 Sprinkle the water over the crumbs. Mix to stiff crumbly-looking paste with round-ended knife
4 Draw together with fingertips, turn out on to lightly floured board. Knead quickly until smooth and crack-free
5 Roll out and use as required
6 If not to be used immediately, transfer to polythene bag or wrap in aluminium foil and leave in refrigerator or cold larder

211

Nut Pastry

For savoury flans, pies, pasties, patties and turn-overs etc.; especially those filled with chicken, veal, eggs or white fish

1 Follow recipe and method for Short Crust Pastry (page 211) but stir in 25 to 40g / 1 to 1½oz very finely chopped shelled walnut halves, salted peanuts or salted cashew nuts before adding water
2 If using salted nuts, reduce quantity of salt by half

Lemon Pastry

For same dishes as Nut Pastry (above)

Follow recipe and method for Short Crust Pastry (page 211) but stir in 1 level teaspoon very finely grated lemon rind before adding water

Rich Short Crust Pastry

For same dishes as Short Crust Pastry

1 Follow recipe and method for Short Crust Pastry (page 211) but use 125g / 5oz of butter and mix with 4 to 5 teaspoons cold water
2 Transfer to polythene bag or wrap in aluminium foil and chill at least ½ hour before rolling out and using

Cheese Pastry

For savoury biscuits and straws; savoury tarts, pies, flans, patties and turnovers

100g / 4oz plain flour
¼ level teaspoon dry mustard
¼ level teaspoon salt
Light shake of Cayenne pepper
65g / 2½oz butter
50g / 2oz very finely grated Cheddar cheese (stale for preference)
Yolk of 1 standard egg
2 to 3 teaspoons cold water

1 Sift flour, mustard, salt and Cayenne pepper into bowl
2 Add butter, cut into flour with knife, then rub in with fingertips
3 Add cheese and toss ingredients lightly together. Mix to very stiff paste with egg yolk and water
4 Turn out on to lightly floured board. Knead quickly until smooth and crack-free
5 Transfer to polythene bag or wrap in aluminium foil
6 Chill at least ½ hour before rolling out and using

Puff Pastry

For vol-au-vents; pastries such as cream horns, Mille feuilles

225g / 8oz butter
225g / 8oz plain flour
¼ level teaspoon salt
1 teaspoon lemon juice
Chilled water to mix

1 Put butter into clean cloth. Squeeze well to remove surplus moisture and to make it soft and pliable. Shape into 2cm / ¾in brick
2 Sift flour and salt into bowl. Mix to soft paste (about same consistency as butter) with lemon juice and water
3 Turn out on to floured board and knead well. Roll into rectangle measuring 30cm × 15cm / 12in × 6in.
4 Stand butter on lower half of rectangle. Bring top half over so that butter is completely enclosed
5 Press open edges firmly together with rolling pin. Put into polythene bag or wrap in aluminium foil. Chill 15 minutes
6 Remove from bag. With fold on right, roll into 45cm × 15cm / 18in × 6in rectangle
7 Fold in three as for Flaky Pastry (page 214). Seal edges, wrap and chill
8 Repeat, until pastry has been rolled, folded and chilled 7 times
9 Return to polythene bag or wrap in aluminium foil. Chill at least 30 minutes before rolling out (to ½cm / ¼in thickness) and using
10 After shaping, let dishes etc rest 30 minutes in cool before baking

Suet Crust Pastry

For sweet and savoury roly-polys and boiled and steamed puddings

200g / 8oz self-raising flour
½ level teaspoon salt
1 level teaspoon baking powder
100g / 4oz finely grated or shredded beef suet
About 125ml / ¼ pint cold water to mix

1 Sift flour, salt and baking powder into bowl
2 Add suet and toss ingredients lightly together
3 Mix to soft paste with water
4 Turn out on to floured board. Knead until smooth and roll out to about ¼cm / ⅛in thickness
5 Use as required: preferably immediately

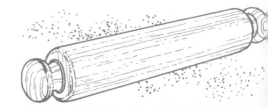

Cream Slices (page 242) using Puff Pastry (page 212)

Rough Puff Pastry

For sweet and savoury pies, patties, turnovers and sausage rolls

200g / 8oz plain flour
¼ level teaspoon salt
150g / 6oz butter
125ml / ¼ pint chilled water
1 teaspoon lemon juice

1 Sift flour and salt into bowl
2 Cut butter into tiny dice
3 Mix together water and lemon juice
4 Add butter to flour. Using knife, mix to fairly soft crumbly paste with water and lemon juice. Take care not to cut or break down butter any further
5 Draw together with fingertips. Turn out on to floured board and shape into block
6 Roll into ½cm / ¼in thick rectangle, measuring about 45cm × 15cm / 18in × 6in. Fold in three, envelope style, by bringing bottom third over middle third and folding top third over
7 Seal open edges by pressing firmly together with rolling pin. Give pastry a quarter turn so that folded edges are to right and left
8 Roll out. Fold and turn three more times

If possible, put folded pastry into polythene bag (or wrap in aluminium foil) and chill about 15 minutes between rollings

Hot Water Crust Pastry

For raised pies such as pork, veal, veal and ham and game

300g / 12oz plain flour
½ level teaspoon salt
Yolk of 1 standard egg
4 tablespoons milk
4 tablespoons water
25g / 1oz butter
75g / 3oz lard

1 Sift flour and salt into bowl and warm slightly. Make a well in centre
2 Beat yolk with 1 tablespoon milk and pour into well
3 Pour rest of milk and water into saucepan. Add butter and lard. Heat slowly until butter and lard melt. Bring to a brisk boil
4 Pour into well. Mix with wooden spoon until ingredients are well blended
5 Turn out on to floured board. Knead quickly until smooth
6 Put into bowl or basin standing over pan of hot water. Cover with clean tea-towel and leave to rest ½ an hour
7 Roll out warm pastry to ½cm / ¼in thickness and use as required
8 When making pies, cut off piece for lid first. Leave it (covered with towel), in bowl over hot water

Cream Cheese Pastry

This is a light, slightly puffy pastry, particularly good for sausage rolls, little savoury patties and jam turnovers

100g / 4oz plain flour
100g / 4oz butter
100g / 4oz cream cheese

1 Sift flour into bowl
2 Add butter and cheese. Cut both into flour with two knives held in same hand until mixture looks like coarse breadcrumbs
3 Draw together with fingertips and shape lightly into a ball
4 Transfer to polythene bag or wrap in aluminium foil and chill overnight
5 Roll out to about ¼cm / ⅛in thickness. Use as soon as it is rolled

Flaky Pastry

For same dishes as Rough Puff Pastry (page 213)

150g / 6oz butter
200g / 8oz plain flour
¼ level teaspoon salt
125ml / ¼ pint chilled water
1 teaspoon lemon juice

1 Divide butter into 4 equal portions. Chill 3 portions
2 Sift flour and salt into bowl. Rub in unchilled portion of butter
3 Mix to soft paste with water and lemon juice. Turn out on to floured board. Knead thoroughly
4 Put into polythene bag or wrap in aluminium foil. Chill ½ an hour
5 Roll out into ½cm / ¼in thick rectangle, measuring about 45cm × 15cm / 18in × 6in
6 Using tip of knife, spread second portion of butter (in small flakes) over top and middle third of rectangle to within 2cm / 1in of edges. Dust lightly with flour
7 Fold in three, envelope style, by bringing bottom third over middle third and folding top third over
8 Seal open edges by pressing firmly together with rolling pin. Put into polythene bag or wrap in aluminium foil and chill 15 minutes
9 Remove from bag or unwrap. With folded edges to left and right, roll out again into 45cm × 15cm / 18in × 6in rectangle
10 Cover with third portion of butter as before. Fold, seal and chill
11 Repeat again, adding last portion of butter, and chill
12 Roll out again. Fold and seal, return to polythene bag or wrap in aluminium foil. Chill at least 30 minutes before rolling out (to ½cm / ¼in thickness) and using
13 After shaping, let dishes etc. rest 30 minutes in cool before baking

Sweet Flan Pastry

For sweet flans, tarts, tartlets and small and large pies

Yolk of 1 standard egg
2 level teaspoons sifted icing sugar
100g / 4oz plain flour
Pinch of salt
65g / 2½oz butter
1 to 2 teaspoons cold water

1 Mix egg yolk and sugar well together
2 Sift flour and salt into bowl
3 Add butter, cut into flour with knife, then rub in with fingertips
4 Mix to very stiff paste with yolk, sugar and water
5 Turn out on to lightly floured board. Knead quickly until smooth
6 Transfer to polythene bag or wrap in aluminium foil
7 Chill at least ½ hour before rolling out and using

Milk 'Puff' Pastry

For same dishes as Rough Puff Pastry (page 213)

200g / 8oz self-raising flour
¼ level teaspoon salt
150g / 6oz butter
4 to 5 tablespoons cold milk

1 Sift flour and salt into bowl
2 Add butter and cut into flour until pieces are no larger than peas
3 Mix to stiff paste with milk. Draw together with fingertips
4 Quickly shape into ball and transfer to polythene bag or wrap in aluminium foil
5 Chill 1 hour before rolling out and using

Choux Pastry

For sweet and savoury buns and éclairs etc

75g / 2½oz plain flour
Pinch of salt
150ml / ¼ pint water
50g / 2oz butter
2 standard eggs, well beaten

1 Sift flour and salt twice
2 Put water and butter into saucepan. Heat slowly until butter melts, then bring to brisk boil
3 Lower heat and tip in all the flour
4 Stir briskly until mixture forms soft ball and leaves sides of pan clean
5 Remove from heat and cool slightly. Add eggs very gradually, beating hard until mixture is smooth, shiny and firm enough to stand in soft peaks when lifted with spoon
6 Use immediately. Otherwise leave in saucepan and cover with lid to prevent pastry drying out

Scone Mixtures

Tea Scone (below)

Do **not** use pasteurised or other heat-treated milk, which has turned sour, for scone making. The souring may have been caused by other than natural souring processes. Instead use half milk with soured cream, yogurt or buttermilk.

Freshly baked scones should be pulled gently apart with fingers. Cutting spoils the texture and makes them doughy. As scones stale quickly it is preferable to make and eat them on the same day

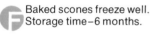 Baked scones freeze well.
Storage time–6 months.

Sultana Scones

1 Follow recipe and method for Tea Scones (right)
2 Add 25 to 50g / 1 to 2oz sultanas with sugar.
Makes 16 to 18 Scones

Currant Scones

1 Follow recipe and method for Tea Scones (right)
2 Add 25 to 50g / 1 to 2oz currants with sugar.
Makes 16 to 18 Scones

Tea Scones

200g / 8oz self-raising flour
½ level teaspoon salt
50g / 2oz butter
25g / 1oz caster sugar
125ml / ¼ pint milk
Extra milk for brushing

1 Sift flour and salt into bowl
2 Rub in butter finely
3 Add sugar
4 Add milk all at once. Mix to soft, but not sticky, dough with knife
5 Turn out on to lightly floured board. Knead quickly until smooth
6 Roll out to about 1cm / ½in thickness. Cut into 16 to 18 rounds with 4 to 5cm / 1¾ to 2in fluted biscuit cutter
7 Transfer to buttered baking tray. Brush tops with milk
8 Bake towards top of hot oven (230°C / 450°F or Gas No 8) for 7 to 10 minutes (or until well risen and golden)
9 Cool on wire rack
10 Serve fresh with butter or whipped fresh double cream or clotted cream and jam.
Makes 16 to 18 Scones

Date & Walnut Scones

1 Follow recipe and method for Tea Scones (page 215)
2 Add 25g / 1oz very finely chopped dates and 15g / ½oz very finely chopped shelled walnut halves with sugar.
Makes 16 to 18 Scones

Spice Scones

1 Follow recipe and method for Tea Scones (page 215)
2 Sift 1 level teaspoon mixed spice with flour and salt
3 Use 25g / 1oz soft brown sugar instead of caster
4 Serve warm.
Makes 16 to 18 Scones

Lemon & Raisin Scones

1 Follow recipe and method for Tea Scones (page 215)
2 Add ½ level teaspoon finely grated lemon rind and 50g / 2oz seedless raisins with sugar.
Makes 16 to 18 Scones

Orange & Cherry Scones

1 Follow recipe and method for Tea Scones (page 215)
2 Add with the sugar ½ level teaspoon finely grated orange rind and 40g / 1½oz finely chopped glacé cherries (which should be well washed and dried first). **Makes 16 to 18 Scones**

Cinnamon Scones

1 Follow recipe and method for Tea Scones (page 215)
2 Sift 1 level teaspoon cinnamon with flour and salt. **Makes 16 to 18 Scones**

Syrup or Honey Scones

1 Follow recipe and method for Tea Scones (page 215)
2 Mix to dough with 1 level tablespoon golden syrup or clear honey (slightly warmed) and 7 tablespoons milk
3 Serve warm.
Makes 16 to 18 Scones

Syrup and Ginger Scones

1 Follow recipe and method for Syrup Scones (left)
2 Sift ½ level teaspoon ground ginger with flour and salt
3 Serve warm. **Makes 16 to 18 Scones**

All-Purpose Scones

200g / 8oz self-raising flour
½ level teaspoon salt
50g / 2oz butter
125ml / ¼ pint milk
Extra milk for brushing

1 Sift flour and salt into bowl
2 Rub in butter finely
3 Add milk all at once. Mix to soft, but not sticky, dough with knife
4 Turn on to lightly floured board. Knead quickly until smooth
5 Roll out to about 1cm / ½in thickness
6 Cut into 9 or 10 rounds with 6cm / 2½in biscuit cutter
7 Transfer to buttered baking tray. Brush tops with milk
8 Bake towards top of hot oven (230°C / 450°F or Gas No 8) for 7 to 10 minutes (or until well risen and golden brown)
9 Cool on wire rack. Serve with butter or whipped cream and jam, or butter and cheese.
Makes 9 to 10 Scones

Cheese Scones

1 Follow recipe and method for All-Purpose Scones (above)
2 Sift 1 level teaspoon dry mustard and pinch of Cayenne pepper with flour and salt
3 Mix in 50g / 2oz very finely grated Cheddar cheese before adding milk. **Makes 9 to 10 Scones**

Ham & Parsley Scones

1 Follow recipe and method for All-Purpose Scones (above)
2 Sift ½ level teaspoon dry mustard with flour and salt
3 Mix in 25g / 1oz very finely chopped ham and 1 level tablespoon very finely chopped parsley before adding milk. **Makes 9 to 10 Scones**

Sugar & Spice Rings

200g / 8oz self-raising flour
¼ level teaspoon salt
40g / 1½oz butter
125ml / ¼ pint milk

Filling
25g / 1oz butter, melted
50g / 2oz caster sugar
1 level teaspoon cinnamon
40g / 1½oz currants

1 Sift flour and salt into bowl
2 Rub in butter finely
3 Add milk all at once. Mix to soft, but not sticky, dough with knife
4 Turn on to lightly floured board. Knead quickly until smooth then roll into rectangle approximately 20cm ×30cm / 8in × 12in
5 Brush with butter to within 1cm / ½in of edges
6 Mix sugar with cinnamon and currants then sprinkle over butter
7 Moisten edges of dough lightly with water. Roll up like a Swiss roll, starting from one of the longer sides
8 Cut into 12 slices. Arrange, cut sides down, in 20cm / 8in, well-buttered round cake tin or fairly deep sandwich tin
9 Bake towards top of hot oven (220°C / 425°F or Gas No 7) for 15 to 20 minutes (or until well risen and golden)
10 Turn out on to wire cooling rack. Leave until lukewarm
11 Gently pull apart to separate rings. Serve as they are or with extra butter.
Serves 4 to 6

Soured Cream Scones

200g / 8oz self-raising flour
¼ level teaspoon salt
40g / 1½oz butter
4 tablespoons soured cream
4 tablespoons milk
Extra milk for brushing

1 Sift flour and salt into bowl
2 Rub in butter finely
3 Add cream and milk all at once. Mix to soft, but not sticky, dough with knife
4 Turn out on to lightly floured board. Knead quickly until smooth
5 Roll out to about 1cm / ½in thickness
6 Cut into 9 or 10 rounds with 6cm / 2½in biscuit cutter
7 Transfer to buttered baking tray. Brush tops with milk
8 Bake towards top of hot oven (230°C / 450°F or Gas No 8) for 7 to 10 minutes (or until well risen and golden brown)
9 Cool on wire rack. Serve with butter and jam.
Makes 9 to 10 Scones

Yogurt Scones

1 Follow recipe and method for Soured Cream Scones (left)
2 Use 4 tablespoons natural yogurt instead of soured cream. **Makes 9 to 10 Scones**

Buttermilk Scones

1 Follow recipe and method for Soured Cream Scones (left)
2 Use 150ml / ¼ pint buttermilk instead of soured cream and milk. **Makes 9 to 10 Scones**

Dropped Scones

200g / 8oz self-raising flour
¼ level teaspoon salt
1 level tablespoon caster sugar
1 standard egg
250ml / ½ pint milk
25 to 50g / 1 to 2oz butter, melted

1 Sift flour and salt into bowl
2 Add sugar
3 Mix to smooth creamy batter with whole egg and half the milk
4 Stir in rest of milk
5 Brush large heavy frying pan with melted butter. Heat
6 Drop small rounds of scone mixture (about twelve in all), from a spoon, into pan
7 Cook until bubbles show on surface (2½ to 3 minutes)
8 Carefully turn over with knife. Cook for further 2 minutes
9 Pile Scones in clean, folded tea-towel to keep warm and moist
10 Serve immediately with butter and jam, golden syrup or honey. **Serves 4**

Dropped Scones with Spice

1 Follow recipe and method for Dropped Scones (above)
2 Sift 1 level teaspoon mixed spice with flour and salt
3 Use 1 level tablespoon soft brown sugar instead of caster. **Serves 4**

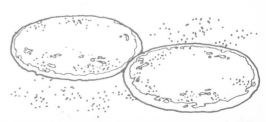

Raspberry Shortcakes

1 recipe Tea Scones (page 215)
Milk for brushing
50 to 75g / 2 to 3oz butter
225g / 8oz raspberries
50g / 2oz sifted icing sugar
4 tablespoons fresh double cream, whipped

1 Roll out Tea Scone dough to 2cm / 1in thickness
2 Cut into 4 rounds with 7cm / 3in biscuit cutter
3 Stand on buttered baking tray. Brush tops with milk
4 Bake towards top of hot oven 220°C / 425°F or Gas No 7) for 15 to 20 minutes (or until well risen and golden)
5 Transfer to wire cooling rack. Leave until lukewarm
6 Pull apart gently with fingers and butter thickly
7 Sandwich each together with whole raspberries mixed with sugar
8 Put tablespoon of cream on each
9 Serve warm. **Serves 4**

Strawberry Shortcakes

1 Follow recipe and method for Raspberry Short-cakes (above) omitting raspberries
2 Sandwich together with 225g / 8oz sliced straw-berries mixed with 50g / 2oz sifted icing sugar.
Serves 4

Wholemeal Scones

100g / 4oz wholemeal flour
100g / 4oz plain flour
2 level teaspoons baking powder
½ level teaspoon salt
40g / 1½oz butter
125ml / ¼ pint milk
Extra milk for brushing

1 Sift flours, baking powder and salt into bowl
2 Rub in butter finely
3 Add milk all at once. Mix to soft, but not sticky, dough with knife
4 Turn on to lightly floured board. Knead quickly until smooth
5 Roll out to about 1cm / ½in thickness. Cut into 9 or 10 rounds with 6cm / 2½in biscuit cutter
6 Transfer to buttered baking tray. Brush tops with milk
7 Bake towards top of hot oven (230°C / 450°F or Gas No 8) for 7 to 10 minutes (or until well risen and golden)
8 Cool on wire rack
9 Serve with butter and Cottage cheese
Makes 9 or 10 Scones

Dropped Scones with Ham

200g / 8oz self-raising flour
½ level teaspoon salt
1 level teaspoon dry mustard
50g / 2oz very finely chopped lean ham
1 standard egg
250ml / ½ pint milk
25 to 50g / 1 to 2oz butter, melted

1 Sift flour, salt and mustard into bowl. Add ham
2 Mix to smooth creamy batter with whole egg and half the milk
3 Stir in rest of milk
4 Brush large heavy frying pan with melted butter. Heat
5 Drop small rounds of scone mixture (about twelve in all), from a spoon, into pan
6 Cook until bubbles show on surface (2½ to 3 minutes)
7 Carefully turn over with knife. Cook for further 2 minutes
8 Pile Scones in clean folded tea towel to keep warm
9 Serve immediately with butter and Wensleydale or Double Gloucester cheese. **Serves 4**

Ring Doughnuts

300g / 12oz self-raising flour
¼ level teaspoon salt
½ level teaspoon cinnamon
½ level teaspoon mixed spice
100g / 4oz butter
50g / 2oz caster sugar
1 standard egg
125ml / ¼ pint milk
Deep fat or oil for frying
Extra caster sugar

1 Sift flour, salt, cinnamon and spice into bowl
2 Rub in butter finely
3 Add caster sugar
4 Beat egg with milk. Add, all at once, to dry ingredients
5 Mix to soft, but not sticky, dough with knife
6 Turn out on to lightly floured board. Knead quickly until smooth
7 Roll out to 1cm / ½in thickness
8 Cut into rounds with 5cm / 2in biscuit cutter. Remove centres with 2cm / 1in cutter. Re-roll and cut into more rings
9 Fry, a few at a time, in hot fat or oil for 2 to 3 minutes, turning once
10 Remove from pan. Drain thoroughly on soft kitchen paper
11 Toss in caster sugar. Serve while still warm.
Makes 20 Doughnuts

Biscuits

Plain Biscuits (below) Rich Shortbread (page 220) Butter Whirls (page 223) Ginger Snaps (page 223) Coffee Walnut Cookies (page 223)

Biscuits freeze successfully.
Storage time – 3 months.

Plain Biscuits

225g / 8oz self-raising flour
Pinch of salt
150g / 5oz butter
100g / 4oz caster or sifted icing sugar
Beaten egg to mix

1 Sift flour and salt into bowl
2 Rub in butter finely
3 Add sugar
4 Mix to very stiff dough with beaten egg
5 Turn out on to lightly floured board. Knead gently until smooth
6 Put into polythene bag or wrap in aluminium foil. Chill 30 minutes
7 Roll out fairly thinly. Cut into about 30 rounds with 5cm / 2in plain or fluted biscuit cutter
8 Transfer to buttered baking trays. Prick biscuits well with fork
9 Bake in centre of moderate oven (180°C / 350°F or Gas No 4) for about 12 to 15 minutes (or until pale gold)
10 Leave on trays for 2 to 3 minutes. Transfer to wire cooling rack
11 Store in airtight tin when cold.
About 30 biscuits

Walnut Biscuits

1 Follow recipe and method for Plain Biscuits (left)
2 Add 40g / 1½oz very finely chopped shelled walnut halves with sugar and ½ teaspoon vanilla essence with egg.
Cut into about 30 Biscuits

Almond Biscuits

1 Follow recipe and method for Plain Biscuits (left)
2 Add 50g / 2oz ground almonds with sugar, and ½ teaspoon almond essence with egg.
Cut into 30 to 36 Biscuits

Lemon or Orange Biscuits

1 Follow recipe and method for Plain Biscuits (left)
2 Add 1 level teaspoon finely grated lemon or orange rind with sugar.
Cut into about 30 Biscuits

Currant Biscuits

1 Follow recipe and method for Plain Biscuits (page 219)
2 Add 50g/2oz currants with sugar.
Cut into about 30 Biscuits

Cherry Biscuits

1 Follow recipe and method for Plain Biscuits (page 219)
2 Add 50g/2oz very finely chopped glacé cherries with sugar. **Cut into about 30 Biscuits**

Spice or Cinnamon Biscuits

1 Follow recipe and method for Plain Biscuits (page 219)
2 Sift 1½ level teaspoons mixed spice or cinnamon with flour and salt. **Cut into about 30 Biscuits**

Coconut Biscuits

1 Follow recipe and method for Plain Biscuits (page 219)
2 Add 50g/2oz desiccated coconut with sugar and ½ teaspoon vanilla essence with egg.
Cut into about 30 Biscuits

Chocolate Flake Biscuits

1 Follow recipe and method for Plain Biscuits (page 219)
2 Add 50g/2oz grated plain chocolate with sugar.
Cut into about 30 Biscuits

Jam Sandwich Biscuits

1 Follow recipe and method for Plain Biscuits (page 219)
2 When Biscuits are cold, sandwich together with raspberry or apricot jam
3 Dust tops with sifted icing sugar.
About 15 Sandwich Biscuits

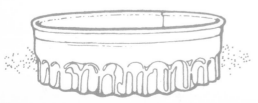

Sugar-topped Biscuits

1 Follow recipe and method for any of the previous biscuits
2 Before baking brush with lightly beaten egg white and sprinkle with caster sugar.
Makes 30 Biscuits

Chocolate Drops

100g/4oz softened butter
50g/2oz caster sugar
½ teaspoon vanilla essence
90g/3½oz plain flour
15g/½oz cocoa powder

1 Cream butter with sugar and essence until light and fluffy
2 Stir in flour sifted with cocoa
3 Drop 18 to 20 teaspoons of mixture, well apart, on to buttered baking tray
4 Bake just above centre of moderately hot oven (190°C/375°F or Gas No 5) for 17 minutes
5 Leave on tray 1 or 2 minutes before transferring to wire cooling rack
6 Store in airtight tin when cold.
Makes 18 to 20 Drops

Rich Shortbread

100g/4oz softened butter
50g/2oz caster sugar
125g/5oz plain flour
25g/1oz semolina
Extra caster sugar

1 Cream butter and sugar together until light and fluffy
2 Using fork, gradually stir in flour and semolina
3 Draw mixture together with finger tips. Press into lightly buttered 18cm/7in sandwich tin
4 Prick well all over. Either pinch up edges with finger and thumb or ridge with prongs of fork
5 Bake in centre of moderate oven (160°C/325°F or Gas No 3) for about 40 minutes (or until colour of pale straw)
6 Leave in tin for 5 minutes
7 Cut into 8 triangles. Dredge with extra caster sugar. Remove from tin when cold
8 Store in airtight tin. **Makes 8 Shortbreads**

Lemon or Orange Shortbread

1 Follow recipe and method for Rich Shortbread (above)
2 Add 1 level teaspoon finely grated lemon or orange rind with flour and semolina.
Makes 8 Shortbreads

Almond Shortbread Biscuits

100g / 4oz softened butter
50g / 2oz caster or sifted icing sugar
100g / 4oz plain flour
50g / 2oz ground almonds
25g / 1oz semolina
A little beaten egg for brushing
Extra caster sugar

1 Cream butter and sugar together until light and fluffy
2 Using fork, gradually stir in flour, almonds and semolina
3 Draw together with fingertips. Turn on to lightly floured board
4 Shape into ball. Either put into polythene bag or wrap in aluminium foil. Chill for at least 30 minutes
5 Roll out to $\frac{1}{2}$cm / $\frac{1}{4}$in thickness. Cut into approximately 18 rounds with 5cm / 2in fluted biscuit cutter
6 Transfer to buttered trays and prick well with fork. Brush with egg
7 Bake in centre of moderate oven (160°C / 325°F or Gas No 3) for 20 to 25 minutes (or until pale gold)
8 Transfer to wire cooling rack. Dredge with caster sugar
9 Store in airtight tin when cold.
Makes 18 Biscuits

Treacle Bites

100g / 4oz self-raising flour, sifted
75g / 3oz rolled oats
25g / 1oz desiccated coconut
100g / 4oz butter
125g / 5oz caster sugar
2 level tablespoons treacle
1 level teaspoon bicarbonate of soda
1 tablespoon milk

1 Combine flour with oats and coconut
2 Put butter, sugar and treacle into saucepan. Very slowly bring to boil, stirring all the time
3 Remove from heat. Add bicarbonate of soda dissolved in milk
4 Pour hot mixture on to dry ingredients. Mix thoroughly. Leave on one side for 30 minutes or until firm
5 Break off 24 pieces of mixture and roll into marbles
6 Transfer to buttered baking trays (leaving room between to allow for spreading). Bake in centre of moderate oven (180°C / 350°F or Gas No 4) for 15 minutes
7 Leave on trays 1 or 2 minutes before transferring to wire cooling rack. Store in airtight tin when cold.
Makes 24 Treacle Bites

Vanilla Refrigerator Biscuits

200g / 8oz plain flour
1 level teaspoon baking powder
100g / 4oz butter
150g / 6oz caster sugar
1 level teaspoon vanilla essence
1 standard egg, beaten

1 Sift together flour and baking powder
2 Rub in butter finely
3 Add sugar. Mix to dough with vanilla and beaten egg
4 Shape into long sausage. Transfer to length of aluminium foil
5 Wrap foil round 'sausage' and twist ends. Work backwards and forwards to form evenly shaped roll about 5cm / 2in diameter
6 Refrigerate overnight

Shaping and baking
Full quantity of mixture makes between 50 and 60 Biscuits. For only 10 or so, slice these very thinly from roll and stand (well apart to allow for spreading) on buttered baking tray. Bake in centre of moderately hot oven (190°C / 375°F or Gas No 5) for 10 to 12 minutes (or until pale gold). Cool on wire rack. Store in airtight tin when cold. Remainder of roll can be returned to refrigerator and left – up to about a week – until more Biscuits are wanted

Chocolate Refrigerator Biscuits

1 Follow recipe and method for Vanilla Refrigerator Biscuits (above)
2 Add 50g / 2oz very finely grated plain chocolate with sugar. **Makes 50 to 60 Biscuits**

Ginger Refrigerator Biscuits

1 Follow recipe and method for Vanilla Refrigerator Biscuits (above)
2 Omit vanilla
3 Sift $1\frac{1}{2}$ level teaspoons ground ginger and $\frac{1}{2}$ level teaspoon mixed spice with flour and baking powder. **Makes 50 to 60 Biscuits**

Orange or Lemon Refrigerator Biscuits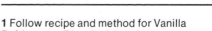

1 Follow recipe and method for Vanilla Refrigerator Biscuits (above)
2 Omit vanilla
3 Add 2 level teaspoons finely grated orange or lemon rind with sugar.
Makes 50 to 60 Biscuits

Brandy Snaps

50g / 2oz butter
50g / 2oz granulated sugar
65g / 2½oz golden syrup
50g / 2oz plain flour
1 level teaspoon ground ginger
2 teaspoons lemon juice
150ml / ¼ pint fresh double cream

1 Put butter, sugar and syrup into pan. Stand over low heat until melted
2 Sift together flour and ginger. Add to melted mixture with lemon juice
3 Drop 4 teaspoons of mixture (well apart to allow for spreading) on to large buttered baking tray
4 Bake in centre of moderate oven 160°C / 325°F or Gas No 3) for 8 minutes
5 Leave 1 minute. Lift off with palette knife. Roll quickly and loosely round buttered handle of wooden spoon
6 Leave until firm and slide off handle
7 Repeat with rest of mixture
8 When cold, fill both ends of each with stiffly whipped cream.
Makes 16 Brandy Snaps

Florentines

75g / 3oz butter
4 tablespoons milk
100g / 4oz sifted icing sugar
40g / 1½oz plain flour
75g / 3oz chopped mixed peel
50g / 2oz finely chopped glacé cherries
75g / 3oz flaked almonds
1 teaspoon lemon juice
100g / 4oz plain chocolate
7g / ¼oz extra butter

1 Cover 2 large baking trays with rice paper
2 Put butter, milk and sugar into saucepan. Stand over low heat until butter melts
3 Remove from heat. Stir in flour, peel, cherries, almonds and lemon juice
4 Leave on one side until completely cold
5 Spoon equal amounts of mixture (well apart to allow for spreading) on to baking trays
6 Bake just above centre of moderately hot oven (190°C / 375°F or Gas No 5) for 10 minutes (or until pale gold)
7 Leave until lukewarm. Carefully lift off trays and remove surplus rice paper round edges
8 Cool completely on wire cooling rack
9 Melt chocolate and extra butter in basin standing over saucepan of hot water
10 Put a heaped teaspoonful on to rice paper side of each Florentine
11 Spread evenly with knife
12 Mark wavy lines with fork on each. Leave until chocolate hardens before serving
13 Store in airtight tin.
Makes 12 Florentines

Nut Refrigerator Biscuits

1 Follow recipe and method for Vanilla
Refrigerator Biscuits (page 221)
2 Add 50g/2oz very finely chopped or ground
walnuts or hazelnuts with sugar.
Makes 50 to 60 Biscuits

Spicy Refrigerator Biscuits

1 Follow recipe and method for Vanilla
Refrigerator Biscuits (page 221)
2 Omit vanilla
3 Sift 2 level teaspoons mixed spice with flour and
baking powder. **Makes 50 to 60 Biscuits**

Coconut Refrigerator Biscuits

1 Follow recipe and method for Vanilla
Refrigerator Biscuits (page 221)
2 Add 50g/2oz desiccated coconut with sugar.
Makes 50 to 60 Biscuits

Raisin Refrigerator Biscuits

1 Follow recipe and method for Vanilla
Refrigerator Biscuits (page 221)
2 Add 50g/2oz very finely chopped, seedless
raisins with sugar. **Makes 50 to 60 Biscuits**

Butter Whirls

150g/6oz softened butter
50g/2oz sifted icing sugar
½ teaspoon vanilla essence
150g/6oz plain flour
8 or 9 halved glacé cherries

1 Cream butter with sugar and vanilla until light
and fluffy
2 Stir in flour
3 Transfer mixture to forcing bag fitted with
star-shaped meringue tube
4 Pipe 16 to 18 flat whirls on to buttered baking
tray or trays. Put half a cherry on to each
5 Bake in centre of moderate oven (160°C/325°F
or Gas No 3) for 20 minutes (or until pale gold)
6 Leave on trays 5 minutes. Transfer to wire
cooling rack
7 Store in airtight tin when cold.
Makes 16 to 18 Whirls

Florentines (page 222)

Flapjacks

100g/4oz butter
75g/3oz golden syrup
75g/3oz soft brown sugar
200g/8oz rolled oats

1 Put butter, syrup and sugar into saucepan and
stand over low heat until melted
2 Stir in oats and mix well
3 Spread into buttered Swiss roll tin, approximately 20cm × 30cm/8in × 12in, and smooth top
with knife
4 Bake in centre of moderate oven (180°C/350°F
or Gas No 4) for 30 minutes
5 Leave in tin 5 minutes, then cut into 24 fingers
6 Remove from tin when cold
7 Store in airtight tin. **Makes 24 Flapjacks**

Ginger Snaps

100g/4oz self-raising flour
1 level teaspoon ground ginger
¼ level teaspoon mixed spice
50g/2oz butter
40g/1½oz caster sugar
1 level tablespoon melted black treacle
Milk to mix

1 Sift flour, ginger and spice into bowl
2 Rub in butter finely
3 Add sugar. Mix to very stiff paste with treacle
and milk
4 Roll out very thinly and cut into 26 to 30 rounds
with 5cm/2in biscuit cutter
5 Transfer to buttered baking trays
6 Bake just above centre of moderate oven
(180°C/350°F or Gas No 4) for 10 minutes
7 Leave on trays for 1 to 2 minutes before
transferring to wire cooling rack
8 Store in airtight tin when cold.
Makes 26 to 30 Ginger Snaps

Coffee Walnut Cookies

100g/4oz softened butter
50g/2oz caster sugar
50g/2oz finely chopped walnuts
100g/4oz plain flour
2 level teaspoons instant coffee powder

1 Cream butter with sugar until light and fluffy
2 Add walnuts. Stir in flour sifted with coffee
powder
3 Put 18 to 20 teaspoons of mixture, well apart, on
to buttered baking tray
4 Bake just above centre of moderately hot oven
(190°C/375°F or Gas No 5) for 15 to 20 minutes
5 Leave on tray 1 or 2 minutes before transferring
to wire cooling rack
6 Store in airtight tin when cold.
Makes 18 to 20 Cookies

Chocolate Cherry Cookies

100g / 4oz softened butter
50g / 2oz caster sugar
½ teaspoon vanilla essence
25g / 1oz finely chopped glacé cherries
25g / 1oz finely chopped plain chocolate
100g / 4oz sifted plain flour

1 Cream butter with sugar and vanilla until light and fluffy
2 Add cherries and chocolate. Stir in flour
3 Put 18 to 20 teaspoons of mixture, well apart, on to buttered baking tray
4 Bake just above centre of moderately hot oven (190°C / 375°F or Gas No 5) for 15 to 20 minutes
5 Leave on tray for 1 or 2 minutes before transferring to wire cooling rack
6 Store in airtight tin when cold.
Makes 18 to 20 Cookies

Date Cookies

1 Follow recipe and method for Chocolate Cherry Cookies (above)
2 Add 50g / 2oz very finely chopped dates instead of chocolate and cherries.
Makes 18 to 20 Cookies

Peanut Crisps

50g / 2oz plain flour
¼ level teaspoon bicarbonate of soda
50g / 2oz softened butter
25g / 1oz caster sugar
50g / 2oz soft brown sugar
½ teaspoon vanilla essence
50g / 2oz peanut butter
1 standard egg

1 Sift together flour and bicarbonate of soda
2 Cream butter with sugars, vanilla and peanut butter until very light and fluffy
3 Beat in egg then stir in dry ingredients
4 Drop 24 teaspoons of mixture, 2cm / 1in apart, on to unbuttered baking trays
5 Bake in centre of moderate oven (180°C / 350°F or Gas No 4) for 10 to 12 minutes
6 Leave on trays for 1 or 2 minutes. Transfer to wire cooling rack
7 Store in airtight tin when cold. **Makes 24 Crisps**

Almond Macaroons

Whites of 2 standard eggs
100g / 4oz ground almonds
200g / 8oz caster sugar
15g / ½oz ground rice
½ teaspoon vanilla essence
¼ teaspoon almond essence
A little extra egg white
9 blanched and split almonds

1 Brush 1 or 2 baking trays with melted butter. Line with rice paper
2 Beat egg whites until foamy but not stiff
3 Add almonds, sugar, ground rice and essences. Beat well
4 Pipe or spoon 18 mounds of mixture, well apart, on to prepared tray or trays. Brush with egg white
5 Put half an almond on middle of each
6 Bake in centre of moderate oven (160°C / 325°F or Gas No 3) for 20 to 25 minutes (or until pale gold)
7 Leave on trays for 5 minutes
8 Carefully lift off and remove rice paper round edges of each
9 Cool on wire rack
10 Store in airtight tin when cold.
Makes 18 Macaroons

Butter Digestive Biscuits

75g / 3oz wholemeal flour
15g / ½oz plain flour
¼ level teaspoon salt
½ level teaspoon baking powder
15g / ½oz oatmeal
40g / 1½oz butter
40g / 1½oz caster sugar
3 tablespoons milk

1 Sift flours, salt and baking powder into bowl. Add oatmeal
2 Rub in butter finely. Add sugar
3 Mix to stiff paste with milk
4 Turn out on to lightly floured board. Knead well
5 Roll out thinly. Cut into 12 rounds with 6cm / 2½in fluted biscuit cutter
6 Transfer to buttered baking tray and prick well
7 Bake in centre of moderately hot oven (190°C / 375°F or Gas No 5) for 15 to 20 minutes (or until light gold)
8 Transfer to wire cooling rack
9 Store in airtight tin when cold.
Makes 12 Biscuits

Meringues

Fruit and Cream Pavlovas (page 227)

Meringues may be frozen unfilled, and packed in a box to prevent breakages.
Storage time–3 months.

Basic Meringues

Whites of 2 standard eggs
100g / 4oz caster sugar
Pinch of cream of tartar (optional)
25g / 1oz granulated sugar

1 Brush large baking tray with salad oil. Cover with double thickness of greaseproof paper. Do **not** brush paper with more oil
2 Put egg whites into clean dry bowl. Add cream of tartar, if used. Beat until stiff and peaky
3 Add half the caster sugar
4 Continue beating until meringue is shiny and stands in firm peaks
5 Add rest of caster sugar. Beat until meringue is very stiff and silky-looking and texture is fairly close. Gently fold in granulated sugar
6 Pipe or spoon 16 rounds or ovals on to prepared tray

7 Bake in centre of very slow oven (110°C / 225°F or Gas No ¼) for 1½ hours
8 Remove from oven. Carefully peel away from paper and gently press a small hole in the base of each with thumb
9 Stand upside down on baking tray. Return to oven and dry out for further ¾ to 1 hour
10 Transfer to wire cooling rack.
Makes 16 Meringue Halves

If flavoured meringues are preferred, add flavouring essence to taste
If preferred, leave in oven for total cooking time of 2½ hours (or until meringues are crisp and firm)

Coffee Meringues

1 Follow recipe and method for Basic Meringues (page 225)
2 Add 2 level teaspoons instant coffee powder with granulated sugar
3 Sandwich together with whipped cream or Coffee Butter Cream Frosting (page 246).
Makes 8 Filled Meringues

Hazelnut Meringues

1 Follow recipe and method for Basic Meringues (page 225)
2 Add 50g / 2oz very finely chopped hazelnuts with granulated sugar
3 Sandwich together with Chocolate Butter Cream Frosting (page 246).
Makes 8 Filled Meringues

Almond Coffee Kisses

1 Follow recipe and method for Basic Meringues (page 225)
2 Add 50g / 2oz ground almonds with granulated sugar
3 Sandwich together with Coffee Butter Cream Frosting (page 246).
Makes 8 Filled Coffee Kisses

Raspberry or Strawberry Cream Meringues

1 Follow recipe and method for Basic Meringues (page 225)
2 Flavour with raspberry or strawberry culinary flavouring or add 1½ level teaspoons raspberry or strawberry blancmange powder with the granulated sugar
3 Sandwich together with whipped cream.
Makes 8 Filled Meringues

Walnut Chocolate Fingers

1 Follow recipe and method for Basic Meringues (page 225)
2 Add 50g / 2oz very finely chopped shelled walnut halves with granulated sugar
3 Pipe twenty 7cm / 3in lengths of mixture on to baking tray
3 Sandwich together with Chocolate Butter Cream Frosting (page 246).
Makes 10 Filled Fingers

Lemon or Orange Meringues

1 Follow recipe and method for Basic Meringues (page 225)
2 Add ½ level teaspoon very finely grated lemon or orange rind with granulated sugar
3 Sandwich together with whipped cream or Lemon Butter Cream Frosting (page 244) or Orange Butter Cream Frosting (page 246).
Makes 8 Filled Meringues

Cream Meringues

1 Follow recipe and method for Basic Meringues (page 225)
2 Sandwich together, in pairs, with 150ml / ¼ pint fresh double cream, beaten until thick with tablespoon of milk.
Makes 8 Filled Meringues

Chocolate Cream Meringues

1 Follow recipe and method for Basic Meringues (page 225)
2 Add 1½ level teaspoons chocolate-flavoured blancmange powder with granulated sugar
3 Sandwich together with whipped cream.
Makes 8 Filled Meringues

If preferred, omit chocolate blancmange powder. Add 25g / 1oz grated plain chocolate with granulated sugar

Meringue Basket

1 recipe Basic Meringues (page 225)

1 Make up Meringue mixture as directed for Basic Meringues (page 225)
2 Lightly oil baking tray. Cover with 4 thicknesses of greaseproof paper
3 Outline 20cm / 8in round on centre of paper, using cake tin or plate as guide
4 Spread Meringue mixture thickly over round
5 Make shallow sides by spooning or piping small mounds of mixture all the way round edge
6 Put into centre of very slow oven (110°C / 225°F or Gas No ¼). Bake until Basket is firm and set (2½ to 3 hours)
7 Carefully peel away from paper. Stand upside down on baking tray
8 Return to oven for further 45 minutes to dry out thoroughly
9 Fill when cold (see Cold Desserts Section page 157). **Serves 6**

Meringue Topping

Whites of 2 standard eggs
50 to 75g/2 to 3oz caster sugar
1 level tablespoon granulated sugar

1 Put egg whites into clean dry bowl. Beat until stiff and peaky (when bowl is turned upside down the whites should stay where they are)
2 Gently fold in caster sugar with large metal spoon
3 Pile meringue over pie or pudding, etc., and sprinkle with granulated sugar

Baking
Quick cooking is essential if meringue is used as decoration on frozen or chilled desserts; therefore **flash bake** dish towards top of hot oven (230°C / 450°F or Gas No 8) until meringue just starts turning gold. (About 1 to 3 minutes but no longer)

If meringue is on a **pudding** or **pie** that is made to be served cold later, it is important to dry out the meringue thoroughly, otherwise it will sag on standing and become wet and syrupy; therefore put dish into centre of very slow oven (110°C / 225°F or Gas No $\frac{1}{4}$) and bake for 1$\frac{1}{2}$ to 2 hours (or until meringue is firm, crisp and golden)

For a **hot pudding** topped with meringue, bake in centre of slow oven (150°C / 300°F or Gas No 2) for 20 to 30 minutes (or until pale gold)

Coconut Pyramids

Whites of 2 standard eggs
125g/5oz caster sugar
150g/6oz desiccated coconut
10 to 12 glacé cherries, halved

1 Line 1 or 2 unbuttered baking trays with rice paper
2 Beat egg whites to stiff snow
3 Stir in sugar and coconut. Mix well
4 Place about 20 to 24 mounds of mixture on to trays. Shape into pyramids with fork
5 Bake in centre of slow oven (150°C / 300°F or Gas No 2) for 20 minutes. Put half a cherry on top of each
6 Return to oven. Bake until pale gold (15 to 20 minutes)
7 Remove from trays
8 Trim away surplus rice paper
9 Cool on wire rack
10 Store in airtight tin when cold.
Makes 20 to 24 Pyramids

Golden Coconut Pyramids

2 standard eggs
200g/8oz desiccated coconut
125g/5oz caster sugar

1 Line 1 or 2 unbuttered baking trays with rice paper
2 Beat eggs well. Stir in coconut and sugar
3 Leave to stand for 20 minutes
4 Dip hands in cold water. Shape mixture into about 24 Pyramids
5 Place on tray or trays
6 Put into centre of moderate oven (180°C / 350°F or Gas No 4). Bake until pale gold (about 25 to 30 minutes)
7 Remove Pyramids from trays and trim away surplus rice paper
8 Cool on wire rack
9 Store in airtight tin when cold.
Makes about 24 Pyramids

Fruit & Cream Pavlovas

1 recipe Basic Meringues (page 225)
150ml / $\frac{1}{4}$ pint fresh double cream
1 tablespoon milk
Fresh or canned fruit

1 Cover 2 oiled baking trays with double thickness of greaseproof paper. Outline three 7cm / 3in rounds on each
2 Cover each round with Meringue mixture, about $\frac{1}{2}$cm / $\frac{1}{4}$in thick
3 Put into centre of slow oven (140°C / 275°F or Gas No 1) and bake for 35 to 45 minutes (or until Pavlovas are pale gold and crisp looking). Insides should be fairly soft
4 Carefully peel away from paper. Cool on wire rack
5 Before serving, whip cream and milk together until stiff
6 Spread two-thirds over Pavlovas
7 Cover with fresh raspberries, halved strawberries or well-drained canned mandarins or peach slices
8 Top each with a whirl of cream and serve immediately. **Serves 6**

Jam and Cream Sandwich (below)

 Cakes freeze successfully alone or with filling and coating of either Butter Cream Frostings or sweetened whipped cream.
Storage time – 6 months

Victoria Sandwich

100g / 4oz softened butter
100g / 4oz caster sugar
2 standard eggs
100g / 4oz self-raising flour, sifted

1 Prepare two 18cm / 7in sandwich tins (page 229)
2 Cream butter and sugar together until very pale in colour, light in texture and fluffy
3 Beat in whole eggs, one at a time, adding a tablespoon of flour with each
4 Gently fold in remaining flour with metal spoon
5 Transfer to prepared tins and smooth tops with knife
6 Bake in centre of moderate oven (180°C / 350°F or Gas No 4) for 25 to 30 minutes (or until well risen, golden brown and firm)
7 Leave in tins for 2 to 3 minutes. Turn out on to wire cooling rack. Strip off paper and leave until cold. **About 8 portions**

Jam Sandwich

1 Follow recipe and method for Victoria Sandwich (left)
2 When cakes are cold, sandwich together with 2 to 3 level tablespoons jam
3 Dust top of cake with sifted icing sugar.
About 8 portions

Jam & Cream Sandwich

1 Follow recipe and method for Victoria Sandwich (left)
2 When cakes are cold, sandwich together with 2 to 3 level tablespoons jam and 3 to 4 tablespoons fresh double cream, whipped until thick
3 Dust top of cake with sifted icing sugar. **About 8 portions**

PREPARATION OF CAKE TINS

Materials for lining Use greaseproof paper, brushed with melted butter, non-stick paper which will not require greasing, or a tin with a non-stick finish which will not need greasing or lining before use.

Sponge Cakes Grease tins, then dust with a mixture of equal parts of flour and caster sugar.

Sandwich Cakes Grease tins then line bottoms of tins with a round of greaseproof paper and grease this. For Genoese sandwiches, grease and dust tins with flour in addition to lining.

Fruit Cakes and Rich Mixtures Grease and line whole tin. For mixtures requiring a long cooking period, use double-thickness greaseproof paper to prevent any overcooking of the outside of the cake.

To line a deep tin

1 Place tin on piece of greaseproof paper and draw round base

2 Cut piece of greaseproof paper just inside pencil mark

3 Cut a strip of greaseproof paper to the size of the depth of the tin, plus 5cm / 2in longer and deeper. Then make a 2.5cm / 1in fold along length of strip and cut diagonally up to the fold at 1cm / $\frac{1}{2}$in intervals

4 Grease inside the tin with melted butter

5 Insert the strip of greaseproof paper, ensuring that snipped part lies flat against base of tin. Place base circle in position

6 Grease all paper surfaces

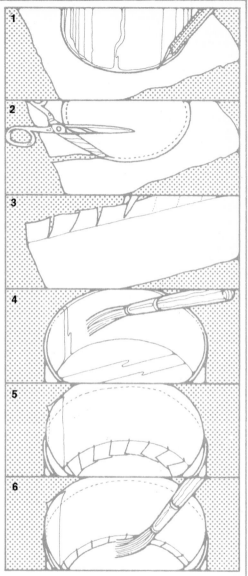

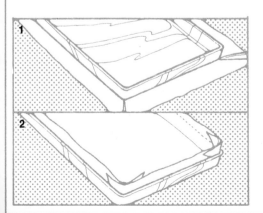

To line a Swiss Roll tin

1 Cut a piece of greaseproof paper 5cm / 2in larger all round than tin. Place tin on it and cut from each corner of paper to corner of tin.

2 Grease tin and put in paper so that it fits closely and overlaps at corners. Grease all paper surfaces

Lemon Sandwich

1 Follow recipe and method for Victoria Sandwich (page 228)
2 Cream butter and sugar with 1 level teaspoon finely grated lemon rind
3 When cakes are cold, sandwich together with either 4 tablespoons fresh double cream, whipped until thick, half a recipe Lemon Butter Cream Frosting (page 244) or Lemon Velvet Frosting (page 243)
4 Dust top of cake with sifted icing sugar.
About 8 portions

Orange Sandwich

1 Follow recipe and method for Victoria Sandwich (page 228)
2 Cream butter and sugar with 1 level teaspoon finely grated orange rind
3 When cakes are cold, sandwich together with either 4 tablespoons fresh double cream, whipped until thick, half a recipe Orange Butter Cream Frosting (page 246) or Orange Velvet Frosting (page 243)
4 Dust top of cake with sifted icing sugar.
About 8 portions

Pineapple Sandwich

1 Follow recipe and method for Victoria Sandwich (page 228)
2 When cakes are cold, sandwich together and cover top with double recipe Pineapple Velvet Frosting (page 244)
3 Decorate top with pieces of crystallized pineapple. **About 8 portions**

Walnut Coffee Sandwich

1 Follow recipe and method for Victoria Sandwich (page 228)
2 Stir 25g / 1oz very finely chopped walnuts into mixture after beating in eggs
3 When cakes are cold, sandwich together with half a recipe Coffee Butter Cream Frosting (page 246) or half a recipe Coffee Cream Frosting (page 246). Dust top of cake with sifted icing sugar.
About 8 portions

Chocolate Sandwich

1 Follow recipe and method for Victoria Sandwich (page 228)
2 When cakes are cold, sandwich together with half a recipe Chocolate Butter Cream Frosting (page 246)
3 Dust top of cake with sifted icing sugar.
About 8 portions

Fresh Fruit Sandwich

1 Follow recipe and method for Victoria Sandwich (page 228)
2 When cakes are cold, sandwich together with Whipped Cream Frosting (page 246) or Whipped Cream Frosting with Rum, Sherry or Brandy (page 246)
3 Spread more Frosting thickly over top. Then cover with 100 to 175g / 4 to 6oz halved fresh strawberries or whole raspberries or loganberries
4 Brush fruit with 1 to 2 tablespoons melted redcurrant jelly or apricot jam
5 Pipe small whirls or rosettes with remaining Frosting round top edge of cake
6 Chill lightly before serving. **Makes 8 portions**

Genoese Sandwich

50g / 2oz butter
3 standard eggs
75g / 3oz caster sugar
75g / 3oz plain flour, sifted twice

1 Prepare two 18cm / 7in round tins as given for Victoria Sandwich (page 229)
2 Melt butter over low heat. Strain into clean basin through muslin or coffee filter paper
3 Put eggs into large bowl standing over saucepan of hand-hot water. Whisk for 2 minutes
4 Add sugar. Continue whisking for further 8 to 10 minutes (or until mixture is very light in colour, fairly thick in texture – consistency of softly whipped cream – and at least double its original volume)
5 Remove bowl from saucepan. Continue whisking for further 5 minutes until egg mixture is cool
6 With large metal spoon, gently fold in half of the melted and cooled butter and half of the flour. Repeat with rest of butter and flour
7 Transfer to prepared tins. Bake in centre of moderate oven (180°C / 350°F or Gas No 4) for 25 to 30 minutes (when cakes should have shrunk slightly away from sides of tins and be golden brown on top)
8 Leave in tins for 1 minute. Turn out on to folded tea-towel. (A wire cooling rack is inclined to sink into these very light cakes and leave deep lines)
9 Carefully peel away paper. Sandwich together as for Victoria Sandwich cakes (page 228).
About 8 portions

Genoese Cake

1 Follow recipe and method for Genoese Sandwich (page 230)
2 Transfer mixture to prepared 18cm/7in deep cake tin (see page 229)
3 Bake in centre of moderate oven (180°C/350°F or Gas No 4) for 40 to 45 minutes (or until wooden cocktail stick, inserted into centre, comes out clean)
4 Leave until cold. Slice into 1 or 2 layers. Sandwich together and cover top with filling and frosting to taste. (See Fillings and Frostings Section, page 243). **Serves 8**

Mixed Fruit Sandwich

1 Follow recipe and method for Fresh Fruit Sandwich (page 230)
2 Instead of strawberries, raspberries or loganberries, cover top of cake with rings or lines of well drained canned peach slices; halved and de-seeded black or green grapes and drained and halved canned red cherries. **Makes 8 portions**

Fairy Cakes

1 Follow recipe and method for Victoria Sandwich (page 228)
2 Stir 50g/2oz currants or sultanas into mixture after beating in eggs
3 Transfer equal amounts to 18 paper cases standing in 18 ungreased bun tins
4 Bake just above centre of moderately hot oven (190°C/375°F or Gas No 5) for 20 to 25 minutes (or until well risen and golden). Cool on wire rack.
Makes 18 cakes

Chocolate Chip Cakes

1 Follow recipe and method for Fairy Cakes (above)
2 Stir in 50g/2oz chopped plain chocolate instead of currants or sultanas. **Makes 18 Cakes**

Chocolate Layer Cake

100g/4oz self-raising flour
2 level tablespoons cocoa powder
100g/4oz butter
100g/4oz caster sugar
25g/1oz golden syrup
½ teaspoon vanilla essence
2 standard eggs
4 teaspoons milk

1 Prepare a deep 20cm/8in round sandwich tin (see page 229)
2 Sift flour twice with cocoa
3 Cream butter, sugar, syrup and essence together until very pale in colour, light in texture and fluffy
4 Beat in whole eggs, one at a time, adding tablespoon of sifted dry ingredients with each
5 Fold in milk and remaining dry ingredients with metal spoon
6 Transfer to prepared tin and smooth top with a knife
7 Bake in centre of moderate oven (180°C/350°F or Gas No 4) for 35 to 40 minutes (or until wooden cocktail stick, inserted into centre of cake, comes out clean)
8 Turn out on to wire rack, strip off paper and leave until cold
9 Cut cake into 2 or 3 layers
10 Fill and cover top with either 300ml/½ pint fresh double cream, whipped until thick, Caramel Cream Frosting (page 246), Whipped Cream Frosting with Nuts (page 246) or Vanilla Butter Cream Frosting (page 244). **Makes 8 portions**

Lime & Chocolate Layer Cake

1 Follow recipe and method for Chocolate Layer Cake (above)
2 When cake is cold, cut into 2 layers
3 Sandwich together and cover top with double recipe Lime Velvet Frosting (page 244)
4 Decorate with small leaves cut from angelica. **Makes 8 portions**

Mocha Layer Cake

1 Follow recipe and method for Chocolate Layer Cake (above)
2 When cake is cold, cut into 2 layers
3 Sandwich together with Coffee Velvet Frosting (page 244)
4 Decorate with 1 to 2 level tablespoons grated plain chocolate and 8 halved glacé cherries.
Makes 8 portions

Madeleines (below) Butterfly Cakes (page 233)

Madeleines

1 Follow recipe and method for Victoria Sand-wich (page 228)
2 Transfer equal amounts of mixture to 12 to 14 well-buttered Dariole moulds
3 Bake just above centre of moderate oven (180°C / 350°F or Gas No 4) for 20 to 25 minutes (or until well risen and golden)
4 Turn out and cool on wire rack
5 When completely cold, trim slice off wide part of each so that Madeleines stand upright without toppling
6 Brush with melted apricot jam, roll in desiccated coconut then put $\frac{1}{2}$ glacé cherry and 2 leaves cut from angelica on top of each.
Makes 12 to 14 Madeleines

Small Iced Cakes

1 Follow recipe and method for Victoria Sand-wich (page 228)
2 Transfer equal amounts of mixture to 18 paper cases standing in 18 ungreased bun tins
3 Bake just above centre of moderately hot oven (190°C / 375°F or Gas No 5) for 20 to 25 minutes (or until well risen and golden). Cool on wire rack
4 When completely cold cover tops with either a Velvet Frosting, Butter Cream Frosting or Glacé Icing to taste (see Fillings & Frostings Section, page 243). Decorate with halved glacé cherries, pieces of angelica, chocolate buttons, grated chocolate, whole hazelnuts, pieces of shelled walnut halves or halved and toasted almonds.
Makes 18 Cakes

Butterfly Cakes

1 Follow recipe and method for Victoria Sandwich (page 228)
2 Transfer equal amounts of mixture to 18 well buttered bun tins
3 Bake just above centre of moderately hot oven (190°C / 375°F or Gas No 5) for 20 to 25 minutes (or until well risen and golden)
4 Cool on wire rack
5 To make Butterflies cut a slice off the top of each cake. Cut slices in halves (for wings)
6 Pipe 3 lines of Butter Cream Frosting (page 244) of choice on top of each cake
7 Put halved slices into cream at an angle to form wings. Dust lightly with sifted icing sugar.
Makes 18 Cakes

Sponge Sandwich

3 standard eggs
75g / 3oz caster sugar
75g / 3oz self-raising flour, sifted twice

1 Prepare two 18cm / 7in sandwich tins (see page 229). Dust sides of tins with sifted plain flour
2 Put eggs into large bowl standing over saucepan of hand-hot water
3 Whisk for 2 minutes
4 Add sugar. Continue whisking further 8 to 10 minutes (or until mixture is very light in colour, thick in texture – consistency of softly whipped cream – and at least double its original volume)
5 Remove bowl from saucepan. Continue whisking further 5 minutes (or until egg mixture is cool)
6 Gently fold in flour with large metal spoon
7 Transfer to prepared tins. Bake in centre of moderate oven (180°C / 350°F or Gas No 4) for 20 minutes (or until well risen and golden)
8 Turn out on to sheet of sugared greaseproof paper resting on folded tea-towel. Carefully peel off lining paper. Leave until completely cold.
About 8 portions

Deep Sponge Cake

1 Follow recipe and method for Sponge Sandwich (above) but use plain flour instead of self-raising
2 Transfer mixture to prepared 18cm / 7in deep cake tin (see page 229)
3 Bake in centre of moderate oven (180°C / 350°F or Gas No 4) for 40 to 45 minutes (or until wooden cocktail stick, inserted into centre, comes out clean)
4 Leave until cold. Slice into 1 or 2 layers
5 Sandwich together and cover top with Filling and Frosting to taste. (See Fillings and Frostings Section, page 243).
Makes 8 portions

Jam Sponge Sandwich

1 Follow recipe and method for Sponge Sandwich (left)
2 When cakes are cold, sandwich together with 2 to 3 level tablespoons jam
3 Dust top of cake with caster sugar.
About 8 portions

Jam & Cream Sponge Sandwich

1 Follow recipe and method for Sponge Sandwich (left)
2 When cakes are cold, sandwich together with 2 to 3 level tablespoons jam and 4 tablespoons double cream, whipped until thick
3 Dust top of cake with caster sugar.
About 8 portions

Swiss Roll

1 Follow recipe and method for Sponge Sandwich (left)
2 Transfer mixture to prepared 30cm × 20cm / 12in × 8in Swiss Roll tin (see page 229).
3 Bake towards top of moderately hot oven (200°C / 400°F or Gas No 6) for 10 to 12 minutes (or until well risen and firm)
4 Turn out on to sheet of sugared greaseproof paper resting on folded tea-towel. Carefully peel off paper
5 Cut away crisp edges with sharp knife. Spread quickly with 4 tablespoons warm jam
6 Roll up tightly and hold in position for 1 minute. Cool on wire rack. **Makes 8 to 10 slices**

Chocolate Swiss Roll

1 Follow recipe and method for Swiss Roll (above)
2 When making up sponge mixture, use 65g / 2½oz self-raising flour sifted twice with 15g / ½oz cocoa powder. **Makes 8 to 10 slices**

Cream-filled Swiss Roll

1 Follow recipe and method for Swiss Roll (above) or Chocolate Swiss Roll (above)
2 After trimming away crisp edges, roll up loosely with paper inside to prevent sticking. Cover with damp tea-towel and leave until completely cold
3 Unroll carefully, remove paper and fill with 150ml / ¼ pint fresh double cream, whipped until thick
4 Roll up again and hold in position for about 1 minute. **Makes 8 to 10 slices**

Small Seed Cakes

1 Follow recipe and method for Victoria Sandwich (page 228)
2 Stir 2 level teaspoons caraway seeds into mixture after beating in eggs
3 Transfer equal amounts to 18 paper cases standing in 18 ungreased bun tins
4 Bake just above centre of moderately hot oven (190°C/375°F or Gas No 5) for 20 to 25 minutes (or until well risen and golden)
5 Cool on wire rack. **Makes 18 Cakes**

Coffee Hazelnut Gâteau

3 Victoria Sandwich Cakes (1½× recipe page 228)
Double recipe Coffee Butter Cream Frosting (page 246)
50g/2oz finely chopped nuts
About 25g/1oz whole hazelnuts

1 Sandwich Cakes together with Frosting
2 Cover top and sides smoothly with more Frosting
3 Press chopped hazelnuts against sides
4 With remaining Frosting, pipe lines in trellis design over top of Cake. Decorate top and lower edges with small piped whirls or rosettes
5 Decorate top with hazelnuts
6 Chill lightly before serving.
Makes 8 to 10 portions

Caramel & Almond Gâteau

1 Genoese Cake (page 231) or
  Deep Sponge Cake (page 233)
1 recipe Caramel Cream Frosting (page 246)
50 to 75g/2 to 3oz flaked and toasted almonds
12 blanched and toasted almonds

1 Cut Cake into 2 layers
2 Sandwich together with Frosting
3 Spread more Frosting around sides. Cover with flaked almonds
4 Swirl rest of Frosting over top of Cake. Decorate with whole almonds
5 Chill lightly before serving. **About 8 portions**

Genoese Slab

1 Follow recipe and method for Genoese Sandwich (page 230)
2 Transfer mixture to prepared 30cm× 20cm/12in× 8in Swiss Roll tin (see page 229)
3 Bake in centre of moderate oven (180°C/350°F or Gas No 4) for 15 to 20 minutes (or until well risen and firm)
4 When cold, cut into 25 to 35 fingers or squares and serve plain. **Serves 6 to 8**

Rich Butter Cake

175g/6oz softened butter
175g/6oz caster sugar
3 standard eggs
225g/8oz plain flour, sifted
2 tablespoons milk
1¼ level teaspoons baking powder

1 Prepare 20cm/8in round cake tin (see page 229)
2 Cream butter with sugar thoroughly for 3 to 4 minutes, until light and fluffy. Beat in whole eggs, one at a time, adding a tablespoon of flour with each. Beat in milk with a tablespoon of flour
3 Gently fold in rest of flour sieved together with baking powder with large metal spoon
4 Transfer to prepared tin and smooth top with knife
5 Bake in centre of moderate oven (160°C/325°F or Gas No 3) for 1½ to 1¾ hours (or until wooden cocktail stick, inserted into centre of cake, comes out clean)
6 Leave in tin for 5 minutes. Turn out on to wire cooling rack
7 Carefully peel off paper when cake is cold
8 Store cake in an airtight tin.
Makes 8 to 10 portions

The creaming of the butter and caster sugar must be done very thoroughly to build as much air as possible into the mixture.

Traditional Madeira Cake

1 Follow recipe and method for Rich Butter Cake (above)
2 Cream butter and sugar with finely grated rind of 1 medium-sized lemon
3 Before baking cake arrange 2 strips of candied citron or lemon rind on top of mixture.
Makes 8 to 10 portions

Orange Cake

1 Follow recipe and method for Rich Butter Cake (above)
2 Cream butter and sugar with 2 level teaspoons finely grated orange rind.
Makes 8 to 10 portions

Coconut Cake

1 Follow recipe and method for Rich Butter Cake (above)
2 Cream butter and sugar with 1 level teaspoon vanilla essence
3 After beating in eggs stir in 50g/2oz desiccated coconut and 2 further tablespoons milk.
Makes 8 to 10 portions

Dundee Cake

1 Follow recipe and method for Rich Butter Cake (page 234)
2 Cream butter and sugar with finely grated rind of 1 small orange
3 After beating in eggs, stir in 50g/2oz ground almonds, 100g/4oz **each** currants, sultanas and seedless raisins and 50g/2oz chopped mixed peel
4 Before baking cake, cover top of mixture with 25 to 50g/1 to 2 oz blanched and split almonds
5 Bake in centre of slow oven (150°C/300°F or Gas No 2) for 2½ to 3 hours (or until wooden cocktail stick, inserted into centre, comes out clean). **Makes 8 to 10 portions**

Seed Cake

1 Follow recipe and method for Rich Butter Cake (page 234)
2 After beating in eggs stir in 3 level teaspoons caraway seeds. **Makes 8 to 10 portions**

Almond & Raisin Cake

1 Follow recipe and method for Rich Butter Cake (page 234)
2 Cream butter and sugar with ½ teaspoon almond essence
3 After beating in eggs stir in 50g/2oz ground almonds and 100g/4oz seedless raisins.
Makes 8 to 10 portions

Frosted Walnut Cake

1 Follow recipe and method for Rich Butter Cake (page 234)
2 Stir in 50g/2oz very finely chopped shelled walnut halves after beating in eggs
3 When cake is cold, cut into 2 layers. Sandwich together with American Boiled Frosting (page 247)
4 Quickly swirl rest of Frosting over top and sides. Decorate with 25 to 50g/1 to 2oz shelled walnut halves. **Makes 8 to 10 portions**

Currant Cake

1 Follow recipe and method for Rich Butter Cake (page 234)
2 Cream butter and sugar with 1 level teaspoon finely grated lemon rind
3 After beating in eggs stir in 175g/6oz currants.
Makes 8 to 10 portions

Sultana Cake

1 Follow recipe and method for Rich Butter Cake (page 234)
2 Cream butter and sugar with 1 level teaspoon finely grated lemon rind and ½ teaspoon vanilla essence
3 After beating in eggs stir in 175g/6oz sultanas.
Makes 8 to 10 portions

Ginger Cake

1 Follow recipe and method for Rich Butter Cake (page 234)
2 Sift flour with 1 level teaspoon ground ginger
3 Add 75g/3oz chopped preserved ginger after beating in eggs. **Makes 8 to 10 portions**

Genoa Cake

1 Follow recipe and method for Rich Butter Cake (page 234)
2 Cream butter and sugar with 1 level teaspoon finely grated lemon rind
3 After beating in eggs stir in 100g/4oz **each** currants, sultanas and chopped mixed peel, 50g/2oz finely chopped glacé cherries and 25g/1oz finely chopped almonds
4 Before baking cake, cover top of mixture with 25 to 50g/1 to 2oz blanched and split almonds
5 Bake in centre of slow oven (150°C/300°F or Gas No 2) for 2½ to 3 hours (or until wooden cocktail stick, inserted into centre of cake, comes out clean). **Makes 8 to 10 portions**

Genoese Fancies

1 Follow recipe and method for Genoese Slab (page 234)
2 When cold, cut into fancy shapes with biscuit cutters. Turn into Fancies by spreading sides of each with Butter Cream Frostings and covering with Glacé Icings (Fillings & Frostings Section, page 243)
3 When each Fancy has set, pipe small rosettes of Butter Cream Frosting along edges
4 Decorate with nuts, glacé cherries, and pieces of angelica.
Makes 24 to 30 assorted-shaped Fancies

Rich Fruit Cake

225g / 8oz plain flour
1 level teaspoon mixed spice
½ level teaspoon cinnamon
½ level teaspoon grated nutmeg
1 level teaspoon cocoa powder
175g / 6oz butter
175g / 6oz soft brown sugar
1 level tablespoon black treacle
1 level teaspoon *each* finely grated orange and lemon rind
4 standard eggs
550g / 1lb 4oz mixed dried fruit (currants, sultanas and seedless raisins)
100g / 4oz chopped mixed peel
50g / 2oz chopped, shelled walnut halves or blanched almonds
50g / 2oz chopped dates
50g / 2oz chopped glacé cherries
1 tablespoon milk

1 Prepare 20cm / 8in round or 18cm / 7in square cake tin (see page 229)
2 Sift flour with spice, cinnamon, grated nutmeg and cocoa
3 Cream butter with sugar, treacle and lemon and orange rind
4 Beat in whole eggs, one at a time, adding tablespoon of sifted dry ingredients with each
5 Stir in currants, sultanas, raisins, chopped peel, nuts, dates and cherries
6 Fold in dry ingredients alternately with milk
7 Transfer to prepared tin and smooth top with knife
8 Bake in centre of slow oven (150°C / 300°F or Gas No 2) for 4 to 4½ hours (or until fine knitting needle, inserted into centre of cake, comes out clean)
9 Leave in tin for 15 minutes. Turn out on to wire cooling rack
10 When completely cold, wrap in aluminium foil and store in airtight tin until needed.
Makes 20 to 30 portions

Iced Christmas Cake

1 Rich Fruit Cake (left)
4 level tablespoons warmed and melted apricot jam
1 recipe Almond Paste (page 245)
1 recipe Royal Icing (page 244)

1 Brush top and sides of Cake with melted jam
2 Turn Almond Paste on to sugared surface (either sifted icing or caster). Roll out about half into 20cm / 8in round or 18cm / 7in square. Use to cover top of Cake
3 Roll out rest of Paste into strip – same depth as Cake – and wrap round sides
4 Press edges and joins well together with fingers dipped in caster sugar
5 When Almond Paste has set (overnight) wrap Cake loosely in aluminium foil. Leave at least 1 week before icing
6 To ice Cake, stand on suitable silver board
7 Spread Royal Icing thickly and evenly over top and sides
8 Flick Icing upwards with back of teaspoon so that it stands in soft peaks
9 Decorate with Christmas ornaments. Leave Cake undisturbed overnight while Icing hardens.
Makes 20 to 30 portions

Iced Celebration Cake

1 Follow recipe and method for Iced Christmas Cake (above)
2 To flat ice the cake follow directions to Royal Ice a Celebration Cake (page 245)
3 Decorate according to the occasion to be celebrated

Iced Celebration Cake (page 236)

Rock Cakes

200g / 8oz self-raising flour
100g / 4oz butter
75g / 3oz caster sugar
100g / 4oz mixed dried fruit
1 standard egg, beaten
2 to 4 teaspoons milk

1 Sift flour into bowl
2 Rub in butter finely
3 Add sugar and fruit
4 Mix to very stiff batter with beaten egg and milk
5 Place 10 spoonfuls of mixture, in rocky mounds, on well-buttered baking tray (allow room between each as they spread slightly)
6 Bake just above centre of moderately hot oven (200°C / 400°F or Gas No 6) for 15 to 20 minutes
7 Cool on wire rack.
Makes 10 Cakes

Date & Lemon Cakes

1 Follow recipe and method for Rock Cakes (left)
2 Use 100g / 4oz finely chopped dates instead of mixed dried fruit
3 Add 1 level teaspoon finely grated lemon rind with dates. **Makes 10 Cakes**

Chocolate Cakes

1 Follow recipe and method for Rock Cakes (left)
2 Sift 175g / 7oz self-raising flour with 25g / 1oz cocoa powder
3 Omit fruit
4 Add 1 teaspoon vanilla essence with egg and milk. **Makes 10 Cakes**

Cherry Cakes

1 Follow recipe and method for Rock Cakes (page 237)
2 Use 75g / 3oz chopped glacé cherries instead of dried fruit.
Makes 10 Cakes

Walnut & Orange Cakes

1 Follow recipe and method for Rock Cakes (page 237)
2 Add 50 to 75g / 2 to 3oz chopped, shelled walnut halves and 1 level teaspoon finely grated orange rind with sugar.
Makes 10 Cakes

Spice & Raisin Cakes

1 Follow recipe and method for Rock Cakes (page 237)
2 Sift 1 level teaspoon mixed spice with flour
3 Add 100g / 4oz seedless raisins instead of mixed dried fruit.
Makes 10 Cakes

Cream Horns

1 recipe Flaky Pastry (page 214)
Milk for brushing
Caster sugar
12 level teaspoons raspberry or strawberry jam
300ml / ½ pint fresh double cream
Sifted icing sugar

1 Brush 12 Cream Horn tins with melted butter
2 Roll out pastry thinly. Cut into twelve 2cm / 1in strips, each about 30cm / 12in long
3 Moisten one side of each strip with water
4 Starting at pointed end of each tin, wind pastry strip round. Make sure moistened side faces inwards and that the strip overlaps by about ½ cm / ¼in
5 Transfer to damp baking tray. Leave for 30 minutes
6 Bake just above centre of hot oven (230°C / 450°F or Gas No 8) for 10 minutes
7 Remove from oven. Brush with milk and sprinkle with caster sugar
8 Return to oven. Bake for further 7 to 10 minutes
9 Transfer to wire cooling rack. Cool for about 5 minutes
10 Carefully remove tins. Leave Horns until completely cold
11 Put teaspoon of jam into each. Fill with cream, whipped until thick and sweetened to taste with icing sugar.
Makes 12 Cream Horns

Gingerbread

150g / 6oz plain flour
2 level teaspoons ground ginger
1 level teaspoon mixed spice
½ level teaspoon bicarbonate of soda
100g / 4oz golden syrup
25g / 1oz butter
25g / 1oz soft brown sugar
1 standard egg, beaten
1 level tablespoon black treacle
2 tablespoons milk

1 Prepare 15cm / 6in cake tin (see page 229)
2 Sift flour, ginger, spice and bicarbonate of soda into bowl. Make a well in centre
3 Put syrup, butter and brown sugar into saucepan. Stir over low heat until butter has melted
4 Pour into well with egg, treacle and milk
5 Stir briskly, without beating, until well combined
6 Transfer to prepared tin. Bake in centre of moderate oven (180°C / 350°F or Gas No 4) for 1 hour (or until wooden cocktail stick, inserted into centre, comes out clean)
7 Turn out on to wire cooling rack. Remove paper when gingerbread is cold.
Makes 10 to 12 portions

Lemon & Almond Ring

100g / 4oz butter
100g / 4oz caster sugar
1 level teaspoon finely grated lemon rind
2 standard eggs
100g / 4oz self-raising flour, sifted
40 to 50g / 1½ to 2oz blanched and finely chopped almonds
1 recipe Lemon Glacé Icing (page 247)

Decoration
Small leaves cut from angelica

1 Brush base and sides of ¾ litre / 1½ pint ring tin with melted butter
2 Cream butter with sugar and lemon rind until light and fluffy
3 Beat in whole eggs, one at a time, adding tablespoon of sifted flour with each
4 Stir in almonds
5 Fold in remaining flour with metal spoon
6 Transfer to prepared tin. Bake in centre of moderate oven (180°C / 350°F or Gas No 4) for 35 to 40 minutes (or until wooden cocktail stick, inserted into centre of cake, comes out clean)
7 Leave in tin for 2 or 3 minutes. Turn out on to wire cooling rack
8 When cake is cold pour Icing over top and allow to run down sides
9 Leave undisturbed until Icing has set. Decorate with angelica.
About 8 portions

Coffee Hazelnut Ring

1 Follow recipe and method for Lemon and Almond Ring (page 238)
2 Use hazelnuts instead of almonds
3 Coat Ring with Coffee Glacé Icing (page 247) instead of Lemon
4 When Icing is set decorate with about 12 whole hazelnuts. **About 8 portions**

Family Fruit Cake

200g / 8oz self-raising flour
100g / 4oz butter
100g / 4oz caster sugar
100g / 4oz mixed dried fruits (currants, sultanas or seedless raisins)
1 level teaspoon finely grated lemon rind
1 standard egg
5 tablespoons milk

1 Prepare 15cm / 6in round cake or 20cm×10cm×6cm / 1lb loaf tin
2 Sift flour into bowl
3 Rub in butter finely
4 Add sugar, fruit and lemon rind
5 Mix to batter with egg and milk
6 Stir with metal spoon until evenly combined. Do **not** beat
7 Transfer to prepared tin
8 Bake in centre of moderate oven (180°C / 350°F or Gas No 4) for 1¼ to 1½ hours (or until wooden cocktail stick, inserted into centre, comes out clean)
9 Leave in tin for 5 minutes. Turn out on to wire cooling rack
10 Peel off paper. Store cake in airtight tin when cold. **Makes 8 portions**

Date & Walnut Cake

1 Follow recipe and method for Family Fruit Cake (above)
2 Sift 1 level teaspoon mixed spice with flour
3 Add 75g / 3oz finely chopped dates and 25g / 1oz finely chopped walnuts instead of mixed fruit
4 Omit lemon rind.
Makes 8 portions

Coconut & Lemon Cake

1 Follow recipe and method for Family Fruit Cake (above)
2 Omit fruit
3 Add 50g / 2oz desiccated coconut with sugar
4 Increase lemon rind to 2 level teaspoons.
Makes 8 portions

Sultana & Orange Cake

1 Follow recipe and method for Family Fruit Cake (left)
2 Use 100g / 4oz sultanas instead of mixed fruit, and orange rind instead of lemon.
Makes 8 portions

Cherry & Ginger Cake

1 Follow recipe and method for Family Fruit Cake (left)
2 Use 50g / 2oz **each** finely chopped glacé cherries and finely chopped preserved ginger instead of mixed fruit. **Makes 8 portions**

Plain Family Cake

1 Follow recipe and method for Family Fruit Cake (left)
2 Omit fruit
3 If preferred, lemon rind can also be omitted and, instead, ½ teaspoon vanilla essence added with egg and milk. **Makes 8 portions**

Cherry Cake

100g / 4oz glacé cherries
200g / 8oz self-raising flour
50g / 2oz semolina
125g / 5oz butter
100g / 4oz caster sugar
1 level teaspoon finely grated lemon rind
½ teaspoon vanilla essence
2 standard eggs, well beaten
2 to 3 tablespoons milk

1 Prepare 18cm / 7in round cake tin (see page 229)
2 Cut cherries into quarters
3 Wash thoroughly to remove syrup
4 Dry well. Mix with 1 tablespoon measured flour
5 Sift rest of flour and semolina into bowl
6 Rub in butter finely
7 Add sugar, lemon rind and cherries
8 Mix to stiff batter with vanilla, eggs and milk
9 Stir briskly, without beating, until well mixed. Transfer to prepared tin
10 Bake in centre of moderate oven (180°C / 350°F or Gas No 4) for 1 hour (or until wooden cocktail stick, inserted into centre of cake, comes out clean)
11 Leave in tin 5 minutes. Turn out on to wire cooling rack
12 Peel away paper. Store in airtight tin when cold. **About 8 portions**

Chocolate Walnut Gâteau

**1 Genoese Cake (page 231) or Deep Sponge
Cake (page 233)**
**Double recipe Chocolate Butter Cream Frosting
(page 246)**
50g/2oz finely chopped walnuts
1 recipe Chocolate Glacé Icing (page 247)
15 to 25g/½ to 1oz shelled walnut halves

1 Cut cake into 3 layers
2 Sandwich together and cover sides with
Frosting
3 Press chopped walnuts against sides
4 Spread Chocolate Glacé Icing over top and
leave Cake undisturbed until icing has set
5 Pipe rosettes or small whirls of remaining
Frosting round top and lower edges of Cake
6 Decorate with walnut halves
7 Chill lightly before serving. **About 8 portions**

Marmalade Cake

200g/8oz plain flour
Pinch of salt
3 level teaspoons baking powder
100g/4oz butter
50g/2oz caster sugar
½ level teaspoon finely grated orange rind
2 standard eggs, beaten
3 level tablespoons orange marmalade
2 to 3 tablespoons milk

1 Prepare 15cm/6in round cake (see page 229)
or 20cm × 10cm × 6cm/1lb loaf tin
2 Sift flour, salt and baking powder into bowl
3 Rub in butter finely
4 Add sugar and orange rind
5 Mix to fairly soft batter with eggs, marmalade
and milk
6 Transfer to prepared tin. Bake in centre of
moderate oven (180°C/350°F or Gas No 4) for
1¼ to 1½ hours (or until wooden cocktail stick,
inserted into centre, comes out clean)
7 Leave in tin for 5 minutes. Turn out on to wire
cooling rack
8 Peel off paper. Store cake in airtight tin when
cold. **Makes 6 to 8 portions**

Marmalade & Walnut Cake

1 Follow recipe and method for Marmalade Cake
(above)
2 Add 50g/2oz finely chopped shelled walnut
halves with sugar. **Makes 6 to 8 portions**

Eccles Cakes

15g/½oz butter
25g/1oz currants
25g/1oz chopped mixed peel
2 level teaspoons soft brown sugar
¼ level teaspoon mixed spice
½ recipe Flaky Pastry (page 214)
Milk for brushing
Extra caster sugar

1 Melt butter in saucepan
2 Stir in currants, peel, sugar and spice. Mix well
3 Roll out Pastry to just under ½cm/¼in thickness
4 Cut into 8 rounds with 8cm/3in biscuit cutter
5 Put heaped teaspoon of fruit mixture on to
centre of each
6 Moisten edges of Pastry with water
7 With fingertips, draw up edges of each round so
that they meet in the centre, completely enclosing
filling
8 Press well together to seal. Turn each cake over
9 Roll to about 1cm/½in thickness
10 Make 3 slits in top of each with sharp knife
11 Brush with milk. Sprinkle thickly with caster
sugar
12 Bake just above centre of hot oven
(220°C/425°F or Gas No 7) for 20 minutes
13 Cool on wire rack.
Makes 8 Cakes

Fruit Cheesecake

Base
100g/4oz self-raising flour
75g/3oz softened butter
50g/2oz sifted icing sugar
1 standard egg

Cheesecake mixture
2 tablespoons cornflour
2 tablespoons single cream
50g/2oz softened butter
2 egg yolks
225g/8oz cream cheese
225g/8oz Cottage cheese
50g/2oz caster sugar
½ teaspoon vanilla essence
2 egg whites

Topping
Fresh or canned fruit

1 Place all ingredients for base in a bowl, beat
until smooth and spread in a loose-bottomed
22cm/9in cake tin
2 Bake in a moderately hot oven (190°C/375°F or
Gas No 5) for 15 minutes. Leave to cool
3 Mix the cornflour and cream to a paste, then
add all remaining ingredients except egg whites
4 Whisk egg whites until stiff. Fold into the cheese
5 Smooth on top of cooked base. Bake in a
moderately hot oven (190°C/375°F or Gas No 5)
for 20 minutes. Allow to cool
6 Decorate with fresh or canned fruit

Marmalade Cake (page 240) Cheesecake (below)

Cheesecake

100g / 4oz digestive biscuits
½ level teaspoon cinnamon
40g / 1½oz butter, melted
350g / 12oz Cottage or curd cheese
Yolks and whites of 3 standard eggs
100g / 4oz caster sugar
2 level tablespoons custard powder or cornflour
1 level teaspoon finely grated lemon rind
4 tablespoons fresh double cream

1 Crush biscuits. Mix with cinnamon and melted butter
2 Use to cover base of 18cm / 7in loose-bottomed buttered round cake tin

3 Rub Cottage cheese, if used, through sieve
4 Add egg yolks, 75g / 3oz sugar, custard powder or cornflour, lemon rind and double cream to Cottage or curd cheese. Mix well
5 Beat egg whites to stiff snow. Gently fold in rest of sugar
6 Fold into cheese mixture with large metal spoon. Pour into tin. Bake in centre of slow oven (150°C / 300°F or Gas No 2) for 1 hour
7 Turn off heat and open oven door. Leave cake in oven for further 30 minutes
8 Gently remove from tin when cold.
About 8 portions

Chocolate Eclairs

1 recipe Choux Pastry (page 214)
300ml / ½ pint fresh double cream
2 tablespoons milk
Sifted icing sugar
1 recipe Chocolate Glacé Icing (page 247)

1 Fit forcing bag with 1cm / ⅓in plain tube
2 Fill bag with pastry. Pipe twelve 10cm / 4in lengths on to buttered baking tray
3 Put into centre of moderately hot oven (200°C / 400°F or Gas No 6) and bake for 10 minutes
4 Reduce temperature to moderate (180°C / 350°F or Gas No 4). Bake for further 20 to 25 minutes (or until Eclairs are well puffed and golden)
5 Remove from oven and make slit in side of each
6 Return to oven for further 5 minutes to dry out
7 Cool on wire rack
8 When completely cold slit each Eclair along one side. Whip cream with milk until thick. Sweeten to taste with icing sugar. Fill Eclairs with cream
9 Cover tops with Icing. Leave until Icing has set.
Makes 12 Eclairs

Coffee Eclairs

1 Follow recipe and method for Chocolate Eclairs (above)
2 Cover tops with Coffee Glacé Icing (page 247) instead of chocolate. **Makes 12 Eclairs**

Almond Slices

1 recipe Short Crust Pastry (page 211)
2 level tablespoons raspberry or apricot jam
100g / 4oz caster sugar
100g / 4oz sifted icing sugar
175g / 6oz ground almonds
1 standard egg
White of one standard egg
½ teaspoon almond essence
25g / 1oz blanched and split almonds

1 Roll out pastry into 25cm × 15cm / 10in × 6in rectangle
2 Transfer to buttered baking tray
3 Pinch up long edges of Pastry between finger and thumb to form raised border
4 Cover base with jam
5 Combine sugars with almonds
6 Mix to paste with whole egg, egg white and almond essence
7 Cover jam with almond mixture, spreading it evenly with knife
8 Decorate with split almonds
9 Bake just above centre of moderately hot oven (200°C / 400°F or Gas No 6) for 25 minutes
10 Cool on wire rack. Cut into 14 slices when cold.
Makes 14 Almond Slices

Chocolate Cream Puffs

1 Follow recipe and method for Chocolate Eclairs (left)
2 Pipe or spoon 16 to 18 equal amounts of mixture, well apart, on to buttered tray
3 Bake, fill and ice as for Eclairs.
Makes 16 to 18 Puffs

Cream Slices

1 recipe Flaky Pastry (page 214) or Puff Pastry (page 212)
300ml / ½ pint fresh double cream
6 level tablespoons jam
Glacé Icing (page 247)

1 Roll out pastry into 40cm × 10cm / 16in × 4in strip
2 Cut into eight 10cm × 5cm / 4in × 2in pieces
3 Transfer to damp baking tray. Leave for 30 minutes
4 Bake towards top of hot oven (230°C / 450°F or Gas No 8) for 15 to 20 minutes (or until well risen, puffy and golden)
5 Transfer to wire cooling rack
6 When completely cold, split in half. Sandwich together with cream, whipped until thick, and jam
7 Cover tops with Icing. Leave until Icing has set.
Makes 8 Cream Slices

Parkin

225g / 8oz plain flour
¼ level teaspoon salt
1 level teaspoon *each* mixed spice, cinnamon and ground ginger
1 level teaspoon bicarbonate of soda
225g / 8oz medium oatmeal
175g / 6oz black treacle
150g / 5oz butter
100g / 4oz soft brown sugar
150ml / ¼ pint milk
1 standard egg, beaten

1 Prepare 18cm / 7in square cake tin
2 Sift flour, salt, spice, cinnamon, ground ginger and bicarbonate of soda into bowl. Add oatmeal. Make a well in centre
3 Put treacle, butter, sugar and milk into saucepan. Stir over low heat until butter has melted
4 Pour into well and add egg. Stir mixture briskly, without beating, until smooth and evenly combined
5 Transfer to prepared tin. Bake in centre of moderate oven (180°C / 350°F or Gas No 4) for 1 hour (or until wooden cocktail stick, inserted into centre, comes out clean)
6 Cool Parkin on wire rack. Store, without removing paper, in an airtight tin about 1 week before cutting.
Makes 12 to 14 portions

Fillings & Frostings

Orange Velvet Frosting (below)

 Frostings and butter cream freeze success-fully apart from boiled frostings. Open freeze rosettes of whipped cream frosting, then pack in layers in a rigid plastic container. Storage time – 2 months.

Lemon Velvet Frosting

Follow recipe and method for Orange Velvet Frosting (right)
Use lemon squash instead of orange. **Sufficient to fill or cover top of 18 to 20cm / 7 to 8in cake**

Orange Velvet Frosting

2 tablespoons butter, melted
2 tablespoons orange squash
175g / 6oz sifted icing sugar

1 Combine butter and squash
2 Gradually stir in icing sugar
3 Beat until icing is fairly thick and creamy, and stiff enough to spread. If Frosting is on the soft side, work in a little extra icing sugar.
Sufficient to fill or cover top of an 18 to 20cm / 7 to 8in cake

243

Lime Velvet Frosting

1 Follow recipe and method for Orange Velvet Frosting (page 243)
2 Use 2 tablespoons lime cordial instead of orange squash.
**Sufficient to fill or cover top of an
18 to 20cm / 7 to 8in cake**

Pineapple Velvet Frosting

1 Follow recipe and method for Orange Velvet Frosting (page 243)
2 Use 2 tablespoons pineapple juice instead of orange squash.
**Sufficient to fill or cover top of an
18 to 20cm / 7 to 8in cake**

Grapefruit Velvet Frosting

1 Follow recipe and method for Orange Velvet Frosting (page 243)
2 Use 2 tablespoons grapefruit juice instead of orange squash.
**Sufficient to fill or cover top of an
18 to 20cm / 7 to 8in cake**

Coffee Velvet Frosting

1 Follow recipe and method for Orange Velvet frosting (page 243)
2 Use 2 tablespoons liquid coffee essence instead of orange squash.
**Sufficient to fill or cover top of an
18 to 20cm / 7 to 8in cake**

Almond Butter Cream Frosting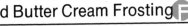

1 Follow recipe and method for Basic Butter Cream Frosting (right)
2 Add $\frac{1}{2}$ to 1 teaspoon almond essence with milk
3 If liked, colour pale pink or green.
**Sufficient to fill and cover top of a 2-layer,
18cm / 7in sandwich cake**

Lemon Butter Cream Frosting

1 Follow recipe and method for Basic Butter Cream Frosting (right)
2 Beat 1 level teaspoon finely grated lemon rind with butter before adding sugar and milk
3 If liked, colour pale yellow with yellow food colouring.
**Sufficient to fill and cover top of a 2-layer,
18cm / 7in sandwich cake**

Basic Butter Cream Frosting

**100g / 4oz softened butter
200g / 8oz sifted icing sugar
2 tablespoons cold milk
Red or green food colouring (optional)**

1 Beat butter until soft
2 Gradually beat in sugar alternatively with milk
3 Continue beating until Frosting is light and fluffy
4 If liked, colour pale pink or green with colouring. Refrigerate Frosting until it thickens a little.
**Sufficient to fill and cover top of a 2-layer,
18cm / 7in sandwich cake**

Vanilla Butter Cream Frosting

1 Follow recipe and method for Basic Butter Cream Frosting (above)
2 Add $\frac{1}{2}$ to 1 teaspoon vanilla essence with milk
3 If liked, colour pale pink or green.
**Sufficient to fill and cover top of a 2-layer,
18cm / 7in sandwich cake**

Royal Icing

**Whites of 2 standard eggs
450g / 1lb sifted icing sugar
$\frac{1}{2}$ teaspoon lemon juice
2 to 3 drops glycerine**

1 Beat egg whites until foamy
2 Gradually beat in icing sugar, lemon juice and glycerine (glycerine prevents icing from becoming too hard to cut)
3 Continue beating hard a good 5 to 7 minutes (or until icing is snowy-white and firm enough to stand in straight points when spoon is lifted out of bowl)
4 If too stiff, add a little more egg white or lemon juice. If too soft, beat in a little more sifted icing sugar
5 If coloured icing is required, beat in a few drops of food colouring.
**Sufficient to cover top and sides of an
18 to 20cm / 7 to 8in cake**

It is best to use Royal Icing a day after it is made to give air bubbles time to disperse. **Always** keep the Icing in an airtight, rigid plastic container until ready for use

Royal Icing for Piping

1 Follow recipe and method for Royal Icing (above)
2 Omit glycerine
3 Make up $\frac{1}{4}$ to $\frac{1}{2}$ quantity only

Almond Paste

225g/8oz ground almonds
225g/8oz sifted icing sugar
225g/8oz caster sugar
Yolks of 2 standard eggs
1 teaspoon lemon juice
½ teaspoon *each* vanilla and almond
essences

1 Combine almonds with both sugars
2 Mix to fairly stiff paste with remaining ingredients
3 Turn out on to board or table covered with sifted icing sugar. Knead lightly with fingertips until smooth, crack-free and pliable.
Sufficient to cover top and sides of a
20 to 23cm/8 to 9in rich fruit cake fairly thickly

To Almond Paste or Marzipan a Celebration Cake

The almond paste acts as a foundation for Royal Icing to prevent the rich cake from staining the white surface. The cake should have a flat surface for the almond paste to go on.
1 Dredge the working surface with a little sifted icing sugar. Knead the almond paste into a ball and divide in half
2 Roll out one half to fit the top of the cake and then brush the almond paste with a little sieved apricot jam
3 Place the cake upside down on the almond paste, press firmly, trim edges and then carefully place the right way up
4 Measure the circumference and depth of the cake with a piece of string. If the cake is round, cut remaining almond paste into two and roll out each until the correct shape to encircle the cake. If the cake is square, divide the almond paste into four
5 Brush almond paste with sieved apricot jam and place almond paste on the cake as for top
6 Use a rolling pin to ensure that the sides and top have a neat finish. Stand the cake on a suitable silver board, 5cm/2in larger than the base of the cake.
Leave the cake for a week before icing

To Royal Ice a Celebration Cake

Before icing the cake be sure that the almond paste has been allowed to dry.
1 With the cake on the cake board, place on an icing turntable, upturned mixing bowl or cake tin. Spoon a little Royal Icing over the almond paste
2 Spread with a palette knife evenly across the top of the cake and at the same time burst any air bubbles
3 With a warm steel rule, draw the rule at an angle firmly across the cake to obtain a smooth surface. Remove surplus icing. Allow to dry for 24 hours
4 Repeat this process for the sides of the cake using a knife, holding it vertically against the side of the cake
5 For a square cake, the two opposite sides should be iced and allowed to dry before icing the other two sides. Apply two or three more thin layers of icing to the surface until a good finish is obtained
6 Decorate according to the occasion to be celebrated

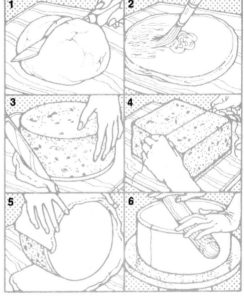

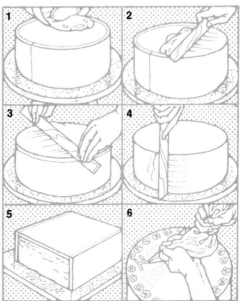

Orange Butter Cream Frosting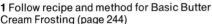

1 Follow recipe and method for Basic Butter Cream Frosting (page 244)
2 Beat 1 level teaspoon finely grated orange rind with butter before adding sugar and milk
3 If liked, colour pale orange with orange food colouring. **Sufficient to fill and cover top of 2-layer, 18cm / 7in sandwich cake**

Coffee Butter Cream Frosting

1 Follow recipe and method for Basic Butter Cream Frosting (page 244)
2 Sift 3 to 4 level teaspoons instant coffee powder with icing sugar.
Sufficient to fill and cover top of 2-layer, 18cm / 7in sandwich cake

Chocolate Butter Cream Frosting

1 Follow recipe and method for Basic Butter Cream Frosting (page 244)
2 Beat in 50g / 2oz melted and cooled plain chocolate with sugar and only 2 teaspoons milk.
Sufficient to fill and cover top of 2-layer, 18cm / 7in sandwich cake

Whipped Cream Frosting

150ml / ¼ pint fresh double cream
1 tablespoon milk
1 level tablespoon caster sugar

1 Whip cream and milk together until thick
2 Gently stir in caster sugar.
Sufficient to fill thickly and cover top of 2-layer, 18cm / 7in sandwich cake

Coffee Cream Frosting

1 Follow recipe and method for Whipped Cream Frosting (above)
2 Add 1 level teaspoon instant coffee powder with caster sugar. **Sufficient to fill thickly and cover top of 2-layer, 18cm / 7in sandwich cake**

Vanilla Cream Frosting

1 Follow recipe and method for Whipped Cream Frosting (above)
2 Whip cream and milk with ½ teaspoon vanilla essence. **Sufficient to fill thickly and cover top of 2-layer, 18cm / 7in sandwich cake**

Whipped Cream with Rum, Sherry or Brandy

1 Follow recipe and method for Whipped Cream Frosting (left)
2 After adding caster sugar, stir in 1 or 2 teaspoons rum, sherry or brandy.
Sufficient to fill thickly and cover top of a 2-layer, 18cm / 7in sandwich cake

Whipped Cream Frosting with Nuts

1 Follow recipe and method for Whipped Cream Frosting (left)
2 After adding caster sugar, stir in 1 level tablespoon very finely chopped shelled walnut halves, hazelnuts or toasted almonds
Sufficient to fill thickly and cover top of 2-layer, 18cm / 7in sandwich cake

Coffee Fudge Frosting

50g / 2oz butter
100g / 4oz soft brown sugar
3 tablespoons liquid coffee essence
1 tablespoon fresh single cream
450g / 1lb sifted icing sugar

1 Put butter, sugar, coffee essence and cream into saucepan
2 Stand over low heat, stirring, until butter melts and sugar dissolves
3 Bring to boil. Boil briskly for 3 minutes only
4 Remove from heat. Gradually stir in icing sugar
5 Beat until smooth. Continue beating further 5 minutes (or until Frosting has cooled and is stiff enough to spread). **Sufficient to fill and cover top and sides of 2-layer, 18cm / 7in sandwich cake**

Caramel Cream Frosting

25g / 1oz caster sugar
2 teaspoons water
300ml / ½ pint fresh double cream, chilled

1 Put sugar and water into saucepan and stand over low heat until sugar dissolves
2 Bring to boil. Cover pan and boil half a minute
3 Uncover. Continue to boil steadily until syrup turns a light caramel colour
4 Remove from heat. Quickly stir in 2 tablespoons of measured cream
5 Leave until cold. Add rest of cream and whip until thick. **Sufficient to fill and cover top of three 20cm / 8in sandwich cakes or fill and thickly cover top and sides of 2-layer, 18cm / 7in sandwich cake**

Glacé Icing

225g / 8oz sifted icing sugar
2 tablespoons hot water

1 Put sugar into bowl. Gradually add water
2 Stir briskly until smooth and thick enough to coat back of spoon without running off
3 If too thick, add a little more water; if too thin, stir in more sifted icing sugar. If liked, colour to taste with food colouring
4 Use immediately. **Sufficient to cover top of an 18 to 20cm / 7 to 8 in cake**

Do not disturb cake until Icing has set, or cracks will form

Orange or Lemon Glacé Icing

1 Follow recipe and method for Glacé Icing (above)
2 Add 1 level teaspoon very finely grated orange or lemon rind to sifted sugar
3 Mix with 2 tablespoons strained and warmed orange or lemon juice instead of water. If liked, colour with orange or lemon food colouring. **Sufficient to cover top of 18 to 20cm / 7 to 8in cake**

Coffee Glacé Icing

1 Follow recipe and method for Glacé Icing (above)
2 Dissolve 2 level teaspoons instant coffee powder in hot water before adding to sugar. **Sufficient to cover top of an 18 to 20cm / 7 to 8in cake**

Chocolate Glacé Icing

50g / 2oz plain chocolate
15g / ½oz butter
2 tablespoons warm water
¼ teaspoon vanilla essence
175g / 6oz sifted icing sugar

1 Break up chocolate and put, with butter and water, into basin standing over saucepan of hot water
2 Leave until melted, stirring once or twice
3 Add vanilla. Gradually beat in icing sugar
4 Use immediately. **Sufficient to cover top of an 18 to 20cm / 7 to 8in cake**

Mocha Glacé Icing

1 Follow recipe and method for Chocolate Glacé Icing (left)
2 Add 2 level teaspoons instant coffee powder to chocolate, butter and water in basin. **Sufficient to cover top of 18 to 20cm / 7 to 8in cake**

Cocoa Glacé Icing

2 level tablespoons sifted cocoa powder
2 tablespoons boiling water
15g / ½oz butter, melted
225g / 8oz sifted icing sugar

1 Mix cocoa to smooth paste with boiling water
2 Add butter
3 Gradually stir in icing sugar
4 Use immediately. **Sufficient to cover top of 18 to 20cm / 7 to 8in cake**

American Boiled Frosting

This Frosting is soft inside and crisp outside

450g / 1lb granulated sugar
150ml / ¼ pint water
Whites of 2 standard eggs
Pinch of cream of tartar
1 teaspoon vanilla essence

1 Put sugar and water into saucepan. Stir over low heat until sugar dissolves
2 Bring to boil. Cover pan and boil 1 minute
3 Uncover. Continue to boil fairly briskly, without stirring, for further 5 minutes (or until small quantity of mixture, dropped into cup of very cold water, forms soft ball when gently rolled between finger and thumb). Temperature on sugar thermometer, if used, should be 115°C / 238°F
4 Meanwhile, beat egg whites and cream of tartar to a very stiff snow
5 When sugar and water have boiled for required amount of time, pour on to egg whites in slow, steady stream, beating all the time
6 Add vanilla. Continue beating until Frosting is cool and thick enough to spread
7 Quickly use to fill cake (it is important to work quickly: Frosting hardens rapidly when once it has cooled). Swirl remainder over top and sides. **Sufficient to fill and cover top and sides of three 18cm / 7in sandwich cakes or one deep 18 to 20cm / 7 to 8in cake, cut into two layers**

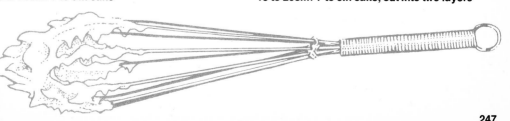

Yeast Recipes

Wholemeal Bread (page 250) Brown Rolls (page 250) Poppy Seed Plaits (page 251) Hot Cross Buns (page 251) Malt Loaf (page 252)

Flour   For best results (especially for bread-making) use a strong plain flour which, with kneading, develops quickly into a firm elastic dough to produce goods with a large volume and a light open texture. A good quality household plain flour will also give good results.

Yeast   Fresh or dried yeast can be used. Fresh yeast should be creamy in colour, firm to touch and easy to break. It can be stored in a cold place for 4 to 5 days. Dried yeast can be used instead of fresh yeast and will keep up to 6 months if stored in an airtight container. Allow 7g/¼oz (or 2 level teaspoons) dried yeast for every 15g/½oz fresh yeast recommended in a recipe. To reconstitute dried yeast, dissolve a teaspoon of sugar in a little of the measured liquid, which should be warm. Sprinkle the yeast on top. Leave in a warm place until frothy (about 10 minutes) and add to the dry ingredients with the rest of the warm liquid.

Kneading and Rising   All doughs must be kneaded thoroughly after mixing to ensure a good rise and even texture. To allow time for the yeast to work, the dough must be risen at least once before baking. The dough must be covered or placed in a lightly greased polythene bag during rising to prevent a skin forming on the surface. The rising time varies with temperature and type of dough – it will take about 1 hour in a warm place or 1½ to 2 hours at room temperature (18 to 21°C/65 to 70°F). To save time the dough may be made up the night before and left to rise

for 8 to 12 hours (overnight) in a cold room, larder or refrigerator. The dough should then be allowed to reach room temperature before shaping. Richer doughs take longer to rise than plain ones and give best results when given a slow rise. Once risen all mixtures must be kneaded quickly to make the dough firm and ready for shaping.

Testing for Baking   When cooked, loaves etc shrink slightly from the sides of the tin, sound hollow when tapped underneath with the knuckles and have golden brown crusts.

🅕 Yeast will freeze successfully in 25g/1oz pieces.
Storage time – 4 to 6 weeks. For immediate use, grate the yeast coarsely or thaw at room temperature for about 30 minutes.

Unrisen dough can be frozen successfully but for best results the quantity of yeast should be increased, eg, use 20g/¾oz instead of 15g/½oz yeast.
Storage time 1 month – in buttered polythene bag. To defrost and rise before use, the dough may be left overnight in the refrigerator or at room temperature for 3 to 4 hours, then shaped as desired.

Baked yeast recipes freeze successfully.
Storage time – white or brown bread – 6 months. The crust of crisp crusted loaves and rolls tends to "shell off" after 1 week. Enriched bread and rolls – 4 months.

White Bread

450g / 1lb plain flour
2 level teaspoons salt
15g / ½oz butter
15g / ½oz fresh yeast
300ml / ½ pint warm water

For Brushing
Milk or beaten egg

1 Sift flour and salt into bowl
2 Rub in butter
3 Mix yeast to smooth and creamy liquid with a little of the warm water. Blend in rest of water
4 Add all at once to dry ingredients. Mix to firm dough, adding more flour if needed, until dough leaves sides of bowl clean
5 Turn out on to lightly floured board. Knead thoroughly 10 minutes
6 Cover and leave to rise until dough doubles in size
7 Turn out on to lightly floured board and knead until firm
8 Shape to fit 20cm × 10cm × 6cm / 1lb loaf tin. Brush tin with melted butter then put in dough
9 Cover and leave to rise until dough doubles in size and reaches top of tin
10 Brush with milk or beaten egg and milk. Bake in centre of hot oven (230°C / 450°F or Gas No 8) 30 to 40 minutes (or until loaf shrinks slightly from sides of tin and crust is golden brown)
11 Cool on wire rack. **Makes 1 Loaf**

Quick White Bread

The quick method of bread making shortens the time of making to approximately 1¾ hours. By adding a small amount of ascorbic acid (vitamin C) to the warm yeast liquid, it is possible to eliminate the first rising of the dough. Ascorbic acid (vitamin C) tablets are available from most large chemists in 25mg, 50mg and 100mg sizes.

It is recommended that fresh yeast be used with this method as dried yeast tends to prolong the time required for rising.

25g / 1oz fresh yeast
350ml / 14fl oz warm water
25mg tablet of ascorbic acid (vitamin C)
600g / 1lb 8oz plain flour
15g / ½oz salt
1 level teaspoon sugar
15g / ½oz butter
Milk or beaten egg for brushing

1 Blend yeast and warm water and crush tablet into yeast liquid
2 Put flour, salt and sugar into bowl. Rub in butter. Add yeast liquid and mix thoroughly until dough leaves side of bowl clean
3 Turn on to a lightly floured board and knead for about 10 minutes
4 Shape to fit 20cm × 13cm × 9cm / 2lb loaf tin. Brush tin with melted butter then place dough in tin. Cover with lightly buttered polythene and leave in a warm place until almost doubled in size
5 Remove polythene, brush with milk or egg. Bake in centre of hot oven (230°C / 450°F or Gas No 8) for 30 to 35 minutes. **Makes 1 Loaf**

Quick Brown Bread

225g / 8oz brown flour
225g / 8oz plain white flour
2 level teaspoons salt
2 level teaspoons granulated sugar
15g / ½oz butter
15g / ½oz fresh yeast
150ml / ¼ pint lukewarm water
150ml / ¼ pint lukewarm milk
Salted water
1 or 2 tablespoons cracked wheat or crushed cornflakes

1 Sift flours, salt and sugar into bowl
2 Rub in butter finely
3 Mix yeast to smooth and creamy liquid with a little of the warm water. Blend in rest of water and milk
4 Add all at once to dry ingredients. Mix to fairly soft dough that leaves sides of bowl clean
5 Turn out on to floured board. Knead 10 minutes (or until smooth and elastic)
6 Cut into 2 and shape each to fit a 20cm × 10cm × 6cm / 1lb loaf tin
7 Brush tins with melted butter. Put in dough
8 Brush tops of loaves with salted water. Sprinkle with cracked wheat (if available) or crushed cornflakes
9 Cover and leave to rise until loaves have doubled in size and spring back when pressed lightly with floured finger
10 Put into centre of hot oven (230°C / 450°F or Gas No 8). Bake 30 to 40 minutes
11 Turn out and cool on wire rack.
Makes 2 Loaves

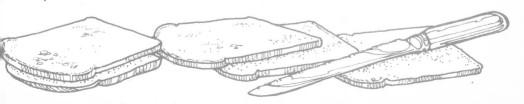

Wholemeal Bread

1¼kg / 3lb wholemeal flour
2 level teaspoons salt
2 level teaspoons caster sugar
25g / 1oz butter
50g / 2oz fresh yeast
600ml / 1 pint lukewarm water
300ml / ½ pint lukewarm milk
Salted water

1 Sift flour, salt and sugar into bowl and rub in butter
2 Mix yeast to smooth and creamy liquid with a little of the warm water
3 Mix dry ingredients with yeast liquid, milk, and sufficient of remaining water to make firm dough that leaves sides of bowl clean
4 Turn out on to lightly floured board. Knead thoroughly 10 minutes (or until dough is smooth and elastic and no longer sticky)
5 Cover and leave until double in size
6 Turn out on to floured board. Knead well and cut in half
7 Shape each piece to fit 20cm × 13cm × 9cm / 2lb loaf tin. Brush tins with melted butter then put in dough
8 Brush top of loaves with salted water. Cover and leave to rise until dough reaches tops of tins
9 Bake in centre of hot oven (230°C / 450°F or Gas No 8) 40 to 45 minutes (or until loaves shrink slightly from sides of tins)
10 Turn out and cool on wire rack.
Makes 2 Loaves

White Bread Rolls

1 Follow recipe and method for White Bread (page 249)
2 After first rising, divide dough into 12 equal-sized pieces and shape into round rolls, miniature plaits and tiny cottage loaves
3 Put on to buttered baking tray, cover and leave to rise until double in size
4 Brush with milk or beaten egg and milk. Bake towards top of hot oven (230°C / 450°F or Gas No 8) 20 to 25 minutes (or until brown and crisp)
5 Cool on wire rack. **Makes 12 Rolls**

Quick Bread Rolls

1 Follow recipe and method for Quick White Bread (page 249) to stage 4
2 Divide dough into 18-20 equal-sized pieces and shape into round rolls
3 Place on buttered baking tray, cover and leave to rise until almost double in size
4 Remove cover, brush rolls with milk or beaten egg and milk. Bake in centre of hot oven (230°C / 450°F or Gas No 8) for 15-20 minutes.
Makes 18-20 Rolls

Crusty Brown Rolls

1 Follow recipe and method for Quick Brown Bread (page 249) but divide dough into 12 equal-sized pieces after kneading
2 Roll into balls. Place 2cm / 1in apart on lightly buttered and floured baking tray
3 Brush tops with salted water. Sprinkle with cracked wheat (if available) or crushed cornflakes
4 Cover and leave to rise until rolls have doubled in size. Bake towards top of hot oven (230°C / 450°F or Gas No 8) 20 to 30 minutes
5 Cool on wire rack. **Makes 12 Rolls**

Scottish Bap or Flat Loaf

450g / 1lb plain flour
1 level teaspoon salt
50g / 2oz butter
15g / ½oz fresh yeast
150ml / ¼ pint lukewarm water
150ml / ¼ pint lukewarm milk

1 Sift flour and salt into bowl. Rub in butter
2 Mix yeast to smooth and creamy liquid with a little of the warm water. Blend in rest of water and milk
3 Add all at once to dry ingredients. Mix to firm dough, adding a little extra flour if necessary, until dough leaves sides of bowl clean
4 Turn out on to lightly floured board. Knead 10 minutes (or until smooth and elastic)
5 Cover and leave to rise until dough doubles in size
6 Turn out on to floured board. Knead lightly and shape into ball
7 Roll out to 2cm / ¾in thick round, transfer to lightly buttered and floured baking tray and dredge with plain flour
8 Cover and leave to rise until double in size
9 Lightly dent top of Bap in 3 places with fingers (to prevent blistering)
10 Bake just above centre of moderately hot oven (200°C / 400°F or Gas No 6) for 20 to 25 minutes
11 Cool on wire rack.
Makes 1 Bap

Small Baps or Flat Loaves

1 Follow recipe and method for Scottish Bap (above)
2 After first rising, divide dough into 10 equal-sized pieces. Roll each into 1cm / ½in thick ovals
3 Transfer to lightly buttered and floured baking tray. Dredge with flour
4 Cover and leave to rise until double in size
5 Make 3 shallow dents in top of each. Bake just above centre of moderately hot oven (200°C / 400°F or Gas No 6) 15 to 20 minutes
6 Cool on wire rack.
Makes 10 Small Baps

Milk Loaf

450g / 1lb plain flour
1 level teaspoon sugar
15g / ½oz fresh yeast or 2 level teaspoons dried
    yeast
200ml / 7fl oz lukewarm milk
1 level teaspoon salt
50g / 2oz butter
1 standard egg, beaten
Extra milk for brushing

1 Put one third of flour into large bowl. Add sugar,
yeast (fresh or dried) and milk. Mix well. Leave in
warm place for 20 minutes (or until frothy)
2 Meanwhile, sift rest of flour and salt into bowl.
Rub in butter then add, with beaten egg, to yeast
mixture. Mix well
3 Turn out on to lightly floured board. Knead for
10 minutes (or until dough loses its stickiness)
4 Cover and leave to rise until double in size
5 Turn out on to floured board. Knead lightly
6 Shape to fit 20cm × 10cm × 6cm / 1lb loaf tin.
Brush tin with melted butter. Put in dough
7 Cover and leave to rise until dough doubles in
size and reaches top of tin
8 Brush with milk. Bake in centre of moderately
hot oven (190°C / 375°F or Gas No 5) for 45 to 50
minutes (or until loaf shrinks slightly from sides of
tin and crust is golden brown)
9 Cool on wire rack. **Makes 1 Milk Loaf**

Poppy Seed Plaits

1 Follow recipe and method for Milk Loaf (above)
2 After dough has risen for first time, turn out on
to floured board, knead lightly and cut in half
3 Cut each half into 3 pieces
4 Shape each piece into long thin roll and plait
together (two plaited loaves)
5 Stand on buttered and floured baking tray.
Brush with a little beaten egg. Sprinkle with 5 to 6
level teaspoons poppy seeds
6 Cover and leave to rise until double in size
7 Put into centre of moderately hot oven
(190°C / 375°F or Gas No 5). Bake for 45 to 50
minutes (or until bases of loaves sound hollow
when tapped and tops and sides are lightly
brown)
8 Cool on wire rack. **Makes 2 Loaves**

Hot Cross Buns

450g / 1lb plain flour
50g / 2oz caster sugar
25g / 1oz fresh yeast or 1 level tablespoon dried
    yeast
150ml / ¼ pint lukewarm milk
4 tablespoons lukewarm water
1 level teaspoon salt
1 level teaspoon mixed spice
½ level teaspoon cinnamon
100g / 4oz currants
50g / 2oz chopped mixed peel
50g / 2oz butter, melted and cooled
1 standard egg, beaten

Glaze
50g / 2oz granulated sugar
3 tablespoons milk

1 Sift 100g / 4oz flour into bowl. Add 1 teaspoon
sugar
2 Blend yeast with milk and water. Add to sifted
flour and sugar
3 Mix well and leave 20 to 30 minutes (or until
frothy)
4 Meanwhile sift remaining flour, salt and spices
into another bowl. Add rest of sugar, currants and
peel. Toss lightly together
5 Add to yeast mixture with butter and beaten
egg. Mix to fairly soft dough that leaves sides of
bowl clean
6 Turn out on to floured board and knead
5 minutes (or until dough is smooth and no
longer sticky)
7 Cover and leave to rise until double in size
8 Turn out on to floured board. Knead lightly and
divide into 12 equal-sized pieces
9 Shape each into round bun. Stand well apart on
lightly buttered and floured baking tray
10 Cover and leave to rise 30 minutes (or until
dough feels springy when pressed lightly with
floured finger)
11 Cut a cross on top of each with a sharp knife.
Bake just above centre of hot oven (220°C / 425°F
or Gas No 7) 20 to 25 minutes
12 Transfer to wire rack. Brush twice with glaze,
made by dissolving sugar in milk and boiling for
2 minutes. **Makes 12 Hot Cross Buns**

Malt Loaves

75g / 3oz malt extract
2 level tablespoons black treacle
25g / 1oz butter
400g / 1lb plain flour
1 level teaspoon salt
200g / 8oz sultanas
25g / 1oz fresh yeast
170ml / 6fl oz lukewarm water
Clear honey

1 Put malt extract, treacle and butter into pan. Heat through gently. Leave to cool
2 Sift flour and salt into bowl. Add sultanas and toss lightly together
3 Mix yeast to smooth and creamy liquid with a little of the water. Blend in rest of water
4 Add to dry ingredients with cooled malt mixture. Work to soft dough that leaves sides of bowl clean
5 Turn out on to lightly floured board. Knead until dough is smooth and elastic
6 Cut into 2 equal-sized pieces. Shape each to fit 20cm × 10cm × 6cm / 1lb loaf tin
7 Brush tins with melted butter and put in dough. Cover and leave to rise until loaves double in size
8 Put in to centre of moderately hot oven (200°C / 400°F or Gas No 6). Bake 40 to 45 minutes
9 Turn out on to wire rack. Glaze tops of hot loaves with wet brush dipped in honey
10 Leave until cold before cutting.
Makes 2 Malt Loaves

Currant Bread

450g / 1lb plain flour
1 level teaspoon salt
25g / 1oz butter
25g / 1oz caster sugar
100g / 4oz currants
25g / 1oz fresh yeast
150ml / ¼ pint lukewarm water
150ml / ¼ pint lukewarm milk
Clear honey or golden syrup

1 Sift flour and salt into bowl and rub in butter. Add sugar and currants and toss lightly together
2 Mix yeast to smooth and creamy liquid with a little of the warm water. Blend in rest of water and milk
3 Add all at once to dry ingredients. Mix to firm dough, adding little extra flour if necessary, until dough leaves sides of bowl clean
4 Turn out on to lightly floured board. Knead 10 minutes (or until dough is smooth and elastic)
5 Cut into 2 equal-sized pieces. Shape each to fit a 20cm × 10cm × 6cm / 1lb loaf tin
6 Brush tins with melted butter and put in dough
7 Cover and leave to rise until dough reaches tops of tins
8 Put into centre of hot oven (220°C / 425°F or Gas No 7). Bake 40 to 45 minutes
9 Turn out on to wire rack. Glaze tops of hot loaves by brushing with wet brush dipped in clear honey or golden syrup
10 Leave until cold before cutting.
Makes 2 Loaves

Yorkshire Tea Cakes

450g / 1lb plain flour
1 level teaspoon salt
25g / 1oz butter
25g / 1oz caster sugar
50g / 2oz currants
15g / ½oz fresh yeast
300ml / ½ pint lukewarm milk

For Brushing
Extra milk

1 Sift flour and salt into bowl and rub in butter
2 Add sugar and currants. Toss lightly together
3 Blend yeast with milk. Add all at once to dry ingredients
4 Mix to firm dough, adding little extra flour if necessary, until dough leaves sides of bowl clean
5 Turn out on to lightly floured board. Knead 10 minutes (or until dough is smooth and elastic)
6 Cover and leave to rise until double in size
7 Turn out on to lightly floured board. Knead well and divide into 6 equal-sized pieces
8 Roll each out into 15cm / 6in round. Transfer to buttered baking tray
9 Brush tops with milk. Cover and leave to rise until almost double in size
10 Bake just above centre of moderately hot oven (200°C / 400°F or Gas No 6) 20 minutes
11 Cool on wire rack
12 To serve, split open and spread thickly with butter. The Tea Cakes can also be split and toasted before being buttered.
Makes 6 Tea Cakes

Babas (below)

Babas

25g / 1oz fresh yeast or 1 level tablespoon dried yeast
5 tablespoons lukewarm milk
225g / 8oz plain flour
½ level teaspoon salt
25g / 1oz caster sugar
4 standard eggs, beaten
100g / 4oz softened butter
100g / 4oz currants

Syrup
4 level tablespoons golden syrup
4 tablespoons water
2 tablespoons rum

Glaze
3 level tablespoons apricot jam
2 tablespoons water

Decoration
300ml / ½ pint fresh double cream

1 Mix yeast with milk and 50g / 2oz flour.
Leave 20 to 30 minutes or until frothy
2 Combine with rest of flour, salt, sugar, beaten
eggs, butter and currants. Beat thoroughly for
5 minutes
3 Brush 16 Dariole moulds with melted butter and
half fill with mixture
4 Cover and leave to rise until moulds are
two-thirds full
5 Bake towards top of moderately hot oven
(200°C / 400°F or Gas No 6) 15 to 20 minutes
6 Cool 5 minutes. Turn out of moulds then
transfer to wire rack with large plate underneath
7 Warm golden syrup, water and rum together.
Pour sufficient over Babas to soak them well
8 Heat jam slowly with water. Strain. Brush thickly
over Babas then leave until cold
9 Transfer to serving dish. Top each with a mound
of cream, whipped until thick. **Serves 8**

Plain Savarin

1 Follow recipe and method for Babas (left) but
omit currants
2 Instead of using Dariole moulds, half-fill one
well-buttered 20cm / 8in ring mould or two
15cm / 6in moulds with mixture
3 After mixture has risen, bake towards top of
moderately hot oven (200°C / 400°F or Gas No 6)
20 minutes
4 Turn out on to dish and prick with skewer
5 Soak with hot syrup made by dissolving
6 tablespoons granulated sugar in 150ml / ¼ pint
water and 2 or 3 tablespoons rum or white wine
6 Serve hot. **Serves 8**

Cherry Savarin

1 Follow recipe and method for Plain Savarin
(above)
2 Fill centre of soaked Savarin with cherries and
pile cream on top. **Serves 8**

Cream Savarin

1 Follow recipe and method for Plain Savarin
(above)
2 Sprinkle soaked Savarin with caster sugar and
fill centre with cream. **Serves 8**

Fruit Savarin

1 Follow recipe and method for Plain Savarin
(above)
2 Decorate with canned fruit, using the syrup to
soak the Savarin. **Serves 8**

Bath Buns

450g / 1lb plain flour
25g / 1oz caster sugar
25g / 1oz fresh yeast or 1 level tablespoon dried yeast
150ml / ¼ pint lukewarm milk
4 tablespoons lukewarm water
1 level teaspoon salt
175g / 6oz sultanas
50g / 2oz chopped mixed peel
50g / 2oz butter, melted and cooled
1 standard egg, beaten

For Brushing
Beaten egg mixed with a little water
Coarsely crushed cube sugar

1 Sift 100g / 4oz flour into bowl. Add 1 teaspoon sugar
2 Blend yeast with milk and water. Add to sifted flour and sugar
3 Mix well and leave 20 to 30 minutes (or until frothy)
4 Meanwhile, sift remaining flour and salt into another bowl. Add rest of sugar, sultanas and peel. Toss lightly together
5 Add to yeast mixture with butter and beaten egg. Mix to fairly soft dough that leaves sides of bowl clean
6 Turn out on to floured board and knead 5 minutes (or until dough is smooth and no longer sticky)
7 Cover and leave to rise until double in size
8 Turn out on to floured board. Knead lightly
9 Put 14 tablespoons of dough on to lightly buttered and floured baking tray
10 Cover and leave to rise 20 minutes (or until dough feels springy when pressed lightly with floured finger)
11 Brush with egg and water, sprinkle with crushed sugar and bake just above centre of hot oven (220°C / 425°F or Gas No 7) 20 to 25 minutes
12 Cool on wire rack.
Makes 14 Bath Buns

Cornish Splits

450g / 1lb plain flour
50g / 2oz caster sugar
25g / 1oz fresh yeast or 1 level tablespoon dried yeast
150ml / ¼ pint lukewarm milk
150ml / ¼ pint lukewarm water
1 level teaspoon salt
50g / 2oz butter, melted and cooled

1 Sift 100g / 4oz flour into bowl. Add 1 teaspoon sugar
2 Blend yeast with milk and water. Add to sifted flour and sugar
3 Mix well and leave 20 to 30 minutes (or until frothy)
4 Meanwhile, sift remaining flour and salt into another bowl. Add rest of sugar
5 Add to yeast mixture with butter. Mix to fairly soft dough that leaves sides of bowl clean
6 Turn out on to floured board. Knead 5 minutes (or until dough is smooth and no longer sticky)
7 Cover and leave to rise until double in size
8 Turn out on to floured board. Knead lightly and divide into 14 equal-sized pieces
9 Shape each into round bun. Stand well apart on lightly buttered and floured baking tray
10 Cover and leave to rise 30 minutes (or until dough feels springy when pressed lightly with floured finger)
11 Bake just above centre of hot oven (220°C / 425°F or Gas No 7) 20 to 25 minutes
12 Cool on wire rack
13 When cold split open and fill with jam and either fresh whipped or clotted cream.
Makes 14 Splits

Brioches

225g / 8oz plain flour
½ level teaspoon salt
15g / ½oz caster sugar
15g / ½oz fresh yeast
6 teaspoons lukewarm water
2 standard eggs, beaten
50g / 2oz butter, melted and cooled

For Brushing
Little extra beaten egg

1 Sift flour, salt and sugar into bowl
2 Mix yeast to smooth and creamy liquid with water
3 Add to dry ingredients with beaten eggs and butter
4 Mix to soft dough. Turn on to floured board and knead 5 minutes (or until dough is smooth and no longer sticky)
5 Cover and leave to rise until double in size
6 Turn out on to floured board. Knead lightly
7 Divide three-quarters of the dough into 12 equal-sized pieces
8 Shape into balls. Put into well buttered deep bun tins or into 8cm / 3in fluted Brioche tins. Press a deep hole in centre of each
9 Divide remaining dough into 12 pieces. Roll into small balls and stand on top of holes
10 Cover and leave to rise in warm place for about 1 hour (or until Brioches are light and well risen)
11 Brush gently with beaten egg. Bake in centre of hot oven (230°C / 450°F or Gas No 8) 10 minutes
12 Transfer to wire rack. Serve warm with butter.
Makes 12 Brioches

Doughnuts

225g/8oz plain flour
1 level teaspoon caster sugar
15g/½oz fresh yeast or 2 level teaspoons dried
  yeast
5 tablespoons lukewarm milk
1 level teaspoon salt
15g/½oz butter, melted and cooled
1 standard egg, beaten
4 level teaspoons red jam
Deep fat or oil for frying
4 level tablespoons caster sugar mixed with
  1 level teaspoon cinnamon

1 Sift 50g/2oz flour into bowl then add sugar and
yeast blended with milk
2 Mix well and leave 20 to 30 minutes or until
frothy
3 Meanwhile, sift remaining flour and salt
together and add to yeast mixture with butter and
beaten egg
4 Mix to fairly soft dough that leaves sides of bowl
clean
5 Turn out on to floured board and knead for
5 minutes (or until dough is smooth and no
longer sticky)
6 Cover and leave to rise until double in size
7 Turn out on to floured board, knead lightly and
divide into 8 equal-sized pieces
8 Shape into balls. Cover and leave to rise
30 minutes (or until dough feels springy when
pressed lightly with floured finger)
9 Press a hole in each ball with finger. Put in
about ½ teaspoon of jam
10 Pinch up edges of dough so that jam is
completely enclosed. Deep fry Doughnuts in hot
fat or oil for 4 minutes
11 Drain thoroughly on soft kitchen paper. Roll in
sugar and cinnamon. **Makes 8 Doughnuts**

For luxury touch, split doughnuts halfway down
and fill with fresh double cream, whipped

Muffins

450g/1lb plain flour
1 level teaspoon salt
25g/1oz fresh yeast
150ml/¼ pint lukewarm milk
6 tablespoons lukewarm water
1 standard egg, beaten
25g/1oz butter, melted

1 Sift flour and salt into bowl
2 Mix yeast to smooth and creamy liquid with a
little milk. Blend in rest of milk and water
3 Add to dry ingredients with beaten egg and
melted butter. Mix to fairly soft dough
4 Turn out on to well-floured board. Knead for
10 minutes (or until dough is smooth and no
longer sticky)
5 Cover and leave to rise until double in size
6 Turn out on to floured board. Knead lightly and
roll out to 1cm/½in thickness
7 Cut into 12 rounds with 9cm/3½in biscuit cutter.
Transfer to well-floured baking tray. Dust with
flour
8 Cover and leave to rise until double in size
9 Bake towards top of hot oven (230°C/450°F or
Gas No 8) 5 minutes
10 Remove from oven. Turn over and bake further
5 minutes. Cool on a wire rack
11 To serve, toast on both sides, pull apart with
fingers, butter thickly and put together again.
Serve hot.
Makes 12 Muffins

Sally Lunns

50g/2oz butter
150ml/7fl oz milk
1 level teaspoon caster sugar
2 eggs
15g/½oz fresh yeast
400g/1lb strong plain flour
1 level teaspoon salt

Glaze
1 tablespoon water
1 tablespoon sugar

1 Melt the butter slowly in a pan, remove from
heat and add milk and sugar
2 Beat the eggs and add to the yeast, with the
warmed milk mixture. Blend well
3 Add to the flour and salt, mix well and lightly
knead
4 Place mixture in two well-greased 10cm/5in
cake tins and leave to rise in a warm place until
the dough fills the tins—about ¾-1 hour
5 Bake in a hot oven (230°C/450°F or Gas No 8)
for 15-20 minutes. Turn onto a wire tray
6 Heat water and sugar in a pan to boiling. Boil
for 2 minutes. Glaze Sally Lunns while still hot.
Makes 2

Grapefruit and Orange Marmalade (page 259) Lemon Curd (page 257) Thick Orange Marmalade (page 259) Strawberry Jam (page 257)

Fruit for jam making should be firm, under-ripe or only just ripe and fresh. Over-ripe fruit lacking in acid or pectin, or both, never makes satisfactory jam since it will not set properly. The fruit should be cleaned, prepared as for other cooking purposes, and as dry as possible.

Choose a good quality jam pan or a strong, roomy saucepan with a heavy base to prevent the jam from sticking and burning. To allow room for the jam to boil vigorously, the pan should be about half full when the sugar has been added – it is a mistake to try to make too much jam at once.

Scum should never be removed until the jam is made as continuous skimming is wasteful and unnecessary. A small piece of butter rubbed over the bottom of the pan helps to avoid scum and prevent sticking. When boiling has finished, remove scum with a metal spoon.

Add the sugar only when the fruit is well cooked and broken down, then boil the jam rapidly until setting point is reached.

To test for setting, pour a scant teaspoonful of the jam on to a cold saucer and leave for 1 minute. Setting point has been reached if the surface sets and crinkles when pushed with the finger. Remove the jam from the heat while this test is being made, otherwise it may boil too rapidly and the setting point may be missed. A sugar thermometer will register about 105°C / 220°F once setting point has been reached.

After removing the scum, allow the jam to cool off slightly before pouring into perfectly clean, dry, warm jars. To prevent strawberries or other whole fruits from rising in the jars, cool the jam in the pan until a thin skin begins to form, then stir gently before potting.

ars should be filled to the brim with hot jam to allow for the considerable shrinkage that takes place during cooling. After filling, press a well-itting waxed tissue on the surface of the jam in each jar and wipe the rim carefully with a hot, damp cloth. Cover the jam while it is still very hot or completely cold.

Label the jam and date; store in a dry, dark, cool, ventilated cupboard.

Note When following the recipes given, slight alterations in the quantities of ingredients will sometimes be advisable. More water may be necessary if large quantities of jam are made or if slow cooking is used. If the fruit is of very good quality, the quantity of fruit may be reduced slightly whereas if the fruit is wet or over-ripe more may be needed.

Fruit in good condition may be frozen when in season for making preserves. Storage time–most 9 to 12 months. Defrost frozen fruit in preserve pan, over heat. Add $\frac{1}{8}$ extra fruit to recipe quantity to make up for the loss of pectin during freezing.

Lemon Curd

100g / 4oz butter
200g / 8oz granulated sugar
3 standard eggs and 1 standard yolk, beaten together
3 medium-sized lemons

1 Melt butter in double saucepan (or basin standing over saucepan of gently simmering water)
2 Add sugar, eggs and extra yolk, and finely grated rind and juice of lemons
3 Cook gently without boiling until Curd thickens sufficiently to coat back of spoon. (This is important because if overheated the mixture may curdle and separate)
4 Pour into clean, dry and warm jars and cover as for Jam.
About 500g / 1lb 4oz

Store in a very cool place and do not keep longer than 2 weeks

Orange Curd

1 Follow recipe and method for Lemon Curd (above)
2 Instead of all lemons, use 2 medium-sized oranges and 1 medium-sized lemon.
About 500g / 1lb 4oz Curd

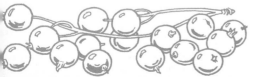

Blackcurrant Jam

1kg / 2lb stemmed and washed blackcurrants
900ml / 1½ pints water
1½kg / 3lb granulated sugar
15g / ½oz butter

1 Put blackcurrants into saucepan and add water
2 Bring to boil, cover pan and reduce heat
3 Simmer gently until fruit is tender (about 45 minutes)
4 Add sugar and stir until dissolved. Bring to boil. Boil briskly for 5 to 10 minutes (or until setting point is reached)
5 Draw pan away from heat. Stir in butter to disperse scum
6 Pot and cover.
About 2½kg / 5lb Jam

Gooseberry Jam

1 Follow recipe and method for Blackcurrant Jam (above)
2 Use gooseberries instead of blackcurrants and halve quantity of water. Boil for 10 to 15 minutes (or until setting point is reached).
About 2½kg / 5lb Jam

Damson Jam

1 Follow recipe and method for Blackcurrant Jam (above)
2 Use damsons instead of blackcurrants and halve quantity of water
3 Boil for 10 to 15 minutes after adding sugar (or until setting point is reached)
4 Remove stones with perforated spoon as they rise to surface.
About 2½kg / 5lb Jam

Strawberry Jam

1¾kg / 3lb 8oz strawberries
Juice of 1 large lemon
1½kg / 3lb granulated sugar
15g / ½oz butter

1 Put strawberries, lemon juice and sugar into pan
2 Heat slowly, stirring all the time, until sugar dissolves
3 Bring to boil. Boil briskly for 10 to 15 minutes (or until setting point is reached)
4 Draw pan away from heat. Stir in butter to disperse scum
5 Leave Jam to cool off in pan until skin forms on surface
6 Stir gently, pot and cover.
About 2½kg / 5lb Jam

Raspberry Jam

1½kg/3lb raspberries
1½kg/3lb granulated sugar
15g/½oz butter

1 Put fruit into saucepan and crush finely with back of wooden spoon
2 Simmer gently for 5 minutes
3 Add sugar and stir until dissolved
4 Bring to boil. Boil briskly for 5 to 7 minutes (or until setting point is reached)
5 Draw pan away from heat. Stir in butter to disperse scum
6 Pot and cover.
About 2½kg/5lb Jam

Loganberry Jam

1 Follow recipe and method for Raspberry Jam (above)
2 Use loganberries instead of raspberries.
About 2½kg/5lb Jam

Raspberry & Loganberry Jam

1 Follow recipe and method for Raspberry Jam (above)
2 Use half loganberries and half raspberries instead of all raspberries.
About 2½kg/5lb Jam

Marrow & Ginger Jam

1½kg/3lb marrow (after peeling and removing seeds)
Finely grated rind and juice of 2 large lemons
40g/1½oz root ginger
1½kg/3lb granulated sugar
15g/½oz butter

1 Cut marrow into small cubes and steam gently for 20 minutes
2 Turn into bowl and add lemon rind and juice, ginger (tied in muslin bag) and sugar
3 Cover bowl and leave to stand 24 hours
4 Transfer to large saucepan and heat slowly, stirring all the time, until sugar dissolves
5 Bring to boil. Boil steadily for 30 to 45 minutes (or until marrow is almost transparent and syrup is thick)
6 Draw pan away from heat. Stir in butter to disperse scum
7 Remove ginger. Pot and cover Jam.
About 2½kg/5lb Jam

This Jam never sets firmly and will always be syrupy

Plum Jam

1½kg/3lb washed plums
450ml/¾ pint water
1½kg/3lb granulated sugar
15g/½oz butter

1 Put plums into saucepan and add water
2 Bring to boil, cover pan and reduce heat
3 Simmer gently until fruit is tender (10 to 20 minutes)
4 Add sugar and stir until dissolved
5 Bring jam to boil. Boil briskly for 10 to 15 minutes (or until setting point is reached). Remove stones with perforated spoon as they rise to surface
6 Draw pan away from heat. Stir in butter to disperse scum
7 Pot and cover.
About 2½kg/5lb Jam

Greengage Jam

1 Follow recipe and method for Plum Jam (above)
2 Use greengages instead of plums.
About 2½kg/5lb Jam

Apple & Blackberry Jam

375g/12oz apples (after peeling and coring)
1kg/2lb blackberries
150ml/¼ pint water
1½kg/3lb granulated sugar
15g/½oz butter

1 Slice apples thinly and put into saucepan with blackberries
2 Pour in water
3 Bring to boil, reduce heat and cover pan
4 Simmer gently for 10 to 15 minutes, crushing fruit against sides of pan until it is soft and pulpy
5 Add sugar and heat slowly, stirring all the time, until sugar dissolves
6 Bring to boil. Boil briskly for 10 to 15 minutes (or until setting point is reached)
7 Draw pan away from heat. Stir in butter to disperse scum
8 Pot and cover.
About 2½kg/5lb Jam

Raspberry & Redcurrant Jam

1 Follow recipe and method for Apple and Blackberry Jam (above)
2 Use 750g/1lb 8oz **each** raspberries and stemmed redcurrants instead of apples and blackberries
About 2½kg/5lb Jam

Mixed Fruit Jam

1 Follow recipe and method for Apple and Blackberry Jam (page 258)
2 Use 1½kg/3lb mixed soft fruit (such as raspberries, strawberries, gooseberries, rhubarb, redcurrants, and loganberries) instead of apples and blackberries.
About 2½kg/5lb Jam

Raspberry & Rhubarb Jam

1 Follow recipe and method for Apple and Blackberry Jam (page 258)
2 Use 750g/1lb 8oz **each** raspberries and trimmed rhubarb (cut into 5cm/2in lengths instead of apples and blackberries.
About 2½kg/5lb Jam

Gooseberry & Redcurrant Jam

1 Follow recipe and method for Apple and Blackberry Jam (page 258)
2 Use 750g/1lb 8oz **each** gooseberries and stemmed redcurrants instead of apples and blackberries.
About 2½kg/5lb Jam

Dried Apricot Jam

500g/1lb dried apricots
1¾ litres/3 pints water
1½kg/3lb granulated sugar
75g/3oz blanched and split almonds
Juice of 1 large lemon
15g/½oz butter

1 Snip apricots into smallish pieces with kitchen scissors. Cover with cold water and leave to soak overnight
2 Drain, put into pan and add 1¾ litres/3 pints water
3 Bring to boil, lower heat and cover pan. Simmer gently about 45 minutes (or until fruit is tender)
4 Add sugar, almonds and lemon juice. Heat slowly, stirring all the time, until sugar dissolves
5 Bring to boil. Boil briskly until setting point is reached
6 Draw pan away from heat. Stir in butter to disperse scum
7 Pot and cover. **About 2½kg/5lb Jam**

Thick Orange Marmalade

750g/1lb 8oz Seville (or bitter) oranges
1¾ litres/3 pints water
Juice of 1 lemon
1½kg/3lb granulated sugar
15g/½oz butter

1 Scrub oranges well
2 Put, without slicing, into large saucepan
3 Pour in water and bring to boil
4 Reduce heat and cover pan. Simmer very gently for 1½ to 2 hours (or until skins of fruit are soft and can be pierced easily with fork or skewer)
5 Lift oranges out of pan. Cool slightly and chop coarsely
6 Collect pips and tie in muslin bag
7 Return chopped oranges to pan with lemon juice and bag of pips
8 Add sugar and heat slowly, stirring all the time, until sugar dissolves
9 Bring to boil. Boil steadily until setting point is reached
10 Draw pan away from heat. Stir in butter to disperse scum
11 Leave Marmalade in saucepan until skin forms on surface
12 Stir gently, pot and cover.
About 2½kg/5lb Marmalade

Sweet Orange Marmalade

1 Follow recipe and method for Thick Orange Marmalade (above)
2 Use 750g/1lb 8oz sweet oranges and juice of 3 medium-sized lemons.
About 2½kg/5lb Marmalade

Grapefruit & Orange Marmalade

1 Follow recipe and method for Thick Orange Marmalade (above)
2 Use 500g/1lb grapefruit, 250g/8oz sweet oranges and juice of 3 medium-sized lemons.
About 2½kg/5lb Marmalade

Coconut Ice (page 262) Uncooked Chocolate Cream Fudge (page 261) Chocolate Rum Truffles (page 262) Peppermint Wafers (page 262)

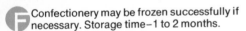 Confectionery may be frozen successfully if necessary. Storage time–1 to 2 months.

Milk Fudge

300ml/$\frac{1}{2}$ pint milk
800g/1lb 12oz granulated sugar
100g/4oz butter
2 teaspoons vanilla essence

1 Pour milk into pan. Bring slowly to boil
2 Add sugar and butter
3 Heat slowly, stirring all the time, until sugar dissolves and butter melts
4 Bring to boil. Cover pan with lid. Boil for 2 minutes
5 Uncover. Continue to boil steadily, stirring occasionally, for further 10 to 15 minutes (or until

a little of the mixture, dropped into cup of cold water, forms soft ball when rolled gently between finger and thumb). Temperature on sugar thermometer, if used, should be 115-116°C/238-240°F
6 Remove from heat. Stir in vanilla. Leave mixture to cool 5 minutes
7 Beat Fudge until it just begins to lose its gloss and is thick and creamy
8 Transfer to buttered 18cm/7in square tin
9 Mark into squares when cool. Cut up with sharp knife when firm and set
10 Store in airtight tin. **About 50 pieces**

Cherry Fudge

1 Follow recipe and method for Milk Fudge (page 260)
2 Add 50g/2oz chopped glacé cherries with vanilla. **About 50 pieces**

Chocolate Fudge

1 Follow recipe and method for Milk Fudge (page 260)
2 Melt 100g/4oz grated plain chocolate in milk before adding sugar and butter. **About 50 pieces**

Coconut Fudge

1 Follow recipe and method for Milk Fudge (page 260)
2 Add 3 level tablespoons desiccated coconut with vanilla. **About 50 pieces**

Fruit & Nut Fudge

1 Follow recipe and method for Milk Fudge (page 260)
2 Add 25g/1oz currants and 25g/1oz blanched and chopped almonds with vanilla.
About 50 pieces

Walnut Fudge

1 Follow recipe and method for Milk Fudge (page 260)
2 Add 50g/2oz finely chopped shelled walnut halves with vanilla. **About 50 pieces**

Uncooked Chocolate Cream Fudge

100g/4oz plain chocolate
50g/2oz butter
3 tablespoons fresh single cream
1 teaspoon vanilla essence
450g/1lb sifted icing sugar

1 Break up chocolate. Put, with butter, in basin standing over saucepan of hot water
2 Leave until both have melted, stirring once or twice
3 Remove basin from pan of water. Stir in cream and vanilla
4 Gradually work in icing sugar. Mix well
5 Transfer to buttered 20cm/8in square tin
6 Leave in the cool until firm and set.
Cut into 60 squares

Uncooked Mocha Cream Fudge

1 Follow recipe and method for Uncooked Chocolate Cream Fudge (left)
2 Add 4 level teaspoons instant coffee powder to chocolate and butter in basin. **About 60 squares**

Marshmallow Raisin Fudge

100g/4oz icing sugar
50g/2oz seedless raisins
100g/4oz marshmallows
2 tablespoons milk
50g/2oz granulated sugar
50g/2oz butter

1 Sift icing sugar into bowl. Add raisins
2 Slowly melt marshmallows in 1 tablespoon milk. Remove from heat. Leave on one side
3 Pour rest of milk into pan. Add sugar and butter
4 Heat slowly, stirring all the time, until sugar dissolves and butter melts
5 Bring to boil. Boil briskly 5 minutes only. Remove from heat
6 Add melted marshmallows and milk. Gradually stir in icing sugar and raisins
7 Mix well. Spread into buttered 15cm/6in square tin
8 Leave until firm and set.
Cut into 36 squares

Marshmallow Almond Fudge

1 Follow recipe and method for Marshmallow Raisin Fudge (above)
2 Add 50g/2oz blanched, toasted and chopped almonds instead of raisins.
About 36 squares

Coffee Wafers

450g/1lb icing sugar
4 level teaspoons instant coffee powder
50g/2oz butter, melted
2 tablespoons lukewarm milk
Extra sifted icing sugar

1 Sift icing sugar into bowl with coffee
2 Combine melted butter with milk. Gradually stir into icing sugar
3 Mix well. Turn out on to board, dusted with sifted icing sugar
4 Knead until smooth. Roll equal amounts of mixture into 40 balls
5 Flatten slightly
6 Transfer to fluted paper sweet cases
7 Leave in the cool until firm.
About 40 Wafers

Peppermint Wafers

1 Follow recipe and method for Coffee Wafers (page 261)
2 Omit coffee powder. Add 1 teaspoon peppermint essence to icing sugar with melted butter and milk
3 Turn out on to board dusted with sifted icing sugar. Roll out to about $\frac{1}{4}$cm/$\frac{1}{8}$in thickness
4 Cut into about 30 rounds with 3cm/1$\frac{1}{2}$in plain biscuit cutter. Leave in the cool until firm.
About 30 Wafers

Chocolate Rum Truffles

100g/4oz plain chocolate
50g/2oz butter
1 tablespoon rum
Yolks of 2 standard eggs
25g/1oz ground almonds
25g/1oz stale cake crumbs
225g/8oz sifted icing sugar
Drinking chocolate

1 Break up chocolate and put, with butter, into basin standing over saucepan of hot water
2 Leave until both have melted, stirring occasionally
3 Add rum and egg yolks. Mix in well
4 Work in remaining ingredients (except drinking chocolate). Transfer mixture to plate. Leave in the cool until firm (about 1$\frac{1}{2}$ hours)
5 Roll equal amounts of mixture into 36 balls. Toss in drinking chocolate
6 Transfer to fluted paper sweet cases.
36 Truffles

Chocolate Sherry Truffles

1 Follow recipe and method for Chocolate Rum Truffles (above)
2 Use sherry instead of rum. **36 Truffles**

Chocolate Whisky Truffles

1 Follow recipe and method for Chocolate Rum Truffles (above)
2 Use whisky instead of rum. **36 Truffles**

Chocolate Orange Truffles

1 Follow recipe and method for Chocolate Rum Truffles (above)
2 Omit rum and add finely grated rind of 1 small orange and 1 tablespoon orange juice with almonds, cake crumbs and icing sugar.
36 Truffles

Chocolate Cream Truffles

50g/2oz plain chocolate
2 tablespoons fresh double cream
1 teaspoon vanilla essence
225g/8oz sifted icing sugar
Chocolate vermicelli

1 Break up chocolate. Put into basin standing over saucepan of hot water
2 Leave until melted, stirring once or twice
3 Add cream and essence. Gradually stir in icing sugar
4 Mix well. Transfer mixture to plate. Leave in cool until firm enough to handle (about 1$\frac{1}{2}$ hours)
5 Roll equal amounts of mixture into 18 balls. Toss in chocolate vermicelli
6 Transfer to fluted paper sweet cases. **18 Truffles**

Coconut Ice

150ml/$\frac{1}{4}$ pint milk
150ml/$\frac{1}{4}$ pint water
900g/2lb granulated sugar
25g/1oz butter
225g/8oz desiccated coconut
1 teaspoon vanilla essence
Red food colouring

1 Pour milk and water into saucepan. Bring to boil
2 Add sugar and butter. Heat slowly, stirring, until sugar dissolves and butter melts
3 Bring to boil. Cover pan. Boil gently for 2 minutes
4 Uncover. Continue to boil, stirring occasionally for 7 to 10 minutes (or until a little of the mixture, dropped into cup of cold water, forms soft ball when rolled gently between finger and thumb). Temperature on sugar thermometer, if used, should be 115°C to 116°C/238°F to 240°F
5 Remove from heat. Add coconut and vanilla
6 Beat briskly until mixture is thick and creamy looking
7 Pour half into buttered 20cm/8in square tin
8 Quickly colour remainder pale pink with food colouring
9 Spread over white layer
10 Leave in the cool until firm and set.
Cut into about 60 pieces

Chocolate Coconut Ice

1 Follow recipe and method for Coconut Ice (above)
2 Instead of colouring second layer pale pink, beat in 1 level teaspoon cocoa powder.
About 60 pieces

Everton Toffee

4 tablespoons water
100g / 4oz butter
300g / 12oz Demerara sugar
2 level tablespoons golden syrup
1 level tablespoon black treacle

1 Put all ingredients into pan
2 Heat slowly, stirring, until butter melts and sugar dissolves
3 Bring to boil. Cover pan. Boil gently for 2 minutes
4 Uncover. Continue to boil, stirring occasionally, for 10 to 15 minutes (or until a little of the mixture, dropped into cup of cold water, separates into hard and brittle threads). Temperature on sugar thermometer, if used, should be about 149°C / 300°F
5 Pour into buttered 15cm / 6in square tin. Leave until hard
6 Turn out on to board. Break up with small hammer. **About 500g / 1lb Toffee**

Honeycomb

3 level tablespoons clear honey
5 level tablespoons granulated sugar
4 tablespoons water
15g / $\frac{1}{2}$oz butter
$\frac{1}{2}$ teaspoon vinegar
$\frac{1}{2}$ level teaspoon bicarbonate of soda

1 Put honey, sugar, water, butter and vinegar into saucepan
2 Heat slowly, stirring, until sugar dissolves and butter melts
3 Bring to boil. Cover pan. Boil gently for 2 minutes
4 Uncover. Continue to boil, without stirring, for about 5 minutes (or until a little of the mixture, dropped into cup of cold water, separates into hard and brittle threads). Temperature on sugar thermometer, if used, should be about 149°C / 300°F
5 Draw pan away from heat. Stir in bicarbonate of soda (mixture will rise in pan)
6 Pour into small buttered tin. Break up when set
7 As Honeycomb does not keep well and very quickly gets sticky it should be made and eaten on the same day. **About 225g / 8oz Honeycomb**

Nut Toffee

1 Follow recipe and method for Syrup Toffee (right)
2 Cover base of buttered tin with 100g / 4oz blanched almonds or 100g / 4oz sliced Brazils before pouring in Toffee.
About 750g / 1lb 8oz Toffee

Syrup Toffee

5 tablespoons water
100g / 4oz golden syrup
2 teaspoons vinegar
450g / 1lb granulated sugar
50g / 2oz butter

1 Pour water and syrup into saucepan. Bring to boil
2 Add vinegar, sugar and butter. Heat slowly, stirring, until sugar dissolves and butter melts
3 Bring to boil. Cover pan. Boil gently for 2 minutes
4 Uncover. Continue to boil, stirring occasionally, for 12 to 15 minutes (or until a little of the mixture, dropped into cup of cold water, forms very hard ball when rolled between finger and thumb). Temperature on sugar thermometer, if used, should be 138°C to 142°C / 280°F to 290°F
5 Pour into buttered 15cm / 6in square tin. Leave until hard
6 Turn out on to board. Break up with small hammer. **About 600g / 1lb 4oz Toffee**

Butterscotch

150ml / $\frac{1}{4}$ pint water
450g / 1lb Demerara sugar
50g / 2oz butter

1 Pour water into pan and bring to boil
2 Add sugar and butter. Heat slowly, stirring, until sugar dissolves and butter melts
3 Bring to boil. Cover pan. Boil gently for 2 minutes
4 Uncover. Continue to boil, without stirring, for about 12 minutes (or until a little of the mixture, dropped into cup of cold water, separates into hard brittle threads). Temperature on sugar thermometer, if used, should be about 149°C / 300°F
5 Pour into buttered 15cm / 6in square tin
6 Mark into squares or bars when almost set with buttered knife
7 Break up when hard and wrap in waxed paper.
About 500g / 1lb Butterscotch

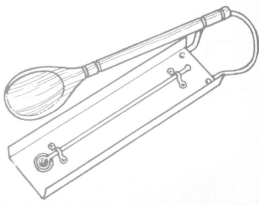

Cold Drinks

Chilled Chocolate Cream (page 265)
Tropical Fruit Shake (page 265)
Raspberry Crush (right)

Raspberry Crush

150ml / ¼ pint raspberry purée (made from fresh, frozen or canned fruit)
600ml / 1 pint chilled milk
Sifted icing sugar
4 tablespoons French Custard Dairy Ice (page 174)

1 Whisk purée and milk well together
2 Sweeten to taste with icing sugar
3 Chill thoroughly
4 Before serving pour into 4 glasses
5 Add tablespoon of Dairy Ice to each. **Serves 4**

Minted Orange Cups

4 unpeeled slices of orange
150ml / ¼ pint fresh orange juice
600ml / 1 pint chilled milk
2 tablespoons fresh double cream, whipped
Fresh mint leaves

1 Slit each orange slice from centre to outside edge. Slot over rims of 4 tumblers
2 Whisk orange juice and milk well together
3 Pour into glasses
4 Top each with whipped cream and mint leaves. **Serves 4**

Chocolate Peppermint Sizzlers

75g / 3oz grated plain chocolate
2 level tablespoons caster sugar
900ml / 1½ pints milk
1 teaspoon peppermint essence
2 tablespoons fresh double cream, whipped
Mint leaves

1 Slowly melt chocolate and sugar in 150ml / ¼ pint milk
2 Stir in rest of milk with peppermint essence. Chill
3 Just before serving pour into 4 glasses
4 Top each with cream and mint leaves. **Serves 4**

Yogurt Strawberry Cooler

150g / 5oz carton strawberry fruit yogurt
300ml / ½ pint chilled milk
A few crushed strawberries

1 Whisk yogurt and milk well together
2 Pour into 2 glasses
3 Top with crushed berries. **Serves 2**

Chilled Chocolate Cream

2 heaped tablespoons drinking chocolate
3 tablespoons boiling water
900ml / 1½ pints chilled milk
1 teaspoon vanilla essence
2 tablespoons fresh double cream, whipped
4 level tablespoons grated milk chocolate

1 Mix drinking chocolate to smooth liquid with water
2 Whisk in milk and vanilla
3 Pour into 4 tumblers
4 Top each with cream and sprinkle with chocolate. **Serves 4**

Chilled Mocha Cream

1 Follow recipe and method for Chilled Chocolate Cream (above)
2 Mix 3 to 4 level teaspoons instant coffee powder with drinking chocolate before adding water.
Serves 4

Chocolate Shake

2 heaped teaspoons drinking chocolate
3 tablespoons boiling water
900ml / 1½ pints chilled milk
4 heaped tablespoons bought vanilla dairy ice cream

1 Mix drinking chocolate to smooth liquid with water
2 Whisk in milk and 2 tablespoons ice cream
3 Divide remaining ice cream equally between 4 tumblers
4 Fill with milk mixture
5 Serve immediately. **Serves 4**

Mocha Shake

1 Follow recipe and method for Chocolate Shake (above)
2 Mix 3 to 4 level teaspoons instant coffee powder with drinking chocolate before adding water.
Serves 4

Milk Shake Float

200ml / ⅓ pint chilled milk
2 rounded tablespoons bought vanilla dairy ice cream
2 tablespoons milk shake syrup (flavour to taste)

1 Whisk milk, 1 tablespoon ice cream and syrup well together. Pour into glass
2 Float remaining ice cream on top. **Serves 1**

Banana Rose Hip Shake

2 medium-sized bananas
4 tablespoons rose hip syrup
750ml / 1¼ pints chilled milk
3 heaped tablespoons bought vanilla dairy ice cream, softened
Nutmeg

1 Mash bananas finely
2 Whisk in rose hip syrup, milk and ice cream
3 Pour into 4 tumblers
4 Sprinkle tops lightly with nutmeg
5 Serve immediately.
Serves 4

Tropical Fruit Shake

2 medium-sized bananas
Finely grated rind and juice of 1 medium-sized orange
4 tablespoons pineapple juice
600ml / 1 pint milk
4 heaped tablespoons bought vanilla dairy ice cream

1 Mash bananas finely. Whisk in orange and pineapple juice and milk
2 Divide ice cream between 4 tumblers
3 Fill with milk mixture
4 Sprinkle tops lightly with orange rind
5 Serve immediately.
Serves 4

Iced Coffee

300ml / ½ pint freshly made double strength black coffee
450ml / ¾ pint milk
Sugar to taste
2 tablespoons fresh double cream, whipped

1 Combine coffee with milk
2 Sweeten to taste. Chill
3 Pour into 3 or 4 tumblers just before serving
4 Top each with swirl of lightly whipped fresh double cream.
Serves 3 to 4

Silk on the Rocks

Crushed ice
450ml / ¾ pint chilled milk
Whisky

1 Half-fill 4 tumblers with crushed ice
2 Two-thirds fill with milk
3 Top up with whisky to taste
4 Sip through straw.
Serves 4

Chocolate Ginger Frappé

Crushed ice
2 heaped tablespoons drinking chocolate
3 tablespoons boiling water
900ml / 1½ pints chilled milk
2 tablespoons ginger wine
2 tablespoons fresh double cream, whipped

1 Cover base of 4 tumblers with crushed ice
2 Mix drinking chocolate to smooth liquid with water
3 Whisk in milk and ginger wine
4 Pour into glasses
5 Top each with cream
6 Serve immediately. **Serves 4**

Milk & Orange Nog

600ml / 1 pint chilled milk
3 standard eggs
4 level tablespoons sifted icing sugar
1 level teaspoon finely grated lemon rind
6 tablespoons fresh orange juice
1 or 2 tablespoons sherry or brandy (optional)
Crushed ice
Nutmeg

1 Whisk milk and eggs well together
2 Whisk in sugar, lemon rind, orange juice and sherry or brandy if used
3 Cover base of 4 tumblers with crushed ice
4 Fill with milk mixture
5 Sprinkle each with nutmeg and serve immediately. **Serves 4**

Malted Honey Whip

75ml / ⅛ pint chilled milk
1 level tablespoon clear honey
2 rounded tablespoons Dairy Cream Ice (page 171) or bought vanilla dairy ice cream
1 standard egg
1 heaped teaspoon malted-milk powder

1 Put all ingredients into bowl. Beat well with rotary whisk until frothy
2 Pour into glasses and serve. **Serves 2**

Rose Hip Shake

4 to 5 tablespoons rose hip syrup
900ml / 1½ pints chilled milk
3 heaped tablespoons bought vanilla dairy ice cream, softened

1 Stir rose hip syrup into milk
2 Whisk in softened ice cream
3 Pour into 4 tumblers
4 Serve immediately. **Serves 4**

Hot Drinks

Irish Coffee

2 tablespoons Irish whiskey
3 cubes sugar or 2 teaspoons brown sugar
Freshly made strong coffee
Fresh double cream

1 Warm a stemmed goblet or medium-sized coffee cup with hot water. Quickly wipe dry
2 Pour in whiskey, add sugar and fill with coffee to within 2cm / 1in of rim
3 Stir briskly to dissolve sugar
4 Top up with cream, by pouring it into goblet or cup over back of teaspoon
5 Serve immediately. **Serves 1**

Scotch Coffee

1 Follow recipe and method for Irish Coffee (above)
2 Use Scotch whisky instead of Irish whiskey.
Serves 1

Russian Coffee

1 Follow recipe and method for Irish Coffee (above)
2 Use vodka instead of whiskey.
Serves 1

French Coffee

1 Follow recipe and method for Irish Coffee (above)
2 Use brandy instead of whiskey. **Serves 1**

Jamaican Coffee

1 Follow recipe and method for Irish Coffee (above)
2 Use rum instead of whiskey. **Serves 1**

Spanish Coffee

1 Follow recipe and method for Irish Coffee (above)
2 Use sherry instead of whiskey. **Serves 1**

Dutch Chocolate Cups

300ml / ½ pint milk
150ml / ¼ pint fresh single cream
150ml / ¼ pint water
3 heaped tablespoons drinking chocolate
¼ bottle Advocaat
Cinnamon

1 Pour milk, cream and water into pan. Bring just up to boil
2 Remove from heat
3 Whisk in drinking chocolate and Advocaat
4 Pour into 4 cups
5 Sprinkle lightly with cinnamon. **Serves 4**

Hot Spiced Milk

750ml / 1¼ pints milk
2 level tablespoons black treacle
2 tablespoons fresh double cream
Cinnamon

1 Bring milk and treacle just up to boil, stirring all the time
2 Pour into 4 cups
3 Float cream on each by pouring it into cups over back of teaspoon
4 Sprinkle lightly with cinnamon
5 Serve immediately. **Serves 4**

Hot Coffee Foam

Yolks and whites of 2 standard eggs
1 level tablespoon caster sugar
2 tablespoons Tia Maria (coffee liqueur)
300ml / ½ pint hot strong black coffee
300ml / ½ pint hot milk
Grated nutmeg

1 Beat egg yolks and sugar together until very thick and pale colour. Gently whisk in Tia Maria, coffee and milk
2 Beat egg whites to stiff snow
3 Put equal amounts into 4 cups
4 Pour hot coffee liquid into cups over egg whites
5 Sprinkle each lightly with nutmeg
6 Serve immediately. **Serves 4**

Chocolate Marshmallow Floats

750ml / 1¼ pints milk
2 heaped tablespoons drinking chocolate
8 marshmallows

1 Bring milk just up to boil
2 Remove from heat and whisk in drinking chocolate
3 Pour into 4 cups
4 Float 2 marshmallows on top of each. **Serves 4**

Chocolate Cream Nog

Yolks and whites of 2 standard eggs
1 level tablespoon caster sugar
50g / 2oz grated plain chocolate
300ml / ½ pint milk
300ml / ½ pint fresh single cream

1 Whisk egg yolks and sugar together until very thick and pale in colour
2 Beat egg whites to stiff snow
3 Put chocolate and milk into saucepan. Stand over low heat until chocolate has melted
4 Add cream and bring just up to boil
5 Whisk gently into egg yolk mixture
6 Quickly stir in beaten whites
7 Pour into 4 or 5 cups or glasses. **Serves 4 or 5**

Winter Milk Punch

1 litre / 2 pints milk
25g / 1oz ground almonds
100g / 4oz granulated sugar
1 level teaspoon finely grated orange rind
Whites of 2 standard eggs
4 tablespoons rum
6 tablespoons brandy

1 Pour milk into large pan
2 Add almonds, sugar and grated rind
3 Bring just up to boil and remove from heat
4 Beat egg whites to stiff snow
5 Add to hot milk mixture with rum and brandy
6 Whisk gently until Punch is frothy
7 Ladle into cups. **Serves 8**

Hot Egg & Milk Nog

Yolks and whites of 2 standard eggs
2 level tablespoons caster sugar
600ml / 1 pint milk
Nutmeg

1 Whisk egg yolks and sugar together until very thick and pale in colour
2 Beat egg whites to stiff snow
3 Bring milk just up to boil and whisk into yolks and sugar
4 Quickly stir in beaten whites
5 Transfer to 3 tumblers
6 Sprinkle lightly with nutmeg
7 Serve immediately. **Serves 3**

Hot Sherry, Brandy or Rum Nog

1 Follow recipe and method for Hot Egg and Milk Nog (above)
2 Add 1 or 2 tablespoons sherry, brandy or rum with the hot milk. **Serves 3**

Fondues

Cheddar Cheese Fondue (page 269)

Fondues lend themselves ideally to a relaxed, informal way of entertaining friends. The fondue originates from Switzerland: made from cheese and wine and eaten on cubes of crusty bread. The saying is that if a girl loses a piece of bread from her fork into the fondue, she forfeits a kiss to all the men present. Should a man commit the same 'crime', he buys yet another bottle of wine for each of the guests. Should anyone lose their bread for a second time, they have to give the next fondue party.

Meat fondues, traditionally Fondue Bourguignonne, originate from France. Tender cuts of steak, such as fillet or rump, are used, cut into bite-size cubes and cooked in hot oil.

Sweet fondues are rather more unusual, but can provide an enjoyable sweet course for a dinner party or can even be used at children's parties if the liqueur is omitted and the fondue is well supervised.

In all cases the fondues are served with a variety of 'dippers and dunkers' which can be speared on the fondue fork.

Cheese Fondue

Hints and tips for Cheese Fondues

Cheese fondue pans are usually thick-based, flame-proof, and generally either metal or pottery

Cheese may tend to burn over the fondue flame so stir from time to time

Always use a dry wine or cider in the fondue. A little lemon juice helps to make the wine drier

Lemon juice also helps to prevent the fondue from curdling

A little more cheese or blended cornflour will help to thicken a thin fondue

Alternatively, carefully blend in a little wine to a thick fondue

Cheddar Cheese Fondue

1 clove garlic
300ml / ½ pint dry white wine or dry cider
1 teaspoon lemon juice
500g / 1lb grated Cheddar cheese
1 level tablespoon cornflour
25g / 1oz butter
Black pepper
Pinch ground nutmeg
2 tablespoons Kirsch

Accompaniments
1 crusty French loaf

1 Rub inside of cheese fondue pan with cut garlic clove
2 Pour in wine or cider and heat gently. Gradually add cheese and cornflour mixed together. Add butter
3 Heat, stirring continuously, until all the cheese has melted, and the mixture is thick and creamy. Stir in remaining ingredients
4 Serve hot with cubes of French bread.
Serves 4-6

Cheese and Tomato Fondue

225g / 8oz grated Cheshire cheese
50g / 2oz grated Stilton cheese
275g / 10oz condensed tomato soup
1 teaspoon Worcestershire sauce
3 tablespoons sherry

Accompaniments
1 crusty French loaf cubed

1 Place all ingredients except sherry in cheese fondue pan
2 Heat, stirring continuously, until cheese melts and the mixture is thick and creamy. Do not boil
3 Serve hot, with cubes of French bread.
Serves 4

Devilled Fondue

1 Follow recipe and method for Cheddar Cheese Fondue (left)
2 Omit nutmeg and Kirsch. Stir in 1 teaspoon of Worcestershire sauce, 1 teaspoon horseradish relish and ½ teaspoon paprika pepper.
Serve with a selection of accompaniments.
Serves 4-6

Anchovy Fondue

1 Follow recipe and method for Cheddar Cheese Fondue (left)
2 Omit nutmeg and Kirsch. Stir in 2 teaspoons anchovy sauce, a few drops of Tabasco sauce and 2 tablespoons of dry sherry.
Serve with a selection of accompaniments.
Serves 4-6

Onion Fondue

1 Follow recipe and method for Cheddar Cheese Fondue (left)
2 Stir in two finely grated onions, cooked until tender in a little of the white wine. Serve with a selection of accompaniments. **Serves 4-6**

Bacon and Corn Fondue

1 Follow recipe and method for Cheddar Cheese Fondue (left)
2 Stir in 100g / 4oz canned creamed sweetcorn, 75g / 3oz chopped fried bacon and 1 tablespoon chopped parsley
Serve with a selection of accompaniments.
Serves 4-6

Almond Cheese Fondue

1 Follow recipe and method for Cheddar Cheese Fondue (left)
2 Add 25g / 1oz ground almonds and 50g / 2oz chopped toasted almonds. Serve with a selection of accompaniments. **Serves 4-6**

Curry Fondue

1 Follow recipe and method for Cheddar Cheese Fondue (left)
2 Stir in 2 tablespoons curry powder (or to taste) when the cheese is added to the wine
3 Serve with cubes of French bread. **Serves 4-6**

Rosé Fondue

Follow recipe and method for Cheddar Cheese Fondue (page 269) but substitute a dry rosé for a dry white wine. Serve hot with cubes of crusty French bread. **Serves 4-6**

Mediterranean Fondue

1 Follow recipe and method for Cheddar Cheese Fondue (page 269)
2 Omit nutmeg and Kirsch. Stir in 3 chopped anchovies, 6 thinly sliced stuffed olives and 1 clove crushed garlic
3 Serve with cubes of crusty French bread, cucumber and celery. **Serves 4-6**

Tuna Fondue

1 Follow recipe and method for Cheddar Cheese Fondue (page 269)
2 Stir in 2 tablespoons Worcestershire sauce, 2 tablespoons dry sherry and 225g/8oz can tuna fish, drained and chopped
3 Serve with cubes of crusty French bread, cucumber and celery. **Serves 4-6**

Farmhouse Fondue

1 clove garlic
15g/½oz butter
450g/1lb grated Cheddar cheese
1 level tablespoon cornflour
150ml/¼ pint milk
Salt and pepper
Pinch dry mustard
Pinch ground nutmeg

Accompaniments
Crusty French loaf

1 Rub inside of cheese fondue pan with cut garlic clove
2 Place all ingredients in the pan and heat very gently, stirring continuously, until cheese melts and mixture thickens. Do not boil
3 Serve hot with cubes of French bread.
Serves 4-6

Avocado Fondue

1 clove garlic
25g/1oz butter
1 medium-sized, finely chopped onion
25g/1oz flour
1 medium-sized avocado pear
4 tablespoons lemon juice
Salt and pepper
50g/2oz grated Cheddar cheese
150ml/¼ pint fresh single cream
Few drops Tabasco sauce

Accompaniments
Peeled whole prawns
Selection of bite-size pieces of raw vegetables

1 Rub inside of cheese fondue pan with cut garlic clove
2 Melt butter in pan, add onion and sauté until soft but not brown
3 Stir in flour and cook for 2 minutes. Remove from heat
4 Remove stone and skin from avocado. Mash or liquidise and add to the pan together with the lemon juice and seasoning
5 Heat gently, stirring continuously, for 5 minutes but do not boil
6 Add cheese, and stir until melted. Then stir in the cream and Tabasco sauce
Serve immediately. **Serves 4**

Stilton Cheese Fondue

1 clove garlic
450ml/¾ pint beer
50g/2oz crumbled Stilton cheese
350g/12oz grated Cheddar cheese
1 level tablespoon cornflour

Accompaniments
1 crusty French loaf cubed

1 Rub inside of cheese fondue pan with cut garlic clove
2 Pour in beer and heat gently. Gradually add cheese and cornflour mixed together
3 Heat, stirring continuously, until all the cheese has melted, and the mixture is thick and creamy
4 Serve hot with cubes of French bread.
Serves 4-6

Caerphilly Fondue

Follow recipe and method for Stilton Cheese Fondue (above) but use Caerphilly cheese instead of Stilton and stir in a pinch of ground nutmeg and freshly ground black pepper. Serve with cubes of crusty French bread. **Serves 4-6**

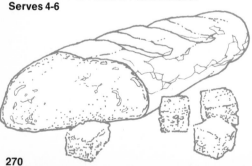

Meat Fondues

Hints and tips for Meat Fondues

Meat fondue pans are usually made from stainless steel or copper

The pan should be only $\frac{2}{3}$ full of oil to avoid danger at the table

It is best to heat the oil on the cooker to 182°C/360°F or until a small cube of bread turns golden in less than a minute when dropped in the oil

The fondue burner should be securely placed on a protected table

The pan should be placed on the burner so that the handle cannot be knocked

Take care not to place too much food in the oil at one time as it can cause the oil to bubble up and rapidly cool

Fondue forks are used only to spear the food for cooking in the oil, not for eating from, as this could burn the mouth

Fondue Bourguignonne

500g/1lb fillet of rump steak
1 recipe Wine Marinade (page 93), optional
Cooking oil

Accompaniments
Onion Dip (page 18)
Soured Cream with Cucumber Dressing
(page 122)
Curry Mayonnaise (page 127)
Curried Barbecue Sauce (page 136)
Jacket Potatoes with Butter (page 102)
Side Salad (see Salad Section, page 114)
Gherkins or stuffed olives

1 Cut beef into bite-size cubes. Marinate the meat for 1-3 hours or overnight
2 Drain and dry thoroughly on kitchen paper to prevent the oil spitting when meat is cooked
3 Half fill the meat fondue pan with oil. Heat gently to 182°C/360°F or until a small cube of bread, dropped into the oil, turns golden within 1 minute. Keep oil hot over the fondue burner on the table.
4 Serve thoroughly drained meat on individual plates and allow each person to spear the meat on their fondue fork and cook to their requirements. Accompany with a variety of sauces (usually four) and salads. **Serves 4**

Lamb Fondue

750g/1lb 8oz leg of lamb
1 recipe Lemon Marinade (page 93)
Cooking oil

Accompaniments
Cumberland Sauce (page 130)
Mint Sauce (page 133)
Avocado Dip (page 18)
Thousand Islands Mayonnaise (page 126)
Side salad (see Salad Section, page 114)
Sauté potatoes (page 101)

1 Cut the lamb into bite-size cubes. Marinate the meat for 1-3 hours or overnight
2 Drain and dry thoroughly on kitchen paper to prevent oil from spitting when meat is cooked
3 Prepare and cook as for Fondue Bourguignonne (left). **Serves 4**

Spicy Fondue

100g/4oz kidney
100g/4oz liver
100g/4oz chicken
100g/4oz fillet of veal
100g/4oz prawns
1 recipe Spice Marinade (page 94)
Cooking oil

Accompaniments
Curried Cream Cheese Dip (page 18)
Creamed Yogurt Dip (page 17)
Louis Mayonnaise (page 126)
Soured Cream with Tomato Dressing (page 122)
Side salad (see Salad Section, page 114)
Fried rice

1 Cut meats into bite-size cubes. Leave prawns whole. Marinate the meat and prawns for 5 hours, or overnight, in the refrigerator
2 Drain and dry thoroughly on kitchen paper to prevent the oil spitting when meat is cooked
3 Prepare and cook as for Fondue Bourguignonne (left). **Serves 4**

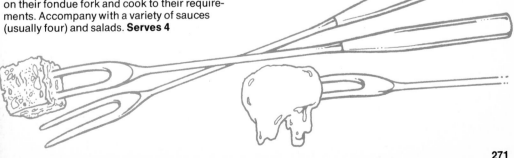

Sweet Fondues

'Dippers and Dunkers' for Sweet Fondues may be a selection of biscuits, plain cake, sponge fingers, macaroons, marshmallows or pieces of fruit.

Chocolate Fondue

225g/8oz plain chocolate
150ml/¼ pint fresh double cream
2 tablespoons Kirsch

1 Grate chocolate and place in the fondue pan with the cream
2 Heat gently, stirring continuously, until chocolate has melted. Do not boil
3 Stir in the Kirsch. Serve hot. **Serves 4**

Chocolate and Orange Fondue

Follow recipe and method for Chocolate Fondue (above) but replace Kirsch with Grand Marnier and add the grated rind of 1 orange. Serve hot. **Serves 4**

Mocha Fondue

225g/8oz milk chocolate
1 tablespoon instant coffee powder
150ml/¼ pint fresh double cream
2 tablespoons Crème de Caçao or Tia Maria liqueur

1 Grate chocolate and mix with instant coffee
2 Place cream in the fondue pan, add chocolate and coffee, and heat gently, stirring continuously, until the chocolate has melted. Add liqueur. Serve hot. **Serves 4**

Banana Fondue

6 bananas
2 tablespoons sugar
50g/2oz plain chocolate
150ml/¼ pint double cream

1 Sieve or liquidise bananas with the sugar
2 Place in fondue pan and heat gently, stirring continuously
3 Grate chocolate and stir into the bananas together with cream. **Serves 4**

Cherry Fondue

2×396g/14oz cans cherry pie filling
2 tablespoons sweet white wine
3 tablespoons fresh double cream
2 tablespoons Cherry Brandy

1 Place cherry pie filling and wine in the fondue pan and heat gently, stirring continuously
2 Stir in cream and Cherry Brandy. Serve hot. **Serves 4**

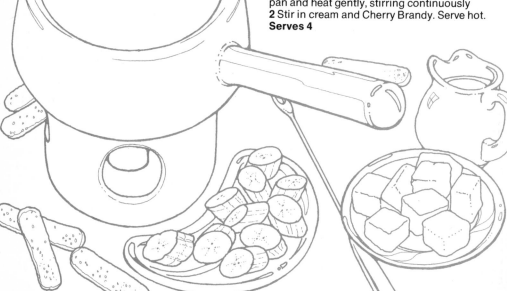

Index

274

283